# HARRAP'S

## Spanish Synonyms

BILINGUAL DICTIONARY OF
SYNONYMS AND ANTONYMS

Compiled by
Louis J. Rodrigues

**HARRAP**
London

Distributed in the United States by
**PRENTICE HALL**
New York

*First published in Great Britain 1990*
*by* HARRAP BOOKS Ltd
Chelsea House, 26 Market Square, Bromley, Kent BR1 1NA

ISBN 0 245-60040-X

In the United States, ISBN 0-13-385014-5

Library of Congress Cataloging-in-Publication Data

Harrap's Spanish synonyms: bilingual dictionary of synonyms and
antonyms / compiled by Louis J. Rodrigues.
p.          cm.
ISBN 0-13-385014-5 (U.S.)
1. Spanish language–Synonyms and antonyms–Dictionaries–English.
2. English language–Synonyms and antonyms–Dictionaries–Spanish
I. Rodrigues, Louis J. (Louis Jerome), 1938-    .
PC4591.H37   1991                                        90-3990
463' .21–dc20                                              C

Printed and bound in Great Britain by
Richard Clay, St Ives PLC, Bungay Suffolk.

# FOREWORD

This little book is not intended to replace a standard dictionary of Synonyms and Antonyms either in English or Spanish. It is intended, however, to provide a means of quick reference to a possible range of meanings of the headword as indicated.

For obvious reasons, the number of headwords in each case is limited to those of common occurrence. The synonyms for each headword have been grouped into categories which reflect divisions of meaning; within these categories synonyms are ordered roughly in accordance with their semantic proximity to the headword. Any corresponding antonyms have been arranged in the same way.

It need hardly be said that these categories and hierarchies are subjective and should not be taken as an absolute guide to meaning. Our aim throughout has been to offer simplicity and ease of reference, and the user is always advised to consult a more specialized, preferably monolingual, work in the case of reasonable doubt.

LJR
JBR

# PROLOGO

Este pequeño libro no está ideado para reemplazar un diccionario normal de Sinónimos y Antónimos tanto en inglés como en español. No obstante, su ideal es proporcionar un medio de consulta rápido de los posibles significados diferentes de la palabra principal según se indica.

Por razones obvias, el número de palabras principales en cada caso está limitado a las palabras de uso más corriente. Se han agrupado los sinónimos de cada palabra principal en categorías, las cuales reflejan los significados de las divisiones. Dentro de estas categorías, se relacionan los sinónimos siguiendo, más o menos, su semejanza semántica a la palabra principal. También se ha relacionado siguiendo este criterio, cualquier antónimo correspondiente.

No es necesario decir que estas categorías y jerarquías son subjetivas y no deberían tomarse como una guía perfecta del significado. Nuestra intención ha sido ofrecer simplicidad y facilidad en la consulta, y se aconseja al lector que utilice obras más especializados, preferentemente monolingües, en caso alguna duda razonable.

LJR
JBR

# PART ONE

# ENGLISH – SPANISH

# ABBREVIATIONS

| | |
|---|---|
| aj | Adjective |
| Am | American |
| av | Adverb |
| Br | British |
| fig | Figurative |
| LAm | Latin American |
| pl | Plural |
| s | Substantive |
| v | Verb |

# A

**abandon**

1 abandonar, descuidar, desatender, desasistir, desentenderse
*amparar, atender, cuidar*

2 abandonar, marcharse, irse, apartarse, retirarse
*volver, regresar, permanecer, quedarse*

3 abandonar, renunciar, dejar
*seguir, insistir*

**abandoned**

1 abandonado, descuidado, desidioso, negligente
*cuidadoso, esmerado, atildado, aseado, pulcro, diligente*

2 desasistido, desamparado, dejado
*atendido, cuidado, amparado, asistido*

3 libre, desenfadado

**abate**

1 abreviar, aminorar, atenuar, deducir, depreciar, descargar, descontar, disminuir, mellar, menguar, minorar, rebajar, reducir, restringir, sisar, sustraer
*acrecentar, agrandar, aumentar, ensanchar, dilatar*

2 aplacar, debilitar, moderar

**abatement**

degradación, decadencia, disminución, menoscabo, reducción, mengua, merma, aminoración, decrecimiento, depreciación, descuento, baja
*aumento, incremento, alza*

**abbreviate**

resumir, acortar, disminuir, restringir, compendiar, condensar
*alargar, amplificar, dilatar, prolongar*

**abdicate**

abdicar, ceder, cesar, dimitir, renunciar
*aceptar, asumir, mantener*

**abhor**

abominar, aborrecer, detestar, execrar, maldecir, odiar
*admirar, amar*

**abide**

1 aguantar, padecer, sobrellevar, sufrir, tolerar
*ceder, flaquear, estallar, explotar*

2 morar, habitar, residir, vivir, avecindarse, permanecer

**ability**

capacidad, agudeza, amaño, aptitud, arte, cabeza, competencia, desenvoltura, diplomacia, discernimiento, disposición, don, entendimiento, experiencia, genio, gracia, ingenio, maña, pericia, perspicacia, picardía, política, práctica, saber, sagacidad, sentido, soltura, suficiencia.
*incapacidad, ineptitud, incompetencia, torpeza, inhabilidad*

**abject**

1 bajo, despreciable, indigno, repugnante, servil, ruin, degenerado, rastrero, infame
*noble, digno, respetable, estimable, íntegro, honrado*

2 marginado, paria
*estimado*

**able**

avezado, aparejado, apto, cualificado, capaz, competente, conocedor, digno, entendido, experimentado, experto, hábil, idóneo, nacido para, perito, práctico, sabio
*incapaz, desconocedor, inepto*

**abnormal**

1 anómalo, anormal, desigual, desusado, extraño, irregular, raro
*regular, correcto, normal*

2 excepcional, original, singular
*común, normal, vulgar*

**abolish**
abolir, abrogar, anular, cancelar, derogar, destruir, eliminar, revocar, suprimir
*establecer, mantener, promulgar, restaurar*

**abominable**
abominable, detestable, execrable, incalificable, monstruoso, nefando, pésimo
*agradable, amable, digno de alabanza*

**abominate**
abominar, aborrecer, detestar, execrar, maldecir, odiar
*admirar, alabar, amar, bendecir, enaltecer*

**above-board** *(av)*
abiertamente, claramente, francamente, llanamente, sin rodeos
*bajo mano, con hipocresía, engañosamente, ocultamente*

**above-board** *(aj)*
decente, hombre de bien, honesto, honorable, imparcial, justo, leal, limpio, probo, recto, virtuoso
*corrupto, deshonesto, sucio, vil*

**abridge**
abreviar, abolir, anular, cancelar, derogar, rescindir, revocar, suprimir
*alargar, dilatar, prolongar*

**abrogate**
abolir, abrogar, acortar, compendiar, disminuir, reducir, restringir, resumir
*alargar, dilatar, prolongar*

**abrupt**
1 abrupto, accidentado, áspero, fragoso, intricado
*llano, suave*
2 excesivo, precipitado, repentino
*gradual*

**absence**
1 ausencia, inasistencia
*asistencia, comparecencia, presencia*

2 carencia, defecto, falta, laguna, omisión, supresión
*existencia*
3 abstracción, despiste, distracción, ensimismamiento, preocupación
*atención*

**absolve**
condonar, exculpar, indultar, perdonar, sobreseer
*condenar, inculpar*

**abstain**
abstenerse, contenerse, inhibirse, pararse, refrenarse, renunciar
*consentir, dar rienda suelta*

**abstemious**
abstemio, moderado, sobrio, temperado
*ebrio, intemperante, voraz*

**abstinence**
abstinencia, continencia, moderación, privación
*incontinencia, indulgencia*

**abstruse**
abstruso, enigmático, inasequible, incomprensible, misterioso, oculto, oscuro, profundo, recóndito
*claro, comprensible, concreto*

**absurd**
absurdo, ilógico, irracional, desatinado, ridículo, irrazonable, sin sentido
*consecuente, lógico, racional, atinado, juicioso, sensato*

**absurdity**
absurdo, disparate, incoherencia, tontería, ingenuidad, extravagancia
*sensatez, coherencia, lógica*

**abundance**
abundancia, acopio, afluencia, exuberancia, fecundidad, opulencia, profusión, riqueza
*carencia, escasez, falta, necesidad, pobreza*

**abundant**
abundante, exuberante, fecundo, pingüe, profuso, rico
*escaso, exiguo, falto, limitado, pobre*

**accept**
aceptar, acceder, admitir, ceder, condescender, consentir, convenir, transigir
*negarse, rechazar, rehusar*

**accidental**
1 accidental, casual, contingente, eventual, fortuito, incidental, oportuno
*previsto, preparado*

**accommodating**
amable, atento, complaciente, considerado, cortés, desinteresado, servicial
*desatento, desconsiderado, descortés, maleducado*

**accumulate**
1 acumular, juntar, amontonar, apilar, almacenar, hacinar, acopiar, aglomerar
*esparcir, disgregar*
2 achacar, colgar, echar la culpa, atribuir
*defender, exculpar*

**accurate**
exacto, fiel y cabal, justo, cierto, estricto, correcto, verdadero, conforme, preciso, textual
*inexacto, impreciso*

**actual**
verdadero, real, cierto, genuino, categórico, efectivo, presente, actual
*irreal, inexacto, potencial*

**adipose**
adiposo, graso, gordo, obeso, sebáceo
*seco, delgado*

**adjacent**
contiguo, vecino, colindante, cercano, (ángulo) adyacente
*lejano, distante*

**adjust**
1 modificar, cambiar, rectificar
*conservar, ratificar*
2 arreglar, corregir, resolver
*desordenar, revolver*
3 adaptar, acomodar, (máquinas) ajustar, graduar, regular
*desajustar, desacomodar*

**admit**
1 reconocer, confesar, aceptar, admitir, conceder
*rechazar, despreciar, negar, refutar*
2 dar entrada, dejar entrar, admitir, (LAm) hacer pasar
*rechazar*

**adore**
1 adorar, idolatrar, reverenciar, venerar
*despreciar, faltar al respeto*
2 querer, adorar, apreciar, estimar, admirar
*odiar, aborrecer*

**adorn**
1 adornar, ataviar, acicalar, embellecer, decorar, engalanar, ornamentar
*desfigurar, afear*
2 elevar, encomiar, engrandecer
*rebajar, empobrecer, menguar*

**adult**
1 adulto, maduro, crecido, grande, medrado
*niño, menor, inmaduro*
2 pleno, formado, desarrollado, perfecto
*inmaduro, subdesarrollado*

**adventurous**
1 aventurero, arriesgado, atrevido, emprendedor, temerario, osado, impetuoso
*sencillo, temeroso, cobarde, cauto*
2 peligroso, arriesgado
*seguro*

**adversary**
adversario, antagonista, contendiente, rival, oponente
*amigo, compañero, camarada, socio*

**adverse**
1 contrario, contradictorio, repugnante, antagonista, hostil, opuesto
*semejante, parecido*
2 dañino, perjudicial
*beneficioso*

**adversity**
desgracia, infelicidad, adversidad, desdicha, aflicción, miseria, catás-

trofe, calamidad, tragedia, fatalidad
*felicidad, suerte, fortuna*

**advertise**
1 anunciar, publicar, proclamar, hacer saber, avisar, informar, notificar, declarar, promulgar
*ocultar, callar*
2 *(comercial)* anunciar

**affectation**
afectación, amaneramiento, pedantería, presunción, petulancia, aire de suficiencia
*naturalidad, espontaneidad, sencillez, simplicidad*

**affirm**
afirmar, asegurar, sostener, aseverar, declarar, confirmar, atestiguar, mantener, ratificar
*negar, denegar, desmentir*

**affront** *(v)*
afrentar, abusar, insultar, enfadarse, ofender, provocar, fastidiar
*respetar*

**affront** *(s)*
afrenta, ultraje, vejación, abuso, insulto, ofensa
*cumplido, gentileza, cortesía*

**aggravate**
1 agravar, cargar, aumentar, empeorar, agudizar
*aligerar, mitigar, reducir, aminorar*
2 irritar, provocar, exasperar, fastidiar, molestar, sacar de quicio, crispar
*calmar, tranquilizar*

**agitate**
1 agitar, sacudir, remover, mover, blandir
*dejar quieto, detener*
2 inquietar, perturbar, alterar, excitar
*tranquilizar, pacificar, calmar*
3 discutir, deliberar, debatir, disputar, *(fig)* ventilar

**alarm** *(v)*
alarmar, asustar, sobresaltar, inquietar, atemorizar, aterrar, amedrantar
*tranquilizar, calmar*

**alarm** *(s)*
1 alarma, susto, inquietud, ansiedad, consternación, aprensión, terror
*sosiego, calma*
2 señal de socorro, timbre de alarma, *(fig)* voz de alarma

**alert** *(aj)*
alerta, listo, vigilante, activo, ágil, enérgico, rápido
*distraído, ido, lento*

**alien** *(aj)*
ajeno, extraño, impropio
*propio, personal*

**alien** *(s)*
extranjero, forastero
*nativo*

**alike**
igualmente, ídem, lo mismo, así, al igual, a la par, por igual, indistintamente
*al contrario, en cambio, por el contrario*

**alive**
vivo, activo, diligente, laborioso, enérgico, avispado, eficaz, dinámico, animado, vigoroso
*inactivo, ineficaz, apático, abúlico*

**allay**
aliviar, aquietar, apaciguar, disipar, aplacar, calmar, mitigar, tranquilizar, pacificar
*agravar, intranquilizar, excitar, afligir*

**allege**
1 afirmar, declarar, pretender, sostener, aseverar, mantener
*negar, desmentir*
2 alegar, pretextar, aducir

**allegiance**
lealtad, deber, obediencia, obligación, fidelidad, homenaje
*deslealtad, traición*

**alliance**
alianza, afiliación, afinidad, pacto, asociación, combinación, convenio, unión, coalición, confederación, acuerdo, lazo, conexión
*ruptura, separación, discordia, desunión*

**allow**

1 permitir, autorizar, tolerar, aprobar, aguantar, sufrir, consentir
*prohibir, desautorizar*

2 aceptar, saber, admitir, conceder, confesar, reconocer
*repudiar, negar*

**ally** *(v)*

asociarse, ligarse, fusionarse, unirse
*desunirse, separarse, romper*

**alone** *(aj)*

solo, aislado, abandonado, incomunicado, solitario, recogido, recoleto
*acompañado, comunicado*

**alter**

1 cambiar, alterar, rectificar, diversificar, convertir, transmutar, metamorfosear, modificar, transformar, variar, remodelar
*permanecer, conservar, mantener*

2 *(Am)* castrar

**amass**

acumular, juntar, amontonar, apilar, acopiar, aglomerar, recoger, reunir
*esparcir, separar, dispersar, disgregar*

**ambiguity**

ambigüedad, oscuridad, confusión, doble sentido
*precisión, claridad*

**ameliorate**

1 mejorar, beneficiar, aumentar, promocionar, reformar
*empeorar, deteriorar, agravar*

2 aliviarse, restablecerse
*agravarse*

**amend**

enmendar, corregir, modificar, reparar, rectificar, mejorar, reformar
*estropear, empeorar*

**amenity**

amenidad, agrado, afabilidad, encanto, simpatía
*desabrimiento, antipatía*

**amiable**

amable, agradable, encantador, atractivo, gracioso, cordial, simpá-tico, sociable, atento, cortés, cariñoso, complaciente
*abominable, aborrecible, desagradable, descortés, odioso, desatento, seco, antipático*

**amicable**

afable, amigable, amistoso, afectuoso, cariñoso, cordial, paternal
*arisco, antipático, poco amistoso*

**amity**

amistad, camaradería, compañerismo, cordialidad, bondad
*enemistad, aversión, rivalidad*

**amnesty**

amnistía, gracia, indulto, olvido, perdón, remisión
*pena, castigo*

**amorous**

amoroso, afectivo, cariñoso, cordial, afectuoso, entrañable, tierno, mimoso, benévolo, ardiente
*frío, arisco, seco*

**ample**

amplio, extenso, espacioso, dilatado, ancho, abundante, grande, vasto
*angosto, breve, corto, estrecho, pequeño, reducido*

**amplify**

aumentar, ampliar, alargar, agrandar, engrosar, engrandecer, acrecentar
*abreviar, disimular, decrecer, mermar, reducir*

**analogy**

analogía, correspondencia, correlación, relación, parecido, semejanza, similitud, afinidad
*disimilitud, desemejanza, diferencia*

**analysis**

1 análisis, disociación, disección, separación, segregación
*síntesis, unión*

2 *(Am)* psicoanálisis

**anathema**

1 anatema, excomunión, prohibición, veto
*inclusión, aceptación*

2 condenación, execración, imprecación, maldición
*alabanza, bendición*

**ancestry**
ascendencia, estirpe, linaje, cuna, descendencia, familia, genealogía, pedigrí, sucesión
*posteridad*

**ancient** *(aj)*
anticuado, antiguo, pasado de moda, primitivo, inmemorial, arcaico, *(persona)* anciano, viejo
*moderno, actual*

**anger** *(s)*
cólera, exasperación, enojo, furor, furia, rabia, indignación, rencor, irritación, ira, resentimiento
*serenidad, paciencia, paz*

**anger** *(v)*
enfadar, enojar, enfurecer, exasperar, fastidiar, irritar, indignar, molestar, provocar, ofender, afrentar
*calmar, apaciguar*

**anguish** *(s)*
angustia, agonía, aflicción, congoja, punzada, pesar, pena, tormento
*consuelo, alivio*

**animate** *(v)*
1 animar, avivar, alentar, excitar, vivificar, inspirar, instigar, encender, incitar, estimular, envalentonar
*desanimar, descorazonar*
2 alegrar, alborozar, regocijar
*aburrir, aquietar*

**animosity**
rencor, animosidad, amargura, aborrecimiento, antipatía, enemistad, odio, rabia, malicia, malevolencia, virulencia
*bondad, benevolencia, simpatía*

**annex**
1 anejar, anexar, anexionar, adscribir, incorporar
*segregar, desvincular, separar*
2 adjuntar, agregar, juntar, unir, acompañar, añadir
*despegar*

**annihilate**
aniquilar, abolir, anular, exterminar, extinguir, eliminar, destruir, invalidar, suprimir
*mantener, preservar, conservar*

**announce**
anunciar, declarar, divulgar, exponer, promulgar, proclamar, relatar, revelar
*disimular, ocultar*

**annoy**
acosar, fastidiar, contrariar, irritar, molestar, importunar, provocar, incomodar, impacientar
*apaciguar, calmar, suavizar*

**anomaly**
anomalía, anormalidad, irregularidad, extravagancia, excepción, rareza
*normalidad, regularidad, conformidad*

**anonymous**
anónimo, desconocido, ignorado, misterioso, sin nombre
*firmado, reconocido por*

**antagonist**
adversario, antagonista, contrario, competidor, enemigo, oponente
*amigo, aliado, colaborador*

**antecedent**
antecedente, antecesor, anterior, precedente, precursor, predecesor
*siguiente, subsiguiente, posterior*

**anticipation**
anticipo, anticipación, esperanza, expectativa, presentimiento, previsión
*imprevisión, desesperanza*

**antipathy**
aborrecimiento, antipatía, aversión, odio, oposición, repugnancia
*simpatía, afición*

**anxiety**
aflicción, inquietud, duda, preocupación, pena, presentimiento, recelo, temor, *(medicina)* ansiedad, angustia
*contento, seguridad*

**anxious**
    alborotado, angustiado, apenado, afligido, inquieto, preocupado, receloso, temeroso
    *seguro, confiado*

**apathy**
    apatía, calma, estoicismo, frialdad, flema, impasibilidad, indiferencia
    *ansiedad, preocupación*

**appal,** *(Am)* **appall**
    aterrar, alarmar, asombrar, aterrar, intimidar, consternar
    *envalentonar*

**apparent**
    aparente, notable, indudable, manifiesto, claro, obvio, ostensible, visible
    *dudoso, incierto*

**appease**
    aliviar, apaciguar, aplacar, calmar, pacificar, tranquilizar, sosegar
    *agravar, perturbar*

**appetite**
    1 apetito, hambre
    *desgana*
    2 *(fig)* deseo, ansia, anhelo, inclinación, propensión
    *apatía, desinterés*

**applaud**
    1 aplaudir, palmotear
    2 *(fig)* aclamar, aplaudir, ovacionar, vitorear
    *abuchear, patear*

**application**
    1 aplicación, atención, diligencia, esfuerzo, perseverancia, laboriosidad, tentativa
    *pereza, distracción, desatención*
    2 súplica, petición, instancia
    3 ejercicio, práctica, uso

**apposite**
    apto, apropiado, adecuado, conveniente, oportuno, pertinente
    *inapropiado, inadecuado*

**appreciate**
    apreciar, aumentar el valor de, estimar, reconocer, valorar
    *depreciar, perder valor, menospreciar*

**apprehend**
    1 aprehender, arrestar, capturar, coger, detener, prender
    *soltar, libertar*
    2 entender, adivinar, concebir, percibir, saber
    *desconocer, ignorar*
    3 recelar, temer
    *confiar, fiar*

**apprehension**
    1 apresamiento, arresto, detención, captura, prendimiento, reclusión
    *libertad, excarcelación*
    2 comprensión, entendimiento, inteligencia, juicio, talento, visión
    *incomprensión, ofuscación*
    3 recelo, aprensión, temor
    *confianza, seguridad*

**appropriate** *(aj)*
    apto, adecuado, apropiado, conveniente, idóneo, oportuno, pertinente
    *inapropiado, inadecuado, impropio, inoportuno*

**appropriate** *(v)*
    1 apropiar, coger, incautarse, quitar
    *dejar, abandonar*
    2 asignar, destinar, dedicar, indicar, señalar

**approximate** *(v)*
    acercar, alcanzar, aproximar, avecinar
    *alejar, apartar(se) de*

**apt**
    1 pertinente, aplicable, relativo
    *independiente*
    2 apropiado, adecuado, conveniente, oportuno
    *inconveniente, inapropiado*
    3 educable, experto, diestro, hábil, inteligente, talentoso, listo
    *torpe, inepto*

**aptitude**
    1 aptitud, capacidad, facultad, inteligencia, habilidad, talento
    *ineptitud, inhabilidad*
    2 disposición, inclinación, propensión, predisposición, tendencia

**archaic**
>     antiguo, anticuado, arcaico, añejo,
>     pasado, obsoleto, primitivo
>     *moderno, contemporáneo, actual*

**ardent**
>     apasionado, ardiente, entusiasta,
>     fervoroso, fogoso, intenso, vehe-
>     mente
>     *apagado, frío, indiferente*

**ardour,** *(Am)* **ardor**
>     ardor, ansia, deseo, fervor, calor,
>     entusiasmo, pasión, vehemencia,
>     efusión
>     *apatía, frialdad, indiferencia*

**arduous**
>     agotador, angustioso, arduo, gra-
>     voso, oneroso, difícil, duro, labo-
>     rioso, dificultoso, penoso
>     *fácil, asequible, sencillo*

**argue**
>     debatir, discutir, cuestionar, dispu-
>     tar, protestar, tratar de, contro-
>     vertir, razonar, convencer, *(LAm)*
>     pelearse
>     *aprobar, asentir, consentir*

**arid**
>     árido, estéril, infecundo, sin hume-
>     dad, seco
>     *fértil, fecundo, húmedo*

**aromatic**
>     odorífero, aromado, aromático,
>     balsámico, fragante, perfumado,
>     oloroso
>     *fétido, maloliente*

**arouse**
>     1 espabilar, despertar, recobrar
>     *adormecer*
>     2 *(fig)* animar, estimular, avivar,
>     mover, incitar
>     *calmar*

**arrest** *(s)*
>     arresto, apresamiento, detención,
>     prendimiento, captura, obstruc-
>     ción
>     *libertad, excarcelación*

**arrest** *(v)*
>     1 detener, arrestar, prender, apre-
>     hender, encarcelar, encerrar
>     *soltar, excarcelar, libertar*

>     2 demorar, retardar, parar, obsta-
>     culizar
>     *seguir, acelerarse*

**arrive**
>     1 llegar, acercarse, venir
>     *partir, marchar, salir*
>     2 alcanzar, abarcar, conseguir, lo-
>     grar

**arrogance**
>     altanería, arrogancia, insolencia,
>     impertinencia, apostura
>     *sencillez, modestia*

**artful**
>     1 artero, astuto, engañoso, fraudu-
>     lento, falso, intrigante
>     *leal, abierto*
>     2 ingenioso, diestro, agudo, astuto,
>     sagaz, hábil, mañoso
>     *torpe*

**artificial**
>     1 artificial, ficticio, falso, engaño-
>     so, fingido, contrahecho, forzado,
>     simulado
>     *auténtico, verdadero, genuino, na-
>     tural*
>     2 fabricado, elaborado
>     *natural, bruto*

**artless**
>     abierto, candoroso, cándido, inge-
>     nuo, inocente, sencillo, llano, fran-
>     co, crédulo, sincero, natural, sim-
>     ple
>     *astuto, ladino, sinuoso*

**ascend**
>     1 ascender, alzar, elevar, levantar,
>     izar, montar, empinar, subir
>     *bajar, descender*
>     2 avanzar, ganar, mejorar, pro-
>     gresar, prosperar, *(empleo)* subir
>     puestos, ascender de puesto
>     *retrasarse, retroceder, estancarse*

**ascendancy**
>     dominio, influencia, influjo, domi-
>     nación, autoridad, predominio, so-
>     beranía, mando
>     *inferioridad, debilidad, superiori-
>     dad, supremacía*

**ascertain**

    averiguar, determinar, descubrir, enterarse, establecer, hallar, indagar, verificar

    *imaginar, suponer*

**ask**

  1  preguntar, informarse de, cuestionar, solicitar, interpelar, interrogar

    *responder, contestar*

  2  pedir, rogar, implorar, exigir, solicitar, suplicar, reclamar

    *conceder, acceder*

  3  invitar, *(LAm)* convidar

**asperity**

  1  aspereza, acrimonia, amargura, severidad, rigor, acritud, acidez, rudeza, dureza, tosquedad

    *afabilidad, alegría*

  2  escabrosidad, desigualdad, fragosidad, abruptez

    *llanura, lisura*

**aspersion**

    calumnia, abuso, censura, detracción, difamación, deshonra, injurias, vituperio

    *elogio, encomio*

**assemble**

    convocar, agrupar, acopiar, acumular, reunir, juntar, congregar

    *separar, dispersar*

**assent** *(s)*

    aprobación, acuerdo, asentimiento, aceptación, consentimiento, consenso, convenio, conformidad, pacto

    *desaprobación, rechazo, censura*

**assert**

    afirmar, asegurar, asentir, mantener, sostener

    *negar, desmentir*

**asseverate**

    aseverar, afirmar, declarar, sostener

    *negar, contradecir*

**associate** *(v)*

    acompañar, afiliarse, juntarse, unirse

    *separarse, oponerse*

**astute**

    astuto, agudo, inteligente, listo, ladino, penetrante, sagaz, perspicaz

    *lerdo, incauto, bobo*

**atrocious**

  1  atroz, diabólico, cruel, escandaloso, horrible, infame, infernal, monstruoso, vil, malvado

    *humano, caritativo, bondadoso*

  2  enorme, notorio

    *insignificante*

**attach**

  1  sujetar, retener, trabar, atar, afianzar

    *soltar, aflojar*

  2  acoplar, ajustar, conectar, ensamblar, soldar

    *desacoplar, desajustar*

  3  adjuntar, acompañar, agregar, anexionar, juntar, unir

    *separar, desunir*

**attack** *(v)*

  1  atacar, arremeter, acometer, asaltar, agredir, culpar, censurar, embestir, impugnar

    *defender, resistir*

  2  *(fig)* acometer, tratar de resolver

**attack** *(s)*

    ataque, asalto, acometida, agresión, embestida, invasión, censura

    *defensa, resistencia*

**attain**

    alcanzar, ganar, conseguir, adquirir, lograr, obtener

    *perder*

**attention**

  1  atención, alerta, aplicación, cuidado, interés

    *distracción, descuido*

  2  cortesía, deferencia, consideración, urbanidad

    *descortesía, desatención, desconsideración*

**attentive**

    atento, consciente de, cortés, considerado, cuidadoso, respetuoso, urbano

    *desatento, descortés, maleducado*

**attenuate**

atenuar, adulterar, debilitar, diluir, disminuir

*aumentar, avivar*

**attest**

afirmar, atestiguar, manifestar, declarar, testificar, confirmar, aseverar, asegurar

*negar, refutar*

**attire** (v)

vestir, equiparse, ataviarse, trajearse, uniformarse, ponerse, engalanarse, arroparse

*desnudarse, desvestirse, quitarse, desarroparse*

**attire** (s)

vestido, equipo, traje, indumentaria, uniforme, ropa, vestimenta, hábito, atavío, prenda

*desnudez*

**attract**

atraer, fascinar, granjearse las simpatías, ganarse, encantar, seducir, tentar, cautivar

*repeler, rechazar*

**attractive**

atractivo, atrayente, amable, interesante, simpático, sugestivo, fascinante, agradable, seductor, encantador, tentador, (LAm) lindo

*repulsivo, desagradable, disuasivo, antipático*

**audacious**

audaz, atrevido, arriesgado, osado, precipitado, intrépido, valiente, imprudente, temerario, descarado, emprendedor, decidido, valeroso

*tímido, cobarde, prudente, poco emprendedor*

**augment**

aumentar, agrandar, ampliar, alargar, crecer, engrosar, acrecentar, dilatar, realzar, intensificar, extender

*disminuir, decrecer, mermar, reducir*

**augmentation**

1 aumento, ampliación, desarrollo, engrandecimiento, engrosamiento, alargamiento

*disminución, merma, reducción*

2 añadidura, adición

*deducción*

**august**

augusto, exaltado, distinguido, grandioso, impresionante, majestuoso, regio, suntuoso, magnífico, solemne

*indigno, bajo, innoble*

**austere**

austero, estricto, duro, inflexible, adusto, riguroso, severo, rígido, serio

*blando, indulgente, afable, genial*

**authentic**

auténtico, autorizado, exacto, correcto, fiel, fidedigno, genuino, verdadero, real, legítimo, seguro, cierto, puro

*falso, ficticio*

**auxiliary** (s)

1 auxiliar, ayudante, subalterno, suplente

*jefe, director*

2 aliado, confederado

**avarice**

avaricia, avidez, codicia, miseria, mezquindad, rapacidad, tacañería

*prodigalidad, generosidad*

**avenge**

vengar, castigar, pagar, desagraviar, desquitar

*perdonar, condonar, absolver*

**aversion**

aversión, aborrecimiento, antipatía, repugnancia, repulsión, rencor, odio

*simpatía, amor, afición, deseo*

**avidity**

avidez, ansia, apetito, avaricia, afán, apetencia, anhelo, codicia, deseo, voracidad

*aversión, saciedad*

**avoid**
> evitar, evadir, esquivar, eludir, escapar, contenerse, abstenerse de, rehuir

**avow**
> afirmar, admitir, asegurar, aseverar, confesar, declarar, reconocer
> *refutar, renunciar*

**award** *(v)*
> adjudicar, asignar, asentir, conceder, conferir, dar, dispensar, otorgar
> *denegar, recibir*

**awe** *(s)*
> asombro, temor, miedo, horror, terror, pavor, espanto
> *confianza, tranquilidad*

**awe** *(v)*
> atemorizar, asustar, alarmar, aterrorizar, acobardar, desalentar, intimar, sobresaltar

> *animar, envalentonar*

**awful**
> 1 alarmante, espantoso, horroroso, detestable, terrible, horrible, horrendo, tremendo, inquietante, repugnante
> *corriente, normal*
> 2 majestuoso, portentoso, solemne, venerable
> *insignificante, menudo*

**awkward**
> 1 difícil, dificultoso, penoso, complicado, intrincado
> *accesible, sencillo*
> 2 inoportuno, importuno, impertinente, incongruente, inconveniente, indiscreto
> *oportuno, conveniente*
> 3 incómodo, inconveniente, irritante, irritable, molesto, inconfortable, desagradable

# B

**back** *(s)*
final, conclusión, parte posterior, reverso, revés, espalda
*anverso, cara, frente*

**back** *(v)*
1 ayudar, asistir, apoyar, secundar, respaldar, aprobar, mantener, tolerar, sostener
*oponerse, desaprobar*
2 confirmar, ratificar, corroborar
*rechazar*
3 retroceder, recular, desandar, volver grupas
*avanzar*

**backslide**
reincidir, recaer, volver a las andadas, volver a caer
*enmendarse, corregir*

**bad**
1 malo, malicioso, diabólico, ruin, vicioso, malvado, vil, inmoral, tramposo, criminal, falso, abominable, canallesco, mezquino
*bueno, magnánimo*
2 nefasto, funesto, pernicioso, nocivo, peligroso, dañoso, dañino, perjudicial, lastimoso
*bueno, beneficioso*
3 travieso, revoltoso
*bueno, obediente*
4 enfermo, indispuesto, malo
*sano, saludable*
5 difícil, penoso, molesto
*fácil, ameno*
6 usado, malo, de baja calidad, estropeado
*nuevo, flamante, fresco*

**baffle**
1 impedir, parar, detener, dar mate, frenar, entorpecer, estorbar, atar de manos, cortar las alas
*ayudar, facilitar*
2 desconcertar, aturdir, dejar perplejo, confundir, desorientar, turbar
*concertar*

**baleful**
1 siniestro, calamitoso, desastroso, devastador, hiriente, pernicioso, funesto, lastimero, nocivo, dañoso
*bueno, beneficioso, saludable*
2 ceñudo, hosco

**baneful**
dañoso, nocivo, pernicioso, perjudicial, dañino, malo, maléfico, negativo
*inofensivo, bueno, saludable*

**bar** *(s)*
1 obstáculo, barricada, barandilla, impedimento, valladar, estorbo, freno, medida, valla, verja
*facilidad*
2 barra, palanca
3 *(jabón, chocolate)* pastilla, *(chocolate)* tableta
4 bar, *(LAm)* cantina

**bar** *(v)*
1 estorbar, dificultar, entorpecer, impedir, frenar, bloquear, refrenar, reprimir
*facilitar, permitir*
2 excluir, exceptuar
*permitir, admitir*

**barbarous**
1 bárbaro, brutal, inhumano, feroz, cruel, fiero, violento, crudo, bruto
*dulce, cariñoso, humano*
2 ignorante, tosco, cerril, inculto, rudo, grosero, torpe, primitivo, basto, burdo
*refinado, culto, educado*

**bare**
1 desnudo, desvestido, descubierto, desabrigado, destapado, desarropado, desprovisto, *(fig)* sin adorno, sencillo, expuesto, claro, evidente
*vestido, cubierto, arropado*
2 escaso, insuficiente, corto
*suficiente*

**barren**
árido, infecundo, improductivo, desierto, estéril, infértil, improductivo, infructuoso, pobre
*fértil, fecundo, productivo*

**base** *(aj)*
infame, degradado, deshonroso, rastrero, servil, indigno, ignominioso, innoble, vil, ruin, maligno, depravado, abyecto, bajo, corrompido, despreciable, traidor, perverso, falso
*bueno, honorable, noble, sublime*

**bashful**
tímido, falto de confianza, vergonzoso, avergonzado, indeciso, irresoluto, modesto, evasivo, reservado, retraído, *(LAm)* apenado
*decidido, resuelto, desenvuelto*

**bawl**
vocear, dar voces, berrear, vociferar, gritar, chillar, bramar, desgañitarse, rugir
*callar, murmurar, susurrar*

**beaming**
radiante, brillante, resplandeciente, luminoso, centelleante, reluciente, fulgurante, precioso
*apagado, mate*

**beautify**
embellecer, ataviar, engalanar, decorar, ornamentar, adornar
*afear, desfigurar, mutilar*

**beauty**
belleza, hermosura, elegancia, encanto, gracia, guapura, atractivo, delicadeza, exquisitez, atracción
*fealdad, insulsez*

**becoming** *(aj)*
decoroso, correcto, decente, conveniente
*indecente, indecoroso*

**beg**
1 suplicar, solicitar, reclamar, pretender, perseguir
*dar, conceder, entregar, acceder*
2 mendigar, pordiosear, limosnear, suplicar, implorar
*donar*

**beggarly**
1 indigente, necesitado, desamparado
*rico, creso, opulento*
2 *(fig)* bajo, infame, pobre, vil, despreciable, avariento, tacaño, mísero

**begin**
iniciar, comenzar, inaugurar, abrir, empezar, emprender
*terminar, acabar, concluir*

**beginning**
comienzo, prólogo, prefacio, preludio, principio, nacimiento, origen, inicio, estreno, apertura, inauguración
*fin, conclusión, clausura*

**behindhand**
atrasado, tardío, retrasado, pospuesto, postergado, demorado, dilatado
*precoz, temprano, adelantado*

**beleaguer**
sitiar, cercar, asediar, rodear, poner cerco, poner sitio, circunvalar, obstruir, dificultar, acosar, perseguir, bloquear, encerrar
*dejar libre, levantar el sitio*

**bellow** *(s)*
bramido, rugido, grito, chillido, vociferación, alarido, gritería, clamor
*murmullo, susurro*

**bellow** *(v)*
gritar, vocear, chillar, bramar, vociferar

**bemuse**
aturdir, dejar perplejo, turbar, perturbar, azorar, confundir, azarar, desconcertar
*serenar, despabilar*

**bend** *(v)*
encorvar, doblar, torcer, arquear, inclinar, plegar, combar, curvar, desviar
*enderezar, estirar*

**benediction**
1 bendición, beatitud, invocación, plegaria, alabanza, enalteci-

miento, ensalzamiento, engrandecimiento
*ofensa, injuria, imprecación*
2 gracia, ayuda, protección, favor
*maldición, castigo*

**beneficial**
beneficioso, provechoso, favorable, útil, productivo, saludable, ventajoso, rentable, lucrativo
*perjudicial, malo, desfavorable*

**benefit** (s)
1 favor, merced, regalo, ayuda, apoyo
*daño, mal, perjuicio*
2 utilidad, ventaja, rendimiento, provecho, beneficio
*pérdida, gasto*

**benevolent**
benévolo, caritativo, altruista, benéfico, filantrópico, bondadoso, afable, benigno, generoso, amable, humano, cariñoso, compasivo
*malintencionado, inclemente, inhumano*

**benign**
benigno, generoso, amable, servicial, atento, afable, humano, afectuoso, complaciente, favorable
*duro, poco servicial*

**bereave**
privar, despojar, desposeer, expropiar, usurpar, desproveer, (fig) desnudar

**besiege**
asediar, sitiar, cercar, acorralar, bloquear, poner cerco, rodear
*dejar libre, levantar el sitio*

**bestir**
menear, animar, vivificar, ejercer, afanarse, estimular, revolver, agitar
*dejar tranquilo*

**betimes**
temprano, pronto, con adelanto, a tiempo, rápidamente
*tarde, tardíamente*

**betray**
1 traicionar, delatar, entregar, descubrir
*ser leal, proteger*

2 revelar, delatar, divulgar, decir, confesar, publicar, cantar
*ocultar, callar*

**better** (aj)
mejor, preferible, superior, perfeccionado, primero, mayor
*peor, inferior, último*

**better** (av)
de manera superior, en forma superior
*peor, en forma inferior, de manera inferior*

**better** (v)
mejorar, remediar, adelantar, aumentar, reformar, corregir, enmendar, perfeccionar, prosperar, aventajar, acrecentar, renovar, desarrollar, superar
*empeorar, deteriorar, pervertir*

**bewitch**
1 hechizar, extasiar, hipnotizar, embrujar, encantar
*desencantar*
2 (fig) cautivar, atraer, seducir, fascinar, embelesar
*repeler, repugnar*

**bias**
1 predisposición, propensión, inclinación, predilección, tendencia, disposición, talento
*desafecto, repelencia, odio*
2 sesgo, diagonal

**bid** (v)
1 ordenar, mandar, decretar, disponer, decidir, preceptuar, prescribir
*revocar, desobedecer*
2 saludar, dar la bienvenida
3 ofertar, ofrecer

**big**
1 grande, amplio, enorme, colosal, considerable, vasto, espacioso, desmesurado, monumental, extenso, mayúsculo, grandioso
*pequeño, mínimo, corto, minúsculo, menudo*
2 ostentoso, fastuoso, arrogante, presuncioso, engreído, altivo, altanero, orgulloso
*humilde*

**bind**

1 atar, liar, amarrar, juntar, enlazar, ligar, unir
*desatar, desamarrar, soltar*

2 atramparse, embarullarse, verse negro, atascarse, embrollarse, entorpecerse, liarse
*desembarazarse, desliarse*

3 obligar, exigir, imponer
*permitir, facultar, eximir*

**birth**

1 nacimiento, parto, *(fig)* origen, principio
*término, fin*

2 ascendencia, línea, familia

**black**

1 negro, tenebroso, obscuro, negruzco, tenebroso, oscuro
*blanco, claro*

2 infeliz, infausto, desventurado, triste, sombrío, melancólico, aciago, apurado, funesto, atroz
*alegre, fausto, venturoso*

**blacken**

1 ennegrecer, calcinar, ensuciar
*limpiar, emblanquecer*

2 *(fig)* difamar, desprestigiar, mancillar, infamar, desacreditar, denigrar, calumniar, ensombrecer
*honrar, ennoblecer*

**blame** *(v)*

culpar, censurar, condenar, acusar, incriminar, atribuir, achacar, reprender
*excusar, exculpar*

**blameless**

inocente, puro, honesto, honrado, inmaculado, irreprochable, perfecto, intachable
*deshonesto, culpable*

**bland**

amable, afable, afectuoso, agradable, simpático, atento, cortés, cariñoso, bonachón, correcto
*desagradable, descortés, desatento, antipático, severo, duro, cruel, tosco, grosero*

**blasphemy**

blasfemia, indignidad, impiedad, profanidad, irreverencia, sacrilegio
*alabanza, bendición*

**bleach** *(v)*

blanquear, emblanquecer, *(fig)* palidecer
*ennegrecer, ensuciar, oscurecer*

**bleak**

desierto, descubierto, solo, vacío, desolado, desolador, triste, sombrío
*habitado, concurrido, frecuentado*

**blemish**

mancha, nota, defecto, borrón, tacha, deshonra, deshonor
*honra, reputación, honor*

**blend** *(v)*

combinar, mezclar, armonizar, integrar, compaginar, casar, acoplar, ordenar
*descomponer, desintegrar*

**bless**

1 bendecir, alabar, dar gracias, glorificar, elogiar, magnificar, ensalzar, honrar, consagrar, santificar
*ofender, injuriar, insultar*

2 amparar, proteger, favorecer, ayudar, asistir
*abandonar, desamparar, castigar*

**bliss**

felicidad, satisfacción, éxtasis, gloria, alegría, gozo, beatitud, bendición
*sufrimiento, aflicción, desdicha*

**blithe**

alegre, vivo, animado, jovial, festivo, gozoso, vivaz
*triste, apenado, apesadumbrado*

**block** *(v)*

impedir, refrenar, obstaculizar, entorpecer, obstruir, atascar, estorbar, impedir, dificultar, *(LAm)* atorar
*facilitar*

**block** *(s)*

  1 estorbo, obstáculo, traba, entorpecimiento, dificultad, atasco, obstrucción
    *ayuda, favor*

  2 *(edificio)* bloque, manzana, *(LAm)* cuadra

**blot** *(v)*

  1 manchar, ensuciar, motear, salpicar, deslustrar, desfigurar, afear, estropear, malograr, arruinar, mancillar, deshonrar
    *purificar, honrar, limpiar*

  2 cancelar, destruir, borrar, tachar, eliminar
    *purificar, honrar, limpiar*

**blot** *(s)*

  borrón, tachadura, mácula, tacha
  *alabanza, elogio*

**blue** *(fig)*

  1 melancólico, abatido, desanimado, desalentado, pesimista, triste, afligido, desilusionado, taciturno, alicaído
    *alegre, contento, jubiloso*

  2 *(obsceno)* verde, *(LAm)* colorado

**bluff** *(aj)*

  franco, abierto, directo, abrupto, áspero, brusco
  *sinuoso, cerrado, hosco*

**bluff** *(v)*

  engañar, mentir, burlar, falsificar, falsear
  *desengañar, abrir los ojos*

**blunt**

  1 despuntado, desafilado, embotado

  2 *(fig)* brusco, descortés, abrupto, rudo, áspero, desabrido, descortés, grosero
    *cortés, afable, suave*

**boast** *(s)*

  alarde, jactancia, presunción, fanfarronada, vanagloria
  *disimulo, ocultación*

**boast** *(v)*

  alardear, gallardear, lucir, hacer gala
  *ser discreto*

**boil** *(v)*

  hervir, agitar, burbujear, bullir, hervir, echar espuma, rabiar, estar furioso
  *pararse, aquietarse*

**boisterous**

  borrascoso, clamoroso, vociferante, tempestuoso, tormentoso, furioso, frenético, estrepitoso, turbulento, bullicioso, revoltoso, ruidoso
  *tranquilo, sosegado, silencioso*

**bold**

  audaz, aventurero, emprendedor, osado, atrevido, arriesgado, intrépido, valiente, decidido, firme
  *tímido, prudente, comedido*

**bondage**

  cautiverio, cautividad, aprisionamiento, confinación, esclavitud, encarcelamiento, sujeción, internamiento
  *libertad*

**bonny**

  1 bonito, hermoso, bello, agraciado, precioso, lindo
    *feo*

  2 rechoncho, regordete, rollizo
    *flaco*

**boon** *(s)*

  beneficio, favor, gracia, servicio, don, regalo, donación
  *daño, mal, perjuicio*

**boorish**

  palurdo, tosco, paleto, rudo, zafio, basto
  *culto, refinado, urbano, elegante*

**border** *(s)*

  borde, lindero, orilla, linde, falda, labio, margen, límite
  *centro*

**boss** *(s)*

  1 protuberancia, bulto, saliente, relieve, taco
    *hoyo, depresión*

  2 jefe, empresario, capataz, mayoral, superintendente, inspector, director, patrono, patrón, amo, due-

ño, presidente, *(Am) (política)* cacique
*súbdito, subalterno*

**boss** *(v)*
regir, regentar, gobernar, dirigir, administrar, llevar el timón, mandar
*obedecer*

**bother** *(s)*
molestia, enojo, irritación, agitación, perplejidad, problema, estorbo, inquietud, preocupación, incomodo
*goce, tranquilidad, comodidad*

**bother** *(v)*
molestar, incomodar, importunar, perseguir, irritar, enfadar, contrariar
*agradar, contentar*

**boundless**
ilimitado, inmensurable, enorme, infinito, indefinido
*limitado, finito*

**bravado**
bravata, baladronada, chulería, fanfarronada, jactancia
*humildad, modestia, discreción*

**brave** *(aj)*
bravo, osado, valeroso, heroico, valiente, atrevido, intrépido, bizarro, resoluto, esforzado, audaz, decidido
*cobarde, indeciso*

**brazen**
descarado, descocado, desvergonzado, atrevido, deslenguado, fresco, insolente, cínico, impúdico
*prudente, discreto*

**breach** *(s)*
1 brecha, grieta, hendedura, abertura, quebradura, boquete, raja, fisura, rotura, ruptura, cisura
*cierre*
2 discordia, disputa, cisma, diferencia, desacuerdo, disconformidad, discrepancia
*reconciliación*

**brevity**
brevedad, cortedad, abreviamiento, abreviación, condensación, concisión, laconismo
*duración, extensión*

**brief** *(aj)*
1 breve, corto, limitado, compendioso, brusco, seco, restringido, efímero, sucinto, lacónico, conciso
*largo, extenso*
2 efímero, fugaz, pasajero, transitorio
*largo, prolongado*

**bright**
1 brillante, centelleante, luciente, resplandeciente, radiante, brillador, cegador, deslumbrante, esplendoroso, fulgurante, lustroso, nítido, reluciente, chispeante, luminoso
*opaco, mate, apagado, deslucido*
2 claro, despejado, sin nubes, diáfano, puro, lúcido, translúcido, transparente
*nublado, oscuro*
3 inteligente, agudo, listo, perspicaz, ingenioso, sutil
*torpe, tonto, estúpido*
4 alegre, alborozado, animado, jovial, divertido, gracioso, festivo, gozoso
*triste, apenado, apesadumbrado, afligido*

**bring**
traer, trasladar, atraer, aproximar, acercar, transferir, transportar, trasplantar
*llevar, alejar*

**brisk**
activo, ágil, brillante, vivo, enérgico, avispado, eficaz, dinámico
*inactivo, apático*

**broach**
1 abrir, destapar, descubrir
*cerrar, tapar*
2 aludir, sugerir, insinuar, apuntar, mencionar
*omitir, callar*

**brook** *(v)*
permitir, aguantar, sufrir, consentir, admitir, acceder, tolerar, conceder
*prohibir, negar*

**brook** *(s)*
arroyo, riachuelo, arroyuelo

**burden** *(v)*
1 cargar, gravar, asignar, aumentar
*exonerar, desgravar*
2 molestar, fastidiar, incomodar, importunar
*agradar, satisfacer*

**burning**
1 ardiente, llameante, vivo, incandescente, caliente, ardoroso, candente, abrasador
*frío, helado*
2 *(fig)* fervoroso, fogoso, vehemente, ardiente, exaltado
*calmoso, sosegado, tranquilo*

**burnish**
bruñir, pulir, abrillantar, acicalar, lustrar, renovar, restaurar
*deslustrar, deslucir*

**bury**
1 enterrar, sepultar, soterrar
*desenterrar, exhumar*
2 ocultar, esconder, callar, disimular, encubrir
*revelar, descubrir*

**bustle** *(s)*
bullicio, movimiento, agitación, confusión, tumulto, revuelo, sensación, bulla, alboroto, excitación, precipitación
*quietud, paz*

**busy** *(aj)*
ocupado, activo, ágil, diligente, atareado, trabajador, dedicado
*aliviado, aligerado, descargado*

# C

**cacophony**
cacofonía, inarmonía, malsonancia, discordancia
*asonancia, armonía*

**cadaverous**
cadavérico, pálido, macilento, demacrado, lívido
*radiante, rubicundo, rojizo*

**calamity**
calamidad, adversidad, aflicción, cataclismo, desgracia, infortunio, desdicha, catástrofe, prueba, desastre
*dicha, fortuna, victoria*

**calculate**
1 calcular, considerar, pensar, creer, determinar, meditar, suponer
*adivinar*

2 calcular, ajustar, estimar, tasar, valorar, computar, contar

**callous**
insensible, indiferente, impasible, duro, endurecido, flemático, inconmovible, indiferente, apático
*sensible, impresionable, sentimental*

**calm** (*v*)
tranquilizar, aliviar, mitigar, aquietar, calmar, sedar, sosegar, serenar, satisfacer, moderar, aplacar, apaciguar, pacificar
*inquietar, turbar, destemplar*

**calumniate** (*v*)
calumniar, maldecir, denigrar, desvirtuar, desacreditar, hablar mal de, infamar, difamar, vilipendiar
*honrar*

**calumny**
calumnia, abuso, ultraje, ofensa, injuria, mentira, deshonra, falsedad, difamación, falacia, descrédito, maledicencia, murmuración, vilipendio
*verdad, veracidad*

**cancel**
cancelar, anular, abolir, invalidar, abrogar, suprimir, tachar, borrar, rescindir, suprimir, revocar, eliminar
*confirmar, ratificar*

**candid**
franco, sencillo, sincero, leal, natural, abierto, cordial, llano, honrado, imparcial, ingenuo
*parcial*

**capable**
capaz, apto, calificado, idóneo, experimentado, sabio, hábil, competente, experto, diestro, eficiente, eficaz, talentoso
*incapaz, desconocedor, inepto*

**capacious**
amplio, extenso, dilatado, espacioso, ancho, vasto, grande, complejo, exhaustivo
*angosto, reducido, estrecho*

**capital**
1 capital, principal, fundamental, central, primordial, esencial, trascendental
*secundario, menor, accidental*

2 estupendo, admirable, asombroso, pasmoso, fantástico, sorprendente, maravilloso, portentoso, prodigioso, excelente
*horroroso, espantoso*

**capsize**
volcar, capotar, trastornar, trastocar
*sostener, enderezar*

**captivate**
cautivar, atraer, conquistar, granjearse, ganar, interesar, tentar, captarse la voluntad de, hechizar, encantar, dominar, embelesar, extasiar, hipnotizar, seducir, fascinar
*repeler, rechazar*

**captive**
cautivo, confinado, esclavizado, esclavo, dependiente, sujeto, vasallo
*libre, liberado*

**captivity**
cautiverio, cautividad, confinación, esclavitud, encarcelamiento, reclusión, servidumbre, vasallaje
*libertad*

**capture** *(v)*
capturar, agarrar, apresar, atrapar, arrestar, coger, detener, prender
*soltar, liberar*

**cardinal**
capital, cardinal, esencial, fundamental, importante, principal
*secundario, subordinado*

**care** *(s)*
1 cuidado, atención, delicadeza, esmero, meticulosidad, precaución, solicitud
*descuido, desgana*
2 inquietud, agitación, ansiedad, ansia, excitación, impaciencia, intranquilidad, nerviosismo
*calma, sosiego, paz, tranquilidad*

**careful**
1 cuidadoso, circunspecto, cauto, prudente, precavido, reservado, discreto, considerado, vigilante, solícito
*descuidado, imprevisor*
2 inquieto, preocupado, solícito, activo, desasosegado, confuso, impaciente, dinámico
*sosegado, tranquilo, pacífico*

**carnal**
1 animal, carnoso, impúdico, licencioso, voluptuoso, lujurioso, libidinoso, lascivo, sensual
*puro, casto*
2 terrenal, materialista, epicúreo, carnal, humano, secular, mundano
*espiritual*

**castigate**
castigar, escarmentar, disciplinar, reprender, increpar, reñir, enmendar, reprimir
*indulgir, pasar por alto*

**casual**
casual, fortuito, accidental, imprevisto, contingente, incidental, incierto
*pensado, previsto*

**catastrophe**
1 catástrofe, infortunio, calamidad, aflicción, adversidad, desastre, desgracia, cataclismo, mala suerte
*beneficio*
2 conclusión, terminación, consecuencia, desenlace, fin, final, terminación, resultado
*principio, origen*

**catch** *(v)*
1 coger, asir, atrapar, detener, capturar, entrampar, enredar
*soltar, dejar*
2 *(fig)* hechizar, cautivar, encantar, fascinar, seducir
*repeler*

**caustic**
cáustico, corrosivo, quemante, acre, ardiente, cortante, mordaz, penetrante, punzante, picante, virulento
*apacible, suave, blando*

**caution**
1 cautela, circunspección, discreción, prudencia, maña, cuidado, miramiento, previsión
*ingenuidad, sinceridad, inhabilidad, imprudencia*
2 advertencia, amonestación, aviso, censura, reprimenda
*elogio, encomio*

**cautious**
cauteloso, alerta, circunspecto, discreto, vigilante, reservado, prudente, precavido, cauto
*imprudente, desatento, descuidado*

**cease**
cesar, culminar, acabar, concluir, desistir, detener, finalizar, interrumpir, parar, terminar
*empezar, continuar*

**cede**
abandonar, abdicar, ceder, conceder, dimitir, entregar, otorgar,

rendir, renunciar, transferir, someter

*mantener, aguantar*

**celebrated**

célebre, eminente, famoso, conocido, ilustre, magnífico, notable, glorioso, renombrado

*desconocido, oscuro*

**celebrity**

celebridad, distinción, eminencia, fama, gloria, honor, notoriedad, popularidad, renombre, reputación

*anónimo, oscuridad*

**celerity**

celeridad, prisa, precipitación, prontitud, presteza, diligencia, rapidez, velocidad, vivacidad

*lentitud, tardanza*

**censure** *(s)*

censura, condenación, condena, crítica, culpa, desaprobación, protesta, reparo, reproche, reprensión, reprimenda

*elogio, alabanza, encomio*

**ceremonious**

ceremonioso, cortés, correcto, civil, fino, elegante, formal, meticuloso, puntilloso, respetuoso, solemne

*informal*

**certain**

cierto, constante, auténtico, infalible, incuestionable, seguro, irrefutable, manifiesto, palpable, evidente, indubitable, incontestable, positivo, indiscutible, inequívoco, claro, patente, verdadero

*dudoso, incierto, discutible*

**certainty**

certeza, certidumbre, inevitabilidad, certitud, seguridad, convicción, evidencia, verdad, convencimiento

*duda, inseguridad, incertidumbre*

**certify**

certificar, afirmar, aseverar, asegurar, hacer constar, dar fe, declarar, verificar, mostrar

*negar, rechazar*

**cession**

cesión, capitulación, concesión, otorgamiento, renuncia, entrega, traspaso, transmisión, abandono

*resistencia*

**champion** *(s)*

campeón, protector, vencedor, desafiador, defensor, héroe, vindicador

*perdedor*

**champion** *(v)*

apoyar, abogar por, defender

*oponerse, atacar*

**chance** *(aj)*

fortuito, imprevisto, casual, accidental

*previsto*

**chance** *(s)*

casualidad, azar, ocasión, oportunidad, suerte, posibilidad, probabilidad

*certeza*

**chance** *(v)*

arriesgar, exponer, ocurrir, acontecer

*proteger, guardar*

**change** *(s)*

1 cambio, alteración, alternación, innovación, mutación, novedad, revolución, renovación, sustitución, transición, transmutación, transformación, variedad, variación, vuelta

*conservación, permanencia*

2 moneda suelta, suelto, vuelta, *(LAm)* sencillo, feria, vuelto

**change** *(v)*

cambiar, modificar, desplazar, diversificar, fluctuar, variar, trasladar, mover, sustituir, reemplazar, transmitir, girar, convertir, transformar

*permanecer*

**changeable**

cambiable, mudable, modificable, inconstante, irregular, veleidoso, movedizo, inestable, variable, versátil, volátil

*constante, exacto, firme, fijo, estable*

## changeless

inmutable, firme, estable, constante, inalterable, fijo, irrevocable, imperturbable, impasible, permanente

*cambiante, mudable, mutable, alterable*

## chaos

caos, anarquía, confusión, desorden

*orden*

## charitable

1 benevolente, caritativo, benéfico, bondadoso, amable, bueno, pródigo, generoso

*tacaño, agarrado*

2 tolerante, liberal, considerado, atento, comedido, indulgente

*inconsiderado*

## charity

1 caridad, benevolencia, benignidad, compasión, magnanimidad, liberalidad, generosidad, filantropía, altruismo

*egoísmo*

2 socorro, limosna, protección, auxilio

*abandono, desamparo*

## charm (s)

1 hechizo, atracción, fascinación, éxtasis, encanto, embrujamiento, encantamiento, prodigio, embeleso

*repulsión*

2 atracción, fascinación, magia, seducción, encanto

*repulsión, repugnancia*

## charm (v)

1 hechizar, embrujar, encantar, extasiar

*desencantar*

2 cautivar, atraer, seducir, enamorar, deleitar, fascinar, embelesar

*repeler, repugnar*

## chary

cauteloso, silencioso, circunspecto, cuidadoso, reservado, prudente, precavido, callado, astuto, cauto

*imprudente*

## chaste

casto, decente, inmaculado, incorrupto, modesto, puro, virtuoso, honesto, incorrupto, limpio, púdico, platónico

*sensual, lujurioso, libidinoso, impuro*

## chasten

castigar, afligir, reprender, increpar, reñir, reprimir

*indulgir, pasar por alto*

## chastise

castigar, corregir, escarmentar, disciplinar, azotar, flagelar, golpear

*perdonar, absolver*

## cheap

1 barato, saldado, asequible

*caro, costoso*

2 vulgar, ordinario, tosco, basto, de mal gusto, ridículo

*fino, elegante, refinado, superior*

## check (v)

1 parar, detener, impedir, frenar, sujetar, inmovilizar, paralizar, contener, espantar, estancar, retener, estacionar

*movilizar, mover, marchar*

2 controlar, comprobar, examinar, censurar, verificar, criticar, inspeccionar, contrastar, vigilar, intervenir

*descuidar, omitir*

3 reprender, corregir, amonestar, reñir, regañar, reprochar, reconvenir, sermonear, increpar, reprobar, censurar

*encomiar, ensalzar, felicitar*

## cheerful

alegre, radiante, contento, satisfecho, animado, jovial, divertido, gozoso, dichoso, agradable

*triste, apenado, apesadumbrado, afligido, melancólico*

## cheerfulness

alegría, dicha, felicidad, contento, gozo, satisfacción, regocijo, placer, alborozo

*pena, tristeza, pesadumbre, aflicción*

**cheerless**
triste, abatido, desanimado, deprimido, desconsolado, afligido, amargado, nostálgico, taciturno, dolorido, tristón, sombrío, melancólico
*alegre, contento, alborozado, regocijado, radiante*

**cherish**
cuidar, confortar, animar, entretener, guardar, atender, velar, mimar
*abandonar, descuidar, desatender*

**chief** *(aj)*
principal, fundamental, primordial, capital, importante, esencial, trascendente, inexcusable, básico, cardinal
*secundario, accesorio, menor*

**chief** *(s)*
jefe, superior, director, patrono, patrón, amo, capitán, presidente, líder
*inferior, súbdito, vasallo, esclavo, subalterno*

**child**
niño, bebé, pequeño, mocoso, chico, chaval, muchacho, criatura, infante
*adulto*

**childish**
pueril, infantil, pequeño, aniñado, inocente, tierno, ingenuo
*resabiondo, retorcido*

**circuitous**
tortuoso, ambiguo, sinuoso, serpentino, torcido
*recto, llano*

**circulate**
difundir, diseminar, hacer circular, propalar, circular, esparcir, saber, divulgar, transmitir, propagar, publicar, trascender, cundir
*ocultar, encubrir*

**citizen**
ciudadano, habitante, vecino, morador, hombre libre, residente, súbdito
*extranjero*

**civil**
1 municipal, civil, nacional, interior, político
2 refinado, culto, servicial, complaciente, atento, afable, civilizado, cortés, fino, correcto, educado
*mal educado, rudo*

**claim** *(v)*
pedir, demandar, requerir, exigir, cuestionar, insistir
*renunciar*

**clamour** *(s)*
estrépito, clamor, estruendo, exclamación, barahúnda, vocería, vocerío, tumulto, ruido, grito, alboroto, escándalo, vociferación
*quietud*

**clarify**
aclarar, limpiar, purificar, refinar
*manchar, deshonrar*

**clash** *(v)*
sonar, hacer ruido, contender, luchar, diferir, discrepar, interferir, chocar
*estar de acuerdo*

**clasp** *(s)*
alfiler de pecho, prendedor, hebilla, pestillo, broche, pasador, gancho

**clasp** *(v)*
sujetar, apretar, empuñar, agarrar, asir, atar, abrazar, conectar
*aflojar, soltar*

**classify**
clasificar, disponer, arreglar, ordenar, convenir, disponer, colocar, distribuir
*desarreglar, descomponer*

**clean**
1 impecable, intachable, sin defecto, perfecto, sin tacha, inmaculado
*sucio, manchado*
2 aclarado, purificado, sin mezcla, puro, no adulterado, no contaminado
*impuro*
3 casto, honrado, inocente, virtuoso, puro, inmaculado
*inmoral*

4 delicado, elegante, pulcro, esmerado, acicalado, aseado, arreglado
*desmañado*

**clear** *(aj)*

1 claro, brillante, despejado, cristalino, límpido, transparente, luminoso, lustroso, iluminado
*oscuro*

2 aparente, comprensible, inconfundible, visible, evidente, inteligible, manifiesto, obvio, patente, claro

3 vacío, libre, sin estorbos, ilimitado, sin obstáculos, despejado
*obstruido*

4 inocente, libre de culpa, virtuoso, puro, inmaculado
*impuro*

**clear** *(v)*

1 limpiar, asear, purificar, depurar, refinar
*contaminar, ensuciar*

2 absolver, perdonar, exonerar, disculpar, vindicar, justificar
*condenar*

3 emancipar, liberar, soltar
*esclavizar*

4 soltar, desasir, desatar, aflojar
*obstruir, cerrar*

**clever**

listo, inteligente, hábil, apto, diestro, ingenioso, rápido, talentoso, experto
*estúpido, bobo*

**climb**

trepar, subir, escalar
*descender, bajar*

**close** *(v)*

1 atrancar, obstruir, impedir, bloquear, atascar, tapar, cerrar
*abrir, destapar*

2 cesar, completar, concluir, acabar, terminar, completar
*empezar, comenzar, iniciar*

**clutch** *(v)*

apretar, sujetar, empuñar, coger, agarrar, asir, estrechar, arrebatar
*soltar, aflojar*

**coalition**

alianza, asociación, combinación, convenio, pacto, confederación, conjunción, conspiración, liga, unión
*separación*

**coarse**

descarado, descortés, mal educado, inoportuno, rudo, brutal, palurdo, grosero, borde, bruto, bronco, brusco, inculto
*refinado, fino, educado*

**coherence**

coherencia, concordancia, conformidad, coalición, cohesión, congruencia, conexión, correspondencia, unión, unidad
*incongruencia, desacuerdo*

**collect**

acumular, juntar, acopiar, agregar, reunir, amontonar, recoger
*extender, propagar, difundir*

**collection**

1 reunión, colección, asamblea, grupo, multitud, montón, acumulación
*dispersión*

2 limosna, contribución, ofrecimiento, ofrenda

**colossal**

enorme, colosal, gigante, hercúleo, inmenso, monstruoso, vasto, prodigioso
*diminuto*

**combat** *(s)*

combate, batalla, acción, conflicto, contienda, lucha, pelea, escaramuza
*paz*

**combat** *(v)*

batallar, contender, luchar, combatir, enfrentarse, luchar, resistir, oponerse, forcejear

**combine**

combinar, amalgamar, asociar, mezclar, combinar, componer, colaborar, mezclar, unir
*separar*

**comfort** (s)

alivio, ayuda, socorro, favor, mitigación, consolación, disfrute, protección, apoyo
*irritación, enojo*

**comfort** (v)

aliviar, mitigar, animar, alegrar, consolar, alentar, regocijar, fortalecer, vigorizar, estimular
*perturbar, inquietar*

**comfortable**

grande, espacioso, cómodo, agradable, acogedor, encantador, delicioso, grato, próspero
*incómodo, molesto*

**command** (s)

mando, control, dominio, por orden de, asalto, orden, instrucción, gobierno, mandato, precepto, regla
*ruego, súplica*

**command** (v)

ordenar, mandar, obligar, controlar, exigir, reclamar, dirigir, dominar, gobernar, requerir, regir
*suplicar*

**commence**

empezar, comenzar, inaugurar, iniciar, originar, principiar
*terminar, acabar, finalizar*

**commend**

1 aplaudir, aprobar, alabar, elogiar, encomiar, ensalzar
*desaprobar*

2 comprometerse, confiar, entregar, dar, rendir

**commendation**

aprobación, consentimiento, encomio, estímulo, coraje, fomento, panegírico, recomendación
*culpa, censura*

**common**

1 acostumbrado, corriente, común, frecuente, general, habitual, ordinario, usual, normal, *(LAm)* ordinario, vulgar

2 general, común, popular, público, universal
*limitado*

**communicate**

avisar, comunicar, informar, anunciar, escribirse, declarar, revelar, divulgar, impartir, hacer saber, publicar
*ocultar, disimular, encubrir*

**compact** (aj)

1 cerrado, compacto, denso, firme, condensado, comprimido, sólido
*suelto, flojo*

2 conciso, breve, lacónico, compendiado, sucinto
*largo, extenso*

**compact** (s)

1 pacto, convenio, arreglo, contrato, estipulación

2 *(Am) (automóvil)* utilitario

**company**

1 compañía, reunión, colección, círculo, grupo, comunidad, sociedad, muchedumbre, corporación, sindicato, tropa
*individuo*

2 compañerismo, invitados, visitantes, fiesta, guateque
*solicitud*

**compare**

asimilar, cotejar, comparar, competir, parecerse a, asemejarse
*contrastar*

**compass** (s)

área, límite, circunferencia, círculo, circuito, extensión, cercado, recinto, recorrido

**compass** (v)

1 acosar, perseguir, asediar, sitiar, bloquear, circunscribir, cercar, rodear
*excluir*

2 conseguir, ejecutar, efectuar, realizar, cumplir, obtener
*fallar*

**compel**

coaccionar, obligar, forzar, conducir, hacer cumplir, impulsar, incitar, instar
*persuadir*

**compensation**
  compensación, expiación, indemnificación, pago, recompensa, premio, salario, remuneración, gratificación
  *privación*

**complacent**
  1 afable, civil, cortés, educado, servicial, agradecido, reconocido
  *rudo, grosero, descortés*
  2 satisfecho, complaciente, contento
  *descontento, insatisfecho*

**complain**
  lamentar, quejarse, deplorar, acongojarse, afligirse, refunfuñar, gemir
  *resignarse, ser sumiso*

**complete**
  consumado, experto, hábil, diestro, suficiente, adecuado, completo, entero, total, intacto, integral
  *incompleto*

**complication**
  combinación, complicación, complejidad, confusión, enredo, embrollo, mezcla
  *simplificación*

**compliment** (*s*)
  admiración, elogio, encomio, cortesía, atención, favor, adulación, halago, alabanza, homenaje
  *desprecio, insulto*

**compliment** (*v*)
  alabar, elogiar, felicitar, ensalzar, adular
  *insultar*

**complimentary**
  elogioso, de felicitación, encomiador, adulador, ensalzador, panegírico
  *despreciativo, despectivo*

**compose**
  1 componer, integrar, hacer, juntar
  2 construir, inventar, crear, imaginar, endilgar
  3 ajustar, arreglar, regular
  *desarreglar*

  4 apaciguar, aplacar, calmar, suavizar, tranquilizar, pacificar, aliviar
  *excitar, entusiasmar*

**comprehend**
  1 percibir, discernir, comprender, saber, ver, entender
  *interpretar mal, entender mal*
  2 abarcar, constar de, contener, incorporar, encerrar, incluir

**comprehensive**
  amplio, extenso, grande, espacioso, completo, voluminoso, vasto, ancho
  *limitado, reducido*

**concession**
  concesión, privilegio, reconocimiento, beneficio, otorgamiento
  *denegación, negativa*

**concise**
  conciso, breve, compacto, sólido, compendioso, global, abreviado, lacónico, corto, sucinto, sumario
  *prolijo*

**conclude**
  1 cerrar, concluir, terminar, completar, finalizar, acabar
  *empezar, iniciar*
  2 decidir, determinar, deducir, sacar consecuencia de que, inferir, optar por algo, resolverse por, (*Am*) decidir hacer

**condemn**
  1 culpar, censurar, desaprobar, reprochar
  *aprobar, estar de acuerdo*
  2 condenar, sentenciar
  *absolver, exonerar*

**condone**
  condonar, tolerar, disculpar, perdonar, olvidar, dispensar
  *castigar*

**confess**
  1 confesar, reconocer, admitir, conceder, permitir
  *negar*
  2 atestiguar, confesar, declarar, confirmar

**confidence**
1 confianza, creencia, fe, dependencia
*desconfianza, recelo*
2 aplomo, serenidad, audacia, coraje, firmeza, independencia
*aprensión, temor*

**confidential**
1 confidencial, íntimo, privado, secreto
*público*
2 fiel, exacto, fidedigno, confiable, de confianza
*de poca confianza*

**confirm**
1 confirmar, asegurar, establecer, fijar, consolidar, determinar
*refutar, rebatir*
2 confirmar, aprobar, dar por bueno, corroborar, verificar, autorizar
*refutar, confutar*

**congregate**
congregarse, reunirse, convocar a alguien, encontrarse, juntarse
*dispensarse, separarse*

**connect**
asociar, juntar, conectar, adherirse, fusionar, unir, ensamblar
*separar*

**connection**
1 alianza, asociación, unión, enlace, conexión
*disyunción*
2 afinidad, comercio, entendimiento, correspondencia, relación

**conquer**
conquistar, dar mate, aniquilar, destruir, vencer, derrotar, subyugar, triunfar, imperar, predominar
*perder, someter*

**consent** (s)
consentimiento, asentimiento, acuerdo, aprobación, conformidad, permiso
*negativa, denegación*

**consent** (v)
consentir, asentir, acceder, estar de acuerdo, conceder, permitir, ceder
*rehusar, negar, denegar*

**consequence**
consecuencia, efecto, resultado, fin, suceso
*causa*

**consider**
1 considerar, examinar, meditar, reflexionar, consultar, rumiar *(fig)*, ponderar, estudiar
2 respetar, considerar, tener cuidado de
*despreciar, desdeñar*

**considerate**
considerado, atento, comedido, caritativo, circunspecto, prudente, atento, solícito, abnegado, altruista
*egoísta, interesado*

**conspicuous**
aparente, discernible, distinguido, eminente, famoso, manifiesto, notable, obvio, perceptible, remarcable
*insignificante, oscuro*

**constant**
1 constante, firme, fijo, inmutable, estable, perpetuo, permanente, uniforme, regular
*mutable, inestable*
2 resuelto, enérgico, impertérrito, firme, inquebrantable
3 fiel, constante, leal, dedicado
*inconstante, voluble*

**consult**
consultar, preguntar, considerar, meditar, deliberar, interrogar
*dictar, ordenar*

**consume**
consumir, deteriorar, destruir, desperdiciar, agotar, reducir, rebajar, gastar, desvanecerse
*salvar, ahorrar*

**contain**
contener, comprender, incorporar, encerrar, incluir
*excluir*

**contempt**
desdén, desprecio, ignominia, desacato, falta de respeto, indiferencia, insulto, desaire
*honra, respeto*

**content** *(aj)*
   agradable, simpático, satisfecho, contento

**content** *(s)*
   contento, alivio, paz, sosiego, tranquilidad, satisfacción
   *descontento, desagrado, enojo*

**content** *(v)*
   satisfacer, contentar, encantar, deleitar, alegrar, regocijar, complacer, consentir
   *desagradar, ofender*

**continue**
   continuar, durar, extender, perdurar, permanecer, resistir, prolongar, quedar, quedarse, estar, mantener, permanecer
   *parar, cesar*

**continuous**
   continuo, conectado, extendido, prolongado, ininterrumpido
   *cortado, roto*

**contrast** *(s)*
   contraste, comparación, contrariedad, diferencia, diferenciación, distinción, oposición
   *similitud, semejanza, parecido*

**contrast** *(v)*
   comparar, contrastar, diferenciar, distinguir, oponer

**control** *(s)*
   control, mando, gobierno, dirección, guía, supremacía, superintendencia, maestría, autoridad, dominio

**control** *(v)*
   comprobar, controlar, mandar, ordenar, dominar, gobernar, dirigir, regular, manejar, supervisar
   *libertar*

**convenience**
   conveniencia, comodidad, ventaja, confort
   *inconveniencia*

**convenient**
   adaptable, apropiado, beneficioso, cómodo, conveniente, adecuado, hecho a medida, práctico, provechoso, adecuado, útil
   *inconveniente*

**correct** *(aj)*
   exacto, correcto, justo, regular, verdadero, estricto, preciso, equitativo
   *inexacto, incorrecto, erróneo*

**correct** *(v)*
   corregir, ajustar, curar, enmendar, reformar, modificar, mejorar, rectificar, regular, remediar
   *desajustar, estropear*

**correspond**
   1 corresponder, acordar, coincidir, estar de acuerdo, conformarse, armonizar, emparejar, concordar
      *diferir, discrepar*
   2 corresponderse, comunicarse con, escribirse

**corruption**
   adulteración, corrupción, infección, polución, putrefacción
   *pureza*

**costly**
   caro, costoso, valioso, estimable, de precio elevado, lujoso, precioso, espléndido, suntuoso
   *barato*

**courage**
   coraje, audacia, osadía, valor, valentía, atrevimiento, intrepidez, firmeza, fortaleza, resolución
   *cobardía*

**courageous**
   audaz, atrevido, bravo, valeroso, heroico, intrépido, osado, firme, resoluto, valiente, resuelto
   *tímido*

**courteous**
   cortés, afable, atento, ceremonioso, complaciente, civil, elegante, educado, refinado, respetuoso
   *descortés*

**courtesy**
   cortesía, afabilidad, urbanidad, elegancia, buenas maneras, educación, amabilidad
   *descortesía*

**crazy**
   1 deshecho, muy decaído, raquítico, tambaleante
      *entero, intacto*

2 loco, chiflado, disparatado, delirante, demente, desquiciado, idiota, imbécil, tonto, lunático, insensato
*sano, juicioso, sensato*

**create**
1 crear, producir, motivar, causar, originar, constituir, inventar, hacer
*destruir*
2 (*Br*) protestar, armar un lío

**crime**
crimen, delincuencia, falta, delito, culpa, culpabilidad, perversidad, ofensa, pecado, violación, equivocación, debilidad
*sin culpa*

**cripple** (*v*)
estropear, inutilizar, destruir, mutilar, debilitar, dañar, perjudicar, estorbar, restringir
*reforzar, fortalecer*

**cross** (*aj*)
arisco, malhumorado, enojado, criticón, grosero, poco afable, irritable, irascible, displicente, petulante, enojadizo
*agradable, simpático, afable, amistoso*

**cross** (*s*)
(*fig*) infortunio, desgracia, carga, miseria, problema

**cross** (*v*)
1 atravesar, cruzar, pasar por
2 estorbar, dificultar, obstruir, impedir

**crude**
1 crudo, sin cocer, indigesto, sin preparar, inmaduro, verde
*cocido, maduro*
2 (*fig*) ordinario, grosero, inculto
*culto*

**cruel**
bárbaro, brutal, amargo, implacable, feroz, fiero, duro, insensible, inhumano, inexorable, severo, rudo, despiadado, implacable, agresivo
*gentil, amable, benévolo, apacible, compasivo, misericordioso*

**culture**
cultura, civilización, ascenso, mejora, finura, educación
*ignorancia*

**cunning** (*aj*)
1 astuto, artero, taimado, agudo, sagaz, perspicaz
*torpe, ingenuo*
2 diestro, hábil, mañoso, ingenioso, experto
*torpe, lerdo, desmañado*
3 (*Am*) precioso, mono

**curious**
1 curioso, interrogativo, fisgón, mirón, entrometido
*despreocupado*
2 curioso, extraordinario, maravilloso, original, insólito, raro, singular, extraño, único, inusual
*común, ordinario*

**current** (*aj*)
corriente, circulante, común, general, acostumbrado, popular, prevaleciente, presente, extenso, amplio
*poco común, extraño, insólito*

**current** (*s*)
curso, corriente, progresión, río, arroyo, riachuelo, progreso

**custom**
1 costumbre, convención, moda, forma, formalidad, hábito, manera, modo, observación, práctica, regla, utilidad, uso
2 aduana, importación, tasa, tributo, peaje

# D

**daft**

absurdo, atolondrado, bobo, estúpido, imbécil, ingenuo, insensato, idiota, necio, simple
*cuerdo, inteligente, sensato*

**dainty**

1 delicado, elegante, encantador, esmerado, exquisito, fino, pulcro, primoroso, refinado
*grosero, torpe, tosco*

2 apetitoso, delicioso, gustoso, sabroso, tierno
*de mal sabor, incomible*

3 escrupuloso, exigente, fastidioso, quisquilloso

**damage** *(s)*

daño, detrimento, mal, perjuicio, deterioro, pérdida
*beneficio, ganancia*

**damages**

compensación, multa, indemnización, reparación, satisfacción

**damp** *(s)*

bruma, humedad, niebla
*aridez, sequedad*

**danger**

aventura, inseguridad, peligro, riesgo
*seguridad*

**dangerous**

arriesgado, inseguro, peligroso
*seguro*

**dare**

atreverse, aventurar, arriesgar, desafiar, osar, poner en peligro, pretender

**dark**

1 atezado, moreno, negro, oscuro
*iluminado*

2 cubierto, encapotado, nublado, oscuro, sin sol
*claro, soleado*

3 abstruso, enigmático, incomprensible, místico, misterioso, oscuro, oculto, recóndito
*claro, llano, obvio*

4 afligido, melancólico, pesimista, sombrío, taciturno, tétrico, triste
*alegre, de buen amor*

5 indocto, ignorante, no enseñado, poco instruido
*enterado, instruido*

6 atroz, diabólico, detestable, infernal, infame, horrible, pecaminoso, vil, satánico
*limpio, bueno*

**date**

1 fecha, edad, época, era, tiempo

2 cita, compromiso

3 *(Am)* novio, acompañante, pareja

**dawdle**

gandulear, haraganear, holgazanear, perder el tiempo, retardar, retrasar
*apresurarse, darse prisa*

**dawn** *(s)*

alba, amanecer, aurora, salida del sol
*ocaso, puesta del sol*

**dawn** *(v)*

amanecer, aparecer, alborear, elevarse, empezar, brillar, salir, subir

**dead**

1 desaparecido, difunto, exánime, extinguido, inanimado, muerto, falto de aliento
*vivo, activo*

2 apático, apocado, frío, frígido, indiferente, inactivo, insensible, torpe
*animado, activo, vivaz*

3 árido, estéril, inactivo, inoperante, improductivo, inmóvil, quieto
*fértil, fecundo, activo*

**deaden**

amortiguar, aliviar, aminorar, debilitar, deteriorar, mitigar, paralizar, reducir, suavizar
*avivar, animar*

**deadly**

siniestro, funesto, dañino, destructivo, fatal, mortal, mortífero, da-

ñoso, nocivo, pernicioso, venenoso, rencoroso
*inofensivo, inocuo, sano*

**deal** *(s)*

1 reparto, cantidad, porción, distribución, grado, parte

2 pacto, convenio, acuerdo, transacción, trato, negocio

**deal** *(v)*

1 asignar, destinar, repartir, distribuir, conceder, dar, dispensar, dividir, premiar, recompensar
*recoger, recaudar, acumular*

2 negociar, tratar, traficar, regatear, vender

**dear**

1 querido, estimado, amado, apreciado; *(fig)* tesoro, mi vida, mi cielo
*persona no estimada*

2 caro, costoso, de precio elevado
*barato, económico*

**death**

cese, destrucción, desolución, extinción, fallecimiento, fin, final, mortalidad, muerte, partida
*nacimiento, comienzo, origen*

**debase**

1 degradar, despreciar, envilecer, deshonrar, humillar, avergonzar
*exaltar, enaltecer*

2 adulterar, contaminar, corromper, degradar, deteriorar, falsificar, polucionar, teñir
*depurar, purificar*

**debate** *(v)*

debatir, argumentar, deliberar, contender, discutir, disputar, preguntar
*estar de acuerdo, coincidir*

**debt**

atrasos, deber, deuda, obligación, saldo deudor
*crédito, haber*

**decadence**

decadencia, decaimiento, declinación, disminución, degeneración, deterioro, caída, retroceso, retrogradación
*progreso, evolución, aumento*

**decay** *(v)*

decaer, declinar, degenerar, deteriorar, menguar, disminuir, perecer, pudrirse, estropear
*aumentar, desarrollarse, extenderse*

**decease**

muerte, fallecimiento, partida, marcha, disolución
*nacimiento, origen*

**deceit**

engaño, artificio, fraude, trampa, astucia, duplicidad, maña, hipocresía, imposición, pretensión, impostura, cambio, truco
*honestidad*

**deceitful**

engañoso, fraudulento, falso, falsificado, ilusorio, intrigante, falaz, astuto, mañoso, vil, tramposo
*sincero, honesto*

**decent**

decente, adecuado, apropiado, decoroso, conveniente, casto, gentil, delicado, modesto, puro, respetable, tolerable
*indecente, inapropiado*

**decision**

decisión, conclusión, determinación, firmeza, juicio, resolución
*indecisión*

**deck** *(v)*

adornar, aparejar, arreglar, embellecer, decorar, vestir, ornamentar
*desvestir*

**decrease** *(v)*

disminuir, bajar, reducir, rebajar, degradar, acortar, restringir, amainar
*aumentar, extender, ensanchar*

**deduction**

1 conclusión, consecuencia, deducción, inferencia

2 disminución, reducción, rebaja, descuento, renuncia, retirada
*adición*

**deep**

1 profundo, intenso, insondable, oscuro, *(música)* bajo, grave
*poco profundo, superficial*

2 abstracto, oscuro, escondido, misterioso, recóndito, secreto

3 astuto, sagaz, taimado, intrigante, perspicaz, pernicioso, listo, prudente
*simple, ingenuo*

4 absorbente, grave, serio, importante

**default** *(s)*
defecto, destitución, fallo, falta, lapso, negligencia, omisión
*suministro, provisión*

**defeat** *(s)*
conquista, desconcierto, confusión, frustración, derrota, ruina, vencimiento
*victoria*

**defect** *(s)*
defecto, deficiencia, error, tacha, mancha, fallo, falta, imperfección
*perfección*

**defective**
defectuoso, deficiente, imperfecto, incompleto, insuficiente, escaso
*adecuado, perfecto*

**defend**
1 defender, fortificar, cubrir, guardar, preservar, proteger, asegurar, resguardar
*atacar, acosar*

2 justificar, mantener, abogar, defender, vindicar, sostener
*acusar*

**defer**
diferir, aplazar, prorrogar, posponer, retrasar, ganar tiempo, *(LAm)* postergar
*expedir, acelerar*

**deference**
atención, complacencia, condescendencia, consideración, deferencia, estima, honor, cuidado, respeto, reverencia, veneración
*desacato, falta de respeto*

**defiance**
desafío, reto, desobediencia, desprecio, oposición
*reverencia*

**definite**
cierto, claro, exacto, seguro, explícito, fijo, positivo, preciso, específico
*incierto, poco concluyente*

**deform**
deformar, desfigurar, distorsionar, estropear, arruinar, echar a perder
*arreglar, embellecer*

**deft**
hábil, diestro, mañoso, experto, listo, inteligente
*torpe*

**defy**
desafiar, retar, desdeñar, despreciar, descuidar, provocar, enfrentarse con, rechazar
*ayudar, apoyar, animar*

**degrade**
1 degradar, corromper, deteriorar, deshonrar, humillar, herir, pervertir, viciar, desacreditar
*exaltar, fomentar*

2 destituir, degradar, deponer, bajar, reducir al rango inferior
*ascender*

**delay** *(v)*
1 diferir, posponer, prolongar, retrasar, aplazar, ganar tiempo, prorrogar
*dar prisa, adelantar*

2 arrestar, detener, obstruir, retardar, parar, reducir

3 malgastar, perder tiempo, holgazanear, rezagarse, quedarse atrás

**deliberate** *(aj)*
1 considerado, premeditado, intencionado, estudiado, pensado
*fortuito*

2 cuidadoso, cauto, metódico, pausado, cauteloso
*desatento, descuidado*

**delicate**
1 frágil, delicado, quebradizo, calumnioso, débil, sensible
*fuerte*

2 delicado, elegante, exquisito, fino, primoroso, respetable
*basto, burdo, tosco*

3 cuidadoso, discernidor, crítico, escrupuloso, delicado, quisquilloso

**delight** (s)
éxtasis, alegría, júbilo, felicidad, placer
*disgusto*

**delight** (v)
encantar, gratificar, satisfacer, alegrar, dar gusto, dar satisfacción
*desagradar, ofender*

**demand** (v)
pedir, preguntar, cuestionar, reclamar, exigir, interrogar
*abandonar, renunciar*

**demolish**
aniquilar, demoler, destruir, desmantelar, arruinar, echar abajo, derrumbar
*construir, levantar*

**demonstrate**
demostrar, establecer, exhibir, ilustrar, enseñar, mostrar, indicar, manifestar, probar
*refutar*

**denounce**
acusar, atacar, denunciar, procesar, censurar, marcar, proscribir, amenazar
*condenar*

**dense**
1 compacto, cerrado, condensado, denso, pesado, opaco, sólido, sustancial
*delgado, diáfano*
2 denso, lento, estúpido, torpe
*inteligente, ingenioso*

**deny**
1 negar, contradecir, oponer, refutar
*estar de acuerdo, estar conforme*
2 renunciar, abjurar, rechazar, negar, renegar, repudiar
*aceptar*
3 rehusar, rechazar, desestimar
*recibir, aceptar*

**depart**
1 marchar, ausentarse, irse, desaparecer, divergir, apartarse, emigrar, largarse, evaporarse
*llegar*

2 morir, fallecer

**departure**
1 salida, retirada, marcha, ida
*llegada*
2 (fig) abandono, desviación, eliminación, variación, supresión
3 (fig) muerte, fallecimiento

**deplore**
llorar, lamentar, afligirse, acongojarse, sentir
*alegrar, regocijar*

**depress**
1 degradar, humillar, rebajar, bajar, deprimir, abatir, desalentar, oprimir, entristecer, desanimar
*animar, levantar*
2 presionar, rebajar

**deprive**
privar, despojar, desposeer, robar, desnudar, quitar
*proporcionar, dar, deparar*

**descent**
1 declive, bajada, pendiente, caída, cuesta
*ascenso, subida*
2 genealogía, linaje, extracción, familia, transmisión
3 asalto, ataque, incursión, invasión, correría

**desire** (v)
desear, preguntar, pedir, ansiar, suplicar, anhelar, solicitar, añorar
*rehusar, rechazar*

**despair** (s)
desespero, desesperación, desaliento, abatimiento, pesimismo, desánimo
*confianza, esperanza*

**despise**
desdeñar, desatender, descuidar, despreciar, rechazar
*admirar*

**destitute**
indigente, necesitado, pobre, desamparado, afligido, miserable, muy pobre
*rico*

**destroy**
destruir, aniquilar, demoler, derrumbar, devastar, extinguir, extirpar, matar, arruinar, desperdiciar
*crear*

**detach**
desconectar, desunir, dividir, separar
*juntar, unir*

**detail** *(v)*
1 enumerar, alinear, describir, detallar, especificar, representar, individualizar
*generalizar*
2 fijar, señalar, destacar, enviar

**detention**
detención, encierro, confinamiento, estorbo, restricción, limitación
*libertad*

**deteriorate**
degenerar, deteriorar, estropear(se), degradar, depravar, depreciar, perjudicar, dañar, empeorar
*mejorar, perfeccionar*

**determination**
1 determinación, constancia, firmeza, persistencia, resolución
*indecisión*
2 determinación, conclusión, decisión, juicio, objetivo, resultado

**detest**
detestar, aborrecer, despreciar, odiar, execrar, desdeñar
*amar, querer, apreciar*

**deviate**
apartar, partir, salir, diferir, variar, divergir, errar, equivocarse
*continuar, seguir*

**devour**
1 devorar, engullir, comer rápidamente, consumir, tragar
*vomitar, arrojar*
2 desaparecer, desvanecerse, palidecer, declinar, menguar
*crecer, aumentar*

**differ**
1 diferir, cambiar, variar
*corresponder*
2 discutir, altercar, pelear, oponerse, disputar, no estar de acuerdo, reñir
*estar de acuerdo*

**difference**
1 diferencia, distinción, diversidad, variedad, variación
*similitud, semejanza*
2 diferencia, argumento, discusión, debate, desacuerdo, disputa, discordancia, pelea
*acuerdo*

**difficulty**
1 dificultad, obstáculo, impedimento, labor dura, oposición, tenacidad, terquedad
*facilidad, complacencia*
2 dilema, desgracia, turbación, desconcierto, perplejidad, problema

**dig**
1 desguazar, parcelar, excavar, cavar, ahuecar, vaciar
*llenar*
2 punzar, picar, clavar, hincar

**digest**
1 digerir, asimilar, confeccionar, incorporar, macerar
2 arreglar, clasificar, codificar, disponer, sistematizar, tabular, reducir
*exponer*
3 asimilar, considerar, meditar, estudiar, ponderar

**diligent**
diligente, activo, asiduo, atento, ocupado, cuidadoso, constante, trabajador, infatigable, laborioso, perseverante, persistente
*holgazán, vago*

**dim** *(aj)*
1 nublado, oscuro, tenebroso, brumoso
*claro*
2 imperfecto, indefinido, indistinto, obtuso, manchado, deslustrado
3 *(Br)* lerdo

**diminish**
disminuir, abatir, acortar, abreviar, restringir, cortar, reducir, encoger

*aumentar*

**direct** *(aj)*

1 directo, recto, sin tergiversaciones, sin tapujos
*enrevesado, rebuscado*

2 absoluto, categórico, franco, obvio, inequívoco, ambiguo, abierto
*intricado, enrevesado*

**dirty** *(aj)*

1 sucio, mugriento, puerco, asqueroso, repugnante
*limpio, aseado*

2 nublado, oscuro, fangoso, lodoso

**disagree**

1 diferir, variar, desviarse

2 argumentar, debatir, no estar de acuerdo, diferir, disputar, discutir
*estar de acuerdo*

**disappear**

desaparecer, cesar, marchar, desvanecer
*aparecer*

**disaster**

accidente, adversidad, calamidad, desastre, infortunio, reverso
*buena suerte*

**discern**

1 contemplar, discernir, descubrir, espiar, notar, observar, percibir, ver, reconocer

2 diferenciar, hacer discriminaciones, distinguir, juzgar
*confundir*

**disciple**

discípulo, seguidor, aprendiz, partisano, alumno, estudiante
*maestro*

**discipline** *(s)*

control, corrección, cultura, disciplina, educación, enseñanza, ejercicio, instrucción, regulación, entrenamiento

**disclose**

comunicar, descubrir, hacer saber, divulgar, exponer, impartir, destapar, revelar, decir
*callar, esconder*

**discomfort**

enojo, contrariedad, inquietud, problema, desasosiego
*confort, comodidad, tranquilidad*

**discord**

discordia, desacuerdo, diferencia, disensión, oposición, ruptura, variación, riña, discusión
*armonía, acuerdo*

**discount** *(s)*

descuento, deducción, reducción, subvención, rebaja
*añadidura*

**discourage**

1 avergonzar, atemorizar, desalentar, deprimir, asustar, intimidar
*alentar, animar*

2 desfavorecer, disuadir, desalentar, estorbar, dificultar
*aprobar, tolerar*

**discredit** *(v)*

1 no creer, dudar, cuestionar
*creer*

2 reprochar, desacreditar, deshonrar
*honrar*

**discrepancy**

discrepancia, diferencia, desacuerdo, discordancia, inconsistencia, variación
*acuerdo*

**disguise** *(v)*

encubrir, disimular, enmascarar, esconder, ocultar, tapar
*revelar, demostrar*

**disgust** *(v)*

aborrecer, abominar, disgustar, no agradar, repeler, causar náuseas
*agradar, gustar*

**dishonest**

deshonesto, corrompido, astuto, engañoso, fraudulento, bellaco, bribón, pérfido, traicionero
*honesto, honrado*

**dishonour**, *(Am)* **dishonor** *(s)*

degradación, descrédito, deshonra, deshonor, infamia, ignominia, odio, escándalo, vergüenza
*honor*

**disinterested**
> imparcial, desinteresado, indiferente, sin interés, sin perjuicios
> *parcial*

**dislike** *(s)*
> antagonismo, aversión, desaprobación, disgusto, desinclinación, desagrado
> *gusto, afición, cariño*

**dismay** *(s)*
> alarma, consternación, miedo, temor, horror, terror
> *seguridad*

**dismiss**
> desterrar, destituir, desechar, descartar, dispersar, rechazar
> *guardar, mantener*

**disorder** *(s)*
> 1 confusión, desorden, desarreglo, irregularidad, revoltijo, lío
> *orden, arreglo*
> 2 clamor, conmoción, griterío, lucha, pelea, rebelión, desorden, alboroto, tumulto
> *orden, tranquilidad*
> 3 *(medicina)* indisposición, desorden, enfermedad, achaque, dolencia

**dispassionate**
> 1 calmado, imperturbable, moderado, quieto, sereno, sobrio, nada excitable, templado
> *excitado*
> 2 cándido, imparcial, desinteresado, indiferente, neutral
> *parcial*

**display** *(s)*
> muestra, exhibición, demostración, ostentación, espectáculo, boato

**disprove**
> refutar, confutar, rebatir, rechazar
> *confirmar*

**dispute** *(s)*
> altercado, disputa, controversia, debate, discusión, pelea, desacuerdo
> *acuerdo*

**disqualify**
> descalificar, incapacitar, estropear, inhabilitar
> *calificar*

**disregard** *(v)*
> desobedecer, despreciar, desdeñar, ignorar, descuidar, desatender, pasar por alto
> *respetar, obedecer*

**dissent** *(s)*
> diferencia, desacuerdo, oposición, negativa, denegación, disentimiento
> *acuerdo*

**dissent** *(v)*
> disentir, disidir, declinar, diferir, negar, denegar
> *estar de acuerdo*

**distance**
> 1 ausencia, distancia, intervalo, separación, espacio, alejamiento
> *proximidad, cercanía*
> 2 reserva, frialdad, frigidez
> *amistad*

**distant**
> 1 lejano, remoto, distante, apartado, lejos
> *cerca*
> 2 *(fig)* ceremonioso, distante, reservado, frío, altivo, arrogante
> *amistoso, cordial*
> 3 apagado, indirecto, indistinto, ligero
> *claro*

**distaste**
> antipatía, aversión, disgusto, desinclinación, desagrado, descontento, insatisfacción, repugnancia
> *simpatía, afición*

**distinct**
> 1 claro, distintivo, manifiesto, obvio, plano, inconfundible, inequívoco, bien definido
> *indistinto, vago*
> 2 definido, diferente, individual, separado, desconectado

**distinguished**
> 1 distinguido, célebre, famoso, eminente, ilustre, notable
> *común*

2 conspicuo, extraordinario, marcado, notable
*corriente, ordinario*

**distort**

retorcer, deformar, distorsionar, falsificar, torcer, desfigurar, tergiversar
*enderezar, poner derecho, desenmarañar*

**distraction**

1 abstracción, agitación, distracción, conmoción, confusión, discordia, desorden, disturbio
*ecuanimidad*

2 aberración, delirio, *(mental)* desarreglo, frenesí, alucinación, incoherencia, manía, locura, demencia
*cordura, sensatez, juicio*

**distress** *(s)*

adversidad, aflicción, agonía, angustia, ansiedad, calamidad, destitución, pena, indigencia, miseria, necesidad, penuria, pobreza, privación, sufrimiento
*confort, consuelo, alivio, comodidad*

**distribute**

distribuir, administrar, arreglar, asignar, destinar, dar, disponer, dividir, tratar
*reunir, acumular, recaudar*

**disturb**

1 confundir, desquiciar, desarreglar, desordenar, perturbar, trastornar
*arreglar, ordenar, disponer*

2 agitar, enfadar, distraer, excitar, molestar, incomodar, interrumpir
*pacificar, suavizar*

**diversion**

1 diversión, alegría, distracción, entretenimiento, juego, placer, recreo, pasatiempo
*trabajo, tarea, labor*

2 *(Br)* rodeo, desviación, digresión

**divert**

1 distraer, apartar, *(Br)* *(tráfico)* desviar
*enderezar, poner derecho*

2 divertir, gratificar, recrear, disfrutar, entretener
*aburrir*

**divide**

1 dividir, bisecar, cortar, partir, segregar, separar, romper
*juntar, unir*

2 asignar, señalar, aportar, tratar, distribuir, repartir, dividir
*retener, conservar*

3 alienar, desunir, enajenar, apartar
*unir*

**dogged**

malhumorado, arisco, intratable, testarudo, obstinado, perverso, resoluto, terco, hosco, taciturno, desabrido, poco afable, resentido
*dócil, amigable, afable*

**dole** *(v)*

asignar, distribuir, dividir, repartir, señalar, gratificar, dar

**domestic** *(aj)*

1 domiciliario, doméstico, familiar, hogareño, privado
*público*

2 domado, domesticado, manso, dócil
*salvaje*

3 interno, interior, nacional
*extranjero*

**dominion**

1 dominio, autoridad, mando, control, gobierno, jurisdicción, supremacía
*servidumbre, sumisión*

2 país, reino, región, territorio, dominio

**dormant**

durmiente, inactivo, inerte, latente, vago, quieto, reposado, perezoso
*activo*

**doubt** *(s)*

1 duda, indecisión, irresolución, vacilación, suspense
*resolución*

2 desconfianza, recelo, sospecha

## doubtful

1 desconfiado, dudoso, vacilante, irresoluto, sospechoso, escéptico
   *resoluto*
2 ambiguo, dudoso, equívoco, oscuro, precario, inseguro, problemático, cuestionable
   *cierto, seguro*

## draw (v)

1 dibujar, delinear, diseñar, trazar, esbozar, bosquejar
2 tirar, arrastrar, dragar, acarrear, remolcar, tobar
   *empujar*
3 deducir, derivar, inferir
4 atraer, influenciar, tentar, fascinar, inducir, persuadir
5 secar, inhalar, inspirar, chupar

## dreadful

alarmante, horrible, horroroso, monstruoso, chocante, terrible, tremendo
*agradable*

## dream (s)

sueño, ilusión, fantasía, alucinación, imaginación, especulación, visión, trance
*realidad*

## dreary

1 depresivo, triste, solitario, incómodo, tétrico, pesaroso, afligido
   *alegre*
2 monótono, aburrido, tedioso, ininteresante, soso, insípido
   *interesante*

## dress (v)

1 vestir, arreglar, trajear, adornar, embellecer, ataviar, engalanar
   *desvestir, desnudar*
2 ajustar, alinear, arreglar, disponer, preparar
   *desarreglar*

## drift (s)

1 acumulación, pila, montón, diluvio
2 corriente, impulso, ímpetu, ráfaga
3 objetivo, dirección, objeto, propósito, tendencia
   *carencia de objetivo*

## drive (v)

1 ir, conducir, viajar, guiar, *(LAm)* manejar
2 empujar, enviar, lanzar, arrojar, impulsar, propulsar

## drop

1 descender, disminuir, bajar, declinar, menguar, perder valor
   *subir, alzar*
2 abandonar, cesar, desertar, manchar, dejar, remitir, descontinuar
   *aguantar, seguir*

## dry (aj)

1 seco, sediento, árido, estéril
   *mojado, húmedo*
2 *(fig)* aburrido, solitario, incómodo, tedioso, fatigoso, ininteresante
   *interesante*
3 *(fig)* agudo, sagaz, sarcástico, perspicaz

## dubious

1 dudoso, incierto, sin decidir, vacilante, indeciso, irresoluto
   *cierto, seguro*
2 ambiguo, equívoco, oscuro, problemático
   *obvio, claro*

## dunce

burro, asno, cabeza de chorlito, simple, imbécil, bobalicón, bobo, zoquete
*genio*

## dusky

1 oscuro, moreno, tostado
2 algo oscuro, nublado, sombrío, débil, lóbrego, encapotado, cubierto
   *claro, con luz*

## dwell

habitar, vivir, morar, permanecer, residir, estar, parar
*viajar*

## dwindle

decaer, declinar, disminuir, reducir, aminorar, encoger, languidecer, consumirse
*aumentar, crecer*

# E

**eagerness**
    ardor, fervor, avidez, ansia, codicia, avaricia, impetuosidad, vehemencia
    *apatía*

**early** *(aj)*
    temprano, prematuro, delantero, avanzado, oportuno
    *tardío*

**earn**
    ganar, adquirir, merecer, obtener, conseguir, lograr, recoger, *(fig)* cosechar
    *perder, gastar*

**earnest** *(aj)*
    1 ardiente, entusiasta, fervoroso, celoso, apasionado
    *flojo, calmado*
    2 resuelto, enérgico, firme, fijo, grave, absorto, atento, sincero, solemne, estable
    *poco sincero*

**earnings**
    emolumento, salario, paga, beneficios, remuneración, sueldo, estipendo
    *gasto*

**ease**
    1 calma, confort, tranquilidad, felicidad, paz, reposo, relajamiento, serenidad, quietud
    *incomodidad, sin tranquilidad*
    2 facilidad, preparación, buena disposición, disponibilidad
    3 libertad, flexibilidad, informalidad, naturalidad
    *formalidad, seriedad*

**easy**
    1 fácil, ligero, sin dificultad
    *difícil*
    2 confortable, cómodo, satisfecho, tranquilo
    *incómodo*
    3 servicial, complaciente, atento, sumiso, dócil, manejable, tratable, afable, gentil, informal

*exigente, poco natural, formal*

**eccentric**
    excéntrico, anómalo, anormal, aberrante, irregular, extraño, raro, peculiar, singular, inusual
    *normal, natural*

**economize**
    economizar, ahorrar, hacer economías
    *malgastar, despilfarrar, gastar, derrochar*

**edge**
    1 borde, límite, lindero, margen, labio, punta
    *centro*
    2 animación, interés, agudeza, entusiasmo
    *franqueza, brusquedad*

**educate**
    educar, cultivar, desarrollar, disciplinar, enseñar, adoctrinar, instruir, entrenar, ejercitar
    *descuidar, desatender*

**effect**
    1 efecto, consecuencia, evento, acontecimiento, fruto, resultado
    *causa*
    2 eficacia, poder, fuerza, hecho, realidad, peso, validez
    3 impresión, significado, tenor, sentido, intención

**effective**
    capaz, activo, adecuado, correcto, competente, efectivo, eficaz, eficiente, enérgico, poderoso
    *incompetente, ineficaz*

**effeminate**
    afeminado, delicado, femenino, suave, tierno, mujeril
    *masculino, viril, varonil*

**efficient**
    capaz, competente, efectivo, eficaz, enérgico, poderoso, hábil, diestro
    *ineficaz, débil*

**eject**
desterrar, descastar, desechar, rechazar, disponer, emitir, denegar
*retener*

**elaborate** (v)
desarrollar, elaborar, mejorar, producir
*simplificar*

**elated**
animado, alegre, excitado, elevado, sublime, eufórico
*deprimido, abatido*

**elegance**
belleza, elegancia, gracia, garbo, finura, corrección, gusto
*desmaña, torpeza, inferioridad*

**element**
1 base, componente, elemento, factor esencial, ingrediente, partícula, principio, unidad
*compuesto*
2 elemento, esfera, entorno, (medio) ambiente

**elementary**
básico, elemental, fundamental, inicial, introductorio, primario, rudimentario, simple
*avanzado, secundario*

**eliminate**
soltar, eliminar, excluir, expeler, sacar, omitir, separar, rechazar
*incluir*

**elude**
1 evitar, evadir, escapar, eludir, esquivar, rehuir
*confrontar*
2 desconcertar, estorbar, decepcionar, frustrar, impedir
*ayudar*

**embarrass**
avergonzar, confundir, complicar, desconcertar, enfadar, molestar, impedir, enredar, enmarañar, turbar, agitar, (LAm) apenar
*confortar, simplificar*

**embrace**
1 abrazar, agarrar, estrechar, apretujar
*soltar*

2 comprender, compendiar, contener, incluir, cubrir, abarcar
*exceptuar*

**eminent**
célebre, eminente, famoso, distinguido, notable, prominente, renombrado
*común, corriente*

**emotion**
agitación, excitación, emoción, pasión, perturbación, simpatía, trepidación
*apatía*

**employ** (v)
emplear, comisionar, encargar, ocupar, contratar, fichar, alquilar
*despedir*

**empty** (aj)
1 vacío, en blanco, desolado, sin ocupar, vacante, sobrante, superfluo, desocupado
*lleno*
2 inefectivo, irreal, insatisfactorio, insustancial, falso
*satisfactorio*

**enable**
permitir, autorizar, capacitar, comisionar, aprobar, preparar,
*prohibir*

**enact**
1 autorizar, mandar, decretar, promulgar, establecer, ordenar, sancionar
*anular*
2 actuar, representar, escenificar, hacer el papel de

**encircle**
circunscribir, cercar, encerrar, rodear, envolver
*excluir*

**encounter** (v)
1 confrontar, enfrentar, ponerse de cara a, encontrarse con, tropezar con
*evitar, eludir*
2 atacar, combatir, contender, luchar, hacer frente a, esforzarse

**end** *(s)*

1 límite, lindero, extremo, final, fin, extremidad, término

2 objetivo, diseño, ideal, propósito, intención

3 consecuencia, conclusión, terminación, resultado, logro, obtención

**endorse**

confirmar, ratificar, aprobar, apoyar, sostener, mantener
*oponer*

**endurance**

entereza, valor, fortaleza, paciencia, resignación, sumisión, tolerancia
*cesación, suspensión, impaciencia*

**endure**

soportar, continuar, experimentar, sufrir, permanecer, sostener, tolerar, persistir
*cesar, fallar*

**enemy**

enemigo, adversario, antagonista, oponente, rival
*aliado, amigo*

**energy**

energía, actividad, animación, eficacia, eficiencia, fuerza, intensidad, espíritu, vigor, entusiasmo
*inactividad*

**enhance**

agravar, aumentar, elevar, exaltar, mejorar, engrosar
*desmejorar, estropear, disminuir*

**enjoy**

agradar, gustar de, divertirse, pasarlo bien
*tener aversión, desagradar*

**enlarge**

amplificar, agrandar, aumentar, difundir, multiplicar, engrosar
*disminuir, reducir*

**enlighten**

informar, instruir, edificar, educar, iluminar, enseñar
*confundir*

**enough** *(aj)*

bastante, suficiente, abundante, adecuado, amplio
*inadecuado*

**enrich**

adornar, enriquecer, decorar, embellecer, ornamentar, dotar
*mermar, reducir*

**enterprise**

1 aventura, esfuerzo, plan, proyecto, ventura, ensayo, empresa, tarea

2 actividad, audacia, energía, atrevimiento, espíritu, disponibilidad
*prudencia, cautela*

**entertain**

1 recrear, divertir, animar, alegrar, complacer
*cansar*

2 considerar, cuidar, proteger, mantener, soportar, tratar
*rechazar*

**entitle**

1 llamar, denominar, designar, caracterizar, nombrar

2 autorizar a, capacitar, ajustar
*incapacitar, inhabilitar*

**entrance**

1 entrada, acceso, avenida, puerta, portal, verja, ingreso, pasaje
*salida*

2 principio, comienzo, inicio, iniciación, introducción

**entreat**

pedir, suplicar, implorar, importunar, rogar
*demandar*

**envy** *(s)*

envidia, rencor, odio, celos, malicia
*desdén*

**ephemeral**

efímero, breve, evanescente, fugaz, fugitivo, corto, transitorio
*permanente, perdurable*

**epitome**

abreviación, compendio, abstracto, condensación, contracción, resumen, epítome
*expansión*

**equity**

honestidad, imparcialidad, justicia, rectitud, equidad, honradez
*injusticia, deslealtad*

**erase**
    borrar, anular, cancelar, suprimir, tachar, eliminar, destruir, *(Am)* *(matar)* liquidar
    *restaurar*

**erect**
    construir, edificar, erigir, elevar, establecer, fundar, instituir, levantar
    *destruir, demoler*

**erroneous**
    erróneo, falso, inexacto, incorrecto, equivocado
    *correcto*

**error**
    1 metedura de pata, error, error garrafal, sofisma, falacia, incorrección, equivocación
    *corrección*
    2 delincuencia, falta, ofensa, pecado, transgresión, equivocación

**escape** *(v)*
    escapar, evitar, evadir, eludir, volar, esquivar, rehuir
    *enfrentar, confrontar*

**especial**
    especial, distinguido, marcado, particular, principal, específico, inusual
    *corriente, normal*

**essential**
    1 esencial, básico, fundamental, importante, indispensable, inherente, innato, necesario, vital
    *superfluo*
    2 refinado, volátil, rectificado

**establish**
    1 constituir, establecer, actuar, fijar, fundar, inaugurar, instalar, instituir, organizar
    *destruir*
    2 confirmar, demostrar, probar, ratificar, verificar
    *desaprobar*

**eternal**
    eterno, inmortal, inmutable, indestructible, infinito, interminable, perpetuo
    *temporal*

**ethereal**
    celestial, aéreo, delicado, feérico, mágico, espiritual, tenue, volátil
    *material*

**evacuate**
    1 evacuar, descargar, vaciar, expulsar, excretar
    *llenar*
    2 abandonar, marchar, dejar, desertar, renunciar
    *aguantar, mantener*

**evaporate**
    1 evaporar, vaporizar, secar, deshidratar
    *condenar*
    2 *(fig)* esfumarse, desvanecerse

**ever**
    siempre, constantemente, continuamente, eternamente, para siempre, incesantemente, perpetuamente
    *nunca, jamás*

**evil** *(s)*
    1 demonio, mal, corrupción, maldición, depravación, perversión, culpabilidad, malignidad, pecado, equivocación, maldad
    2 calamidad, desastre, daño, miseria, pena, desgracia, infortunio, sufrimiento

**exact** *(aj)*
    1 exacto, cuidadoso, correcto, fiel, literal, metódico, ordenado, preciso, puntilloso
    *inexacto*
    2 riguroso, escrupuloso, estricto, severo
    *impreciso, vago*

**exaggerate**
    exagerar, aumentar, engrandecer, sobreestimar
    *minimizar*

**exalt**
    1 exaltar, elevar, promocionar, dignificar, ennoblecer, enaltecer
    *humillar*
    2 exaltar, glorificar, bendecir, alabar, ensalzar

**excessive**

1 excesivo, desproporcionado, enorme, exorbitante, irrazonable, superfluo, desmedido, desmesurado
*razonable*

2 extremo, inmoderado, intemperado
*sobrio*

**excite**

1 animar, despertar, incitar, inflamar, excitar, estimular, levantar
*calmar, apaciguar*

2 agitar, irritar, provocar, molestar
*calmar, apaciguar*

**exclude**

1 prohibir, excluir, exceptuar, eliminar, omitir, vetar, proscribir
*incluir*

2 arrojar, expeler, expulsar, excluir, sacar
*admitir*

**excuse** (v)

1 excusar, exculpar, absolver, exonerar, perdonar
*condenar*

2 liberar, exentar, eximir, soltar, libertar
*obligar*

**exemption**

exención, absolución, dispensación, excepción, inmunidad, libertad, privilegio
*obligación*

**exhaust** (v)

1 vaciar, secar, filtrar, evacuar
*rellenar*

2 consumir, agotar, gastar, disipar, derrochar, malgastar
*economizar*

3 debilitar, cansar, fatigar, enervar
*reforzar*

**exile** (v)

exiliar, expatriar, expulsar, excluir de la sociedad, proscribir
*repatriar*

**exist**

existir, ser, estar, respirar, continuar, durar, vivir
*cesar, morir*

**expand**

extenderse, desarrollar, difundir, dilatar, distender, engrandecer, aumentar, ampliar, inflar
*contraer*

**expansion**

expansión, desarrollo, difusión, dilatación, distensión, engrandecimiento, aumento, inflación, hinchazón
*contracción*

**expectation**

expectación, anticipación, confidencia, esperanza, perspectiva, expectativa, confianza
*realización*

**expedient** (aj)

apropiado, ventajoso, aconsejable, conveniente, deseable, provechoso, adecuado
*inapropiado, inconveniente*

**expedient** (s)

método, manera, esquema, recurso, estratagema, treta, expediente

**expensive**

caro, costoso, de precio elevado, extravagante
*barato*

**expert**

experto, diestro, hábil, mañoso, apto, inteligente, rápido, listo, preparado
*torpe*

**expire**

1 cesar, cerrar, concluir, terminar, parar
*empezar*

2 emitir, exhalar, espirar

3 marchar, expirar, partir, morir, fallecer

**explain**

clarificar, definir, explicar, exponer, ilustrar, interpretar, justificar, enseñar
*confirmar*

**expose**

1 exponer, mostrar, enseñar, visualizar, exhibir, revelar
*ocultar, disimular*

2 traicionar, denunciar, identificar, detectar, desenmascarar

3 exponer, peligrar, arriesgar, comprometer

**expressive**

1 enfático, energético, vigoroso, animado, fuerte, vivo
*apagado*

2 expresivo, significante, indicativo, sugestivo
*inexpresivo*

**extend**

1 aumentar, continuar, dilatar, engrandecer, extender, prolongar, ampliar
*acortar*

2 dar, ofrecer, otorgar, rendir, deparar

**exterminate**

abolir, aniquilar, destruir, eliminar, exterminar, desarraigar, extirpar
*originar*

**external**

1 exterior, superficial, de afuera, externo
*interno*

2 citar, determinar, seleccionar, extraer

**extraordinary**

extraordinario, excepcional, maravilloso, particular, raro, peculiar, remarcable, singular, inusual
*ordinario, corriente, usual*

**extravagant**

1 excesivo, exorbitante, inmoderado, desmesurado, desmedido, extravagante, pródigo
*económico*

2 absurdo, tonto, ridículo, irrazonable
*razonable*

**extreme**

1 extremo, final, último, mayor, supremo
*inicial*

2 excesivo, inmoderado, irrazonable
*razonable*

**exuberance**

abundancia, copiosidad, exceso, exuberancia, lujuria, profusión, superabundancia
*escasez*

**exuberant**

abundante, copioso, excesivo, exuberante, lujurioso, profuso, rico, superabundante
*escaso*

# F

**fable**
1 fábula, alegoría, apólogo, leyenda, mito, parábola, historia, cuento
2 ficción, invención, mentira, falsedad, quimera
*realidad*

**fabricate**
1 construir, erigir, fabricar, hacer, manufacturar, disponer, idear
*destruir, tirar*
2 *(fig)* acuñar, falsificar, fingir, inventar, aparentar, forjar, fraguar

**face** *(s)*
1 apariencia, aspecto, expresión, mirada, prestigio, reputación
2 confianza, seguridad, aplomo, audacia, atrevimiento, descaro, insolencia
*vergüenza, desconfianza*

**facilitate**
facilitar, expedir, dar, ayudar
*estorbar, dificultar*

**fact**
1 hecho, acto, acción, incidente, ocurrencia, actuación
2 certeza, realidad, verdad
*ficción*

**faction**
1 cábala, confederación, coalición, combinación, grupo, conjunto, partido
2 desacuerdo, disconformidad, rebelión, recalcitración, turbulencia, tumulto
*acuerdo*

**fail**
1 fallar, cesar, declinar, desaparecer, desvanecer, ahogar, debilitar
2 perder, fracasar

**failure**
1 fallo, declive, deficiencia, pérdida, negligencia, omisión, defecto
*éxito*

2 bancarrota, quiebra, insolvencia, caída, ruina

**faint**
desmayar, fallar, debilitar, languidecer, consumirse

**fair** *(aj)*
1 rubio, claro, con luz, intachable, sin tacha, blanco
*oscuro*
2 cándido, franco, honesto, imparcial, derecho
*injusto, no equitativo*
3 mediocre, pasable, tolerable, prometedor, regular
*bueno*
4 atractivo, hermoso, bonito, elegante, gentil, lindo

**fall** *(v)*
1 rebajar, mitigar, declinar, reducir, descender, menguar, decaer, disminuir, caer
*subir, aumentar*
2 errar, equivocarse, caer, ofender, pecar, transgredir
3 morir, desvanecerse, desaparecer

**false**
1 falso, mentiroso, mendaz, informal, ficticio
*verdadero, genuino*
2 deshonesto, deshonrado, falso, infiel, desleal, traidor, pérfido
*leal, honesto*
3 erróneo, incorrecto, impropio, falso, equivocado, infundado
4 falso, engañoso, fraudulento, ilusorio, hipócrita

**fame**
fama, celebridad, eminencia, gloria, honor, notoriedad, renombre, reputación, buena fama
*deshonra, deshonor, descrédito*

**familiar**
1 familiar, acostumbrado, afable, amigable, cordial, informal, ínti-

mo, cercano, poco ceremonioso,
conocido
*poco amistoso*

2 doméstico, domiciliario, común,
familiar

**familiarity**
familiaridad, conocimiento, intimidad, falta de respeto, informalidad, trato, intimidad, libertad,
libertinaje, sociabilidad, entendimiento
*no familiaridad*

**family**
1 clan, familia, antepasados, des-
cendiente, genealogía, linaje, raza,
tribu

2 clase, género, familia, grupo, tipo,
división
*individuo*

**famine**
escasez, indigencia, miseria, hambre, carestía
*abundancia, cantidad*

**famous**
famoso, distinguido, eminente, excelente, ilustre, glorioso, notorio,
remarcable, notable, renombrado
*desconocido*

**fan** *(v)*
1 agitar, excitar, aumentar, estimular
*calmar*

2 refrescar, abanicar, ventilar, aventar

**fanciful**
caprichoso, quimérico, fantástico,
ideal, imaginario, imaginativo, visionario
*práctico*

**fantastic**
fantástico, caprichoso, grotes-
co, imaginario, irreal, quimérico, extraño, visionario, excelente,
*(LAm)* bárbaro
*realista, objetivo, auténtico*

**fascinate**
fascinar, atraer, cautivar, encantar, deleitar, enamorar, hechizar,
encaprichar
*repugnar, rechazar*

**fashionable**
corriente, acostumbrado, moderno, fino, elegante, predominante,
a la moda, *(LAm)* estiloso
*poco elegante, poco atractivo*

**fast** *(aj)*
1 rápido, veloz, ligero, repentino
*lento*

2 constante, firme, fijo, inmovible,
impenetrable, seguro

3 disoluto, extravagante, vistoso,
estrafalario
*sobrio*

**fat** *(aj)*
1 gordo, corpulento, rollizo, carnoso, obeso, rechoncho
*delgado, seco, magro*

2 graso, grasoso, aceitoso

3 fértil, lucrativo, productivo, rico,
fructuoso
*pobre*

**fatal**
1 funesto, fatal, siniestro, calamitoso, desastroso, catastrófico, destructivo, letal, mortal
*inofensivo*

2 condenado, predestinado, inevitable, decretado

**fatigue**
fatiga, agotamiento, penas, labor
pesada, lasitud, trabajo, debilidad
*reposo, descanso*

**fault** *(s)*
1 defecto, falta, imperfección, debilidad, desperfecto
*mérito*

2 error, omisión, fallo, patochada,
falta, desliz, equivocación
*corrección, exactitud*

3 delincuencia, error, delito, fechoría, crimen, ofensa, pecado, tras-
gresión
*bondad*

**favour,** *(Am)* **favor** *(v)*
1 ayudar, asistir, favorecer, patroci-
nar, ofrecer amistad
*desaprobar*

2 mitigar, moderar, disminuir

**favourable,** *(Am)* **favorable**

1 favorable, beneficioso, ventajoso, conveniente, adecuado
*inservible, incompetente*

2 afectuoso, cariñoso, amable, amistoso, amigable
*poco amistoso*

**fear** *(s)*

1 alarma, aprensión, consternación, miedo, pavor, temor, pánico, horror
*coraje, valor*

2 ansiedad, inquietud, preocupación, soledad
*calma, tranquilidad*

3 pavor y respeto, reverencia, veneración
*irreverencia*

**feasible**

alcanzable, realizable, posible, practicable, factible
*imposible, no factible*

**feast** *(s)*

1 banquete, festín, jarana, juerga, entretenimiento, comida, jolgorio, comilona
*ayuno*

2 celebración, festival, fiesta, vacación

3 placer, deleite, fruición

**feed** *(v)*

alimentar, nutrir, dar de comer, sustentar, aprovisionar
*morirse de hambre*

**fell** *(v)*

cortar, nivelar, derribar, telar, tajar, postrar, abatir

**fellow**

compañero, camarada, compinche, asociado, homólogo, igual, amigo, miembro, socio, par
*extraño, desconocido*

**fence** *(s)*

valla, barrera, defensa, guardia, seto, estacada, palizada, terraplén, pared, seguridad

**ferment** *(s)*

1 levadura, fermento

2 *(fig)* agitación, conmoción, fiebre, excitación

**ferocious**

1 fiero, salvaje, rapaz, violento, indomado
*domado*

2 bárbaro, brutal, cruel, inhumano, despiadado, implacable, sin piedad
*gentil*

**fertile**

fértil, abundante, fructuoso, provechoso, productivo, prolífico, rico
*estéril, árido*

**fervent**

animado, ardiente, entusiasmado, excitado, ferviente, vehemente, celoso
*frío, apagado*

**festivity**

festival, festividad, alegría, regocijo, jovialidad, júbilo
*tristeza*

**feud** *(s)*

discusión, contienda, discordia, disensión, enemistad, rencor, hostilidad, pelea, odio
*acuerdo*

**fickle**

caprichoso, inconstante, irresoluto, inestable, vacilante, variable, volátil, voluble, veleidoso
*firme, constante, resuelto*

**fictitious**

artificial, falso, ficticio, imaginario, fingido, ideado, espurio, irreal
*genuino*

**fidelity**

1 fidelidad, lealtad, devoción, integridad, exactitud
*infidelidad, deslealtad*

2 exactitud, precisión, fidelidad, proximidad
*inexactitud*

**fierce**

bárbaro, brutal, cruel, feroz, fiero, furioso, apasionado, salvaje, truculento, violento
*manso, dócil*

**figurative**

1 figurativo, emblemático, metafórico, representativo, simbólico
*claro, franco*

2 florido, poético, vistoso, ornado
*sencillo, llano*

**file** *(s)*

1 línea, lista, nómina, rol

2 carpeta, expediente, archivo, fichero

**fill**

llenar, amueblar, abarrotar, inundar, rellenar, provisional, almacenar, guardar, suministrar, proveer
*vaciar*

**filth**

suciedad, corrupción, grosería, impureza, indecencia, oscuridad, polución
*limpieza*

**final** *(aj)*

final, concluyente, decisivo, definitivo, eventual, último, terminal
*primario, primero*

**find**

1 alcanzar, obtener, lograr, conseguir
*perder*

2 hallar, descubrir, experimentar, observar, percibir, ver, notar
*perder*

3 contribuir, suministrar, proveer

**fine** *(aj)*

1 admirable, elegante, excelente, bonito, exquisito, selecto, espléndido, superior
*inferior*

2 pequeño, menudo, delgado, tenue, fino
*grueso, grande*

3 claro, inalterado, puro, refinado

4 agudo, crítico, penetrante, perspicaz, astuto, mañoso
*franco*

**fine** *(s)*

multa, penalización, castigo

**finish** *(v)*

1 acabar, terminar, cumplir, conseguir, completar, concluir, hacer, ejecutar
*empezar, comenzar*

2 elaborar, perfeccionar, depurar

**firm**

1 compacto, denso, firme, duro, condensado
*suave*

2 constante, firme, resoluto, fuerte, tenaz, enérgico, robusto, fijo, estable
*inestable*

**fitness**

adaptación, conveniencia, propiedad, pertinencia, preparación, corrección, idoneidad
*inadecuación*

**fix**

1 fijar, establecer, localizar, colocar, ubicar, plantar, hacer arraigar

2 fijar, unir, atar, conectar, apretar, asegurar, liar
*separar, desunir*

3 determinar, limitar, definir

4 corregir, reparar, arreglar, enmendar

5 congelar, fijar, solidificar, poner tieso

6 *(Am)* preparar, servir, dar

**flag** *(s)*

bandera, colores, insignia, estandarte, pendón, banderín, banderola

**flag** *(v)*

declinar, caer, fallar, desmayar, sucumbir, languidecer, debilitar, consumir
*fortalecer, reforzar*

**flagrant**

atroz, horroroso, notorio, escandaloso, enorme, manifiesto
*leve, ligero, apacible*

**flame** *(s)*

1 fuego, llama, brillo, fulgor

2 afecto, ardor, entusiasmo, fervor, calor, interés, ilusión
*frialdad*

**flat** *(aj)*

1 plano, llano, horizontal, nivelado, suave, bajo
*desigual*

2 muerto, sin vida, insípido, prosaico, sin interés, soso

3 absoluto, directo, positivo, perentorio, imperativo

**flat** *(s)*

piso, apartamento, alojamiento, vivienda

**flatter**

halagar, engatusar, camelar, cumplimentar, lisonjear, seducir, tentar

*ofender*

**flavour** *(s)*

aroma, olor, sabor, gusto, condimento

*soso, insípido*

**flee**

fugarse, eludir, marchar, escapar, largarse, esquivar, rehuir

*seguir, cazar, perseguir*

**flinch**

recular, esquivar, rehuir, retroceder, retirarse, eludir, asustarse

*continuar*

**flock** *(s)*

colección, grupo, compañía, congregación, convoy, rebaño, multitud, manada

*dispersión*

**flow** *(v)*

1 deslizar, derramar, chorrear, verter, echar, dejar correr, manar

*parar*

2 inundar, anegar

3 emanar, surgir, emerger, resultar, emitir, expedir

**fly** *(v)*

1 volar, aletear, revolotear, flotar, estar suspendido (en el aire), cernerse, remontar, pilotar, dirigir, transportar, *(LAm)* pilotear

2 pasar, transcurrir, escurrir, deslizar, escapar, evitar, correr

*permanecer*

**fond**

1 cariñoso, afectuoso, chocho, amoroso, tierno

2 absurdo, vacío, tonto, indiscreto, vano, débil

*sensible*

**fool** *(s)*

1 tonto, idiota, imbécil, simple, zopenco, bobo, *(LAm)* zonzo

*sabio*

2 bufón, arlequín, payaso, juglar, saltimbanqui

**foolish**

1 sin cerebro, loco, atontado, tonto, idiota, insensato, simple, estúpido, débil

2 absurdo, imprudente, indiscreto, irrazonable, disparatado

*juicioso, prudente*

**forbid**

prohibir, excluir, rechazar, impedir, inhibir, vetar

*permitir*

**force** *(v)*

forzar, obligar, presionar, urgir, necesitar, imponer

*inducir*

**foreign**

1 extranjero, ajeno, distante, exótico, externo, remoto

*nativo*

2 extraño, extrínseco, irrelevante

*pertinente*

**foremost**

primero, delantero, más alto, principal, dirigente

**forfeit** *(s)*

daños, multa, pérdida, penalidad

**forgetful**

olvidadizo, descuidado, negligente, olvidio, inútil

*que piensa*

**forgiveness**

perdón, absolución, exoneración, remisión

*castigo*

**formal**

1 formal, ceremonioso, convencional, correcto, exacto, preciso, puntilloso

*informal, nada ceremonioso*

2 explícito, expreso, metódico, regular, rígido, estricto

**formidable**
formidable, peligroso, horrible, horroroso, amenazante, terrorífico, chocante, tremendo
*inofensivo, agradable*

**forward** *(aj)*
1 avanzado, temprano, prematuro, progresivo
2 atrevido, osado, temerario, impertinente, confiado, lleno de confianza, respondón, presumido, presuntuoso, impulsivo
*modesto*
3 rápido, listo, celoso, irreflexivo, fervoroso

**foul** *(aj)*
1 sucio, impuro, repugnante, asqueroso, ofensivo, polucionado, podrido, putrefacto, fétido, hediondo
*puro*
2 abusivo, blasfemo, ordinario, grosero, indecente, bajo, obsceno
*decente, inocente*
3 abominable, detestable, deshonroso, vil, vergonzoso, escandaloso
*atractivo, agradable*

**foundation**
1 base, fundamento, parte baja, pie, trabajo preliminar
*superestructura*
2 establecimiento, fundación, institución, creación, asentamiento

**fragile**
frágil, rompible, delicado, débil, quebradizo, enfermizo
*fuerte*

**fragrant**
fragante, aromático, balsámico, oloroso, perfumado, de olor agradable
*maloliente*

**frank**
franco, cándido, directo, honesto, ingenuo, abierto, sincero, llano, verídico
*reservado, callado, artero, astuto*

**frantic**
fanático, furioso, loco, enloquecido, frenético, violento, rabioso
*calmado*

**fraudulent**
fraudulento, listo, avispado, deshonesto, vil, falso, traicionero
*honesto, honrado*

**fray** *(s)*
combate, batalla, lucha, refriega, conflicto, pelea, disturbio
*paz*

**fray** *(v)*
raer, rozar, corroer, desgastar, gastar

**freedom**
1 libertad, emancipación, independencia
*esclavitud*
2 franqueza, ingenuidad
3 familiaridad, facilidad, informalidad, licencia, laxitud

**frequent** *(aj)*
frecuente, común, habitual, acostumbrado, usual, repetitivo
*raro, escaso*

**frequent** *(v)*
asistir, atender, frecuentar, visitar, rondar

**fresh**
1 nuevo, novato, reciente
*antiguo, viejo*
2 floreciente, fresco, florido, robusto, saludable, rosado, vigoroso, joven
*pasado, rancio, no fresco*
3 fresco, refrescante, puro, nuevo
*templado*

**friendship**
amistad, afección, concordia, benevolencia, familiaridad, cariño, afecto, intimidad, amor, armonía
*enemistad*

**fruitful**
abundante, copioso, fértil, fecundo, productivo, prolífero, rico
*estéril, árido*

**fugitive** *(aj)*
corto, efímero, momentáneo, evanescente, temporal, inestable, transitorio
*permanente*

**fugitive** *(s)*
> fugitivo, desertor

**fulfil,** *(Am)* **fulfill**
> conseguir, alcanzar, completar, concluir, ejecutar, observar, perfeccionar, realizar, hacer, cumplir
> *fallar*

**fun**
> diversión, felicidad, jolgorio, regocijo, alegría
> *melancolía*

**function** *(s)*
> 1 función, ejecución, operación, actuación
> *negligencia*
> 2 negocios, ceremonia, deber, empleo, ocupación, oficio

**fundamental**
> fundamental, básico, elemental, esencial, importante, indispensable, necesario, primario, principal
> *incidental, casual*

**furious**
> enfadado, furioso, fiero, fanático, impetuoso, loco, turbulento, vehemente, violento, salvaje
> *calmado*

**fuse** *(v)*
> combinar, amalgamar, entremezclar, fundir
> *solidificar*

**future** *(aj)*
> futuro, venidero, próximo, subsiguiente, posterior
> *pasado*

# G

**gaiety**
　animación, alegría, buen humor, hilaridad, júbilo, regocijo, alborozo, vivacidad
　*tristeza, melancolía*

**gain** (v)
　1 lograr, alcanzar, adquirir, conseguir, obtener, ganar, asegurar, realizar
　*perder, no lograr*
　2 conciliar, persuadir, convencer, prevalecer, imponerse

**gale**
　vendaval, tempestad, ráfaga, huracán, tormenta, tornado, tifón
　*céfiro*

**gallant**
　1 bravo, gallardo, valiente, audaz, valeroso, heroico, intrépido, impávido
　*cobarde*
　2 caballeroso, cortés, decoroso, magnánimo, noble, educado
　*mal educado, descortés*

**gallery**
　1 galería, tribuna
　2 pasadizo, corredor

**game** (aj)
　bravo, gallardo, intrépido, resoluto, valiente, valeroso, heroico, audaz
　*cobarde*

**game** (s)
　1 juego, diversión, entretenimiento, pasatiempo, recreación, deporte
　*trabajo, labor, tarea*
　2 aventura, empresa, iniciativa, proyecto, plan, esquema, tarea

**gang**
　banda, grupo, cuadrilla, pandilla, peña, compañía, camarilla, horda

**gap**
　brecha, abertura, grieta, hendidura, fisura, agujero

**garbage** (Am)
　basura, suciedad, porquería, inmundicia, desperdicios, deshecho

**garble**
　corromper, tergiversar, falsificar, falsear, citar mal, desfigurar, mutilar, pervertir
　*citar, aducir*

**garnish** (v)
　adornar, embellecer, decorar, engalanar, ornamentar, mejorar
　*estropear*

**gasp** (s)
　soplo, soplido, jadeo, resuello

**gate**
　puerta, verja, entrada, compuerta

**gather**
　1 reunir, juntar, acumular, coleccionar, congregar, fundir
　*esparcir, separar*
　2 amasar, acumular, coleccionar, recoger, amontonar
　3 asumir, concluir, deducir, aprender, inferir
　4 condensar, crecer, aumentar, engrosar, engordar

**gay**
　1 animado, alegre, contento, jubiloso, feliz, divertido, regocijante, jovial, vivaz
　*triste*
　2 brillante, luminoso, llamativo, chillón, vistoso

**generate**
　generar, engendrar, reproducirse, crear, procrear, formar, producir
　*destruir, exterminar*

**generous**
　1 benevolente, generoso, liberal, caritativo, hospitalario, munificiente, magnánimo, noble
　*tacaño, agarrado*
　2 abundante, copioso, amplio
　*escaso*

**genial**

genial, cordial, agradable, alegre, amigable, jovial, avivador, animado, campechano, inspirador, alborozado
*frígido, frío*

**genteel**

fino, elegante, aristocrático, refinado, cortés, de moda, a la moda
*rudo, mal educado, mal criado*

**gentle**

1 gentil, afable, amable, suave, clemente, dócil, bondadoso, manso, compasivo, apacible, pacífico, plácido, quieto, tratable
*poco amable*

2 aristocrático, gentil, noble, educado, refinado, cortés
*mal educado, mal criado*

3 gradual, moderado, ligero, escaso
*severo, duro*

**genuine**

genuino, auténtico, franco, natural, horrible, malísimo, espectral, pálido
*agradable, grato*

**giant** *(aj)*

colosal, gigante, enorme, grande, monstruoso, prodigioso, vasto
*menudo, pequeño*

**giant** *(s)*

coloso, gigante, monstruo, Hércules
*enano*

**giddy**

1 descuidado, negligente, cambiable, frívolo, desatento, inconstante, irresoluto, irreflexivo, inestable

2 vertiginoso

**gigantic**

gigante, gigantesco, colosal, enorme, hercúleo, inmenso, prodigioso, titánico, tremendo
*diminuto, insignificante, canijo*

**glad**

alegre, contento, encantador, delicioso, regocijado, complacido, satisfecho, feliz, jubiloso
*abatido, triste, desdichado*

**glare** *(s)*

1 brillo, llama, llamarada, destello, rayo, centelleo
*luz trémula, luz ténue*

2 ceño, mirada

**glaze** *(s)*

capa, esmalte, renovación, lustre, vidriado, brillo, laca, maque, barniz, cera
*sombra, palidez*

**gleam** *(s)*

1 claridad, luminosidad, lustre, rayo, esplendor, brillantez, destello
*oscuridad, mate*

2 rayo, haz de luz, luz trémula, destello

**glide** *(s)*

deslizamiento, movimiento, corrimiento
*reposo*

**glitter** *(s)*

llamarada, relámpago, destello, luz, brillo, luminosidad, lustre, centelleo, haz de luz, brillo, claridad, brillantez, rayo, resplandor
*sombrío, lo deslustrado*

**gloom**

1 nube, lo nuboso, oscuridad, lo deslustrado, penumbra, tenebrosidad, sombra
*brillo, claridad*

2 abatimiento, desaliento, depresión, pesimismo, desánimo, melancolía, tristeza
*felicidad, alegría*

**glory**

1 celebridad, dignidad, gloria, distinción, eminencia, fama, honor, alabanza, elogio, renombre
*prestigio*

2 brillo, lustre, magnificencia, pompa, fausto, resplandor, esplendor

**glow** *(s)*

1 brillo, brillantez, luminosidad, incandescencia, enrojecimiento

2 ardor, entusiasmo, excitación, fervor, impetuosidad, vehemencia, calor
*tibieza, falta de entusiasmo*

**glow** (v)

abrillantar, incendiar, quemar, brillar, relucir, destellar, enrojecer, poner de rojo, teñir de rojo, relucir, resplandecer

**glum**

1 grosero, agrio, desabrido, resentido, poco afable, hosco, malhumorado, irritable, brusco, arranque de cólera

*afable, jovial*

2 alicaído, cabizbajo, pesimista, estar melancólico, taciturno, triste, mohíno

*jovial, alegre*

**glutton**

glotón, engullidor

*asceta*

**goad** (v)

molestar, fastidiar, incitar, excitar, atormentar, perseguir, impulsar, instigar, estimular, irritar, agujar, picar, punzar, acuciar, inquietar

*apaciguar, calmar, pacificar*

**goal**

ambición, meta, objetivo, objeto, gol, intención, propósito, diseño, límite

*inicio, comienzo*

**gorge** (s)

desfiladero, fisura, quebrada, paso, puerto, barranco, garganta

**gorge** (v)

engullir, llenar algo de, decorar, comerse, alimentar, llenar, hartar, saciar, glotonear, tragar, hinchar, atiborrar

*morirse de hambre, pasar hambre, padecer hambre*

**gorgeous**

brillante, lujoso, magnífico, deslumbrante, deslumbrador, espléndido, vistoso, llamativo, suntuoso

*raído, viejo, gastado, feo*

**govern**

gobernar, administrar, controlar, dirigir, guiar, mandar, comandar, conducir, manejar, ordenar, pilotar, reinar, supervisar

*obedecer, seguir, gobernar mal, administrar mal*

**government**

1 mando, control, dirección, gobierno, guía, manejo, gerencia, regla, imperio, dominio

*desorden, disturbio, tumulto*

2 administración, gabinete, consejo de ministros, dominio, comisión, gobierno, estado

*anarquía*

**grace** (s)

1 atractivo, belleza, encanto, hermosura, gracia, elegancia, finura, urbanidad, cultura, educación, refinamiento

*desgarbo, torpeza*

2 generosidad, gracia, beneficencia, favor, amabilidad, buena voluntad, benevolencia, bondad

*desaprobación*

3 clemencia, devoción, perdón, misericordia, santidad, compasión, piedad, salvación

*condena, condenación*

4 bendición, gracias, oración

**graceful**

gracioso, agraciado, hermoso, elegante, airoso, natural, favorecedor, lindo, suelto

*desgarbado, torpe*

**gracious**

afable, benévolo, cortés, benigno, civil, amistoso, amigable, amable, educado, apacible

*descortés, grosero*

**gradual**

gradual, aproximado, continuo, progresivo, regular, atrasado, sucesivo, consecutivo

*repentino, accidentado, quebrado*

**grand**

1 augusto, eminente, exaltado, fino, glorioso, gran, ilustre, imponente, majestuoso, magnífico, noble, espléndido, pomposo, real, sublime

*insignificante, pequeño*

2 grande, principal

3 *(Br)* mil libras, *(Am)* mil dólares

**grant** *(v)*

1 asignar, dar, adjudicar, impartir, conceder, otorgar, conferir, ceder

*recibir*

2 traspasar, transferir, transmitir

**grasp** *(s)*

1 broche, corchete, cierre, agarre, asimiento, posesión

2 comprensión, alcance, entendimiento, facultad, envergadura

**grasp** *(v)*

1 agarrar, asir, abrochar, remachar

*soltar, dejar, liberar*

2 entender, comprender, captar

**gratify**

encantar, deleitar, satisfacer, complacer, dar gusto, contentar, recompensar, compensar

*descontentar, no satisfacer*

**gratitude**

gratitud, agradecimiento, reconocimiento, deuda

*ingratitud, desagradecimiento*

**grave** *(aj)*

1 serio, crítico, importante, trascendental, influyente, de peso

*insignificante, no importante*

2 grave, solemne, serio, formal, sabio, sosegado, sobrio, pensativo, meditabundo

**gravity**

importancia, gravedad, trascendencia, seriedad, peso, solemnidad

*trivialidad, sin importancia, frivolidad*

**great**

1 gran, grande, abultado, enorme, gigante, gigantesco, inmenso, vasto

*pequeño*

2 considerable, excesivo, importante, mucho, numeroso

*insignificante*

3 eminente, excelente, famoso, distinguido, célebre, exaltado, elevado, notable, renombrado, ilustre

*más bien mediocre, no eminente*

**green**

1 floreciente, esmeraldino, de color esmeralda, lozano, fresco, nuevo, verde

*marchito, seco*

2 *(fig)* ignorante, inmaduro, inexperto, verde, novato, desmañado

*experto, hábil*

**grief**

pena, aflicción, agonía, angustia, abatimiento, desaliento, queja, miseria, tristeza, lamentación, remordimiento, pesar, dolor, tribulación, sufrimiento, problema

*alegría, gozo, regocijo, júbilo*

**grievance**

aflicción, queja, carga, angustia, pena, infortunio, daño, tribulación, problema, injusticia

*justicia*

**grieve**

1 afligir, herir, dañar, molestar, irritar, contrariar, fastidiar

*confortar, consolar, aliviar*

2 lamentar, quejarse, deplorar, apenarse, afligirse, estar afligido, sufrir, padecer

*alegrarse, regocijarse*

**grind**

1 contundir, magullar, estrujar, triturar, rallar, pulverizar, machacar, majar, estregar, restregar, *(Am) (culinario)* picar

2 afligir, oprimir, acosar, atormentar, perseguir, fastidiar, turbar

*abrir, tranquilizar*

**gross**

1 grande, abultado, denso, masivo, grueso

*pequeño*

2 ordinario, grosero, común, impuro, indecente, antidelicado, bajo, rudo, sensual, vulgar, *(Am)* asqueroso

*decente, puro*

3 aparente, manifiesto, obvio, serio, vergonzoso, notorio, escandaloso

**ground**
1 tierra, campo, suelo, marga, molde, césped, tepe
2 país, dominio, estado, tierra, propiedad, territorio
3 base, causa, factor, motivo, razón, fundamento
4 depósito, sedimento, heces, poso

**group** (s)
1 grupo, colección, manojo, puñado, cacho, ramo, racimo
*individual, propio*

**grovel**
encogerse, arrastrarse, moverse a hurtadillas, deslizarse, agacharse, acurrucarse
*encararse, afrontar, enfrentarse*

**grow**
1 crecer, desarrollar, engrandecer, extender, expandir, aumentar, difundir, cundir
*disminuir, rebajar, empequeñecer*
2 crecer, germinar, lanzar, brotar, echar, engrosar
3 avanzar, mejorar, progresar, volverse, crecer
4 cultivar, producir

**growth**
1 aumento, desarrollo, expansión, extensión, crecimiento
2 cultivo, germinación, producción, vegetación, brote

**grudge** (v)
tener envidia, envidiar, quejarse, codiciar

**guard** (s)
1 protector, guardián, guardia, centinela

2 convoy, escolta, guardia, patrulla
3 defensa, protección, seguridad, escudo, baluarte
*ataque*
4 atención, cuidado, cautela, prudencia, vigilancia, desvelo

**guardian**
guardián, protector, conservador, defensor, vigilante, administrador
*pupilo*

**guess** (v)
1 creer, conjeturar, imaginar, suponer, adivinar, sospechar, figurarse, atreverse a, aventurar
*saber, conocer*
2 estimar, profundizar, penetrar, resolver, solucionar

**guest**
invitado, visitante, compañía, comunicante, huésped, convidado
*anfitrión*

**guide** (v)
guiar, conducir, controlar, dirigir, escoltar, gobernar, manejar, regular, mandar, supervisar, entrenar
*seguir*

**gush** (s)
efusión, ráfaga, corriente, flujo, avenida
*parada, pausa, interrupción*

**gust** (s)
1 ráfaga, racha, viento, tormenta, brisa
*calma, día gris, recalmón*
2 pasión, paroxismo, arranque, acceso
*calma, respiro*

# H

**habit** *(s)*
1 hábito, inclinación, constitución, costumbre, disposición, manera, modo, práctica, tendencia, uso
2 ropa, indumentaria, hábito, vestido, prenda

**habitual**
habitual, normal, acostumbrado, común, corriente, regular, usual
*extraño, insólito, inusual*

**haggard**
1 agobiado, demacrado, chupado, pálido, calavérico, flaco, pobre, ojeroso, arrugado
*robusto, fuerte*
2 intratable, refractario, obstinado, ingobernable, desmandado

**hail** *(v)*
dirigirse a, llamar, saludar, hablar, dar la bienvenida, recibir, entablar conversación
*evitar*

**halt** *(v)*
1 cesar, desistir, terminar, detener, interrumpir, parar
*continuar, seguir*
2 dudar, pararse, balbucir, vacilar
*estar seguro*

**hamper** *(v)*
impedir, atar, reprimir, limitar, estorbar, enredar, trabar, obstruir, prevenir, refrenar
*animar, alentar*

**handsome**
1 elegante, excelente, admirable, favorecedor, gentil, guapo, bien parecido
*feo*
2 considerable, amplio, generoso, liberal, magnánimo, copioso, abundante
*tacaño*

**handy**
1 diestro, hábil, mañoso, inteligente, listo, experto, preparado, cualificado, útil
*terco, difícil*
2 conveniente, práctico, cómodo
*inconveniente*

**harass**
enfadar, molestar, fatigar, acosar, atormentar, perturbar, alterar, confundir, atormentar, inquietar, preocupar
*tranquilizar, aliviar, calmar*

**harbour**, *(Am)* **harbor** *(s)*
1 destino, anclaje, puerto
2 asilo, refugio, retiro, santuario, seguridad

**harbour**, *(Am)* **harbor** *(v)*
proteger, cuidar, ocultar, abrigar, alojar, hospedar, colocar, esconder, guarecer
*desterrar*

**hard**
1 compacto, denso, firme, duro, impenetrable, rígido, sólido, tieso, inflexible
*suave, dúctil, flexible*
2 arduo, exigente, laborioso, fatigoso, penoso
*ligero*
3 complicado, difícil, intrincado, confuso, misterioso, incomprensible
*fácil*
4 cruel, severo, insensible, duro de corazón, obstinado, terco, austero
*amable, afable*

**hardy**
1 valiente, audaz, valeroso, bizarro, heroico, intrépido, fuerte, resuelto
*medroso, apocado*
2 sano, robusto, saludable, fuerte, vigoroso, fornido, corpulento
*débil, flojo*

**harm** *(s)*
daño, perjuicio, mal, maldad, herida, lesión, malicia, diablura
*bondad*

**harsh**
1 ofensivo, injurioso, austero, amargo, brutal, cruel, duro, severo, des-

agradable, punzante, despiadado, poco amable
*gentil, amable*
2 discordante, disonante, áspero, desapacible, adverso, poco melodioso
*armonioso*

**hasten**
acelerar, despachar, apresurar, precipitar, presionar, empujar, apresurar(se), incitar
*retardar, retrasar*

**hate** (*v*)
odiar, abominar, detestar, execrar, aborrecer, tener aversión, tener antipatía
*querer, amar*

**haul** (*v*)
tirar, arrastrar, extraer, remolcar, acarrear, transportar
*empujar*

**haunt** (*v*)
1 frecuentar, rondar, visitar, acudir, concurrir
*desertar, abandonar*
2 perseguir, importunar

**hazard** (*s*)
peligro, riesgo, aventura, accidente
*seguridad*

**headlong** (*aj*)
1 peligroso, impulsivo, inconsiderado, precipitado, temerario, imprudente, irreflexivo
*serio, pensativo, considerado*
2 perpendicular, precipitado, escarpado, abrupto

**headlong** (*av*)
precipitadamente, imprudentemente, temerariamente, irreflexivamente, sin pensar
*cautelosamente*

**health**
robustez, vigor, salud, salubridad, fuerza
*debilidad, enfermedad*

**healthy**
1 activo, ágil, vigoroso, bien de salud, saludable, bueno
*indispuesto, malo*

2 tónico, vigorizante, saludable, higiénico, vigorizador, nutritivo, salubre
*insalubre, nocivo*

**hearty**
1 cordial, genuino, honesto, ilusionado, formal, verdadero, real, entusiasta, celoso
*frío, poco sincero*
2 activo, enérgico, saludable, robusto, fuerte, vigoroso
*débil, flojo*

**heat** (*s*)
calor, calefacción, (*fig*) fuego, ardor, excitación, fervor, impetuosidad, intensidad, pasión, vehemencia, violencia, celo
*frialdad, falta de entusiasmo*

**heaven**
1 firmamento, cielo
*tierra*
2 (*fig*) felicidad, éxtasis, paraíso, edén, transporte, Elíseo
*infierno*

**heavy**
1 pesado, abultado, masivo
*ligero*
2 gravoso, oneroso, difícil, penoso, duro, opresivo, severo, pesado
*fácil*
3 amodorrado, soñoliento, inactivo, indolente, inerte, lento, perezoso, atontado
*alerta, despierto*
4 abundante, copioso, cargado, lleno
5 borrascoso, tempestuoso, violento
*calmado*

**hedge** (*v*)
1 bloquear, encerrar, vallar, obstruir, cercar, circundar, rodear
*admitir*
2 fortificar, guardar, proteger, resguardar, amparar
3 desaparecer, esconder, escurrir el bulto, permanecer oculto

**heed**
atender, considerar, notar, observar, prestar atención, hacer caso, ver
*pasar por alto, no hacer caso de*

**height**
1 altitud, altura, ápice, cumbre, colina, montaña, cima, pico, cenit
*falda, pie, parte baja*
2 dignidad, eminencia, exaltación, magnificencia, sublimidad, grandiosidad
*bajeza, vileza*

**help** (s)
ayuda, asistencia, remedio, socorro, colaborador, colaboración, alivio, consuelo, desahogo

**help** (v)
1 ayudar, asistir, cooperar, respaldar, salvar, secundar, apoyar
*obstruir, dificultar, estorbar*
2 aliviar, mejorar, curar, mitigar, asistir, remediar, devolver la salud, sanar
*agravar, empeorar*
3 evitar, controlar, prevenir, contenerse, resistir, oponerse

**helpless**
abandonado, desamparado, indefenso, minusválido, expuesto, débil, impotente, desprotegido
*fuerte, protegido*

**hesitate**
dudar, deliberar, objetar, vacilar, titubear, tartamudear, balbucir
*resolver, arreglar*

**hesitation**
retraso, indecisión, tartamudeo, suspenso, vacilación, balbuceo, titubeo, reticencia, irresolución, duda
*certeza, seguridad*

**hide** (v)
esconder, encerrar, enterrar, enmascarar, encubrir, ocultar, disimular, velar, cubrir
*revelar, mostrar, enseñar*

**hideous**
abominable, detestable, horrible, horroroso, repulsivo, chocante, terrible, desagradable
*agradable, grato*

**high**
1 elevado, alto, encumbrado
*bajo*

2 arrogante, fanfarrón, déspota, dominante, altanero, altivo, orgulloso, ostentoso, tiránico
3 caro, costoso, suntuoso
*barato*

**hilarious**
jocoso, de risa, ruidoso, alegre, festivo, jovial, jubiloso
*abatido, alicaído*

**hill**
colina, elevación, montaña, prominencia, altura, montículo, otero
*valle, llanura*

**hiss** (v)
1 gritar, chillar, zumbar, runrunear, silbar, sisear
2 condenar, ridiculizar, maldecir, desacreditar, rebajar
*aplaudir, aclamar, vitorear*

**hit** (s)
1 golpe, colisión, choque, enfrentamiento
2 oportunidad, aventura, éxito, fortuna

**hoard** (v)
acumular, agrupar, amasar, coleccionar, atesorar, juntar, salvar, almacenar
*disipar, derrochar, desperdiciar*

**hoist** (v)
elevar, subir, alzar, izar
*bajar, descender*

**holiday** (s)
fiesta, aniversario, celebración, festival, gala, receso, vacaciones
*día laboral*

**hollow** (aj)
1 cavernícola, cóncavo, vacío, hundido, vacante
*lleno*
2 artificial, falso, engañoso, fraudulento, baladí, poco sincero, traicionero
*genuino, real, sincero*

**homage**
1 devoción, fe, fidelidad, lealtad, servicio, obediencia, homenaje, tributo
*deslealtad, infidelidad*

2 adoración, deferencia, deber, honor, respeto, reverencia, veneración
*desacato, falta de respeto*

**honest**

honesto, honrado, cándido, concienzudo, decente, franco, honorable, ingenuo, justo, sincero, virtuoso, estimable, honroso, formal
*deshonesto, tramposo*

**honour,** *(Am)* **honor** *(s)*

1 crédito, dignidad, distinción, elevación, estima, fama, gloria, honor, renombre, reputación

2 deferencia, homenaje, reverencia, respeto, veneración

3 honestidad, integridad, rectitud, probidad

**hope** *(s)*

esperanza, creencia, deseo, fe, confianza, expectativa, dependencia
*desesperación*

**hopeless**

1 desesperado, desamparado, abatido, deprimido, desconsolado
*esperanzado*

2 incurable, irremediable, indefenso

3 imposible, inalcanzable, impracticable, imposible de conseguir

**horrify**

horrorizar, asustar, alarmar, aterrorizar, atemorizar, conmocionar
*animar, alentar*

**hostility**

hostilidad, animosidad, antagonismo, antipatía, aversión, odio, oposición, enemistad
*amistad, simpatía*

**hot**

1 ardiente, caliente, que quema, abrasador, llameante
*frío, apagado*

2 picante, acre, punzante, condimentado

3 *(fig)* animado, ferviente, impetuoso, irascible, violento, apasionado, vehemente

**humble** *(v)*

rebajar, reducir, mortificar, degradar, rebajar, envilecer
*exaltar, elevar*

**humorous**

caprichoso, cómico, gracioso, divertido, jocoso, alegre, fantástico, chistoso, ingenioso
*serio*

**humour,** *(Am)* **humor** *(s)*

1 diversión, humor, chiste, gracia, jocosidad, carácter festivo
*seriedad*

2 propensión, humor, ánimo, capricho, antojo, manía

**hungry**

hambriento, codicioso, antojo, deseoso, famélico, ávido, glotón, muerto de hambre
*satisfecho, saciado*

**hunt** *(v)*

1 perseguir, acosar, cazar
*huir de, evitar*

2 buscar, mirar, escudriñar

**hurry** *(s)*

prisa, celeridad, conmoción, expedición, precipitación, rapidez, prontitud, velocidad, urgencia, *(LAm)* apuro
*lentitud*

**hurt** *(v)*

1 herir, dañar, amoratar, perjudicar, debilitar
*sanar, curar*

2 *(fig)* afligir, molestar, apenar, fastidiar, irritar

**husband** *(v)*

economizar, salvar, ahorrar, manejar con prudencia
*gastar, derrochar*

**husky** *(aj)*

1 seco, marchito, arrugado

2 severo, duro, ronco, estridente
*melifluo*

**icy**
  1 frío, helado, glacial, escarchado
    *templado*
  2 *(fig)* frío, frígido, indiferente
**ideal**
  1 intelectual, mental
  2 ideal, imaginario, irreal, visionario, falta de sentido
    *real, verdadero*
  3 completo, ideal, consumado, perfecto
**identity**
    existencia, identidad, individualidad, personalidad, igualdad
    *diferencia*
**idle** *(aj)*
  1 inactivo, indolente, gandul, vago, lento, perezoso, parado, ocioso, holgazán, *(LAm)* flojo
    *trabajador, laborioso*
  2 inefectivo, vano, inútil, fútil, infundado
    *aprovechable*
**ignorant**
    ignorante, analfabeto, poco instruido, indocto
    *sabio*
**ill**
  1 enfermo, indispuesto, mareado
    *bueno, saludable*
  2 malo, endemoniado, diabólico, desafortunado, equivocado, enfadado, hostil, malévolo, odioso, malhumorado
    *bueno*
**illegal**
    ilegal, prohibido, ilícito, impropio, no autorizado, inconstitucional, sin permiso
    *legal, autorizado*
**illegible**
    ilegible, indescifrable, oscuro
    *legible*

**illegitimate**
  1 ilegal, ilícito, ilegítimo, impropio, sin autorizar
    *legítimo*
  2 bastardo, ilegítimo, espurio, falso
    *legítimo*
**illicit**
  1 ilegal, ilegítimo, ilícito, no autorizado, sin permiso
    *legal*
  2 prohibido, culpable, impropio, equivocado
    *apropiado*
**illiterate**
    ignorante, inculto, no enseñado, poco instruido, indocto, analfabeto
    *culto, alfabetizado*
**illusion**
    ilusión, quimera, decepción, error, falacia, fantasía, alucinación
    *realidad*
**imaginary**
    imaginario, asumido, hipotético, ideal, ilusorio, supuesto, irreal, fantástico
    *real*
**imitate**
    imitar, copiar, duplicar, seguir, parodiar
    *deformar, tergiversar*
**immature**
    inmaduro, crudo, verde, imperfecto, prematuro, inacabado, informe
    *maduro*
**immediate**
  1 inmediato, contiguo, cercano, próximo, directo
    *remoto, lejano*
  2 al instante, instantáneo, presente
    *más tarde*
**immobile**
  1 inmóvil, fijo, estable, estacionario, sin movimiento
    *movible*

2 rígido, inmóvil, inactivo, firme,
inflexible, impasible
*flexible*

**immortal**
inmortal, eterno, duradero, impe-
recedero, indestructible, perdurable
*perecedero*

**impair**
dañar, deteriorar, debilitar, perjudicar, enervar, estropear, empeorar
*fortalecer, reforzar*

**impartial**
imparcial, desinteresado, equitativo, justo, recto
*parcial*

**impatient**
abrupto, brusco, impaciente, seco,
lacónico, impetuoso, intolerante,
vehemente, violento, inquieto
*paciente, tranquilo*

**impediment**
impedimento, estorbo, bloque, dificultad, obstáculo, obstrucción,
freno, tropiezo
*ayuda*

**impel**
actuar, forzar, incitar, influir, conducir, instigar, inducir, mover, estimular, empujar
*refrenar, reprimir*

**imperfect**
defectuoso, imperfecto, incompleto, inacabado, dañado, deteriora-
do
*completo, perfecto*

**impertinent**
1 impertinente, insolente, descarado, atrevido, carota, cara dura,
presuntuoso, rudo, incivilizado
*educado*
2 inapropiado, inaplicable, irrelevante, incongruo, disonante
*apropiado*

**impetuous**
impetuoso, vehemente, fiero, furioso, impulsivo, apasionado, violento
*cauto, prudente*

**implement** *(s)*
instrumento, implemento, herra-
mienta, utensilio

**implement** *(v)*
efectuar, ejecutar, realizar, llevar a
cabo
*ignorar, descuidar, desatender, no
cumplir*

**implicit**
1 implícito, entendido, tácito, dedu-
cido
2 absoluto, constante, total, entero,
firme, impertérrito
*dudoso*

**implore**
implorar, pedir, suplicar, rogar,
solicitar
*ordenar, mandar*

**imply**
presagiar, implicar, denotar, significar, querer decir, incluir, involucrar
*declarar*

**import** *(v)*
1 importar, traer, introducir, transportar, comprar
*exportar, vender*
2 denotar, implicar, querer decir,
significar, dar a entender

**importance**
asunto, interés, consecuencia, importancia, significado, trascendencia, valor, peso
*insignificancia*

**improper**
1 erróneo, falso, impropio, inexacto, incorrecto, equivocado
*correcto*
2 indecente, indecoroso, impropio
*apropiado*

**improve**
arreglar, reparar, corregir, enmendar, rectificar
*empeorar*

**improvise**
improvisar, fabricar, inventar,
imaginar
*repetir*

**impulse**
1 fuerza, ímpetu, impulso, empuje, avance
*estirón*

2 *(fig)* sentimiento, impulso, incitación, inclinación, influencia, instinto, motivo, pasión, resolución

**inability**
incapacidad, incompetencia, descalificación, impotencia, ineficacia
*habilidad*

**inadequate**
inadecuado, defectuoso, incompetente, incompleto, insuficiente, desigual, inadmisible
*admisible*

**inane**
vacío, fatuo, frívolo, futil, idiota, pueril, estúpido, vano, sin sentido, *(LAm)* sonso
*sensible*

**incapable**
incapaz, impotente, incompetente, insuficiente, débil
*capaz*

**incite**
animar, excitar, incitar, instigar, provocar, estimular
*calmar*

**include**
comprender, contener, abarcar, incluir, incorporar
*excluir*

**income**
ganancias, sueldo, salario, paga, beneficios, rentas, ingresos, recaudación
*gastos, desembolso, inversión*

**incompatible**
contradictorio, incompatible, inconsistente, irreconciliable, inapropiado
*consistente, compatible*

**incomplete**
incompleto, defectuoso, deficiente, imperfecto, sin acabar, sin terminar
*completo, acabado*

**inconsistent**
incómodo, molesto, inconveniente, problemático, cansado, inoportuno, desventajoso
*cómodo, ventajoso*

**incorporate**
combinar, mezclar, incorporar, unir, abarcar, fusionar, converger
*excluir*

**incorrect**
erróneo, falso, incorrecto, impropio, inadecuado, inexacto, equivocado
*correcto, exacto*

**increase** *(v)*
aumentar, avanzar, dilatar, engrandecer, expander, extender, crecer, multiplicar, prolongar
*rebajar, disminuir*

**indefinite**
indefinido, confuso, dudoso, equívoco, indistinto, oscuro, incierto, indeterminado, vago
*definido*

**independence**
1 autonomía, independencia, autogobierno, separación
*sujeción*

2 libertad, independencia, tranquilidad, facilidad
*dependencia*

**indiscreet**
imprudente, indiscreto, tonto, incauto, inconsiderado, poco juicioso, desatento
*sabio*

**indiscriminate**
mezclado, indiscriminado, confundido, diverso, vario, inconsiderado
*secreto, reservado*

**indispensable**
esencial, necesario, indispensable, requisito
*innecesario*

**indolent**
inactivo, inerte, indolente, vago, apático, indiferente, perezoso
*trabajador, laborioso*

**induce**
1 actuar, animar, incitar, influir, instigar, mover, persuadir, inducir
*desanimar*
2 efectuar, producir, causar

**indulge**
favorecer, permitir, conceder, gratificar, promover, satisfacer, complacer
*negar*

**industrious**
activo, asiduo, ocupado, diligente, trabajador, laborioso, persistente, perseverante
*indolente, perezoso*

**infallible**
cierto, infalible, seguro, veraz, fidedigno
*informal, de poca confianza*

**infamous**
infame, atroz, detestable, deshonroso, de mala fama, ignominioso, odioso, escandaloso, vergonzoso, villano
*honorable, honrado*

**infect**
afectar, infectar, contaminar, envenenar, polucionar, viciar, manchar
*limpiar*

**infer**
concluir, deducir, conjeturar, colegir, inferir, suponer
*saber, conocer*

**infinite**
infinito, ilimitado, enorme, inmenso, interminable, vasto, amplio
*definido, limitado*

**inflame**
inflamar, enfadar, exasperar, encender, arder, estimular, enfurecer
*desanimar, suavizar*

**inflate**
hinchar, inflar, dilatar, extender, engrandecer, aumentar, expandir
*desinflar, rebajar*

**inform**
informar, comunicar, avisar, instruir, notificar, enseñar, decir
*ocultar*

**information**
aviso, consejo, información, instrucción, conocimiento, noticias
*encubrimiento, disimulación*

**infringe**
romper, desobedecer, infringir, transgredir, violar
*obedecer*

**ingenious**
capaz, apto, hábil, diestro, ingenioso, listo, brillante, inventivo, experto
*inexperto, desmañado*

**inherent**
incongénito, inherente, de nacimiento, innato, intrínseco, natural
*adquirido*

**inhibit**
impedir, inhibir, imposibilitar, obstruir, desanimar, prohibir
*apoyar*

**initial** *(aj)*
principal, inicial, temprano, primero, incipiente, naciente
*final*

**initiate**
empezar, comenzar, iniciar, inaugurar, introducir, abrir, originar
*finalizar, acabar*

**injury**
daño, detrimento, mal, injusticia, perjuicio, ruina, equivocación
*beneficio*

**innocent**
ingenuo, sencillo, inocente, honesto, inmaculado, impecable, inofensivo, puro, simple, recto, sin mancha
*culpable*

**inquiry**
pregunta, duda, interrogación, búsqueda, escrutinio, estudio
*respuesta*

**insane**
1 loco, demente, lunático, desquiciado
*sano, cuerdo*
2 estúpido, insensato
*sensato*

**insecure**

peligroso, inseguro, expuesto, incierto, débil, sin protección, no defendido

*seguro*

**insidious**

mañoso, astuto, artero, insidioso, criminal, engañoso, falso, fraudulento, taimado

*honesto, honrado, probo*

**insignificant**

insignificante, inconsiderable, trivial, sin importancia, baladí, vil

*importante, significativo*

**insinuate**

1 insinuar, aludir, sugerir

2 inculcar, inyectar, introducir, infundir

*retirar*

**insist**

insistir, demandar, persistir, presionar, instar

*entregar, ceder*

**inspire**

1 inspirar, inhalar, respirar

*exhalar*

2 *(fig)* animar, inspirar, avivar, imbuir, infundir, inculcar

*desanimar*

**instant** *(aj)*

1 instantáneo, inmediato, rápido, pronto

*lento, despacio*

2 corriente, presente, actual

**instigate**

actuar, animar, incitar, instigar, influir, mover, persuadir, provocar, levantar, inculcar, estimular

*desanimar*

**instinctive**

automático, intuitivo, instintivo, involuntario, natural, espontáneo

*razonado*

**instruct**

1 disciplinar, educar, enseñar, iluminar, instruir, guiar, informar, entrenar

*aprender*

2 mandar, comandar, dirigir, ordenar, *(Br)* instruir, dar instrucciones a

*aprender, obedecer*

**insult** *(s)*

abuso, afrenta, ofensa, insulto, ultraje, insolencia, atentado

*cumplido, piropo*

**insult** *(v)*

abusar, afrontar, injuriar, ofender

*respetar*

**intact**

intacto, virgen, inmaculado, puro, completo, sin dañar

*dañado*

**intelligence**

1 aptitud, inteligencia, viveza, ingenio, capacidad, habilidad, perspicacia, entendimiento, razón

2 información, conocimiento, noticias, notificación, rumor

*ignorancia*

**intelligent**

inteligente, agudo, apto, brillante, listo, instruido, conocedor, informado, habilidoso, vivo

*estúpido, tonto*

**intense**

1 agudo, profundo, excesivo, extremo, gran

2 intenso, ardiente, enérgico, apremiante, vehemente, vigoroso

**intent** *(s)*

intento, objetivo, final, intención, objeto, plan, propósito

**inter**

enterrar, sepultar, inhumar

*exhumar*

**intercourse**

comercio, comunicación, comunión, conexión, conversión, correspondencia, intimidad, tratos, relaciones

*separación, silencio*

**interest** *(s)*

1 atracción, atención, curiosidad, interés, simpatía

2 ventaja, beneficio, autoridad, influencia, prima, parte
*pérdida*

**interfere**
intervenir, entrometer, interferir, colisionar, chocar, tomar parte, interponerse
*confirmar, aprobar*

**interior**
1 interior, de dentro, interno
*exterior*
2 *(geografía)* tierra adentro, lejano, distante

**interpose**
1 arbitrar, interceder, mediar
2 interferir, interponer, intervenir, entrometerse
3 insertar, introducir, poner
*sacar, retirar*

**interrupt**
interrumpir, romper, cortar, desconectar, retardar, retrasar, dividir, desunir, interferir, separar, parar, suspender
*reanudar, continuar*

**intimate** *(aj)*
cercano, confidencial, amistoso, íntimo, privado, secreto
*distante, lejano*

**intimate** *(s)*
socio, compañero, camarada, confidente, amigo, familiar, compinche, íntimo
*enemigo*

**intolerable**
insufrible, intolerable, insoportable, inaguantable
*aguantable, tolerable*

**intrigue** *(s)*
artificio, cábala, conspiración, conjuración, maquinación, complot, estratagema
*franqueza*

**intrinsic**
1 esencial, genuino, intrínseco, real, verdadero
*artificial*

2 inherente, nativo, natural, innato
*adquirido, extrínseco*

**introduce**
empezar, comenzar, inaugurar, iniciar, introducir
*retirar, sacar*

**introduction**
1 inauguración, presentación, introducción
*retirada*
2 principio, preámbulo, prefacio, prólogo, preludio
*conclusión*

**intuitive**
instintivo, involuntario, espontáneo, intuitivo
*calculado, planeado*

**invalid** *(aj)*
1 frágil, enfermo, débil
*fuerte, sano*
2 inválido, falso, nulo, infundado, falaz, erróneo, engañoso
*válido*

**invaluable**
costoso, inestimable, inapreciable, valioso
*sin valor, inútil*

**invariable**
constante, inmutable, invariable, incambiable, uniforme, inalterable
*variable, mutable*

**invention**
1 invención, creación, diseño, descubrimiento, invento
*copia, imitación*
2 invención, engaño, fraude, ficción, falsificación

**invite** *(v)*
1 invitar, pedir, solicitar, llamar, rogar, convocar
*convidar*
2 atraer, tentar, fascinar, sugerir, inducir
*rechazar, repeler*

**invoke**
suplicar, implorar, invocar, rogar, conjurar, pedir, solicitar
*insistir*

## involve

1 envolver, cubrir, arropar
   *destapar*
2 envolver, complicar, conectar, implicar, mezclar, combinar, entrelazar

## irrational

1 irracional, absurdo, tonto, irrazonable, imprudente
   *racional, prudente*
2 loco, demente, aberrante, chiflado, tarado
   *racional, cuerdo, juicioso*

## irregular

anormal, subnormal, irregular, caprichoso, excéntrico, excepcional, inmoderado, incierto, inusual, variable, desordenado, nada metódico
   *regular, normal, corriente, uniforme*

## irritate

enfadar, irritar, molestar, exasperar, ofender, provocar, inquietar, indignar, encolerizar
   *suavizar, encantar, deleitar*

## isolate

desconectar, separar, desvincular, segregar, aislar
   *unir, juntar*

## isolation

desconexión, aislamiento, segregación, separación, soledad, retiro
   *compañía, sociedad*

# J

**jam** *(s)*
aglomeración, multitud, atasco, obstrucción, montón, muchedumbre, tropel, embotellamiento, caravana, *(LAm)* tapón

**jam** *(v)*
aglomerar, atascar, obstruir, apretar, presionar, atestar, apretujar

**jar** *(v)*
perturbar, inquietar, alterar, molestar, irritar, ofender

**jargon**
1 tonterías, galimatías, guirigay, disparates
*sentido, juicio*
2 argot, jerga, dialecto

**jealous**
1 celoso, envidioso, codicioso, resentido, ofendido, rival
*satisfecho*
2 inquieto, preocupado, aprensivo, ansioso, atento, suspicaz, vigilante
*despreocupado, alegre*

**jeer** *(v)*
chancearse, bromear, ridiculizar, mofarse, burlarse de, insultar
*alabar, elogiar*

**jeopardize**
poner en peligro, arriesgar, exponer, aventurar, estar en peligro, exponerse, comprometer
*preservar, proteger, conservar*

**jest** *(v)*
bromear, ridiculizar, mofarse, burlarse de, insultar

**jingle** *(v)*
hacer sonar, hacer tintinear, traquetear, tañer, repicar

**join** *(v)*
unir, juntar, acompañar, añadir, incluir, adherir, anexionar, adjuntar, consolidar, conectar, emparejar, atar
*aflojar, soltar, desunir*

**joint** *(aj)*
combinado, unido, colectivo, conjunto, coordinado

**joint** *(s)*
articulación, conexión, gozne, bisagra, juntura, unión, conyuntura, nudo

**joke** *(s)*
chiste, broma, chanza, burla, juego, agudeza, ocurrencia, dicho gracioso

**jolly**
1 alegre, de buen humor, festivo, sociable, retozón, divertido, gracioso, regocijante, jovial, jubiloso, alborozado, juguetón
*triste, desdichado, desgraciado*
2 rechoncho, gordinflón, robusto, regordete, rollizo
*flaco, chupado, desvaído*

**jovial**
jovial, confiado, alegre, sociable, festivo, contento, regocijante, jocoso, gracioso, jubiloso
*triste, sombrío, infeliz*

**joy**
alegría, regocijo, felicidad, encanto, delicia, éxtasis, exaltación, fiesta, gusto, satisfacción, embeleso
*pesar, pena*

**judgment**
1 raciocinio, lógica, perspicacia, discernimiento, sabiduría, inteligencia, prudencia, sagacidad, sentido, juicio
*estupidez*
2 arbitraje, sentencia, fallo, conclusión, decisión, decreto, determinación, opinión, sentencia, veredicto

**judicious**
juicioso, cauteloso, precavido, prudente, considerado, discreto, perspicaz, discernidor, prudente, racional, razonable, sagaz, sensible, diestro, bien calculado, sabio
*indiscreto, imprudente*

**jumble** *(v)*
confundir, desarreglar, descomponer, desordenar, mezclar, embrollar
*arreglar, organizar, disponer*

**jump** *(v)*
saltar, botar, brincar, saltar a la pata coja, dar un salto

**junction**
1 alianza, combinación, unión, juntura, acoplamiento, conexión, ligadura
*separación*
2 *(carreteras)* cruce, *(LAm)* crucero

**just** *(aj)*
1 intachable, concienzudo, equitativo, justo, imparcial, bueno, honesto, honorable, puro
*deshonesto, injusto*

2 exacto, correcto, precio, verdadero, regular
*equivocado, erróneo, inexacto*
3 apropiado, apto, legítimo, meritorio, verdadero, adecuado

**justice**
justicia, equidad, imparcialidad, integridad, rectitud, ley
*prejuicio, predisposición, parcialidad*

**justify**
justificar, absolver, autorizar, defender, exculpar, exonerar, disculpar, perdonar, aprobar
*acusar*

**juvenile** *(aj)*
juvenil, de muchacho, inmaduro, pueril, joven
*maduro*

# K

**keen**
1 ardiente, vehemente, fervoroso, apremiante, apasionado
*apático*
2 agudo, mordaz, cortante, penetrante
*franco*
3 astuto, rápido, sagaz, listo, perceptivo
*estúpido, tonto, corto*

**keep** (s)
1 comida, alimento, mantenimiento, sustento, pensión
2 castillo, mazmorra, calabozo, torre, fortaleza, plaza, fuerte

**keep** (v)
1 mantener, guardar, sostener, conservar, proteger, retener, contener, apoyar
*perder*
2 observar, atenerse a, obedecer, ejecutar, cumplir
3 permanecer, estar, morar, durar, perdurar

**kick** (fig)
oponerse, protestar, rebelarse, resistir, reaccionar, quejarse, desdeñar
*obedecer*

**kid** (s)
1 cabrito, chivo, cabritilla, carne de cabrito
2 chiquillo, chaval, niño, crío, pequeño, (LAm) pibe, escuincle
*adulto*

**kidnap**
raptar, secuestrar, capturar, eliminar, llevarse, robar
*devolver, libertar*

**kill** (v)
1 matar, asesinar, dar muerte, hacer una carnicería, despachar
*crear, dar vida*
2 (fig) calmar, sofocar, hacer abandonar, frustrar, suprimir

**kind** (aj)
amable, afable, agradable, amigable, cariñoso, afectuoso, benéfico, benigno, benévolo, benevolente, generoso, caritativo, clemente, compasivo, simpático, amistoso, generoso, humano, de buen corazón, tierno, educado
*poco amable, nada amistoso*

**kindle** (s)
fuego, ignición, llama, lumbre
*extinción*

**kindle** (v)
animar, estimular, despertar, exasperar, mover, excitar, fomentar, incitar, provocar, motivar, agitar

**king**
rey, monarca, soberano
*plebeyo, súbdito*

**knack**
destreza, aptitud, habilidad, pericia, facilidad, presteza, inteligencia, agilidad
*torpeza, desmaña, terquedad*

**knave**
pillo, canalla, tramposo, pícaro, bribón, tunante, sinvergüenza
*caballero*

**knob**
protuberancia, bulto, manojo, tirador de mano, puño, tachón, clavo

**knot** (s)
1 lazo, vínculo, unión, junta
2 colección, manojo, puñado, grupo, racimo

**knot** (v)
atar, liar, complicar, enredar, enmarañar, entrelazar, (fig) prometerse, casarse
*desatar, desliar*

**know**
saber, comprender, averiguar, discernir, distinguir, aprender, reconocer, entender
*desconocer, no comprender*

**knowledge**

1 conocimiento, educación, erudición, luz, instrucción, aprendizaje, estudio, ciencia, saber, sabiduría, prudencia

*ignorancia*

2 percepción, comprensión, discernimiento, entendimiento, perspicacia, juicio

3 información, aviso, conocimiento

# L

**laborious**

1 arduo, difícil, fatigoso, duro, oneroso, cansado, laborioso
*fácil*

2 laborioso, diligente, trabajador, incansable, concienzudo, esmerado
*vago, holgazán*

**lack** *(s)*

deficiencia, escasez, insuficiencia, miseria, necesidad, cortedad, indigencia
*abundancia, cantidad*

**lame** *(aj)*

1 cojo, lisiado, mutilado, defectuoso, retrasado, minusválido
*sano, robusto*

2 *(fig)* débil, insuficiente, pobre, insatisfactorio
*satisfactorio*

**lament** *(s)*

1 lamento, lamentación, queja, quejido, gemido, protesta

2 canto fúnebre, requiem, elegía, lamento

**lament** *(v)*

lamentar, quejar, gemir, llorar, deplorar, sentir
*alegrarse*

**land** *(s)*

1 tierra, suelo

2 país, nación, distrito, barrio, región, territorio, provincia

**landlord**

1 propietario, dueño, amo
*inquilino*

2 *(Br)* anfitrión, patrón, mesonero, hotelero, posadero
*convidado, invitado, huésped*

**language**

1 lenguaje, dialecto, idioma, habla, lengua, terminología, jerga

2 lenguaje, dicción, expresión, estilo, fraseología

**last** *(aj)*

último, el que cierra, concluyente, extremo, decisivo, final, postrero, terminal
*primero, inicial*

**last** *(v)*

durar, persistir, continuar, permanecer
*fallar*

**late** *(aj)*

1 difunto, muerto, fallecido, finado
*vivo*

2 tarde, atrás, por detrás, retardado, lento, tardío
*temprano, adelantado*

**latent**

latente, escondido, oculto, invisible, potencial, secreto, velado
*abierto, a la vista*

**launch** *(v)*

1 echar, arrojar, despachar, lanzar, proyectar, tirar
*coger, asir*

2 empezar, comenzar, inaugurar, abrir

3 disertar, extender, aumentar

**lavish** *(aj)*

excesivo, extravagante, generoso, inmoderado, imprevisor, liberal, pródigo, profuso, irrazonable, desenfrenado
*tacaño*

**lead** *(v)*

1 dirigir, gobernar, conducir, encabezar, mandar, escoltar, acompañar, llevar, guiar
*seguir*

2 influir, persuadir, prevalecer, atraer, inducir

**lean** *(aj)*

1 delgado, huesudo, demacrado, flaco, chupado, desvaído, escaso, magro, escuálido, esbelto
*gordo, relleno, obeso*

2 pelado, raso, estéril, árido, infecundo, improductivo
*fértil, fecundo*

**lean** *(v)*

1 apoyarse en, inclinarse, reclinar, reposar, descansar, desviar, torcer, tender a

2 confiar, tener confianza en, depender, creer
*desconfiar*

**leap** *(v)*

saltar, botar, rebotar, brincar, retozar

**learn**

aprender, adquirir, memorizar, descubrir, lograr, conseguir, juntar, oír
*olvidar*

**learned**

enseñado, erudito, experimentado, experto, astuto, culto, alfabetizado, cualificado, especializado, versado, bien informado
*ignorante, desconocedor*

**least**

el más débil, último, el más bajo, más pequeño, más diminuto
*el mayor*

**leave** *(v)*

1 dejar, abandonar, marchar, ir, retirar, partir, desertar
*llegar*

2 cesar, parar, desistir, abstenerse, refrenarse

3 dejar, permitir, conceder

4 legar, dejar, transmitir

**legal**

legal, permisible, lícito, autorizado, constitucional, legítimo, legalizado, correcto, aprobado, *(Am)* oficial
*ilegal, ilícito, no autorizado*

**legalise**

1 autorizado, genuino, legal, propio, real, permitido
*ilegal, ilícito*

2 correcto, justificable, legal, lógico, sensible, válido
*irrazonable*

**leisure**

comodidad, libertad, oportunidad, recreación, ocio, tiempo libre, vacaciones
*trabajo*

**lend**

prestar, adelantar, conferir, dejar, dar, impartir, ofrecer, presentar
*pedir prestado, tomar prestado*

**lenient**

compasivo, clemente, gentil, indulgente, misericordioso
*despiadado*

**lethargy**

apatía, coma, sopor, estupor, modorra, somnolencia, flojeza, inacción, inercia, flema
*vigor, ánimo*

**level** *(v)*

1 destruir, demoler, igualar, allanar, aplanar, alisar
*restaurar*

2 apuntar, dirigir, hacer

**lewd**

impuro, lascivo, licencioso, libidinoso, lujurioso, disoluto, libertino, impúdico
*casto*

**liability**

responsabilidad, deber, obligación, tendencia, riesgo, carga
*inmunidad, exención*

**liberal**

1 abundante, generoso, liberal, pródigo, profuso, caritativo, comprensivo, de buen corazón

2 de amplias miras, criterio amplio, liberal, noble, altruista, magnánimo, tolerante, sin prejuicios
*fanático, intolerante*

**liberty**

libertad, emancipación, liberación, independencia, inmunidad
*restricción*

**lie** *(s)*

mentira, falsedad, invención, tergiversación
*verdad*

**lie** (*v*)

1 falsificar, mentir, inventar, tergiversar, buscar evasivas
*decir la verdad*

2 ser, estar, reclinar, permanecer, reposar, descansar en
*incumbir*

**light** (*s*)

1 luz, amanecer, brillo, luz del día, fosforescencia, rayo, destello
*oscuridad*

2 luz, lámpara, vela, linterna, antorcha, faro, bujía, cerilla, farola

3 (*fig*) aspecto, comprensión, ilustración, información, instrucción, conocimiento

**like** (*aj*)

igual, parecido, análogo, paralelo, correspondiente
*diferente*

**like** (*s*)

preferencia, gusto, afición

**like** (*v*)

gustar, agradar, aprobar, elegir, desear, estimar, querer, preferir, seleccionar, amar
*desagradar, no gustar*

**limit** (*s*)

límite, borde, frontera, limitación, restricción, lindero, precinto
*principio*

**limp** (*aj*)

fláccido, flexible, fofo, blanducho, ágil, relajado
*rígido*

**link** (*v*)

unir, juntar, conectar, atar, empalmar
*separar*

**listen**

oír, escuchar, atender, obedecer, observar, hacer caso de, tener en cuenta
*desatender, no hacer caso de*

**litter** (*s*)

1 confusión, desorden, basura, desarreglo, fragmentos, suciedad
*limpieza, pulcritud, orden*

2 ropa de cama, canapé, sofá, bastidor, camilla

3 camada, cría, familia, prole, generación

**little**

1 pequeño, diminuto, menudo, pigmeo, infinitesimal, breve, escaso
*grande, enorme*

2 breve, insignificante, inconsiderable, trivial, sin importancia, baladí
*importante*

3 iliberal, intolerante, tacaño, avaro, egoísta, interesado

**live** (*v*)

1 ser, estar, existir, respirar, alimentar, subsistir, pasar, vivir
*morir*

2 continuar, morar, vivir, permanecer, residir

**lively**

activo, vivo, ágil, alerta, animado, contento, vivaz, entusiasta, rápido, vigoroso
*apagado, inactivo, flojo*

**living** (*aj*)

activo, vivo, animado, existente, enérgico, fuerte, vigoroso
*muerto, apagado*

**load** (*s*)

1 carga, bulto, opresión, presión, peso, estorbo, íncubo, responsabilidad, agobio

2 flete, carga, cargamento

**load** (*v*)

cargar, gravar, tomar cargamento
*aligerar*

**lock** (*v*)

1 cerrar, encerrar, confinar, atar, juntar, sellar, unir, parar, reprimir, refrenar
*abrir, separar*

2 abrochar, abrazar, envolver, rodear, encerrar, agarrar, apretujar

**lodge** (*v*)

1 habitar, morar, vivir, permanecer, asentar, reposar, pararse, residir

2 acomodar, hospedar, entretener, cubrir, abrigar, alojar, acuartelar, amparar, proteger

**lonely**

1 solo, separado, abandonado, desamparado, sin amigos
*acompañado*

2 desierto, desolado, solo, remoto, solitario, inhabitado, sin frecuentar
*lleno, atestado, concurrido*

**look** *(v)*

1 ver, considerar, contemplar, examinar, ojear, observar, mirar, buscar

2 anticipar, esperar, contar con, imaginar

3 volver la cara a, ponerse de cara a, dar a, estar enfrente de

**loose** *(aj)*

1 libre, movible, sin atar, suelto, liberado, ilimitado, infinito, sin restricción
*atado, sujeto*

2 vicioso, disoluto, desenfrenado, licencioso, impúdico, lascivo, inmoral
*casto, púdico*

3 difuso, indefinido, indistinto, confuso, vago
*conciso*

**lord** *(s)*

1 señor, conde, noble, caballero, par, vizconde
*plebeyo*

2 gobernador, rey, monarca, príncipe, *(Br)* director de colegio
*súbdito*

3 *(religión)* Jesucristo, Dios, el Señor, Jehová

**loss**

1 pérdida, privación, fracaso, derroche, despilfarro

2 daño, derrota, pérdida, destrucción, detrimento, perjuicio, desventaja
*ventaja*

**low** *(aj)*

1 profundo, bajo, hundido, disminuido

2 pequeño, corto, enano

3 abyecto, bajo, degradado, servil, miserable, vil, vulgar, innoble, sórdido

4 vergonzoso, deshonroso, escandaloso, no refinado, de mala fama, indecoroso

5 moribundo, exhausto, enfermo, débil, delgado

6 barato, de precio bajo, moderado, razonable

**loyal**

leal, patriótico, constante, fiel, dedicado
*desleal, infiel*

**ludicrous**

absurdo, burlesco, cómico, divertido, ridículo, gracioso, raro
*serio, formal*

**lukewarm**

1 tibio, templado

2 *(fig)* indiferente, frío, apático, despreocupado
*entusiasta, incondicional*

**lunatic**

1 loco, maníaco
*sano*

2 loco, chiflado, tarado, desquiciado, demente, lunático
*sano, cuerdo*

**luscious**

empalagoso, delicioso, meloso, jugoso, sabroso, apetitoso, suculento
*agrio, cortado, desagradable, incomible*

**luxurious**

1 opulento, lujurioso, rico, espléndido, suntuoso
*sencillo, llano, sin adornos, ordinario*

2 afeminado, epicúreo, sensual, voluptuoso, regalado, amante de los placeres

**luxury**

1 opulencia, lujo, riqueza, suntuosidad, voluptuosidad, desenfreno
*austeridad*

2 confort, bienestar, comodidad, placer, encanto, gratificación, indulgencia, placer
*incomodidad, malestar*

# M

**mad**

1 loco, aberrante, lunático, delirante, demente, desquiciado, fanático, rabioso
*sano, cuerdo*

2 *(fig)* enfadado, exasperado, furioso, irritado, rabioso
*calmado*

3 tonto, imprudente, alocado, insensato, arriesgado, peligroso
*sensato*

**magnificence**

magnificencia, brillantez, lujo, majestuosidad, pompa, esplendor, grandeza
*humildad, mezquindad*

**magnify**

1 ampliar, amplificar, aumentar, engrandecer, exagerar
*disminuir, reducir*

2 celebrar, exaltar, glorificar, magnificar
*menospreciar, denigrar*

**majestic**

majestuoso, augusto, elevado, exaltado, grande, imperial, magnífico, noble, pomposo, real, espléndido, sublime
*humilde*

**majesty**

majestad, dignidad, grandiosidad, sublimidad
*humildad*

**make**

1 hacer, crear, componer, constituir, confeccionar, fabricar, formar, originar, producir, moldear
*destruir, deshacer*

2 adquirir, ganar, conseguir, obtener, alcanzar, asegurar

3 actuar, hacer, establecer, ejecutar, ordenar, practicar

4 pensar, juzgar, suponer, estimar

**malign** *(v)*

abusar, calumniar, difamar, herir, menospreciar, denigrar, injuriar, vilipendiar
*alabar, elogiar*

**man** *(s)*

1 hombre, adulto, ser, cuerpo, humanidad, individuo, macho, persona, personaje, alma
*bestia, animal*

2 asistente, empleado, sirviente, trabajador, ayuda de cámara
*señor, dueño*

**mania**

1 aberración, delirio, locura, manía, demencia, fanatismo
*cordura, sensatez*

2 *(fig)* deseo, entusiasmo, manía

**manifold**

diverso, variado, múltiple, multitudinario, numeroso, vario, variado
*poco*

**manufacture** *(v)*

construir, edificar, componer, crear, fabricar, formar, hacer, amoldar, producir
*destruir*

**mar**

manchar, emborronar, dañar, desfigurar, mutilar, arruinar, estropear, perjudicar
*mejorar*

**margin**

borde, margen, límite, lindero
*centro, exterior*

**marriage**

1 matrimonio, nupcias, casamiento, boda
*celibato*

2 alianza, asociación, confederación, unión
*separación*

**marshal** *(s)*

mariscal, oficial, *(Am)* alguacil, oficial de justicia

**marshal** *(v)*
arreglar, disponer, colocar, recoger, reunir, ordenar, mandar, guiar
*dispersar, esparcir*

**martial**
marcial, bravo, heroico, militar, belicoso, guerrero
*pacífico*

**marvellous,** *(Am)* **marvelous**
1 maravilloso, asombroso, pasmoso, extraordinario, milagroso, estupendo
*ordinario*
2 improbable, increíble, sorprendente
*creíble*

**master** *(s)*
1 capitán, jefe, comandante, gobernador, propietario, principal, superintendente, *(Br) (colegio)* director, rector
*sirviente*
2 instructor, pedagogo, preceptor, maestro, director de escuela, tutor
*estudiante*

**mature** *(aj)*
maduro, completo, crecido, añejo, perfecto, listo
*inmaduro, verde*

**meagre,** *(Am)* **meager**
1 demacrado, magro, desvaído, chupado, seco, delgado, pobre, en los huesos, hambriento
*rollizo, regordete, obeso*
2 deficiente, desprovisto, pobre, escaso, improductivo, infértil
*copioso*

**mean** *(v)*
significar, denotar, diseñar, expresar, indicar, significar, proponer

**means** *(s)*
1 expediente, medida, instrumento, método, modo, manera
*fin*
2 dinero, ayuda, bienes, recursos, sustancia, riqueza, abundancia
*pobreza*

**meddlesome**
entrometido, intruso, malicioso, juguetón, oficioso, fisgón, curioso
*no entrometido*

**meek**
calmado, dócil, gentil, modesto, paciente, pacífico, sumiso, indulgente, apacible, manso
*arrogante, deshonesto, descarado*

**meet** *(v)*
1 enfrentar, confrontar, contactar, hallar, encontrar, abordar
2 contestar, responder, acatar, desempeñar, cumplir, satisfacer, complacer
3 conectar, unir, juntar, convergir
4 agrupar, coleccionar, congregar, reunir, recoger, juntar

**melancholy** *(s)*
melancolía, depresión, tristeza, abatimiento, desaliento, pesimismo
*alegría*

**mellow**
1 delicado, sabroso, condimentado, maduro, suculento, muy dulce, añejo, meloso, suave
*verde, inmaduro*
2 alegre, divertido, jovial, tranquilo

**melt**
1 disolver, fundir, difundir, licuar, deshelar, derretir
*solidificar*
2 *(fig)* relajar, apaciguar, calmar, templar, mitigar
*endurecer*

**mention** *(v)*
mencionar, aludir, citar, comunicar, declarar, divulgar, impartir, referir, revelar, decir
*ocultar, disimular*

**mercy**
benevolencia, caridad, clemencia, compasión, perdón, gracia, amabilidad, lenidad
*crueldad*

**merit** *(s)*
virtud, mérito, bondad, honor, mérito, recompensa
*inutilidad, falta de valor*

**mess**

1 lío, confusión, desorden, enredo, mezcla, suciedad, desperdicios
*limpieza, orden*

2 *(fig)* dificultad, perplejidad, confusión, crisis, situación apremiante

**might**

habilidad, capacidad, eficacia, energía, fuerza, poder, valor
*debilidad*

**mild**

1 amigable, calmado, clemente, compasivo, gentil, indulgente, amable, moderado, plácido, agradable, tranquilo, suave
*poco amable, poco compasivo*

2 emoliente, lenitivo, apaciguador, calmante, tranquilizador
*severo, duro*

**mind** *(s)*

1 cerebro, inteligencia, seso, razón, sentido, espíritu, entendimiento
*cuerpo*

2 disposición, deseo, inclinación, intención, propósito, tendencia, voluntad

3 creencia, opinión, juicio, sentimiento, pensamiento

4 memoria, recolección, recuerdo

**mingle**

mezclar, alear, combinar, confundir con, entremezclar, mezclar, unir
*disolver, separar*

**minute** *(aj)*

1 diminuto, fino, pequeño, microscópico, delgado, tenue
*grande*

2 crítico, detallado, exacto, preciso
*inexacto, vago*

**mirth**

alegría, fiesta, regocijo, hilaridad, jovialidad, placer, animación, satisfacción
*tristeza, melancolía*

**misdeed**

crimen, falta, delito, fechoría, mala conducta, ofensa, pecado, transgresión, error, equivocación
*derecho, justicia, bien*

**miserable**

1 afligido, desconsolado, melancólico, miserable, infeliz, triste, abatido, desanimado
*feliz, contento*

2 pobre, miserable, necesitado, sin dinero, indigente, desamparado
*rico, adinerado*

3 miserable, malo, bajo, abyecto, vil, despreciable
*bueno*

**misery**

1 aflicción, agonía, angustia, calamidad, pena, infortunio, miseria, tormento, tortura, pesar, desdicha
*alegría, júbilo, deleite*

2 *(fig)* aguafiestas, quejicoso

**misfortune**

accidente, adversidad, aflicción, calamidad, fallo, dureza, desgracia, percance, revés
*suerte, fortuna*

**mislead**

engañar, dirigir mal, informar, erróneamente, aconsejar mal, despistar
*dirigir*

**mist**

1 niebla, neblina, *(fig)* nube, velo
*claridad*

2 *(fig)* oscuridad, perplejidad, aturdimiento
*claridad*

**mistake** *(s)*

error, fallo, inexactitud, cálculo erróneo, falta, equivocación
*precisión, exactitud*

**mistrust** *(v)*

dudar, temer, sospechar, desconfiar, recelar
*confiar*

**misty**

nublado, oscuro, encapotado, nebuloso, brumoso
*claro, despejado*

**misunderstanding**

1 error, incomprensión, equivocación, no interpretar correctamente
*entendimiento, comprensión*

2 diferencia, dificultad, desacuerdo, discordia, pelea
*acuerdo*

**mix** (v)

mezclar, asociar, combinar, incorporar, juntar, unir, componer
*separar*

**mixture**

mezcla, amalgamación, asociación, combinación, conglomeración, revoltijo, confusión, unión, fusión
*elemento*

**moan** (v)

lamentar, deplorar, afligirse, acongojarse, gemir, quejarse, llorar, suspirar

**mockery**

contumelia, engaño, irrisión, mofas, befas, imitación, burlas, ridículo, parodia
*aprobación, consentimiento*

**moderate** (aj)

1 moderado, abstemio, limitado, comedido, refrenado, serio, formal, templado, razonable, juicioso
*inmoderado*

2 barato, mediocre, ordinario, regular

**modern**

moderno, nuevo, último, novato, actual, presente, reciente
*viejo, antiguo, obsoleto*

**modest**

1 tímido, modesto, vergonzoso, decoroso, conveniente, reservado, humilde, sumiso, retraído, sin pretensiones
*valiente, audaz*

2 casto, virtuoso, puro, de mente pura
*corrupto*

**moist**

húmedo, mojado
*seco*

**molest**

enfadar, molestar, enojar, atacar, distraer, incomodar, irritar, acosar, importunar, plagar, atormentar, preocupar
*dar gusto, agradar, contentar*

**monotonous**

aburrido, monótono, tedioso, pesado, uniforme, cansado
*variado*

**moral** (aj)

1 moral, ético, intachable, irreprochable, bueno, honesto, justo, honorable, virtuoso
*inmoral, amoral*

2 abstracto, ideal, intelectual, mental

**morose**

poco afable, hosco, malhumorado, irritable, pesimista, malévolo, malicioso, taciturno, maleducado
*de buen humor, alegre*

**mortal** (aj)

mortal, destructivo, fatal, letal, vital, humano, perecedero
*inmortal*

**motion**

1 cambio, movimiento, paso, marcha, funcionamiento
*repaso*

2 proposición, sugerencia, moción

**mould** (v)

tallar, grabar, esculpir, formar, moldear, crear, hacer
*deformar*

**mount** (v)

1 montar, subir, ascender, levantar, remontar, escalar
*descender, bajar*

2 embellecer, ornamentar, adornar

**mournful**

calamitoso, deplorable, afligido, lamentable, melancólico, infeliz, doloroso, penoso, triste, pesaroso
*feliz, alegre, animado, optimista*

**move** (v)

1 mover, avanzar, ir, marchar, proceder, progresar, andar, caminar
*parar, permanecer*

2 cambiar, mover, operar, funcionar, impulsar, conducir, empezar

3 actuar, afectar, agitar, excitar, impresionar, inducir, influir, instigar, persuadir, instar

4 proponer, sugerir, recomendar

**muddle** *(s)*

confusión, desorden, mezcla, enredo, situación apremiante, apuro

*orden*

**mundane**

mundano, terrenal, secular, temporal, terrestre

*espiritual, sobrenatural*

**muscular**

atlético, fornido, musculoso, poderoso, robusto, fuerte, vigoroso

*débil, fofo, blanducho*

**mute**

mudo, silencioso, taciturno, sin voz, estupefacto

*vocal, ruidoso*

**mysterious**

misterioso, oscuro, enigmático, escondido, inexplicable, incomprensible, recóndito, secreto

*claro, inteligible, abierto*

# N

**nag** *(v)*
molestar, fastidiar, acosar, atormentar, irritar, provocar, inquietar
*suavizar, apaciguar, mitigar*

**naïve**
cándido, sencillo, franco, ingenuo, abierto, sin afectar
*sofisticado, astuto*

**naked**
1 desnudo, destapado
*vestido*
2 manifiesto, obvio, evidente, llano, simple, franco, sin disfraz, abierto
*exagerado*

**narrow**
1 circunscrito, limitado, confinado, cerrado, encogido, escaso, corto, insuficiente
*ancho, extenso, amplio*
2 avaricioso, avariento, avaro, tacaño, codicioso, poco generoso, mercenario
*generoso*
3 parcial, intolerante, iliberal, de miras estrechas
*tolerante, liberal*

**nasty**
1 nauseabundo, sucio, desagradable, asqueroso, repugnante, ofensivo
*limpio, aseado*
2 sucio, viciado, indecente, impuro, grosero, lascivo, lujurioso, obsceno, procaz
*decente*
3 pesado, importuno, malhumorado, displicente, de mal genio, antipático, grosero
*agradable, simpático, atento*

**native** *(aj)*
1 nativo, congénito, innato, ingénito, indígena, natal, natural
*adquirido*
2 genuino, real, original
*falso, viejo*

3 nacional, vernáculo, natal
*extranjero*

**natural**
1 legítimo, natural, normal, regular, ordinario, usual
*sofisticado*
2 cándido, franco, genuino, abierto, real, sencillo, ingenuo

**naughty**
1 tremendo, travieso, malo, desobediente, perverso, juguetón, malicioso
*bueno, obediente*
2 *(fig) (chiste)* escabroso, picante, atrevido, verde, *(LAm)* colorado

**near** *(aj)*
1 cercano, adyacente, contiguo, vecino, colindante, tocante
*lejano, remoto*
2 inminente, cercano, próximo, venidero
*lejano*
3 familiar, íntimo, querido

**neat**
1 elegante, primoroso, ordenado, pulcro, aseado, acicalado, arreglado
*sucio, desordenado*
2 apto, listo, experto, diestro, mañoso, hábil, perito
*torpe, desmañado*
3 puro, sin mezcla, sin diluir
*diluido*
4 *(Am)* estupendo, fantástico

**necessary**
necesario, obligatorio, esencial, indispensable, inevitable, involuntario, ineludible
*superfluo, innecesario*

**need** *(s)*
1 adversidad, carencia, falta, necesidad, pobreza, penuria, privación, miseria
2 emergencia, necesidad, urgencia, exigencia

**neglect** *(s)*
negligencia, descuido, falta de atención, despreocupación, olvido
*atención, cuidado*

**neglect** *(v)*
olvidar, descuidar, pasar por alto, fallar, omitir, ignorar
*observar, recordar*

**negligent**
negligente, descuidado, olvidadizo, indiferente
*cuidadoso*

**neighbourhood**
vecindario, cercanía, barrio, región, proximidad
*distancia*

**negotiate**
negociar, arreglar, tratar, pactar, discutir, deliberar, acordar

**nerve**
1 nervio, coraje, energía, fuerza, firmeza, resolución, resistencia, valor, ánimo, vigor
*debilidad, flojedad*

**neutral** *(aj)*
neutral, imparcial, indiferente, indistinto, indeciso, neutro
*parcial*

**new**
1 nuevo, fresco, moderno, original, sin usar, a la moda
*viejo, antiguo*
2 adicional, complementario, supletorio

**nice**
1 agradable, cortés, amigable, amable, educado, fino, refinado, enseñado, simpático
*desagradable, descortés*
2 elegante, primoroso, fino, sutil, aseado, pulcro, ordenado, acicalado, arreglado
*desharrapado, mal vestido*
3 exacto, preciso, riguroso, crítico, severo, exigente, escrupuloso, estricto
*vago, impreciso, incierto*

4 guapo, hermoso, *(LAm)* lindo
*feo*

**nimble**
activo, ágil, alerta, brusco, vivaz, ligero, rápido, listo, inteligente
*lento, torpe, desmañado*

**noble** *(aj)*
1 aristocrático, noble, linajudo, señorial, patricio
2 distinguido, noble, elevado, eminente, excelente, grande, honorable, espléndido, impresionante, sublime
*innoble, plebeyo*

**noble** *(s)*
noble, aristócrata, lord, caballero, par, hidalgo
*plebeyo*

**noise**
ruido, clamor, sonido, estrépito, estruendo, tumulto, alboroto, *(fig)* escándalo
*paz, silencio, tranquilidad*

**noisy**
ruidoso, clamoroso, estrepitoso, tumultuoso, turbulento, vocífero, alborotado
*quieto, tranquilo, silencioso*

**normal**
normal, natural, ordinario, típico, usual, corriente, regular
*anormal, inusual, extraño*

**note** *(s)*
1 nota, anotación, comentario, comunicado, comunicación, epístola, carta, minuta, memorándum, registro
2 indicación, nota, símbolo, marca, señal, indicio, muestra
3 celebridad, distinción, eminencia, fama, renombre, reputación, nombradía

**notice** *(v)*
notar, distinguir, discernir, observar, percibir, ver, marcar, fijarse
*pasar por alto, olvidar*

**notorious**

1 notorio, deshonesto, deshonrado, sin reputación, infame, oprobioso
*loable, estimable*

2 notorio, famoso, celebrado, conocido, renombrado
*desconocido*

3 obvio, abierto, evidente, patente, indiscutible
*oscuro, escondido*

**nourish**

1 alimentar, nutrir, atender, suministrar, proveer, criar
*hacer pasar hambre, matar de hambre*

2 confortar, animar, alentar, sustentar, estimular, sostener
*descuidar*

**novice**

novato, aprendiz, neófito, noviciado, novicio, converso, alumno, principiante
*maestro*

**nuisance**

enojo, contrariedad, irritación, aburrimiento, molestia, lata, ofensa, peste, plaga, problema
*placer, deleite*

**nullify**

anular, rescindir, cancelar, invalidar, neutralizar, abolir
*llevar a cabo, efectuar*

**number** (s)

1 número, dígito, cifra, cuenta, figura, numeral, suma, total

2 conjunto, muchedumbre, colección, compañía, multitud, horda, grupo

**numerous**

numeroso, abundante, muchos, incontable
*pocos*

**nurse** (v)

alimentar, asistir, nutrir, lactar, atender, cuidar, amamantar, criar
*descuidar, olvidar*

# O

### obedience
obediencia, acuerdo, conformidad, deber, respeto, reverencia, sumisión
*desobediencia, negativa*

### obese
corpulento, gordo, gordinflón, obeso, rollizo
*delgado, chupado, seco*

### obey
obedecer, seguir, cumplir, observar, atenerse a, someter
*desobedecer*

### object (s)
1 hecho, fenómeno, cosa, objeto, realidad
2 blanco, intención, meta, motivo, objetivo, propósito, plan

### object (v)
objetar, contravenir, oponerse, poner reparos, protestar
*estar de acuerdo*

### obligatory
coactivo, forzoso, inevitable, necesario, obligatorio
*voluntario*

### oblige
1 coaccionar, forzar, obligar, requerir, exigir, imponer, hacer cumplir
*sonsacar*
2 acomodar, favorecer, beneficiar, contentar, gratificar, servir

### obliging
considerado, cortés, amistoso, amable, civil, atento, educado, servicial
*poco servicial*

### oblivious
descuidado, negligente, olvidadizo, despreocupado, desatento, distraído
*atento, preocupado*

### obscene
obsceno, sucio, desagradable, impuro, inmoral, indecente, licencioso, ofensivo, pornográfico, vergonzoso, impúdico, relajado, disoluto
*decente*

### obscure (aj)
1 oscuro, nublado, encapotado, cubierto
*claro, despejado*
2 ambiguo, dudoso, incomprensible, intrincado, misterioso, vago, complejo, enrevesado
*obvio, claro*
3 humilde, ignominioso, desconocido, anónimo, innominado, desapercibido
*distinguido, conocido*

### observe
1 observar, detectar, descubrir, notar, percibir, ver, atestiguar
*pasar por alto, olvidar*
2 observar, mencionar, comentar, decir, notar
*callar*
3 observar, obedecer, cumplir, seguir, hacer, actuar, realizar, tener en cuenta
*hacer caso omiso, ignorar*
4 celebrar, recordar, solemnizar

### obstacle
obstáculo, barrera, dificultad, impedimento, interferencia, interrupción, obstrucción, revés, contratiempo
*ayuda, asistencia*

### obstinate
obstinado, firme, persistente, contumaz, tenaz, cabeza cuadrada, terco, testarudo, perverso
*dócil, domable, sumiso*

### obstruct
obstruir, atascar, impedir, interferir, prevenir, obstaculizar, interrumpir, retardar
*asistir, ayudar*

**obtain**

obtener, conseguir, alcanzar, ganar, lograr
*perder*

**obvious**

obvio, aparente, claro, distintivo, evidente, manifiesto, palpable, patente, perceptible, llano, visible
*oscuro, oculto, indistinto*

**occasional**

accidental, casual, infrecuente, irregular
*frecuente, normal*

**occupy**

1 emplear, utilizar, alquilar
2 habitar, ocupar, poseer, ser dueño de
3 ocupar, invadir, capturar, apoderarse de
*evacuar, desocupar*

**occur**

ocurrir, acontecer, aparecer, surgir, producir, producirse, aventurar, motivar

**odd**

anormal, diferente, raro, extraño, excéntrico, excepcional, extraordinario, peculiar, original, inusual, fantástico, desigual, curioso
*común, normal, igual*

**offence**, *(Am)* **offense**

1 ofensa, crimen, delincuencia, falta, felonía, transgresión, pecado, delito
2 enfado, indignación, ira, resentimiento
*encanto, delicia*
3 agresión, ataque, asalto, arremetida

**offend**

1 ofender, molestar, herir, dañar, insultar, irritar, molestar, provocar, fastidiar, contrariar, mortificar
*agradar, contentar, dar gusto a*
2 ofender, pecar, transgredir, errar, equivocarse

**offer** *(v)*

ofrecer, dar, mover, presentar, proporcionar, proveer, proponer, ofertar
*rehusar, rechazar, denegar*

**old**

viejo, anciano, antiguo, anticuado, cariado, de edad, mayor, obsoleto, pasado de moda, primitivo, senil
*nuevo, joven*

**omission**

omisión, falta, fallo, negligencia, descuido, equivocación, olvido
*cumplimiento, realización*

**omit**

omitir, dejar, eliminar, excluir, perder, olvidar, pasar por alto
*incluir*

**open** *(v)*

1 abrir, empezar, comenzar, iniciar
2 exhibir, revelar, explicar, mostrar, descubrir

**opening**

1 abertura, brecha, hendura, fisura, agujero, grieta, perforación, línea, ranura
*cierre*
2 principio, comienzo, inicio, inauguración
*final, conclusión*

**operation**

1 operación, negocio, acción, asunto, esfuerzo, manipulación, movimiento, actuación, procedimiento, proceso
*cese, suspensión*
2 *(medicina)* operación, intervención quirúrgica

**opponent**

oponente, rival, adversario, antagonista, competidor, contendiente, contrincante, enemigo
*aliado, amigo*

**oppress**

oprimir, maltratar, cargar, aniquilar, aplastar, dominar, subyugar, tiranizar
*liberar, librar, aliviar*

## oppressive

1 opresivo, cruel, déspota, pesado, inhumano, severo, injusto, tiránico
*ligero*

2 opresivo, cerrado, sofocante, asfixiador, bochornoso
*aireado, fresco*

## order (v)

1 ordenar, decretar, mandar, dirigir, prescribir, requerir
*dejar, obedecer*

2 ajustar, arreglar, ordenar, controlar, disponer, regular, clasificar
*enredar, desordenar*

## ordinary

1 ordinario, corriente, común, habitual, normal, usual, regular, cotidiano
*irregular*

2 indiferente, ordinario, inferior, mediocre, malo, de segunda mano
*superior, bueno*

## organise

1 organizar, arreglar, disponer, coordinar, establecer, formar, constituir, determinar, hacer
*desorganizar, arruinar*

2 (Am) sindicarse, afiliarse a un partido/sindicato

## origin

1 origen, principio, causa, inicio, derivación, fundación, raíz, fuente
*final*

2 nacimiento, linaje, familia, origen
*muerte, fallecimiento, final*

## original (aj)

1 original, aborigen, primario, primitivo, primordial, prístino
*secundario*

2 original, inventivo, nuevo, insólito
*anticuado, viejo*

## originate

1 originar, empezar, emanar, fluir, proceder, hacer surgir, levantar
*finalizar, acabar*

2 crear, descubrir, formar, inventar, idear, producir

## ornament (s)

adorno, ornamento, decoración, diseño, embellecimiento
*mancha, tacha*

## ornament (v)

adornar, embellecer, arreglar, decorar, engalanar, aderezar
*estropear, deslucir*

## ostentatious

ostentoso, fanfarrón, jactancioso, engreído, extravagante, gallardo, pomposo, presumido, pretencioso, vanidoso
*modesto, módico*

## outrage (v)

abusar, injuriar, insultar, afrontar, indignar, ofender, maltratar, violar
*cumplimentar*

## outrageous

abominable, atroz, excesivo, extravagante, furioso, inmoderado, loco, alocado, violento, terrible, monstruoso, escandaloso
*moderado, tranquilo*

## overcharge

1 sobrecargar, cargar, oprimir, agobiar, hartar
*cobrar menos, rebajar*

2 exagerar

## overcome

vencer, conquistar, ganar, aniquilar, destruir, derrotar, prevalecer, subyugar
*rendirse, someterse*

## overlook

1 perdonar, condonar, disculpar
*castigar*

2 olvidar, ignorar, dejar pasar, omitir, pasar, perder
*incluir, recordar*

3 examinar, inspeccionar, indagar, supervisar, revisar, estudiar

## own (v)

1 poseer, tener, ser dueño de

2 reconocer, aceptar, admitir, confesar, conceder, permitir
*negar, denegar*

# P

**pacify**

pacificar, aliviar, mejorar, calmar, moderar, conciliar, tranquilizar, suavizar, mitigar
*provocar*

**pain** *(s)*

1 pena, dolor, aflicción, agonía, angustia, aspereza, incomodidad, sufrimiento, tormento, tortura, vejación
*placer*

2 *(fig)* persona latosa

**painful**

1 doloroso, agonizante, molesto, desagradable, penoso, provocador, grave, atroz
*inofensivo, indoloro*

2 arduo, difícil, duro, laborioso, severo
*fácil*

**pale** *(aj)*

pálido, ceniciento, de ceniza, sin color, blanco, cetrino, amarillento
*subido, rojizo*

**pamper**

mimar, acariciar, complacer, satisfacer, consentir, estropear
*desatender*

**panic**

alarma, consternación, miedo, pánico, temor, horror, terror
*calma*

**parade** *(s)*

1 muestra, ostentación, pompa, fausto
*freno, control, restricción*

2 desfile, parada, ceremonia, procesión, espectáculo, revista

**pardon**

perdón, absolución, amnistía, condonación, excusa, gracia, indulgencia, remisión, descargo
*culpa*

**parity**

paridad, analogía, correspondencia, igualdad, equivalencia, semejanza, similitud, parecido
*desigualdad*

**part** *(s)*

1 pieza, parte, componente, constituyente, división, elemento, fracción, fragmento, porción, sección, trozo
*total*

2 interés, asunto, facción, lado, grupo

3 negocio, cargo, deber, función, oficio, responsabilidad, trabajo

**particle**

partícula, átomo, molécula, grano, ápice, pizca, mota, poquitín, pedacito, fragmento
*entero*

**partisan** *(s)*

partisano, discípulo, seguidor, partidario, partidista
*líder, maestro*

**passage**

1 pasaje, avenida, curso, sendero, ruta, camino, carretera
*barrera*

2 canal, viaje, tour, cruce, trayecto

3 pasillo, galería, vestíbulo, puerta, entrada, portal

**pastime**

diversión, entretenimiento, recreo, pasatiempo
*trabajo*

**patent** *(aj)*

aparente, claro, evidente, indiscutible, manifiesto, obvio, patente, palpable
*oscuro*

**pathetic**

conmovedor, enternecedor, tierno, patético, lastimoso, lastimero
*de risa*

**patience**
paciencia, calma, compostura, diligencia, tolerancia, resistencia, aguante, perseverancia, persistencia, resignación, serenidad, sumisión
*excitación*

**patient** *(aj)*
paciente, calmado, persistente, quieto, resignado, sumiso, sereno, sosegado, tranquilo, indulgente
*excitable*

**patron**
patrón, abogado, guardián, defensor, ayudante, protector, *(artes)* mecenas
*enemigo*

**peace**
paz, acuerdo, armisticio, calma, armonía, descanso, silencio, tranquilidad
*discordia, guerra*

**peak**
1 punta, cénit, cima, cresta, ápice, cumbre
*fondo, asiento*
2 *(fig)* cumbre, apogeo

**peer** *(s)*
1 asociado, compañero, igual, camarada, compinche
2 par, aristócrata, barón, conde, duque, señor, marqués, vizconde, noble
*plebeyo*

**peevish**
acrimonio, criticón, reparón, pueril, aniñado, infantil, malhumorado, irritable, petulante
*amigable*

**penalty**
multa, pérdida, castigo, sanción
*recompensa*

**perception**
percepción, concepción, discernimiento, idea, observación, reconocimiento, sensación
*malentendido*

**perfect** *(aj)*
1 perfecto, completo, completado, entero, consumado, terminado, total
*incompleto*
2 intachable, irreprochable, excelente, inmaculado, puro, espléndido
*impuro*
3 experto, consumado, ducho, hábil, cualificado

**perform**
1 conseguir, acabar, terminar, completar, actuar, hacer, efectuar, ejecutar, observar, satisfacer
*fallar*
2 actuar, escenificar, representar

**periodical** *(aj)*
periódico, intermitente, incidental, sistemático, regular
*irregular*

**perishable**
perecedero, decadente, destructible, agonizante, moribundo, frágil, fugitivo, mortal
*duradero, durable*

**permanent**
constante, duradero, fijo, inmutable, indestructible, invariable, estable, permanente, perpetuo, perdurable, eterno
*temporal, provisional, temporáneo*

**permission**
autorización, consentimiento, libertad, licencia, permiso, tolerancia
*negativa, denegación*

**permit** *(v)*
admitir, acordar, permitir, autorizar, consentir, dejar, tolerar
*negar, denegar*

**perpetual**
constante, continuo, eterno, incesante, duradero, infinito, interminable, permanente, perpetuo, ininterrumpido
*temporáneo, provisional*

**perplex**
1 molestar, distraer, perturbar, alterar, fastidiar, jorobar

2 complicar, embrollar, enredar, enmarañar, involucrar

3 dejar perplejo, confundir, desconcertar, desorientar

**persecute**
afligir, enfadar, molestar, agotar, acosar, hostigar, perseguir, oprimir
*ofrecer amistad*

**perseverance**
constancia, determinación, persistencia, perseverancia, resolución, tenacidad
*inconstancia*

**persist**
1 continuar, durar, permanecer, persistir
*pasar*

2 insistir, perseverar, persistir

**personal**
1 corporal, corpóreo, material, físico, personal
*impersonal*

2 individual, personal, peculiar, privado, especial
*general*

**persuade**
accionar, impulsar, persuadir, aconsejar, convencer, incitar, inducir, influir, prevalecer, urgir
*disuadir*

**pertinent**
aplicable, apropiado, apto, relevante, adecuado, pertinente, oportuno
*irrelevante*

**perturb**
perturbar, confundir, agitar, desordenar, inquietar, alterar, fastidiar
*calmar*

**perverse**
contrario, perverso, tenaz, obstinado, intratable, terco, testarudo, problemático, inmanejable
*obediente, manejable, maleable*

**petition**
petición, memorial, aplicación, solicitud, formulario, ruego, súplica

**petty**
pequeño, diminuto, insignificante, inconsiderable, inferior, menor, trivial, sin importancia
*importante*

**picture**
1 imagen, cuadro, pintura, fotografía, retrato, dibujo, esquema

2 descripción, similitud, impresión, representación, parecido

**piece**
trozo, pieza, fragmento, pedazo, puñado, parte, porción
*todo, entero*

**piety**
devoción, gracia, piedad, santidad, reverencia, veneración
*irreverencia, impiedad*

**pilfer**
sisar, ratear, robar, hurtar
*reemplazar*

**pillage** *(s)*
pillaje, botín, presa, estrago, saqueo, rapiña, robo
*reparación, indemnización*

**pine** *(v)*
1 decaer, declinar, desvanecer, languidecer, consumirse, acabarse, flaquear
*reponer, avivar, restablecer*

2 desear, anhelar, suspirar (por), añorar

**pity** *(s)*
compasión, condolencia, simpatía, pena, afinidad, amabilidad, misericordia
*crueldad*

**placid**
plácido, calmado, frío, gentil, imperturbable, pacífico, quieto, sereno, tranquilo, impasible, ecuánime
*temperamental, excitable, caprichoso*

**plague** *(s)*
1 plaga, contagio, enfermedad, epidemia, infección, peste, pestilencia

2 *(fig)* aflicción, calamidad, mal, molestia, incomodidad, tormento, prueba, fastidio
*beneficio, ventaja*

**plain** (aj)

1 aparente, llano, claro, manifiesto, evidente, obvio, distintivo
*ambiguo, oscuro*

2 franco, llano, abierto, sincero, honesto, cándido, directo, ingenuo
*engañoso, deshonesto*

3 llano, plano, nivelado, suave, recto, igual
*desigual, abrupto*

**plane** (aj)

llano, plano, suave, igual, nivelado
*desigual, abrupto*

**plane** (s)

avión

**play** (v)

1 actuar, representar, escenificar

2 jugar, apostar, especular, (fig) arriesgar, invertir

**plead**

rogar, alegar, argumentar, defender, discutir, mantener, pretextar, suplicar
*negar, denegar*

**pleasant**

agradable, aceptable, divertido, encantador, gratificador, deleitable, jocoso, humorístico, juguetón
*desagradable, antipático, malhumorado*

**pleasure**

1 comodidad, confort, deleite, placer, felicidad, alegría, satisfacción
*pena, pesar*

2 inclinación, preferencia, voluntad, deseo, objetivo
*desinclinación*

**pledge** (s)

bono, depósito, garantía, seguridad, prenda, señal

**plentiful**

abundante, amplio, completo, copioso, fructífero, productivo, profuso
*escaso*

**plot** (s)

1 cábala, complot, conspiración, intriga, maquinación, plan, estratagema

2 historia, materia, tema, hilo

**plump**

rechoncho, regordete, gordo, obeso, fornido, corpulento, rollizo
*delgado, flaco*

**poignant**

punzante, doloroso, amargo, intenso, sarcástico, severo, conmovedor, patético
*suave*

**poisonous**

nocivo, venenoso, corrupto, dañoso, pestilente
*saludable*

**policy**

acción, discreción, procedimiento, regla, plan, estratagema, norma, acierto
*simplicidad, imprudencia, temeridad*

**polish** (v)

lustrar, abrillantar, pulir, renovar, limpiar (frotando), terminar, (LAm) bolear
*manchar*

**polite**

afable, civil, civilizado, complaciente, cortés, educado, gentil, refinado, urbanizado
*mal educado, descortés*

**pollute**

contaminar, corromper, ensuciar, polucionar, manchar, degradar
*purificar, limpiar*

**pompous**

augusto, pomposo, jactancioso, presumido, fanfarrón, ostentoso, suntuoso, vistoso, exagerado, pretencioso
*simple, sencillo*

**ponderous**

abultado, pesado, masivo
*ligero*

**portion**

1 trozo, porción, fragmento, bocado, puñado, pieza, parte, sección
*todo, total, completo*

2 ración, porción, cuota, cantidad, reparto

**possess**
controlar, poseer, tener, mantener, obtener
*perder*

**possession**
control, custodia, ocupación, posesión, propiedad, tenencia
*pérdida*

**possessions**
efectos, acciones, riqueza, posesiones, bienes

**possible**
posible, potencial, factible, probable, verosímil, practicable
*imposible, impracticable*

**posterity**
1 descendencia, familia, hijos, herederos, vástagos
*antepasados*
2 posterioridad, futuro
*pasado*

**postpone**
posponer, aplazar, retrasar, prorrogar, diferir
*acelerar, despachar*

**potent**
capaz, activo, efectivo, eficaz, eficiente, poderoso, fuerte, influyente, potente
*débil, impotente*

**poverty**
1 mendicidad, miseria, pobreza, indigencia, desgracia, necesidad, penuria, privación, escasez
*riqueza, opulencia*
2 deficiencia, esterilidad, aridez, infructuosidad
*fertilidad*

**power**
1 habilidad, capacidad, competencia, energía, facultad, fuerza, poder, potencia, poderío
*incapacidad*
2 autoridad, mando, control, poder, dominio, influencia, regla, soberanía
*sumisión, sujeción, sometimiento*

**practical**
1 práctico, eficiente, experimentado, cualificado, entrenado, adiestrado
*torpe*
2 práctico, servible, útil, utilizable

**praise** (v)
1 aclamar, admirar, aplaudir, aprobar, cumplimentar, elogiar
*condenar, denigrar, culpar*
2 alabar, adorar, rogar, rezar, exaltar, glorificar

**prayer**
1 ruego, súplica, petición, instancia, solicitud
*orden*
2 rezo, ruego, devoción, invocación, letanía, súplica

**precarious**
peligroso, precario, dudoso, molesto, fastidioso, inseguro, incierto, de poca confianza, inestable, inseguro
*seguro, salvo*

**precipitate** (v)
acelerar, avanzar, despachar, expedir, precipitar, presionar, hacer correr
*retrasar, retardar*

**precise**
1 preciso, exacto, correcto, claro, categórico, explícito
*incorrecto*
2 cuidadoso, formal, exacto, preciso, puntilloso, escrupuloso

**preface** (s)
prefacio, introducción, prólogo, preámbulo, preludio, preliminar
*apéndice, epílogo, conclusión*

**prefer**
1 escoger, elegir, desear, preferir, seleccionar, agradar
*rechazar, desechar*
2 avanzar, elevar, promocionar, levantar
*degradar*

**premature**
1 temprano, prematuro, adelantado, inmaduro, verde
*maduro*

2 *(fig)* inconsiderado, precipitado, irreflexivo, intempestivo
*considerado*

**presence**

1 asistencia, presencia, compañía, proximidad, vecindad, vecindario
*ausencia*

2 aire, aspecto, apariencia, presencia, personalidad, porte, andares

**presently**

1 pronto, luego, dentro de poco, en breve
*eventualmente*

2 *(Am)* directamente, inmediatamente, en el acto, ahora, actualmente

**preserve** *(v)*

conservar, continuar, guardar, preservar, defender, mantener, proteger, retener, sostener
*destruir*

**press** *(v)*

1 presionar, comprimir, agarrar, estrujar, apretujar
*soltar, dejar*

2 presionar, empujar, hacer correr, dar prisa, acelerar

**presumption**

1 presunción, anticipación, creencia, conjetura, opinión, probabilidad, suposición

2 presunción, atrevimiento, audacia, osadía, temeridad
*modestia*

**pretence**

afectación, color, excusa, fingimiento, máscara, pretensión, pretexto, semblanza, simulación, velo
*sinceridad, franqueza*

**pretext**

afectación, apariencia, pretensión, excusa, máscara, pretexto, simulación, semblanza, velo
*verdad*

**pretty**

hermoso, bonito, bello, atractivo, elegante, fino, parecido, distinguido, de buen gusto, *(LAm)* lindo
*feo*

**prevailing**

1 común, corriente, general, ordinario, usual, normal
*inusual*

2 reinante, imperante, dominante, predominante, vigente, operante, operativo, eficaz, efectivo

**prevent**

anticipar, bloquear, prevenir, prohibir, impedir, interceptar, parar, obstruir, frustrar, estorbar
*ayudar, apoyar*

**previous**

anterior, antecedente, precedente
*posterior, más tarde*

**pride**

orgullo, arrogancia, insolencia, presunción, vanidad, engreimiento, altanería, desdén, vanagloria
*humildad*

**prim**

formal, etiquetero, presumido, mojigato, pedante, relamido
*informal, cordial, campechano*

**primary**

1 original, aborigen, primordial, primario, originario, radical

2 el mejor, el jefe, el primero, el más alto, principal, líder
*el más bajo*

**prime**

1 primario, primero, original, primitivo, temprano
*posterior*

2 principio, apertura, inicio

3 el mejor, capital, jefe, principal, excelente, de primera clase
*inferior*

**prior**

antecedente, anterior, temprano, previo
*posterior, tardío*

**privacy**

encubrimiento, escondrijo, seclusión, soledad, retraimiento, secreto, reserva, discreción
*publicidad*

**privilege**
   ventaja, privilegio, permiso, derecho, prerrogativa, licencia
   *desventaja*

**prize** *(s)*
   premio, recompensa, botín, presa, trofeo

**prize** *(v)*
   tasar, valorar, apreciar, estimar, clasificar
   *desdeñar*

**proceed**
   1 proceder, continuar, aventajar, progresar
   *retroceder, retirarse*
   2 emanar, originar, resultar, provenir

**proclaim**
   anunciar, proclamar, publicar, circular, declarar, promulgar
   *esconder, encubrir, disimular*

**product**
   producto, consecuencia, efecto, producción, actuación, trabajo, fruto, resultado
   *causa*

**proficient**
   apto, atinado, hábil, experto, capaz, listo, competente, entrenado, versado, cualificado
   *no cualificado, no especializado*

**profit** *(s)*
   beneficios, ventajas, ganancias, ingresos, emolumentos
   *pérdidas*

**profuse**
   abundante, copioso, profuso, excesivo, extravagante, exuberante, pródigo
   *escaso, poco común*

**progress** *(s)*
   adelanto, avance, progreso, desarrollo, crecimiento, progresión, aumento
   *disminución*

**prohibit**
   prohibir, excluir, rechazar, impedir, estorbar, obstruir, prevenir
   *dejar, permitir*

**prologue**
   prólogo, introducción, preámbulo, prefacio, preliminar, preludio
   *conclusión*

**promise** *(s)*
   promesa, acuerdo, garantía, palabra, pacto, convenio, voto, acatamiento
   *negativa, denegación*

**prompt** *(aj)*
   1 ágil, apto, rápido, listo, vigilante, despierto, enérgico, vigoroso
   *lento, parado*
   2 temprano, pronto, puntual, oportuno
   *tardío*

**proper**
   1 apropiado, decente, decoroso, legítimo, educado, respetable, recto, conveniente, correcto
   *indecente, incorrecto*
   2 exacto, preciso, correcto, formal
   *incorrecto*
   3 individual, propio, particular, privado, peculiar, personal, especial

**proposal**
   propuesta, esquema, oferta, plan, proposición, recomendación, sugestión, términos
   *rechazo, denegación*

**propose**
   1 diseñar, intentar, significar, proponer, planificar, esquematizar
   *rechazar*
   2 nominar, proponer, ofrecer, recomendar, sugerir
   *declinar*

**protect**
   defender, guardar, proteger, preservar, salvar, asegurar, amparar
   *atacar, agredir*

**proud**
   1 arrogante, orgulloso, presuntuoso, jactancioso, presumido, fanfarrón, imperioso
   *humilde*
   2 imponente, impresionante, majestuoso, magnífico, ostentoso, espléndido
   *innoble, vil*

**provide**
  1 dar, proporcionar, contribuir, suministrar, producir, ofrecer
    *privar*
  2 arreglar, preparar, reunir, colectar, recaudar, procurar

**provoke**
    enfrentar, afrontar, agravar, enfadar, exasperar, incitar, enfurecer, insultar, irritar, ofender, provocar
    *apaciguar, calmar, aliviar*

**proximity**
    proximidad, cercanía, adyacente, vecindario, vecindad
    *distancia*

**public** *(aj)*
    conocido, abierto, común, general, notorio, público, popular
    *privado, secreto*

**punctual**
    temprano, exacto, preciso, pronto, puntual, estricto
    *tarde, tardío*

**pungent**
    acre, punzante, cáustico, picante, penetrante, intenso, agudo
    *suave, dulce*

**pupil**
    principiante, escolar, estudiante, catecúmeno, discípulo, aprendiz, novicio
    *profesor, maestro*

**purchase** *(v)*
    adquirir, comprar, obtener, ganar, conseguir, gestionar
    *vender*

**purge** *(v)*
    purgar, purificar, depurar, clarificar, limpiar
    *polucionar, ensuciar*

**push** *(v)*
  1 empujar, mover, apartar a codazos, dar empujones, impulsar, impeler
    *tirar*
  2 persuadir, impeler, presionar, acelerar, apresurar, apurar, dar prisas a
    *estar de acuerdo*

**put**
  1 poner, depositar, colocar, traer, ajustar
    *sacar*
  2 expresar, ofertar, ofrecer, proponer, exponer, plantear
  3 incitar, inducir, obligar, forzar, instar

**puzzle** *(s)*
  1 enigma, acertijo, adivinanza, pregunta difícil, misterio
  2 confusión, dificultad, dilema, desconcierto, aturdimiento, turbación, azoramiento

# Q

**quack** *(s)*
charlatán, farsante, impostor, pretendiente, saltimbanqui, *(medicina)* curandero
*víctima*

**quail** *(v)*
encogerse, recular, desanimarse, palidecer, desmayarse, acobardarse, arredrarse, estremecerse, temblar
*confrontar, enfrentarse con, hacer frente*

**quaint**
1 antiguo, anticuado, curioso, bizarro, fantástico, raro, extraño, peculiar, singular, inusual, excéntrico
*normal*
2 recóndito, ingenioso, abstruso, sutil
*ordinario*

**qualification**
1 habilidad, talento, capacidad, aptitud, cualidad, idoneidad, *(LAm)* calificación
*inhabilitación*
2 condición, limitación, estipulación, restricción

**qualified**
apto, cualificado, capacitado, habilitado, listo, sabio
*inepto, incapacitado*

**qualify**
1 adaptar, acomodar, ajustar, capacitar, autorizar a uno, preparar, equipar
*incapacitar, inhabilitar*
2 disminuir, limitar, moderar, modificar, reducir, regular, reprimir, refrenar, debilitar, cambiar

**quandary**
aturdimiento, dificultad, dilema, duda, desconcierto, turbación, perplejidad, apuro
*convicción, creencia*

**quarrel** *(s)*
pelea, lucha, refriega, reyerta, riña, altercado, contienda, controversia, diferencias, disputa, combate, violación, tumulto
*paz, sosiego*

**quarrel** *(v)*
reñir, pelear, luchar, altercar, alborotar, enfrentarse, no estar de acuerdo, diferir, disputar
*llevarse bien, entenderse*

**quarter** *(s)*
barrio, distrito, lugar, localidad, posición, región, territorio, punto
*ciudad, país*

**queer** *(aj)*
raro, curioso, extraño, excéntrico, extraordinario, único, singular, peculiar, inusual, sospechoso, misterioso
*normal, corriente*

**quell**
1 conquistar, dominar, derrotar, vencer, subyugar, suprimir, aplastar, aniquilar, destruir
2 reprimir, calmar, sofocar, aliviar, tranquilizar, mitigar, amortiguar, apaciguar
*excitar, emocionar, incitar*

**quench**
1 detener, refrenar, destruir, finalizar, acabar, suprimir, reprimir, extinguir
*encender, prender*
2 aliviar, refrescar, enfriar, apagar
*excitar, estimular*

**query** *(v)*
1 preguntar, indagar, cuestionar
*responder, contestar*
2 discutir, dudar, poner en duda

**question** *(v)*
1 preguntar, inquirir, examinar, interrogar, investigar
*responder, contestar*

2 poner en duda, cuestionar, dudar, contradecir
*estar de acuerdo*

**question** *(s)*

1 pregunta, interrogación, petición, investigación, cuestión
*contestación, respuesta*

2 controversia, disputa, duda, interrogante, pregunta

3 punto, moción, proposición, tópico, tema, asunto

**quibble** *(s)*

sutileza, objeción, reparo, equivocación, evasión, pretexto, pretensión, evasiva, peculiaridad, subterfugio
*verdad, realidad*

**quick** *(aj)*

1 rápido, activo, ágil, animado, brusco, veloz, vivo, ágil, ligero
*lento, pausado*

2 diestro, inteligente, hábil, agudo, mañoso, perspicaz, experto
*estúpido, tonto*

3 repentino, brusco, seco, excitable, impaciente, irascible, irritable, colérico

*paciente*

4 animado, enérgico, vivo
*muerto*

**quicken**

1 acelerar, dar prisa, apresurar, apurar
*retrasar, retardar, tardar, demorar*

2 animar, excitar, refrescar, vivificar, resucitar, revivir, estimular, revigorizar
*amortiguar, aliviar*

**quit**

1 abandonar, desamparar, dejar, renunciar, retirarse, rendirse, *(Am)* irse, marcharse
*permanecer, estar, quedar*

2 absolver, exculpar, exonerar, liberar, soltar
*encerrar, confinar*

**quiz**

1 acertijo, adivinanza, enigma, misterio

2 interrogatorio, encuesta, examen, *(Am)* test

**quote** *(v)*

citar, dar, aducir, hacer referencia, estimar

# R

**rabble**
> canalla, muchedumbre, tropel, horda, turba, populacho, gentuza, chusma
> *aristocracia*

**race** (s)
> 1 competición, contienda, caza, persecución, prueba
> 2 raza, clan, familia, casa, origen, línea, linaje, tribu, descendiente, descendencia, progenie, prole

**rack** (s)
> percha, perchero, anaquel, estante, estantería, cuelgacapas, *(platos)* escurreplatos, *(tren)* rejilla, *(LAm)* colgadero

**rack** (v)
> 1 forzar, estirar
> 2 organizar, atormentar, molestar, torturar
> *suavizar*

**radiant**
> brillante, efulgente, radiante, resplandeciente, lustroso
> *oscuro*

**radical** (aj)
> 1 radical, esencial, constitucional, arraigado, fundamental, innato, nativo, natural, orgánico, original, primitivo
> *superficial*
> 2 completo, entero, extremo, excesivo, total, fanático

**rage** (s)
> 1 cólera, ira, excitación, furia, frenesí, delirio, locura, pasión, vehemencia
> *calma*
> 2 manía, moda, entusiasmo, rapto

**rail** (v)
> abusar, censurar, condenar, vituperar, mofarse, reprender, despotricar, denostar
> *alabar, elogiar*

**raise** (v)
> 1 avanzar, elevar, erigir, exaltar, levantar, alzar, subir
> *bajar, descender*
> 2 aumentar, agravar, engrandecer, realzar, intensificar
> 3 despertar, evocar, conmover, estimular
> 4 juntar, reunir, obtener, conseguir, recaudar

**rampant**
> 1 excesivo, exuberante, desenfrenado
> *restringido*
> 2 agresivo, dominante, furioso, impetuoso, incontrolable, vehemente, violento
> *moderado, comedido*

**rancour**, *(Am)* rancor
> rencor, animosidad, antipatía, enemistad, odio, malevolencia, malicia, resentimiento, ojeriza, virulencia
> *benevolencia*

**range**
> 1 fila, hilera, grupo, *(montañas)* cordillera, sierra, *(Am)* dehesa, terreno de pasto
> 2 alcance, distancia, recorrido, extensión, escala, gama, serie, amplitud, compás
> 3 clase, tipo, especie, género, categoría

**rapid**
> rápido, veloz, pronto, ligero, apresurado, precipitado
> *lento, tardío*

**rapture**
> beatificación, beatitud, bienaventuranza, éxtasis, entusiasmo, exaltación, felicidad, alegría, ensalmo
> *miseria*

**rare**
1 raro, excepcional, infrecuente, singular, extraño, poco común, inusual
*común, normal*
2 admirable, excelente, incomparable, selecto, escogido
3 crudo, medio cocido, poco hecho

**rash**
aventurero, audaz, descuidado, impetuoso, impulsivo, incauto, precipitado, rápido, temerario, imprudente
*cauto, prudente*

**rational**
1 racional, inteligente, lúcido, sano, cuerdo, sabio, juicioso
*irracional, loco, demente*
2 discreto, juicioso, moderado, razonable
*irrazonable*

**ravage** *(v)*
destruir, devastar, arruinar, estropear, saquear, pillar
*restaurar*

**ravish**
1 cautivar, encantar, seducir, deleitar, embelesar, arrebatar, transportar
*desagradar, ofender*
2 abusar, seducir, desflorar, violar, forzar

**reach** *(v)*
1 alcanzar, llegar, conseguir, obtener
*perder, escapar*
2 extenderse, estirarse, tocar

**ready**
1 listo, preparado, arreglado, completado
*incompleto, sin preparar*
2 apto, listo, inteligente, rápido, experto, agudo, hábil, diestro
*inexperto, inepto*
3 dispuesto, inclinado, deseoso, amable
*desinclinado*

**real**
real, absoluto, actual, auténtico, cierto, esencial, genuino, intrínseco, positivo, sincero, verdadero
*falso*

**realise**
1 comprender, entender, imaginar, coger, darse cuenta
*no entender*
2 conseguir, adquirir, completar, efectuar, ganar, obtener, realizar
*comenzar*

**reality**
realidad, certidumbre, hecho, verdad, verosimilitud
*falsedad, imaginación*

**rear** *(v)*
1 educar, enseñar, subir, entrenar, cuidar, criar
2 elevar, levantar, izar, subir
*bajar*
3 construir, erigir, edificar
*demoler*

**reasonable**
1 razonable, honesto, justo, lógico, propio, derecho
2 inteligente, juicioso, racional, cuerdo, sano, sensible, sobrio, sabio
*irracional*
3 moderado, tolerable
*irrazonable*

**rebel** *(aj)*
rebelde, insubordinado, desobediente, insurrecto
*leal*

**rebel** *(s)*
rebelde, insurrecto, revolucionario
*observante de la ley*

**recall**
1 recordar, acordarse de
*olvidar*
2 anular, cancelar, rescindir, retractar, revocar, renunciar
*reafirmar*

**recede**
1 desistir, retirarse, retroceder
*avanzar*
2 bajar, disminuir

**receive**

1 recibir, obtener, conseguir, adquirir, aceptar
*dar, donar*

2 admitir, recibir, saludar, dar la bienvenida, entretener
*excluir*

**recent**

reciente, fresco, último, moderno, nuevo, actual
*viejo, antiguo, pasado de moda*

**reception**

1 recepción, fiesta, espectáculo, reunión, guateque, banquete, tertulia

2 recepción, recibo, admisión, aceptación

**recess**

1 cavidad, esquina, hueco, nicho, escondrijo, lugar secreto
*saliente, protuberancia*

2 receso, vacaciones, respiro, descanso, *(Am)* recreo
*día laboral, trabajo*

**reckon**

1 calcular, contar, enumerar, computar
*contar mal*

2 considerar, estimar, evaluar, juzgar

3 creer, suponer, imaginar, pensar

**recognise**

1 admitir, reconocer, conceder, confesar
*desconocer, rechazar*

2 identificar, notar, saber, recordar, venir a la memoria
*olvidar*

**recollect**

recordar, acordarse de
*olvidar*

**record** *(s)*

1 cuenta, crónica, entrada, memoria, memorándum, minuta, registro

2 anales, archivos, fichero

**recount**

contar, describir, enumerar, narrar, recitar, relatar, repetir, decir

**recover**

1 recobrar, recuperar, restaurar, reparar, subsanar

2 recuperarse, curarse, reponerse, mejorarse
*empeorar*

**rectify**

1 rectificar, ajustar, enmendar, corregir, mejorar, reformar, regenerar
*falsificar*

2 *(química)* purificar, refinar

**redress** *(v)*

1 ajustar, enmendar, rectificar, reformar, remediar, reparar, reajustar
*destruir, estropear*

2 compensar, aliviar, mitigar

**reflection**

1 consideración, contemplación, deliberación, meditación, opinión, reflexión, pensamiento

2 calumnia, censura, reproche, acusación, imputación
*alabanza, elogio*

**reform** *(v)*

mejorar, enmendar, corregir, reformar, reconstituir, rectificar, regenerar, reorganizar, remodelar, reparar, restaurar
*empeorar, desmejorar*

**refrain** *(v)*

abstenerse, refrenar, cesar, desistir, retener, negar
*persistir*

**refuse** *(s)*

basura, porquería, desperdicios, sedimentos, escoria, trastos, viejos

**refuse** *(v)*

rehusar, declinar, negar, denegar, excluir, repeler, rechazar, repudiar
*aceptar*

**refute**

refutar, confutar, derrumbar, derribar, repeler, silenciar, rebatir
*aprobar, comprobar, justificar, establecer*

**regard** *(v)*
1 mirar, ver, marcar, notar, darse cuenta, observar
2 estimar, admirar, honrar, respetar, reverenciar, valorar
3 contar, creer, estimar, imaginar, suponer

**regret** *(v)*
lamentar, deplorar, afligirse, acongojarse, arrepentirse, *(fig)* llorar
*regocijar, alegrar*

**regular**
1 constante, habitual, establecido, fijo, regular, firme, uniforme
*irregular*
2 formal, metódico, normal, puntual, sistemático, ordenado, usual
*irregular*

**regulate**
ajustar, arreglar, controlar, dirigir, fijar, gobernar, guiar, manejar, ordenar, regular
*desordenar, desarreglar*

**reinforce**
reforzar, aumentar, fortificar, fortalecer, consolidar
*debilitar*

**reject** *(v)*
rehusar, rechazar, declinar, denegar, eliminar, excluir, renunciar, repeler, repudiar
*aceptar*

**relate**
relatar, describir, detallar, narrar, recitar, contar, decir
*ocultar, encubrir, disimular*

**release** *(v)*
1 soltar, librar, descargar, emancipar, liberar, desatar, aflojar
*apretar*
2 absolver, dispensar, exonerar, eximir

**relevant**
aplicable, apropiado, apto, relevante, pertinente, relacionado
*irrelevante*

**reliable**
honesto, de confianza, fidedigno, confiable
*de poca confianza*

**relief**
ayuda, asistencia, comodidad, remedio, socorro, apoyo, sustento, alivio
*aflicción, angustia, miseria*

**relieve**
ayudar, aliviar, asistir, confortar, mitigar, remediar, socorrer, apoyar, sustentar
*aumentar, acrecentar*

**reluctant**
sentir repugnancia, sentir antipatía, tímido, desinclinado, dudoso, indispuesto
*deseoso, entusiasta*

**remain**
permanecer, continuar, durar, estar, vivir, morar, sobrevivir, esperar
*partir, dejar*

**remark** *(s)*
1 atención, nota, aviso, observación
*indiferencia, descuido*
2 comentario, declaración, afirmación, aserto, manifestación
*silencio*

**remarkable**
remarcable, distinguido, extraordinario, famoso, notable, prominente, raro, extraño, inusual, maravilloso
*ordinario, común*

**remedy** *(s)*
1 remedio, antídoto, cura, medicamento, medicina, ayuda, reconstituyente, tratamiento
*enfermedad, dolencia*
2 asistencia, reparación, compensación, ayuda

**remembrance**
1 memoria, recuerdo, reminiscencia, pensamiento
*olvido*
2 memento, recuerdo, souvenir, señal de agradecimiento

**reminiscence**
memoria, recuerdo, recolección

**remission**

1 remisión, exoneración, perdón, indulgencia, absolución, exculpación
*condenación*

2 disminución, reducción, moderación, temperancia, suspenso
*aumento*

**remit** (*v*)

1 enviar, transferir, transmitir, remitir
*guardar*

2 absolver, perdonar, excusar, olvidar
*castigar*

3 disminuir, abatir, decrecer, rebajar, moderar, aflojar
*aumentar*

**remote**

1 distante, remoto, solo, alejado, fuera del camino, apartado, retirado
*cerca, próximo*

2 ajeno, extranjero, sin relacionar
*relacionado*

3 vago, pequeño, inconsiderado, débil
*considerado*

**remove**

1 sacar, llevar, desplazar, eliminar, extraer, mover, transferir, transportar, quitar, suprimir, apartar, alejar
*retener, conservar*

2 (*fig*) eliminar, matar, suprimir, deshacerse de

**remunerate**

compensar, indemnificar, pagar, recompensar, remunerar, reembolsar, gratificar
*agraviar, ofender*

**render**

1 servir, prestar, rendir, dar, pagar, suministrar, devolver
*conservar, retener*

2 causar, hacer, actuar, ejecutar, reproducir

3 interpretar, traducir

**renounce**

abandonar, abdicar, declinar, dejar, desamparar, renunciar, repudiar, pasar sin
*aceptar*

**repair** (*v*)

1 fijar, enmendar, reparar, remendar, renovar, restaurar, subsanar, componer
*destruir*

2 acudir, ir, reunirse con

**repeal** (*v*)

abolir, anular, cancelar, rescindir, repeler, retirar, destruir, revocar
*confirmar*

**repeat** (*v*)

repetir, duplicar, recapitular, reiterar, continuar, referir
*discontinuar*

**replace**

reemplazar, reestablecer, restaurar, reintegrar, devolver, resarcir
*quitar, llevarse*

**report** (*s*)

1 cuenta, anuncio, comunicación, declaración, descripción, detalle, narrativa, noticias, reportaje, recital, rumor, historia
*silencio*

2 detonación, descarga, sonido, ruido, explosión

3 minuta, nota, expediente, informe

**report** (*v*)

anunciar, circular, comunicar, declarar, describir, emitir, divulgar, narrar, proclamar, mencionar, recitar, relatar, publicar

**representative** (*s*)

representante, agente, delegado, comisario, apoderado, suplente, (*Am*) diputado
*principal*

**repress**

castigar, corregir, controlar, reprimir, aniquilar, destruir
*animar, ayudar*

**reproach** (s)

abuso, censura, condena, desaprobación, desgracia, deshonra, ignominia, indignación, oprobio, vergüenza
*aprobación*

**repulsive**

desagradable, nauseabundo, odioso, repelente, asqueroso, repugnante
*agradable*

**request** (v)

cuestionar, pedir, desear, rogar, solicitar, suplicar
*negar*

**require**

1 desear, necesitar, querer, carecer de

2 pedir, ordenar, exigir, requerir
*rehusar, rechazar*

**resemblance**

analogía, imagen, retrato, semejanza, parecido, similaridad
*desigualdad*

**reserve** (v)

reservar, aguantar, mantener, retener, almacenar
*gastar*

**resignation**

1 abandono, abdicación, renuncia, dimisión, sumisión

2 resignación, paciencia, resistencia, aguante, dominio
*impaciencia*

**resist**

resistir, atacar, oponer, repeler, confrontar, refrenar
*someter(se)*

**resolute**

constante, resuelto, determinado, firme, inflexible, perseverante, intencionado, impávido
*débil, indeciso*

**resolve** (v)

1 decidir, determinar, fijar, intentar, resolver, querer hacer
*dudar*

2 aclarar, explicar, resolver, desenmarañar, desenredar

**resort** (s)

1 refugio, retiro, lugar de veraneo

2 recurso, referencia

**respect** (v)

1 respetar, admirar, adorar, estimar, querer, cuidar, honrar, reverenciar, valorar, venerar

2 respetar, atenerse a, hacer caso de, notar, referirse a

**respectable**

respetable, decente, estimable, bueno, honesto, honrado, respetuoso, educado
*mal educado, descortés*

**rest** (v)

1 desistir, parar, estar, cesar, detener, interrumpir
*continuar*

2 relajar, descansar, reclinar, reposar, dormir, tenderse

**restrain**

refrenar, contener, reprimir, moderar, impedir, limitar, mantener, aguantar
*dejar, liberar*

**result** (s)

resultado, conclusión, consecuencia, efecto, decisión, terminación
*causa*

**resume**

empezar de nuevo, reanudar, recomenzar
*parar*

**retire**

1 partir, marchar, retirarse
*llegar*

2 retirar, sacar, quitar, remover
*adelantar*

**retort** (v)

contestar, devolver, responder
*preguntar*

**retract**

retractar, cancelar, renunciar, repudiar, rescindir, revocar, retirar, destituir
*afirmar*

**retreat** (s)

1 retiro, marcha, retirada

**2** retiro, asilo, refugio, guarida, seclusión

**reveal**
anunciar, comunicar, divulgar, impartir, abrir, proclamar, revelar, publicar, mostrar, decir
*esconder, disimular*

**reverse** (*v*)
**1** invertir, girar, volcar, trastornar, transponer, alterar, anular, cambiar
*restaurar*
**2** rescindir, repeler, revocar
*confirmar*

**revoke**
abolir, anular, cancelar, abrogar, invalidar, repudiar, repeler, rescindir
*ratificar*

**revolt** (*v*)
**1** rebelarse, amotinarse, resistir, levantarse contra
*someterse*
**2** disgustar, desagradar, ofender, repeler, marear, causar náuseas
*agradar*

**reward** (*s*)
**1** compensación, recompensa, mérito, premio, remuneración, pago
**2** (*fig*) castigo, desquite, pena merecida

**rich**
**1** rico, afluente, opulento, adinerado
*pobre*
**2** costoso, caro, precioso, suntuoso, de gran valor
*barato*
**3** abundante, amplio, copioso, rico, fértil, fructífero, productivo
*estéril, árido*
**4** delicioso, dulce, sabroso, gustoso
*insípido, soso*

**righteous**
devoto, pío, piadoso, santo, virtuoso, moral, bueno, honesto, justo, equitativo
*deshonesto, malo, inmoral*

**rigid**
austero, seco, inflexible, rígido, riguroso, severo, duro
*flexible*

**rigour**, (*Am*) **rigor**
**1** aspereza, austeridad, dureza, rigor, inflexibilidad, rigidez, exactitud, severidad
*apacibilidad, suavidad, dulzura*
**2** (*tiempo*) severidad, inclemencia

**riot**
confusión, alboroto, conmoción, desorden, disturbio, rebelión, pelea, motín
*paz*

**rise** (*v*)
**1** levantar, ascender, subir, aumentar, montar, ensanchar, engrandecer
*descender, rebajar*
**2** aparecer, emerger, ocurrir, acontecer, originar
**3** amotinar, rebelarse, sublevarse

**robust**
**1** atlético, bravo, musculoso, poderoso, robusto, fuerte, enérgico, vigoroso
*débil, flojo*
**2** rudo, brutal, inconsiderado, ordinario, grosero
*refinado, considerado*

**romantic**
**1** extravagante, romántico, efímero, fabuloso, idílico, quimérico, fantástico, legendario, pintoresco, sentimental
*práctico*
**2** exagerado, ficticio, improbable, irreal
*realista*

**rough**
**1** mellado, desigual, desnivelado, sin pulir, sin forma
*igualado, liso*
**2** brusco, mal educado, incivilizado, francote, abrupto, ordinario, grosero
*educado, refinado*

3 duro, severo, violento, insensible
*amable, sensible*

4 discordante, inarmónico, disonante
*armonioso*

**row** *(s)*
fila, hilera, serie, renglón, gama

**row** *(s)*
conmoción, querella, pelea, disturbio, tumulto, riña, disputa
*paz, sosiego*

**rude**

1 bárbaro, rudo, brusco, ordinario, grosero, vulgar, salvaje, incivilizado, indisciplinado, ignorante, mal educado
*civilizado, enseñado, educado*

2 claro, conciso, rudo, descortés, impertinente, insultante, insolente, grosero
*educado*

3 sin gracia, torpe, desmañado, poco elegante
*elegante*

4 indecente, *(chiste)* verde, *(LAm)* colorado

**ruin** *(v)*

1 demoler, destruir, derrumbar, echar abajo
*restaurar*

2 dañar, desfigurar, estropear, echar a perder
*mejorar*

**rule** *(v)*

1 decidir, decretar, establecer, juzgar

2 mandar, gobernar, dirigir, administrar, controlar, reinar

**rumour,** *(Am)* **rumor** *(s)*
rumor, chafardería, chisme, chismorreo, comadreo, habladuría
*hecho, realidad*

**rush** *(v)*

1 apresurar, correr, volar, presionar, empujar, ir deprisa
*tardar, quedarse atrás*

2 atacar, cargar, vencer, superar

**ruthless**
bárbaro, sin modales, cruel, fiero, feroz, duro, inexorable, inhumano, salvaje, severo, despiadado, implacable
*humano, compasivo, misericordioso*

# S

**sacrifice** *(v)*
sacrificar, perder, inmolar, ofrecer, entregarse, rendirse
*aceptar*

**sad**
1 triste, deprimido, desconsolado, lúgubre, melancólico, furioso, serio, sombrío, abatido, desanimado
*alegre*
2 malo, calamitoso, deplorable, desastroso, grave
*bueno*

**safe**
1 guardado, protegido, salvado, seguro, ileso
*inseguro*
2 serio, fiable, confiable
*desconfiable*

**sage** *(aj)*
agudo, inteligente, juicioso, prudente, sagaz, sabio
*estúpido*

**sanction** *(s)*
aprobación, autorización, confirmación, sanción, soporte
*denegación, negativa*

**sane**
saludable, sano, lúcido, juicioso, sensato, sobrio
*insensato, loco, demente*

**sarcastic**
sarcástico, agudo, cínico, irónico, satírico, mordaz

**satirical**
mordaz, satírico, cortante, agudo, cínico, irónico, sarcástico
*encomiable, elogiable*

**satisfaction**
1 satisfacción, contento, alivio, disfrute, placer, gratificación
*descontento, insatisfacción*
2 expiación, compensación, recompensa, indemnificación, remuneración, restitución, liquidación
*perjuicio, daño*

**satisfy**
1 contentar, gratificar, satisfacer, complacer
*descontentar*
2 compensar, indemnificar, recompensar, remunerar
*perjudicar*

**saucy**
insolente, irrespetuoso, poco serio, ligero, impertinente, impúdico, presuntuoso, rudo
*modesto, serio, formal*

**savage** *(aj)*
1 salvaje, aborigen, nativo, incivilizado, incultivado
*civilizado*
2 bárbaro, bestial, brutal, bruto, cruel, feroz, fiero
*domado, domesticado*
3 sanguinario, despiadado, homicida, implacable, agresivo
*misericordioso, compasivo*

**savoury**, *(Am)* **savory**
agradable, apetitoso, delicioso, sabroso, suculento, gustoso
*incomible, desagradable, repugnante*

**scale** *(v)*
ascender, escalar, montar, trepar
*descender*

**scandalous**
atroz, vergonzoso, escandaloso, ignominioso, odioso, calumnioso, difamatorio
*honroso, formal*

**scarce**
poco, deficiente, infrecuente, insuficiente, raro, poco normal, inusual
*suficiente*

**scarcity**
escasez, falta, carestía, deficiencia, rareza, penuria
*abundancia*

**scare** *(s)*

    alarma, miedo, pánico, terror, temor

**scare** *(v)*

    asustar, alarmar, acobardar, intimidar, consternar, aterrorizar

    *tranquilizar, alentar*

**scatter**

    1 diseminar, divulgar, emitir, difundir, extender, esparcir

    *juntar, recoger*

    2 disipar, dispersar, desunir, separar

    *reunir, juntar*

**scholarship**

    1 talentos, dotes, méritos, educación, conocimiento, aprendizaje

    *ignorancia*

    2 beca, ayuda económica

**scold** *(v)*

    censurar, reñir, culpar, reprender, reprochar, vituperar

    *fomentar, estimular*

**scoundrel**

    bellaco, bribón, sinvergüenza, pillo, pícaro, picaruelo, vagabundo, villano

    *caballero, señor*

**scour**

    limpiar, asear, pulir, renovar, restaurar, depurar, frotar, blanquear, *(medicina)* purgar, *(Am)* restregar

    *ensuciar*

**scrap** *(s)*

    trozo, pedazo, fragmento, pizca, porción, bocado

    *todo, entero*

**screen** *(v)*

    1 cubrir, encubrir, disimular, ocultar, esconder, enmascarar

    *revelar, mostrar*

    2 defender, proteger, guardar, abrigar, amparar, resguardar

**scrub** *(v)*

    limpiar, asear, frotar, depurar

    *ensuciar*

**scuffle** *(s)*

    alteración, refriega, lucha, pelea, reyerta, alboroto, combate

    *paz*

**seal** *(s)*

    garantía, promesa, confirmación, notificación, testimonio, autenticación

**seal** *(v)*

    1 encerrar, cerrar, asegurar, fijar

    *abrir*

    2 asegurar, atestar, autentificar, confirmar, establecer, ratificar

**secluded**

    solo, privado, remoto, retirado, aislado, solitario, poco frecuentado

    *ocupado, público*

**secret** *(aj)*

    1 secreto, cerrado, encerrado, cubierto, oculto, reticente, desconocido, no revelado

    *aparente, a la vista*

    2 recóndito, abstruso, clandestino, cabalístico, latente, misterioso, oculto, manifiesto, claro

**section**

    sección, división, fracción, fragmento, parte, pieza, porción

    *todo, entero*

**sedative**

    calmante, lenitivo, relajante, tranquilizante, tranquilizador, sedante

    *estimulante*

**seize**

    prender, detener, arrestar, capturar, atar, apretar, sujetar, tomar, agarrar

    *perder, dejar, soltar*

**select** *(v)*

    seleccionar, escoger, preferir

**sell**

    1 cambiar, vender, negociar, tratar, hacer negocios

    *comprar*

    2 *(fig)* traicionar

**send**

    1 enviar, despachar, transmitir, mandar, remitir

    *recibir*

    2 emitir, propalar, dar, lanzar, arrojar

    *guardar, mantener*

**sensible**

1 perceptible, tangible, visible, sensible
*insensible*

2 observador, consciente, enterado, convencido, entendedor
*inconsciente*

**sensitive**

susceptible, sensitivo, delicado, impresionable, perceptible, sensible, tierno, quisquilloso
*insensible, duro*

**separate** *(aj)*

1 separado, desconectado, desunido, dividido, divorciado
*unido*

2 solo, aparte, distintivo, independiente, individual

**serene**

1 calmado, tranquilo, sereno, imperturbable, pacífico, plácido, tranquilo
*alborotado, poco tranquilo*

2 sereno, brillante, claro, despejado
*nublado*

**serious**

1 devoto, serio, formal, grave, piadoso, sobrio, solemne, pensativo, constante
*caprichoso, inconstante*

2 crítico, peligroso, grave, importante, trascendental, pesado, importante, influyente
*frívolo, trivial*

**servile**

servil, bajo, abyecto, vil, doméstico
*independiente, magistral*

**shade** *(s)*

1 sombra, oscuridad, penumbra, tenebrosidad
*luz, claridad*

2 persiana, cortina, velo, pantalla

3 color, tinte, mancha, matiz, tono

4 sombra, aparición, fantasma, espíritu, espectro

**share** *(v)*

asignar, distribuir, dividir, repartir, desglosar, asignar
*quedar*

**sharp**

1 agudo, penetrante, mordaz, cortante, afilado
*desafilado, despuntado, franco*

2 alerta, apto, astuto, listo, inteligente, discernidor, observador, conocedor, ingenioso, preparado
*estúpido, torpe*

3 ácido, picante, punzante, agrio, acre, cortado

4 intenso, severo, violento, horrible, fatal, doloroso, penoso
*apacible, pacífico, suave*

**shelter** *(s)*

cubierta, defensa, guarida, puerto, abrigo, albergue, asilo, refugio, santuario, seguridad, *(fig)* protección, resguardo

**shelter** *(v)*

cubrir, resguardar, defender, guardar, abrigar, proteger, escudar
*mostrar, revelar, enseñar, descubrir*

**shine** *(v)*

brillar, destellar, relucir, resplandecer, distinguirse

**shock** *(s)*

colisión, golpe, impacto, sorpresa (desagradable), encuentro, tropiezo

**shock** *(v)*

1 horrorizar, aterrar, asustar, escandalizar

2 causar náuseas, marear, ofender, desagradar, disgustar
*agradar*

**short**

1 corto, breve, compendioso, conciso, lacónico, sucinto, resumido, sentencioso, brusco, *(persona)* bajo, *(LAm)* chaparro
*extenso, largo*

2 deficiente, corto, inadecuado, insuficiente, limitado, pobre, escaso
*adecuado*

3 abrupto, descortés, mal educado, cortante, directo, franco
*educado*

**shrewd**

agudo, astuto, mañoso, inteligente, ingenioso, taimado, perspicaz, sagaz

*estúpido, lerdo, atontado*

**sickness**

enfermedad, desorden, dolencia, achaque, indisposición, *(fig)* malestar, mal

*salud*

**signal** *(aj)*

eminente, extraordinario, famoso, memorable, notable, remarcable

*ordinario, corriente*

**signal** *(s)*

señal, marca, indicación

**silence**

1 calma, paz, quietud, tranquilidad

*ruido*

2 mudez, reticencia, reserva, taciturnidad

*habla*

**silly**

tonto, absurdo, aniñado, frívolo, idiota, imprudente, ridículo, estúpido, sin sentido, bobo, necio, insensato

*juicioso, inteligente*

**similar**

parecido, similar, uniforme, correspondiente, igual

*desigual*

**sincere**

cándido, inofensivo, franco, genuino, honesto, honrado, abierto, sincero, genuino

*falso, insincero, poco franco*

**single**

1 sencillo, singular, simple, individual, distintivo, solo, separado, único, solitario, *(habitación)* individual, *(LAm)* sencillo

*varios, muchos*

2 soltero, sin casar

*casado*

3 sencillo, simple, sin mezclar

*mezclado*

**skilful,** *(Am)* **skillful**

capaz, hábil, diestro, adepto, apto, inteligente, listo, ingenioso, experto, mañoso, conocedor, enseñado, educado, rápido, entrenado

*patoso, inexperto, torpe, desmañado*

**slow**

lento, retrasado, detrás, inactivo, dilatorio, estúpido, tardío, tedioso, cansado

*rápido, veloz*

**sly**

astuto, inteligente, avispado, furtivo, secreto, insidioso, clandestino, sutil

*legítimo, honrado, inocente, candoroso*

**small**

1 pequeño, delgado, ligero, diminuto, en miniatura, insignificante, nimio, *(LAm)* chaparro

*grande, extenso, amplio*

2 inadecuado, insuficiente, trivial, sin importancia

**smart**

1 experto, hábil, ágil, apto, brillante, inteligente, rápido, listo, agudo, perspicaz

*torpe, lerdo*

2 chic, elegante, de moda, fino, acicalado, atractivo, pulcro

*poco elegante, poco atractivo*

**smash** *(v)*

romper, estrellar, estropear, triturar, estrujar, destruir, hacer pedazos

*reparar, restaurar, arreglar*

**smooth** *(aj)*

1 fino, plano, liso, llano, nivelado, pulido, suave, igual, uniforme, *(LAm)* parejo

*desnivelado*

2 agradable, suave, dulce, blando, grasoso, oleaginoso, aceitoso

3 calmado, ecuánime, pacífico, tranquilo

**soak**

mojar, enjuagar, empapar, humedecer, saturar, remojar

*secar*

**sober**

1 abstemio, sobrio, moderado, temperado, abstinente

*borracho, bebido*

2 calmado, compuesto, templado, frío, desapasionado, imparcial, grave, pacífico, quieto, racional, razonador, sereno, serio, solemne, moderado

*inmoderado*

**soften**

1 ablandar, reblandecer

2 disminuir, calmar, mitigar, templar, debilitar, suavizar

*agravar*

**solitary**

solo, solitario, único, desolado, remoto, retirado, retrasado, confiscado, infrecuentado

*ocupado*

**sorrow** (s)

aflicción, pena, dolor, tristeza, problema

*alegría, felicidad*

**sound** (aj)

1 completo, entero, firme, perfecto, robusto, sin dañar, vigoroso, enérgico, sano

*defectuoso*

2 correcto, justo, ortodoxo, apropiado, válido, derecho, verdadero, razonable

**sound** (s)

ruido, resonancia, tono, voz, estruendo, estrépito

*silencio*

**spacious**

amplio, ancho, cómodo, extenso, espacioso, grande, vasto

*reducido*

**spare** (aj)

1 económico, frugal, escaso, insuficiente

*pródigo, despilfarrado*

2 desvaído, delgado, fino, magro, flaco, chupado

*regordete, rollizo, obeso*

**spare** (v)

1 permitir, dar, gratificar, proporcionar

2 ahorrar, economizar, preservar, guardar, reservar

*malgastar, derrochar, desperdiciar*

**speed** (v)

1 expedir, enviar, apresurar, presionar, dar prisas

2 adelantar, avanzar, ayudar, asistir, promover, fomentar

**spend**

consumir, dispensar, disipar, gastar, desembolsar, agotar, expender, malgastar, despilfarrar

*ahorrar*

**splendid**

1 brillante, reluciente, espléndido, lustroso, radiante, refulgente

*sombrío, deslustrado*

2 magnífico, deslumbrante, deslumbrador, vistoso, impresionante, imponente

*corriente, ordinario*

**split** (v)

1 romper, hender, repartir, explotar, dividir, partir, separar

*unir, juntar*

2 hendirse, rajarse

3 *(fig) (Br)* chivatear, soplar

4 *(fig (Am)* largarse, irse

**spoil**

1 pillar, robar, saquear

2 gastar, despilfarrar, malgastar

3 dañar, destruir, desfigurar, arruinar, echar a perder, estropear, deteriorar

*reparar, restaurar*

**spread** (v)

1 dilatar, expandir, extenderse, abrirse, desenrollarse

*contraer*

2 publicar, emitir, circular, diseminar, proclamar, promulgar, propagar

*callar, disimular, encubrir*

**stain** (s)

1 mancha, tacha, borrón, coloramiento

2 (fig) desgracia, deshonra, deshonor, infamia, reproche, vergüenza
*honor*

**stain** (v)

manchar, tachar, emborronar, colorear, teñir, empañar, deslustrar, matizar
*limpiar*

**stand** (v)

1 continuar, permanecer, estar, parar
*mover*

2 soportar, sufrir, tolerar, aguantar, resistir

**start** (v)

1 empezar, iniciar, levantar, comenzar, emitir, originar
*finalizar, acabar*

2 alarmar, molestar, asustar, sobresaltarse, espantar

**station** (s)

1 estación, lugar, puesto, localización, sitio, situación

2 posición social, rango, categoría, status, grado, puesto, empleo, colocación

**stay** (s)

1 retraso, retardo, parada, pausa

2 apoyo, sostén, puntal, soporte

**stay** (v)

1 continuar, retrasar, retardar, parar, permanecer, tardar, quedarse atrás
*marchar, irse*

2 soportar, sostener, apuntalar, apoyar, reforzar

**stem** (s)

rama, tallo, tronco, vástago, renuevo

**stem** (v)

oponer, frenar, resistir, parar, cerrar, aguantar, detener, controlar
*producir, dar, ceder*

**stimulate**

animar, estimular, impeler, fomentar, incitar, inflamar, instigar, provocar, levantar, favorecer, promover
*deprimir*

**stop** (v)

1 cesar, parar, concluir, desistir, discontinuar, terminar
*empezar, comenzar, iniciar*

2 parar, arrestar, bloquear, romper, encerrar, cerrar, impedir, interceptar, interrumpir, obstruir, prevenir
*continuar, seguir*

**storm** (s)

1 tormenta, huracán, viento fuerte, lluvia, ciclón, tempestad, tornado, ventarrón
*calma*

2 (fig) agitación, tormenta, clamor, conmoción, disturbio, revuelo, tumulto, confusión, desorden

3 (fig) asalto, ataque, arremetida, embestida, ímpetu, acometida

**straight**

1 derecho, recto, perpendicular, erecto, vertical
*horizontal, en pendiente*

2 directo, cerca, corto, constante, inquebrantable, firme
*tortuoso, sinuoso*

3 cándido, franco, honesto, justo, de confianza, honorable
*deshonesto*

**strain** (s)

1 esfuerzo, fuerza, tensión, tirantez, arranque, tirón

2 ascendencia, linaje, familia, raza, tribu, rebaño

3 melodía, música, canción, tonada, trova

**strength**

coraje, energía, fuerza, firmeza, potencia, poder, resolución, espíritu, vehemencia, vigor
*debilidad*

**strengthen**
1 animar, fortalecer, vigorizar, fomentar, alentar
*debilitar*
2 confirmar, corroborar, establecer, justificar, apoyar

**strip** *(v)*
1 desvestir, destapar, descubrir, desnudar
*cubrir*
2 privar, despojar, desmantelar, pelar, robar, pillar, saquear, *(fig)* desnudar, descubrir

**strong**
1 atlético, fuerte, vigoroso, eficiente, saludable, muscular, poderoso, robusto, *(protesta)* enérgico, *(café)* cargado, *(color)* intenso, *(característica)* acusado
*débil, flojo*
2 ardiente, firme, tenaz, celoso
3 fuerte, salado, picante, con muchas especies
*suave, flojo*

**stubborn**
tenaz, resuelto, testarudo, inflexible, contumaz, intratable, obstinado, persistente, incontrolable
*dócil*

**studious**
estudioso, cuidadoso, diligente, trabajador, meditativo, reflexivo, pensador, erudito
*desatento, distraído*

**stupid**
estúpido, obtuso, lento, atontado, bobo, simple, insensato
*inteligente*

**subdue**
romper, controlar, conquistar, dominar, avasallar, sojuzgar, reprimir, vencer, derrotar
*rendirse, someterse*

**subject** *(aj)*
sujeto, dependiente, inferior, obediente, subordinado

**subject** *(s)*
1 materia, estudio, tema, objeto

2 dependiente, subordinado
*superior*
3 causa, motivo, razón, fundamento

**submit**
1 someterse, capitular, doblegarse, obedecer, acatar, resignarse, rendirse, tolerar
*resistir, afrontar*
2 proponer, presentar, aducir, referir, rendir

**subservient**
1 inferior, servil, subordinado, sujeto
*superior*
2 auxiliar, conducente, propicio, instrumental, provechoso, útil, subsidiario, servible, servicial

**subsidiary**
auxiliar, cooperativo, secundario, servicial, subordinado, suplementario, provechoso, útil
*primario, principal*

**substitute** *(s)*
agente, sustituto, diputado, equivalente, representante, apoderado, interino
*jefe, principal, cabeza, director*

**subtle**
astuto, mañoso, apto, agudo, taimado, curioso, perspicaz, penetrante, profundo, ingenioso
*simple, ingenuo*

**successful**
favorable, exitoso, fructuoso, feliz, oportuno, afortunado, próspero, victorioso
*desafortunado*

**sudden**
repentino, de repente, rápido, apresurado, inesperado, inusual, brusco, precipitado
*intencionado, pensado, premeditado*

**suffer**
admitir, aguantar, experimentar, permitir, soportar, sentir, sufrir, sostener, tolerar
*resistir, aguantar*

**sufficient**
adecuado, amplio, suficiente, lleno, satisfactorio
*insuficiente*

**suitable**
aplicable, apropiado, adecuado, apto, conveniente, pertinente, relevante
*inconveniente, inapropiado*

**supplement** *(s)*
adición, apéndice, posdata, suplemento, consecuencia, resultado

**supply** *(v)*
contribuir, ofrecer, suministrar, proporcionar, dar, satisfacer, almacenar, donar, ceder, otorgar
*retener, negar, denegar*

**support** *(v)*
1 mantener, sostener, aguantar, nutrir, apoyar
*estorbar, dificultar, impedir*
2 abogar, asistir, confirmar, defender, promocionar, secundar, apoyar
*oponer*
3 aguantar, sufrir, soportar, tolerar, resistir

**suppress**
ganar, vencer, conquistar, subyugar, reprimir, sofocar, ahogar, avasallar, dominar
*dejar libre, liberar, libertar*

**sure**
1 exacto, seguro, cierto, confidente, convencido, positivo, preciso, de confianza, verdadero
*incierto*
2 firme, seguro, sólido, estable

**survive**
sobrevivir, vivir, durar, perdurar
*morir*

**suspect** *(v)*
1 dudar, poner en duda, desconfiar, recelar
2 creer, sospechar, conjeturar, considerar, adivinar, suponer, imaginar
*aceptar*

**sustain**
1 soportar, aguantar, llevar, sentir, sufrir
2 ayudar, asistir, confortar, mantener, nutrir, alimentar, reanimar
*pasar por alto, olvidar*
3 aprobar, sostener, ratificar, confirmar

# T

**tail** *(s)*
    cola, final, conclusión, extremo
    *principio, cabeza*

**taint** *(v)*
    contaminar, manchar, corromper, imbuir, empapar, infectar, polucionar, ensuciar, viciar, deslustrar
    *limpiar*

**take** *(v)*
    1 coger, capturar, agarrar, ganar, sujetar, empuñar, atrapar, obtener, asir, *(fig)* robar
    *dejar*
    2 aceptar, adoptar, asumir, considerar, suponer
    3 beber, comer, tomar, inhalar, tragar

**talent** *(aj)*
    talento, habilidad, aptitud, capacidad, facultad, genio, don, maña, destreza
    *estupidez*

**tame** *(v)*
    conquistar, disciplinar, domar, domesticar, subyugar, reprimir, esclavizar, dominar, reprimir

**tangible**
    tangible, claro, categórico, evidente, palpable, positivo, real, sustancial, táctil, tocable, perceptible
    *abstracto, irreal*

**task**
    tarea, negocio, trabajo, labor, lección, empleo, ocupación
    *ocio, tiempo libre*

**taste** *(s)*
    1 gusto, sabor
    *insipidez*
    2 *(fig)* deseo, predilección, cariño, afición
    3 *(fig)* discriminación, elegancia, estilo, perspicacia, discernimiento

**teach**
    enseñar, aconsejar, dirigir, educar, impartir, disciplinar, inculcar, informar, instruir, entrenar
    *aprender*

**tear** *(v)*
    desgarrar, dividir, lacerar, estropear, rasgar, rajar, romper, separar
    *componer, remediar, zurcir*

**tease** *(v)*
    molestar, incomodar, irritar, fastidiar, provocar, atormentar, preocupar, inquietar, contrariar
    *apaciguar, calmar*

**tedious**
    aburrido, monótono, soso, pesado, prosaico, cansado, poco interesante, fatigoso
    *interesante*

**temper** *(s)*
    1 enfado, disgusto, temperamento, irritabilidad, irritación, pasión, resentimiento, enojo
    *buen humor*
    2 disposición, humor, naturaleza, temperamento, ánimo
    3 tranquilidad, compostura, imperturbabilidad, ecuanimidad

**temperate**
    abstemio, calmado, frío, desapasionado, moderado, pacífico, manso
    *inmoderado*

**tempest**
    tempestad, ciclón, huracán, tormenta, tornado, ventarrón
    *calma*

**tempestuous**
    tempestuoso, ventoso, tormentoso, de mucho viento, borrascoso, turbulento
    *calmado*

**temporary**

breve, efímero, fugaz, pasajero, momentáneo, transitorio, provisional
*permanente, duradero*

**tender** *(aj)*

1 tierno, cariñoso, afectuoso, compasivo, gentil, humano, amable, amoroso, clemente, sentimental, simpático, de buen corazón
*poco amable, despiadado*

2 delicado, frágil, débil
*fuerte*

3 tierno, sensible, doloroso, dolorido

**tender** *(v)*

ofrecer, presentar, proponer, sugerir

**tentative**

experimental, provisional, de prueba, de juguete, de ensayo
*cierto, verdadero*

**terminate**

terminar, cesar, acabar, completar, concluir, finalizar, cerrar, resultar
*empezar, comenzar*

**terrible**

terrible, espantoso, horroroso, tremendo, imponente, horrible, monstruoso, horripilante
*agradable, placentero*

**testify**

testificar, afirmar, atestiguar, certificar, corroborar, declarar, atestiguar, deponer
*negar, denegar*

**testimony**

afirmación, confirmación, corroboración, testimonio, declaración, evidencia, prueba, autenticación, deposición
*encubrimiento, disimulación*

**thick**

1 espeso, compacto, condensado, denso, atestado
*disperso, esparcido*

2 grueso, abultado, gordo, rollizo, sólido, rechoncho
*delgado, fino*

3 abundante, frecuente, numeroso

4 nublado, espeso, brumoso, nebuloso, de niebla
*claro, despejado*

**thin**

delgado, atenuado, delicado, fino, ligero, flaco, chupado, desvaído, magro, en los huesos, transparente, esbelto, escuálido
*gordo, grueso, obeso, rechoncho, espeso*

**thirsty**

1 sediento, seco, árido
*saciado, húmedo*

2 impaciente, ávido, hambriento, anhelante, ansioso
*satisfecho, saciado*

**thoughtful**

1 contemplativo, meditabundo, deliberativo, pensativo, serio, especulativo, estudioso
*irreflexivo, descuidado*

2 atento, cuidadoso, solícito, considerado, circunspecto, prudente, discreto, cauto
*descuidado*

**thoughtless**

irreflexivo, descuidado, inactivo, inconsiderado, indiscreto, negligente, temerario, precipitado, imprudente, distraído
*serio, meditabundo, atento*

**thrash**

golpear, castigar, azotar, apalear, vapulear, maltratar
*cuidar*

**threshold**

1 puerta, umbral, entrada

2 *(fig)* comienzo, principio, apertura
*final*

**throw** *(v)*

echar, volver, arrojar, proyectar, tirar, lanzar, emprender, enviar, impulsar, propulsar
*tener, agarrar, coger, asir*

**tidy**

limpio, nítido, ordenado, pulcro, esmerado, acicalado, aseado, arreglado
*sucio, desarreglado*

**tie** (v)

atar, vincular, encadenar, conectar, unir, ligar, apretar, asegurar
*desatar, desunir, aflojar*

**tight**

apretado, cerrado, compacto, tenso, firme, fijo, tirante
*suelto, flojo*

**timid**

tímido, asustado, cobarde, vergonzoso, evasivo, reservado, medroso, pusilánime, modesto, retraído, temeroso
*intrépido, audaz, valiente*

**tiny**

pequeño, diminuto, microscópico, en miniatura, menudo, pigmeo, enano
*grande*

**tip** (s)

1 aviso, consejo, advertencia, confidencia, notificación, soplo, chivatazo

2 extremidad, final, punta, vértice, tope
*fondo, pie, asiento, parte baja*

3 propina, donación, dádiva, ofrenda, gratificación

**tip** (v)

inclinar, sesgar, ladear, volcar

**tolerate**

aguantar, admitir, permitir, soportar, sufrir, tolerar, resistir, recibir
*oponerse, resistir*

**torment** (s)

tormento, agonía, ansiedad, contrariedad, irritación, pena, aflicción, provocación, persecución, tortura
*calma, paz, consuelo*

**torture** (s)

agonía, angustia, dolor, pena, tormento, tortura
*consuelo*

**torture** (v)

agonizar, atormentar, doler
*aliviar, tranquilizar*

**toss** (v)

1 echar, lanzar, arrojar, tirar, proyectar, propulsar, impulsar

2 agitar, sacudir, retumbar, abatir, retorcerse, debatirse
*descansar, apoyarse*

**tough**

1 durable, duradero, firme, inflexible, duro, tieso, rígido, tenaz
*débil, blando*

2 difícil, insensible, cruel, obstinado, terco, refractario, tenaz, molesto, fastidioso
*tratable, dócil*

**tragedy**

1 adversidad, calamidad, catástrofe, desastre, tragedia, infortunio, desgracia, desventura

2 obra dramática, tragedia, drama

**traitor**

traidor, apóstata, impostor, embustero, sinvergüenza, rebelde, renegado, bellaco, desertor
*leal, legitimista*

**tranquil**

tranquilo, calmado, plácido, quieto, sereno, pacífico, sosegado, imperturbable, ecuánime
*alborotado, poco tranquilo*

**tranquillity**

calma, paz, sosiego, tranquilidad, placidez, serenidad, reposo, quietud, silencio
*excitación*

**transform**

transformar, alterar, cambiar, convertir, transmutar, transfigurar
*mantener*

**transport** (v)

1 transportar, aguantar, llevar, traer, mover, transferir
*dejar*

2 (fig) transportar, encantar, deleitar, extasiar, embelesar

**treat** (s)

banquete, placer, deleite, fruición, festín, refrigerio

**treat** (v)

1 tratar, atender, actuar, manejar, usar, administrar
*manejar mal*

2 entretener, divertir, agasajar, festejar

3 negociar, regatear, pactar

**tremendous**

alarmante, tremendo, horroroso, horrible, terrorífico, espantoso, temeroso, aprensivo
*ordinario, corriente, normal*

**trespass** (s)

1 usurpación, invasión, infracción, violación, intrusión

2 crimen, delincuencia, error, falta, ofensa, pecado, transgresión, maldad, perversión
*observancia, cumplimiento*

**trial**

1 examen, experiencia, experimento, prueba, ensayo, tentativa
*logro, consecución*

2 intento, esfuerzo, tentativa, trabajo

3 aflicción, pena, miseria, dolor, sufrimiento, problema, infortunio

4 acción, caso, proceso, juicio, vista, causa

**trick** (v)

engañar, defraudar, embaucar, timar, estafar
*desengañar, desilusionar*

**trim** (v)

1 cortar, recortar, acortar, reducir, podar, afeitar, esquilar, trasquilar
*aumentar*

2 ajustar, adornar, arreglar, embellecer, decorar, vestir, preparar
*desarreglar*

**triumph** (v)

triunfar, exaltar, prevalecer, florecer, prosperar, alegrar, tener éxito, ganar
*fallar, perder*

**trivial**

trivial, inconsiderable, insignificante, pequeño, baladí, nimio, sin importancia
*importante*

**trouble** (s)

problema, adversidad, aflicción, temor, dificultad, disturbio, pena, inconveniencia, irritación, sufrimiento, tormento, tribulación
*felicidad*

**true**

1 verdadero, auténtico, correcto, exacto, genuino, real, veraz
*falso*

2 constante, honesto, leal, fiel, honorable, puro, sincero, recto
*infiel, desleal*

**trust** (v)

creer, confiar, fiarse de, defender, esperar
*desconfiar, recelar*

**truthful**

1 exacto, preciso, correcto, verdadero, de confianza, de fiar, fiable, confiable
*inexacto, incorrecto*

2 cándido, franco, natural, sencillo, honesto, ingenuo, honrado
*falso, mentiroso*

**tumult**

refriega, riña, altercado, conmoción, desorden, fracaso, pelea, motín, disturbio, tumulto, contienda
*tranquilidad, sosiego*

**tutor** (s)

tutor, guardián, instructor, profesor, preparador, entrenador, preceptor
*alumno, escolar*

**twist**

contorsionar, torcer, enroscar, distorsionar, entrelazar, trenzar
*destorcer*

# U

**ugly**
feo, desagradable, espantoso, horrible, monstruoso, ofensivo, repulsivo, terrible, repugnante, chocante, vil
*atractivo, agradable*

**ultimate**
último, conclusivo, concluyente, decisivo, final, extremo, más remoto
*primero*

**umpire** (s)
árbitro, juez
*jugador, litigante*

**unanimity**
unanimidad, acuerdo, concierto, concordato, armonía, unidad
*desacuerdo*

**unbearable**
insoportable, insufrible, intolerable, inaguantable
*soportable, sufrible, aguantable*

**uncover**
descubrir, exponer, revelar, mostrar, enseñar, desnudar
*cubrir, tapar*

**undeniable**
innegable, cierto, claro, evidente, indudable, obvio, incontestable, incuestionable
*dudoso*

**underhand**
clandestino, fraudulento, furtivo, secreto, ingenioso, disimulado, sigiloso, subrepticio
*abierto, franco*

**understand**
saber, conocer, comprender, entender, concebir, discernir, percibir, reconocer, ver

**unfaithful**
indiferente, insensible, desleal, infiel, pérfido, traidor, informal, de poca confianza
*leal, fiel*

**unfold**
1 desenredar, desenmarañar, abrir, expandir, desplegar, desenroscar
*doblar, plegar*
2 (fig) clarificar, revelar, desarrollar, explicar, ilustrar
*ocultar, no revelar*

**unfortunate**
desgraciado, desafortunado, calamitoso, deplorable, desastroso, malogrado, malhadado, infeliz
*afortunado, agraciado*

**uniform** (aj)
uniforme, parecido, consistente, constante, igual, regular, incambiable, invariable
*variable, irregular*

**union**
1 unión, combinación, juntura
*separación*
2 unión, alianza, asociación, coalición, confederación
*separación*
3 acuerdo, concordia, concordato, armonía, unanimidad, unísono, unidad
*desunión, desacuerdo*

**unique**
único, solo, singular, excepcional, raro, anormal, inusual, poco común
*usual, normal*

**unison**
armonía, acuerdo, concordato, concordia
*desacuerdo*

**unite**
unir, añadir, amalgamar, acoplar, asociar, mezclar, combinar, confederar, conectar, consolidar, incorporar
*separar, desunir*

**unjust**
1 parcial, injusto, con prejuicios, no equitativo
*justo, imparcial*

2 malo, fraudulento, atroz, nefando, equivocado, malvado, perverso
*justo, bueno*

**unlucky**
desafortunado, miserable, nefasto, de mal agüero, poco propicio, desfavorable, desgraciado
*afortunado, de buen agüero, feliz*

**unreasonable**
1 absurdo, tonto, irracional, estúpido, disparatado, ridículo, insensato
*razonable*
2 excesivo, exorbitante, inmoderado, extorsionador, injusto
*razonable, justo*

**unsettle**
perturbar, inquietar, desconcertar, desquiciar, trastornar, alterar
*tranquilizar, calmar*

**unsteady**
inseguro, cambiable, inconstante, irregular, tambaleante, informal, de poca constancia, variable, indeciso, irresoluto
*firme, fijo, estable*

**unusual**
inusual, curioso, excepcional, extraordinario, raro, remarcable, extravagante, extraño, singular, insólito, indeciso, irresoluto
*firme, fijo, estable*

**upright**
1 vertical, derecho, erecto, perpendicular
*horizontal, plano*

2 *(fig)* bueno, honesto, honrado, recto, incorruptible, virtuoso, justo
*deshonesto*

**uproar**
rugido, bramido, clamor, conmoción, confusión, ruido, turbulencia, estrépito, tumulto, desorden, alboroto
*paz, tranquilidad, sosiego, calma*

**upshot**
conclusión, consecuencia, final, resultado, acontecimiento
*inicio, comienzo*

**urge** *(v)*
1 urgir, obligar, forzar, impeler, incitar, estimular, instigar, presionar, empujar
2 implorar, recomendar, rogar, pedir, suplicar

**urgent**
urgente, inmediato, imperativo, importante, insistente, apremiante, acuciante
*sin importancia*

**use** *(v)*
1 utilizar, usar, emplear, ejercitar, practicar, aplicar
*no usar*
2 consumir, gastar, usar, agotar, expender
*ahorrar, salvar*
3 acostumbrarse, familiarizarse, habituarse

**useful**
útil, utilizable, ventajoso, beneficioso, efectivo, provechoso, saludable, servible
*inútil, inservible, inoperante*

# V

**vacant**

1 vacante, vacío, desocupado, libre, pendiente, sin ocupar
*ocupado*

2 distraído, soñador, necio, irreflexivo, inconsciente
*serio, pensativo*

**vagrant** *(aj)*

nómada, vagabundeante, paseante, inhabitado, vagabundo, errante
*aposentado, fijo*

**vagrant** *(s)*

vagabundo, mendigo, pordiosero, ambulante, vago, gandul, caminante
*habitante*

**vague**

vago, dudoso, impreciso, indefinido, indeterminado, indistinto, oscuro, poco claro, desconocido
*definido, claro*

**vain**

1 vano, fútil, improductivo, trivial, sin importancia, inservible, inútil
*productivo*

2 arrogante, egoísta, ostentoso, orgulloso, vanidoso, engreído, presumido, exagerado
*modesto, sencillo*

**valid**

válido, convincente, sólido, concluyente, decisivo, eficaz, eficiente, bueno, justo, lógico, poderoso, sustancial, bien fundado
*inválido, débil*

**valuable**

costoso, caro, de valor, estimable, preciable, servible, práctico, útil
*sin valor, inútil*

**value** *(v)*

1 valorar, estimar, calcular, contar, tasar, evaluar

2 apreciar, estimar, considerar, atesorar, guardar
*no hacer caso de, pasar por alto*

**vanish**

desaparecer, esfumarse, disolver, desvanecerse
*aparecer, surgir*

**vanity**

1 vanidad, arrogancia, presunción, engreimiento, orgullo, egotismo
*modestia*

2 vacío, vaciedad, inutilidad, necedad, fatuidad, trivialidad, irrealidad

**variation**

alteración, cambio, desviación, diferencia, discrepancia, diversidad, marcha, modificación, variación
*acuerdo, trato*

**vary**

alterar, alternar, cambiar, diferir, diversificar, modificar, no estar de acuerdo, transformar, variar
*continuar*

**vast**

inmenso, ilimitado, colosal, enorme, grande, gigante, extenso, amplio
*diminuto, pequeño*

**vault** *(s)*

1 arco, techo, bóveda

2 catacumba, cripta, mausoleo, tumba, bodega, sótano

**vehemence**

vehemencia, ardor, entusiasmo, afán, ansia, seriedad, fervor, impetuosidad, intensidad, ilusión, pasión, violencia, celo
*apatía*

**veil** *(s)*

velo, cortina, persiana, cubierta, disfraz, máscara, pantalla, sombra

**velocity**

velocidad, celeridad, rapidez, prisa
*lentitud*

**venerable**

honorable, respetable, reverenciado, sabio, serio, juicioso, prudente, venerable
*desdeñado*

**venerate**

adorar, estimar, honrar, reverenciar, respetar, loar
*deshonrar*

**venom**

1 veneno, virus
*antídoto*

2 *(fig)* amargura, hiel, bilis, rencor, odio, malignidad, virulencia
*alabanza, elogio*

**verge** *(s)*

margen, límite, borde, canto
*interior*

**verify**

atestiguar, autentificar, confirmar, cerciorar, corroborar, probar, verificar
*desaprobar*

**vernacular**

indígena, materno, nativo, vernáculo, vulgar
*extranjero*

**versatile**

adaptable, cambiable, flexible, inconstante, versátil, variable
*constante, invariable*

**vex**

afligir, agitar, molestar, estorbar, irritar, ofender, provocar, atormentar, fastidiar, contrariar, impacientar
*contentar, agradar*

**vexatious**

acongojante, engorroso, fastidioso, desagradable, molesto, irritante, pesado, guasón, atormentador, importuno
*satisfactorio, agradable*

**vice**

vicio, corrupción, defecto, perversión, depravación, demonio, falta, inmoralidad, imperfección, debilidad, pecado
*virtud*

**vicinity**

vecindad, distrito, barrio, localidad, vecindario, proximidad
*distancia*

**vicious**

1 vicioso, malo, abandonado, corrupto, depravado, degradado, envilecido, inmoral, imperfecto, malicioso, pecaminoso, poco escrupuloso, cínico
*virtuoso*

2 contrario, malévolo, refractario, obstinado, revoltoso, ingobernable

**victory**

conquista, éxito, victoria, autoridad, superioridad, triunfo
*derrota*

**vigilance**

vigilancia, alerta, cuidado, precaución, observancia, circunspección, observación
*desatención, distracción*

**vigorous**

activo, enérgico, vigoroso, efectivo, eficiente, emprendedor, sano, robusto, fuerte, viril, animoso, brioso

**vigour,** *(Am)* **vigor**

vigor, actividad, animación, eficacia, energía, fuerza, salud, viveza, robustez, potencia, virilidad, vitalidad
*debilidad*

**vile**

vil, malo, abandonado, innoble, depravado, despreciable, impuro, miserable, bajo, pecaminoso, vicioso, débil
*respetable, loable*

**vindictive**

implacable, malicioso, maligno, rencoroso, despiadado, vengativo, malévolo
*misericordioso, perdonador*

**violent**

violento, fiero, furioso, impetuoso, intenso, severo, ingobernable,
vehemente, salvaje, turbulento,
atroz, terrible
*calmado, tranquilo*

**virtue**

1 virtud, castidad, moralidad, pureza, bondad
*vicio*

2 eficacia, excelencia, integridad,
justicia, calidad, rectitud, valor

**visible**

aparente, claro, evidente, manifiesto, notable, obvio, patente,
perceptible, visible, distinguible,
observable
*invisible*

**vital**

1 vivo, vital, vivificante, viviente
*muerto, apagado*

2 crítico, vital, esencial, importante,
indispensable, necesario
*no esencial*

**vivacious**

vivaz, animado, alegre, juguetón,
divertido, alborozado, enérgico,
vivo

*torpe, lerdo*

**vivid**

1 brillante, claro, intenso, lúcido

2 activo, animado, enérgico, expresivo, rápido, vivo, fuerte, vigoroso
*sombrío, apagado, inactivo*

**vociferous**

clamoroso, ruidoso, alto, tumultuoso, vociferante
*tranquilo, silencioso*

**voice** *(s)*

voz, articulación, expresión, lenguaje, sonido, tono, palabra
*silencio*

**vow** *(v)*

afirmar, dedicar, consagrar, pro-
meter, jurar
*repudiar*

**vulgar**

1 *(persona)* vulgar, común, ordinario, plebeyo, de humilde cuna
*educado, refinado*

2 general, nativo, vernáculo, vulgar

3 *(indecente)* ordinario, vulgar, grosero, de mal gusto, *(chiste)* verde,
*(LAm)* colorado

# W

**wail** *(s)*
    lamento, lamentación, queja, pena, sufrimiento, gemido, quejido
    *alegría, gozo*

**wail** *(v)*
    lamentar, llorar, deplorar, acongojarse
    *alegrar, regocijar*

**waive**
    abandonar, renunciar, someterse, dimitir, diferir
    *demandar, insistir*

**wake** *(v)*
    1 levantar, despertar
    *dormir*
    2 activar, despertar, animar, excitar, provocar, encender
    *aliviar, disipar, aquietar*

**walk** *(s)*
    1 paseo, caminata, vuelta, excursión
    2 paseo, avenida, pasaje, sendero, camino, senda, acera, vereda

**wander**
    vagar, desviarse, marcharse, recorrer, errar por, pasear, deambular, callejear
    *establecer, colonizar*

**wane** *(s)*
    disminución, moderación, decadencia, declinación, pérdida

**wane** *(v)*
    disminuir, abatir, decaer, declinar, fallar
    *crecer*

**want** *(s)*
    1 deseo, vehemencia, anhelo, ansia, necesidad, exigencia
    *indiferencia*
    2 escasez, deficiencia, insuficiencia, carencia, carestía
    3 indigencia, miseria, penuria, pobreza

**war** *(s)*
    guerra, contienda, hostilidad, enemistad, lucha
    *paz*

**warm** *(aj)*
    1 acalorado, caliente, tibio, templado, soleado, termal
    *frío*
    2 afable, amable, cordial, vivaz, apasionado, entusiasta, entusiasmado, emocionado, fervoroso, amistoso, simpático, vehemente
    *frío, flemático*

**warning**
    advertencia, aviso, amonestación, consejo, augurio, precaución, notificación, premonición, presagio, signo, señal
    *atención, estímulo*

**warrant** *(v)*
    1 afirmar, asegurar, atestiguar, declarar, afianzar
    *rechazar, no aceptar*
    2 aprobar, autorizar, garantizar, justificar

**wary**
    cuidadoso, cauto, circunspecto, prudente, vigilante, observador
    *imprudente*

**wash** *(v)*
    lavar, mojar, bañar, enjuagar, humedecer
    *secar*

**watch** *(s)*
    1 atención, alerta, inspección, observación, vigilancia, interés
    2 centinela, guarda, guardia, guardián, sereno
    3 reloj, cronometrador

**watch** *(v)*
    1 mirar, contemplar, observar, ver, notar, visualizar, marcar
    2 guardar, mantener, proteger, atender
    *descuidar, pasar por alto*

**watchful**
    alerta, atento, circunspecto, cauteloso, cauto, observador, perspicaz, vigilante, prudente
    *imprudente, incauto*

**watery**

1 aguado, mojado, humedecido, húmedo, acuoso
*seco*

2 aguado, diluido, insípido, soso
*concentrado*

**wax** *(s)*

cera, cerumen, cerilla

**wax** *(v)*

crecer, aumentar, ser, armar, montar
*menguar, disminuir*

**weak**

1 débil, delicado, frágil, quebradizo, enfermizo, lánguido, achacoso
*fuerte, saludable*

2 débil, indefenso, expuesto, sin protección

3 tonto, corto, simple, imprudente, irresoluto, débil
*fuerte, listo, avispado*

4 diluido, aguado, rebajado, flojo, insípido
*concentrado*

**weaken**

degradar, debilitar, presionar, rebajar, enervar, deteriorar, reducir
*reforzar, fortalecer*

**wealth**

1 bienes, activo, acciones, fortuna, fondos, dinero, posesiones, propiedad, riqueza
*pobreza, miseria*

2 abundancia, opulencia, afluencia, profusión
*escasez, falta*

**wear**

1 llevar, vestir, ponerse, usar, calzar

2 aguantar, resistir, durar

3 consumir, gastar, usar, estropear, deteriorar
*arreglar*

**weary**

1 cansado, fatigado, exhausto, agotado, hastiado
*fresco*

2 molesto, fastidioso, pesado, fatigoso, agotador

**weave**

trenzar, entrelazar, entremezclar, entretejer, tramar
*deshacer, desenredar, desenmarañar*

**weep**

llorar, lamentar, quejarse, gemir, protestar
*reír*

**weight**

1 peso, bulto, carga, gravedad, pesadez
*ligereza*

2 *(fig)* peso, consecuencia, eficacia, importancia, significado

**welcome** *(s)*

bienvenida, recepción, saludo, recibimiento, acogida

**well** *(aj)*

1 sano, robusto, saludable, bueno
*enfermo, malo*

2 benéfico, dichoso, feliz, provechoso, satisfactorio, útil

**well** *(av)*

1 con precisión, correctamente, bien, adecuadamente, eficientemente

2 abundantemente, copiosamente, ampliamente, totalmente

**wheedle**

halagar, camelar, mimar, cortejar, tentar, seducir, adular, lisonjear, complacer, persuadir
*forzar, rechazar*

**whimsical**

caprichoso, curioso, excéntrico, fantástico, extravagante, peculiar, raro, singular, original
*serio, formal*

**whole**

1 total, todo, completo, entero, integral, indivisible
*parcial, divisible*

2 bueno, sin fallo, perfecto, entero, sin dañar
*imperfecto*

## wicked

amoral, malo, corrupto, abandonado, depravado, demonio, inmoral, impío, irreligioso, pecaminoso, vicioso, vil, villano, disoluto
*virtuoso*

## wide

1 ancho, amplio, espacioso, comprensivo, extenso, grande, vasto
*estrecho, pequeño*

2 distante, remoto
*cercano*

## wild

1 feroz, fiero, salvaje, indomable, indomesticable, indomado
*domado, domesticado*

2 furioso, impetuoso, ruidoso, rebelde, inconsiderado, turbulento, indisciplinado, violento, ingobernable

3 extravagante, fantástico, alocado, insensato, disparatado

4 ansioso, entusiasta, entusiasmado, excitado

5 desierto, incultivable, incivilizado, inhabitado

## win (v)

1 ganar, conseguir, alcanzar, adquirir, conquistar, obtener, lograr, triunfar
*perder*

2 tentar, fascinar, atraer, convencer, influir, persuadir

## wise (aj)

sabio, discreto, erudito, inteligente, juicioso, conocedor, educado, prudente, racional, razonable, sagaz
*tonto, corto*

## wise (s)

manera, modo, guisa

## wit

1 perspicacia, discernimiento, intuición, intelecto, percepción, agudeza, razón
*ignorancia*

2 diversión, jocosidad, humor, chiste

## withdraw

1 partir, marchar, soltar, retirar, retroceder, separarse, secesionarse
*permanecer, estar*

2 renunciar, rechazar, retirar, desdecirse, rescindir, retractar
*mantener*

## withhold

restringir, mantener, rehusar, reservar, resistir, retener
*otorgar, conceder, ceder*

## withstand

confrontar, enfrentar, oponer, resistir
*someter*

## witness (v)

1 atestiguar, testificar, confirmar, corroborar
*desaprobar*

2 marcar, notar, ver, darse cuenta, observar, percibir

## wonder (s)

1 asombro, sorpresa, estupefacción, curiosidad, aturdimiento, perplejidad
*calma*

2 milagro, fenómeno, prodigio, rareza, maravilla

## wonder (v)

maravillarse, preguntarse, meditar, especular, pensar

## wonderful

maravilloso, milagroso, extraño, raro, remarcable, peculiar, fenomenal, sorprendente, asombroso

## work (v)

1 manejar, dirigir, manipular, mover, operar, actuar

2 efectuar, conseguir, ejecutar, hacer, producir

3 trabajar, trabajar como un esclavo, trabajar como un negro, fatigarse, afanarse
*descansar, mandar*

## worry (s)

contrariedad, disgusto, molestia, lata, ansiedad, cuidado, miedo, preocupación, inquietud, recelo,

duda, perplejidad, problema, impaciencia, aflicción
*alegría, júbilo, regocijo*

**worship** *(v)*
adorar, rogar, amar, respetar, honorar, rezar, venerar, reverenciar, idolatrar
*detestar, odiar*

**worth**
1 precio, coste, valor, tasa, tarifa
2 estima, excelencia, buena calidad, mérito, valor, provecho
*inutilidad, falta de valor*

**wound** *(v)*
1 dañar, herir, estropear, lastimar, lesionar, lacerar
*curar, sanar*
2 *(fig)* ofender, molestar, irritar, fastidiar

**wrath**
furia, ira, cólera, exasperación, indignación, pasión, resentimiento

*serenidad, calma*

**wreck** *(s)*
desolación, devastación, destrucción, ruina
*reconstrucción*

**wretched**
desastroso, calamitoso, incómodo, despreciable, vil, deplorable, afligido, angustiado, melancólico, miserable, pobre, desconsolado

**wrinkle** *(s)*
arruga, pliegue, estrujamiento, doblez, surco, fruncido
*liso, terso, sin arrugas*

**wrong** *(aj)*
equivocado, erróneo, falso, ilegal, estropeado, incorrecto, injusto, injurioso
*cierto, acerado*

**wrong** *(s)*
error, injusticia, inmoralidad, equivocación, pecado, debilidad, culpa

# Y

**yarn**
> cuento, historia, anécdota, relato

**yell** *(s)*
> grito, aullido, chillido
> *susurro*

**yell** *(v)*
> gritar, chillar, chirriar, aullar, dar gritos
> *susurrar, cuchichear*

**yield** *(v)*
> 1 dar, proporcionar, producir, proveer, suministrar
> 2 abandonar, abdicar, capitular, ceder, renunciar, dimitir, someterse, rendirse
> *resistir, aguantar*
> 3 permitir, conceder, otorgar, autorizar, tolerar, aceptar
> *rechazar, anular, no aceptar*

**yoke** *(s)*
> 1 lazo, vínculo, cadena, unión, atadura
> 2 esclavitud, cautiverio, servicio, servidumbre, vasallaje
> *libertad*

**yoke** *(v)*
> conectar, acoplar, unir, juntar, liar, atar
> *desunir*

**young**
> joven, nuevo, menor
> *viejo, antiguo, mayor*

**youth**
> 1 juventud, adolescencia, inmadurez
> *edad, madurez*
> 2 joven, adolescente, chico, chaval, muchacho, mozo
> *adulto*

# Z

**zeal**
  celo, ardor, afán, ansia, entusiasmo, fervor, pasión
  *desinterés, frialdad, falta de entusiasmo*

**zealous**
  ardiente, apasionado, apremiante, fervoroso, entusiasta
  *frío, indiferente*

**zenith**
  cenit, ápice, apogeo, clímax, cumbre, cúspide, cima, vértice
  *base, nadir, punto más bajo*

**zest**
  entusiasmo, gusto, ganas, deseo, fruición, sabor, dejo
  *aversión, repugnancia, disgusto*

PART TWO

ESPAÑOL – INGLES

# ABREVIATURAS

| | |
|---|---|
| aj | adjetivo |
| Am | (Norte) Americano |
| av | Adverbio |
| Br | Británico |
| fig | Figurativo |
| LAm | Latinoamericano |
| pl | Plural |
| s | Sustantivo |
| v | Verbo |

# A

**abandonado**
1 abandoned, deserted, (god)forsaken, derelict, vacant
*inhabited, retained*
2 neglected, forlorn, uncared for, (LAm) slovenly, untidy
*looked after*
3 (LAm) perverted

**abandonar**
abandon, desert, forsake, leave, leave behind, relinquish, renounce, resign, surrender, vacate, waive, yield to, quit, withdraw, retire
*cherish, defend, keep, maintain, uphold*

**abarcar**
include, embrace, take in, encompass, span, extend to, contain, comprise, undertake, take on, (LAm) monopolize, corner a market
*exclude, omit*

**abastecer**
supply, provide with, furnish
*withhold, retain*

**abatido**
1 downhearted, crestfallen, dejected, unhappy, depressed, despondent, discouraged, dispirited, downcast, low-spirited, sad
*happy, optimistic*
2 contemptible, base, despicable, low, mean
*commendable, laudable*

**abatir**
1 demolish, dismantle, knock down, cut down, fell, lower, strike, prostrate, lay low
*construct, raise, erect*
2 humiliate, debase, degrade, depress, humble, sadden, discourage, shame
*elevate, raise, encourage, cheer (up)*

**abatirse**
1 drop, fall, swoop, dive
*rise*
2 be depressed, get discouraged

**abdicar**
abdicate, relinquish, renounce, vacate
*maintain, retain*

**abiertamente**
openly, candidly, frankly, plainly, publicly
*secretly, stealthily, privily*

**abismar**
1 humble, crush, debase, degrade, cast down, humiliate
*raise, elevate, exalt*
2 spoil, ruin
*reinstate, restore*

**ablandar**
soften, soften up, appease, calm, diminish, loosen, moderate, mitigate, soothe, temper, (LAm) run in (a car)
*aggravate, exasperate, irritate, provoke*

**abolir**
abolish, annul, cancel, revoke
*establish, reinstate*

**abominable**
abominable, detestable, execrable, abhorrent, odious, loathsome, hateful, invidious

**abominar**
abominate, abhor, detest, execrate, hate, loathe, recoil from, regard with repugnance
*admire, enjoy, like, love*

**abonar**
1 guarantee, vouch for, support, confirm, insure, warrant
*disclaim, disown, refuse, repudiate*
2 pay, pay for, remunerate, settle
3 fertilize, manure

**aborrecer**
1 detest, abhor, hate, loathe
*love, like, appreciate*

2 desert, abandon
3 become bored by

**abreviar**
1 abbreviate, abridge, compress, condense, contract, cut short, epitomize, reduce, shorten
*amplify, enlarge, extend, lengthen, prolong*
2 hasten, advance, bring forward
*retard*

**abrillantar**
1 polish, brighten, burnish, shine, *(LAm)* glaze
*sully, tarnish, discolour, taint, dull*
2 enhance, add lustre to

**abrir**
1 open, open up, cut open, spread out, extend, *(forest) (LAm)* clear
*close*
2 start, begin, commence
*end, finish*
3 open, unfold
*close*
4 *(LAm)* run away, beat it
5 *(LAm)* backtrack, back-pedal

**abrogar**
abrogate, abolish, annul, cancel, rescind, revoke
*enforce, maintain, ratify*

**abrumar**
1 oppress, crush, weigh down, overwhelm
*relieve, free*
2 wear out, exhaust, tire

**abrupto**
1 abrupt, blunt, brusque, curt, discourteous, rude
*civil, courteous, gracious, polite*
2 abrupt, precipitous, steep, sudden, sheer
*gradual, gentle*

**absolver**
absolve, acquit, clear, discharge, excuse, exonerate, pardon, release
*blame, censure, condemn*

**abstinencia**
abstinence, abstemiousness, avoidance, forbearance, restraint
*indulgence, incontinence*

**abstruso**
abstruse, dark, enigmatic, hidden, recondite, difficult, deep, profound, incomprehensible
*clear, concrete*

**absurdo**
1 illogical, absurd, crazy, nonsensical, ridiculous, preposterous, farcical, irrational, silly, foolish
*sensible, wise*
2 eccentric, outlandish, odd, strange, extravagant

**abundancia**
abundance, superabundance, copiousness, plenty, plethora, plenteousness, profusion
*lack, need, scarcity*

**abundante**
1 abundant, copious, plentiful, numerous, plenteous, profuse
*scarce*
2 rich, fertile, fecund, exuberant
*poor*

**aburrimiento**
monotony, boredom, dullness, weariness, tedium
*variety, diversity*

**acabado**
1 complete, consummate, perfect
*incomplete, imperfect*
2 finished, destroyed, consumed
*unfinished*
3 old, worn-out, ruined in health, wrecked

**acabar**
1 finish, conclude, complete, terminate, finalize, come to an end
*begin, commence, initiate, start*
2 consume, exhaust, drain, deplete
3 kill, kill off, *(LAm)* speak ill of
4 *(LAm)* ejaculate, come

**acaloramiento**
1 ardour, suffocation, fatigue, heat
2 vehemence, passion, enthusiasm, exaltation
*apathy, coolness, indifference, unconcern*
3 anger, choler, ire

## acallar
silence, quieten, calm, reassure, placate, hush, assuage, pacify
*provoke, annoy, irritate*

## acatamiento
1 respect (for), docility, obedience, submissiveness
*disobedience, rebelliousness*
2 awe, reverence, veneration
3 deference, regard, esteem
*scorn, disregard, disrespect*

## acatar
1 obey, respect, yield to, submit, *(LAm)* observe, notice
*disobey, resist*
2 hold in awe, revere, reverence, venerate
3 defer to, treat with deference
*disrespect*

## accidental
1 accidental, incidental, unintentional, eventual, casual, secondary, contingent, chance
*designed, planned, essential*
2 provisional, transitory, temporary, brief, transient
*permanent, constant*

## aceptación
1 acceptance, acknowledgement
*refusal, rejection*
2 approval, approbation
*disapproval, disapprobation*
3 popularity, standing
*unpopularity*

## aceptar
1 accept, admit, approve, give, receive
*reject, deny, refuse, repudiate, spurn*
2 accept, face, compromise oneself, bind oneself

## acerado
1 cutting, incisive, sharp
*blunt*
2 *(fig)* incisive, biting, scathing, sharp, cutting, caustic, wounding, sarcastic, trenchant
*kind, mild, gracious*

## acerbo
1 rough, bitter, sour, sharp, harsh
2 unpleasant, cruel
*pleasant, kind*
3 *(fig)* harsh, severe, rigorous, painful, distressing
*gentle*

## acérrimo
1 staunch, constant, faithful, firm, loyal, reliable, stout, true, steadfast, trustworthy, trusty
*disloyal, unfaithful, unreliable*
2 bitter, cruel, fierce, harsh, merciless, ruthless, savage
*kind, merciful*

## acertado
1 correct, right, successful
*improper, unsuccessful*
2 sensible, wise, sound
*unwise*
3 bright, good
4 well-conceived
5 apt, fitting, well-aimed, appropriate, adequate, suitable
*unsuitable, inappropriate, inadequate*

## acertar
1 hit, hit upon, hit the mark
*miss*
2 get, get right, guess, decipher, guess correctly, be right
3 find, discover, come across, succeed in tracing
4 achieve, succeed in reaching
5 manage, be successful
*fail*

## acicalar(se)
1 polish, burnish, clean, *(fig)* polish up, touch up
*dull, dim, stain, sully, tarnish*
2 dress up, bedeck, adorn
3 smarten oneself, spruce oneself up, get dressed up

## aclarar
1 light up, illuminate
2 clarify, thin, thin down, *(LAm)* clear
3 dawn, clear up

4 clarify, explain, make clear, illustrate, elucidate, cast light upon
5 resolve, remove

**acoger**
1 admit, accept, welcome, receive
*repel, reject*
2 protect, shelter, give refuge to, harbour

**acogida**
1 welcome, reception
2 admission, acceptance, approbation
*rejection, repudiation, renunciation*
3 shelter, refuge, asylum, hospitality

**acometer**
1 attack, close (in on), set upon, assail, rush on, charge
*defend, protect*
2 begin, embark on, undertake, attempt, tackle, deal with, try, attempt, take on
3 overcome, seize, take hold of

**acomodadizo**
1 accommodating, obliging, adaptable, acquiescent
*inconsiderate*
2 pliable, easy-going

**acomodado**
1 convenient, opportune, appropriate, suitable, adequate, fit
*inconvenient, inappropriate, unsuitable*
2 moderate, reasonable, moderately priced
*expensive, dear*
3 neat, orderly, presentable, fitting, becoming
4 well-to-do, wealthy, well-off, rich

**acomodar**
1 adjust, accommodate, adapt (to)
2 fit in, find room for, accommodate, take in, lodge
3 suit, adapt (to), match
4 arrange, compose, put in place, put in order, put right, repair, adjust
*disarrange, disorder*
5 reconcile
6 place, give a job to, take on, employ

**acompasado**
1 rhythmic, regular, metrical, measured
*irregular, unsteady, varying*
2 deliberate, considered, purposeful, studied, leisurely, slow

**acongojar(se)**
1 distress, grieve, oppress, afflict, sadden, trouble
*comfort, delight, please*
2 become distressed, get upset

**acopiar**
1 join, unite, assemble, collect, put together, gather together, accumulate, pile up
*disperse*
2 buy up, get a monopoly of
3 collect, hire

**acoplar**
1 *(technical)* couple, join, fit together, fit (into), insert
*uncouple, remove*
2 *(electricity)* connect, join up
*disconnect*
3 *(spaceship)* dock, link up
4 yoke, hitch
5 mate, pair

**acoquinar(se)**
1 intimidate, scare, cow, frighten, threaten, terrify, affright, alarm
*reassure, calm, appease, pacify, lull*
2 get scared, allow oneself to be intimidated

**acordar**
1 decide, resolve, determine
2 grant, accord, agree to, agree on, come to an agreement
*disallow, disagree*
3 reconcile, blend, harmonize, tune

**acortar**
1 shorten, cut down, reduce, abbreviate, abridge, condense, lessen, diminish, *(LAm)* tone down
*enlarge, amplify, expand*
2 limit, restrict, curtail

**acosar**
1 pursue relentlessly, chase, follow, hunt, track
2 *(fig)* hound, harass, badger, importune, molest

## acotar

1 survey, mark out, limit, set bounds to
2 fence in, protect, preserve
3 lop, prune, shorten, truncate, dock, cut (off)
4 annotate, mark elevations on
5 *(fig)* accept, adopt, choose
   *reject*
6 *(fig)* vouch for, guarantee
7 *(fig)* check, verify

## acre

1 *(taste)* sharp, bitter, tart, piquant
2 *(smell)* acrid, pungent, stinging, penetrating
3 sour
4 *(fig)* biting, mordant, caustic, sarcastic, trenchant
   *gentle, mild*

## acrecentar(se)

1 increase, augment, grow
   *abate, decrease, reduce*
2 advance, promote, further the interests of
   *discourage, dissuade, hinder*

## acreditar

1 do credit to, add to the reputation of
2 vouch for, guarantee, warrant
3 prove, justify, confirm, substantiate
4 sanction, authorize, approve, allow, permit
   *disallow, refuse*
5 *(commerce)* credit

## acriminar

incriminate, accuse, impute, blame, censure
*exonerate, acquit, absolve, vindicate*

## activar

1 activate
2 expedite, speed up, hurry along
   *delay*
3 brighten up, poke
4 *(commerce)* stimulate

## activo *(aj)*

1 active, agile, alert, efficient
2 lively, animated, spirited, vivacious
3 prompt, punctual, timely, early, rapid, quick, ready
4 energetic, vigorous, strong, indefatigable, industrious
5 busy, diligent, occupied, employed, engaged

## activo *(s)*

*(commerce)* assets

## actual

1 present, present-day, up-to-date, recent, latest, modern
   *obsolete, old, out-of-date*
2 current, common, prevailing, popular, topical, fashionable
   *uncommon, unfashionable*

## acuciar

1 urge on, goad, prod, spur, stimulate, incite, instigate
2 hasten, expedite, hurry, precipitate
   *delay*
3 harass, mob, press, worry
4 desire keenly, long for, crave, yearn for, hanker after

## acucioso

diligent, zealous, keen, eager, earnest, fervid
*cold, cool, indifferent*

## acudir

1 come, come along, come up, turn up, present oneself
2 come/go to the rescue, go to help, assist, help, appear in court
3 *(agriculture)* produce, yield
4 answer, *(horses)* obey

## acuerdo

1 agreement, union, consonance, conformity, harmony, blend
   *disagreement, discord*
2 determination, *(parliament)* resolution
3 agreement, treaty, contract, pact
4 *(LAm)* consultative meeting

## acumular

accumulate, agglomerate, amass, gather, collect, assemble, pile up, hoard, reunite

## acusación

1 accusation, denunciation

2 *(law)* accusation, charge, indictment, arraignment
*defence, apology*

**acusar(se)**

1 blame, accuse

2 accuse, charge, indict

3 impute, attribute, point to, proclaim the guilt of

4 denounce, reveal, show, betray

5 *(cards)* declare, lay down

6 confess, own up

**achaque**

1 indisposition, infirmity, sickliness, weakness, ailment, malady, menstrual period, monthlies

2 vice, defect, flaw, fault, weakness

3 matter, subject

4 pretext, excuse, apology

**achicar(se)**

1 shorten, cut short, reduce, lessen, contract, diminish

2 *(fig)* dwarf, belittle, diminish, dishonour

3 discourage, dishearten, intimidate, browbeat, frighten, scare

**achuchar**

1 crush, squash, squeeze flat

2 *(fig)* crush, drain, bleed

3 push, shove, jostle, harass, pester

4 urge on a dog

**adamado**

1 effeminate, womanish, womanlike, soft, delicate
*manly, virile*

2 elegant, chic

3 flashy

**adecuado**

1 adequate, fit, suitable
*inadequate, unfit, unsuitable, improper*

2 sufficient, appropriate, requisite, satisfactory
*insufficient, inappropriate, unsatisfactory*

3 well-to-do, well-off

**adecuar**

adapt, adjust, make suitable, prepare, make ready, fit
*disarrange, disorder*

**adefesio**

1 pile of nonsense, absurdity, rubbish

2 queer bird, ridiculous person

3 outlandish dress, ridiculous attire

4 unwanted object, white elephant

**adelantar**

1 move forward, move on, advance, *(sport)* pass on, pass forward

2 speed up, quicken, hurry along, accelerate
*slow down, delay*

3 advance, pay in advance, lend

4 get ahead, outstrip, overtake, pass
*fall behind, fall back*

5 advance, further, promote

6 go ahead, get on, make headway, improve, progress

7 be fast, gain

**adelanto**

1 advancement, progress, growth

2 advance, improvement, betterment

3 *(commerce)* advance, loan

**además**

also, further, furthermore, in addition to, moreover, otherwise, too, besides
*except, save*

**aderezar**

1 make up, put together, beautify, deck, array, adorn, polish, dress up

2 arrange, put in order, prepare, get ready

3 season, garnish

4 tidy up, fix, repair, remedy, compose, mend, patch up

**adhesión**

1 adhesion, adherence, affiliation

2 approval, acceptance, consent
*disapproval, refusal, dissent*

3 union, attachment, devotion, affection

**adicionar**

add, augment, sum up, count up
*deduct, subtract*

**adiestrar(se)**

1 train, teach, coach

2 *(military)* drill
3 guide, conduct, escort, lead
4 practise, train

**adinerado**
rich, wealthy, well-off, well-to-do, moneyed
*poor, impecunious, indigent*

**adjunto** *(aj)*
joined on, attached to, appended, enclosed

**adjunto** *(s)*
1 addition, annex, adjunct, enclosure
2 assistant

**admirar(se)**
1 admire, esteem, regard
2 respect, look up to
3 astonish, surprise, cause to marvel
4 be astonished, be surprised, marvel (at)

**admitir**
1 admit, receive, accept, take, welcome
*refuse, reject*
2 permit, consent to, allow, suffer, endure
*refuse, deny*
3 suppose, concede, open one's doors to, think well of

**adoptar**
1 adopt, foster
*abandon, repudiate*
2 take, accept, admit, approve, welcome
*reject, disapprove*
3 follow, embrace

**adorar**
1 idolize, desire intensely, love intensely
*hate, abhor*
2 adore, worship, revere, venerate
*despise, execrate*

**adornar**
adorn, decorate, beautify, embellish, ornament, deck, array, polish, dress up

**adquirir**
1 get, obtain, reach, achieve, attain
*lose, give, sell*

2 gain, appropriate, take possession of, obtain
*lose, forfeit*
3 contract

**adular**
flatter, compliment, court, humour, inveigle
*offend*

**adulto** *(aj)*
adult, full-grown, mature, of age, ripe
*adolescent, immature*

**advenedizo** *(aj)*
1 foreign, from outside, alien, strange, newly arrived
*native, indigenous*
2 upstart

**adversario**
adversary, opponent, enemy, antagonist, rival, competitor
*ally, friend, partner*

**adversidad**
adversity, misfortune, setback, mishap, calamity, trouble, bad luck
*good fortune, prosperity, happiness*

**advertir**
1 observe, note, notice, take note of, note intently
*overlook*
2 point out, draw attention to
3 warn, caution, inform, notify, advise, counsel

**afable**
affable, amiable, friendly, genial, courteous, attentive unaffected, natural, simple, easy, pleasant, nice
*unfriendly, hostile, uncivil, discourteous*

**afamado**
famous, renowned, celebrated, well-known, distinguished, illustrious, eminent
*undistinguished, unknown*

**afán**
1 desire, urge, eagerness, zeal, anxiety, solicitude
2 earnestness, diligence, great care
3 hard work, industry, exertion, toil, fatigue, tiredness, pain, trouble

**afanoso**
1 hard, heavy, laborious
2 tough, uphill
3 industrious, solicitous
4 feverish, hectic

**afear**
1 make ugly, deface, spoil, disfigure, deform
   *improve, preserve*
2 *(fig)* condemn, censure, decry, reprimand, vituperate
   *approve*

**afección**
1 affection, fondness, tenderness, endearment, inclination
2 *(medicine)* illness, ailment, disease, condition, trouble

**afectación**
   affectation, artificiality, affectedness, unnatural imitation
   *artlessness, unaffectedness*

**afectar**
1 affect, move
2 *(LAm)* hurt, damage, harm
3 *(LAm)* take on, assume

**afectuoso**
   affectionate, loving, tender, lovable, friendly, affable
   *distant, hostile, brusque*

**afeminado** *(aj)*
   effeminate, womanish, womanlike, unmanly
   *manly, virile, masculine*

**aferrar**
1 grasp, grab, seize, grapple, secure, fasten, moor
   *release, disengage, free, unfasten*
2 insist, be obstinate about, not back down

**afianzar**
1 strengthen, fasten, secure, support, prop up
2 guarantee, stand surety (for), answer (for), vouch for
   *repudiate, disclaim*

**afición**
1 inclination, affection, fondness, attachment, devotion, liking (for), taste (for)
   *dislike, aversion*
2 hobby, pastime

**aficionado** *(s)*
   enthusiast, amateur, dilettante, fan, follower, supporter

**afín** *(aj)*
1 similar, related, analogous, equal
2 next, near, contiguous, bordering, adjacent

**afinar**
1 perfect, finish, complete, polish (up), touch (up)
2 specify, determine exactly, fix, be precise, be exact
3 *(technology)* purify, refine, temper, tune (up)
4 sing in tune, play in tune
   *be out of tune*

**afirmar**
1 assure, consolidate, back, strengthen, secure, rest on, be supported by, steady
2 asseverate, confirm, aver, assure, assert, state, affirm
3 ratify, reiterate

**afligir**
1 oppose, impede, grieve, sadden, distress, trouble, torment, mortify
2 distress, lay waste, ruin, depress, afflict
   *console, comfort*
3 *(LAm)* beat, hit

**aflojar(se)**
1 distend, loosen, unfasten, undo, release, set free, let go
   *secure*
2 fork out, pay up, cede
3 abate, weaken, grow cool, get slack, grow weak, get softer
4 come loose, work loose, slacken
   *tighten*

**afluencia**
1 inflow, influx, flow, press, crowd, jam, attendance, number present
2 abundance, plenty
3 eloquence, fluency

**afortunado**
   fortunate, lucky, happy, successful
   *unfortunate*

**afrenta**
>     affront, offence, wrong, dishonour, shame, insult, outrage, abuse, opprobrium, vilification
>     *compliment, courtesy*

**afrentar**
>     offend, insult, injure, vilify, dishonour, outrage, abuse, wrong
>     *praise, honour*

**agarrar(se)**
>     1 grasp, grip, seize, catch hold of, grab, clutch, pick up
>     2 get, wangle
>     3 *(commerce)* corner the market in, pile up stocks of
>     4 take hold (of), stick, *(Br)* take root
>     5 fight, have a fight, quarrel
>     6 hold on
>     *release, let go*
>     7 *(LAm)* pick, catch

**agasajar**
>     1 treat well, fête, give a royal welcome to, feast, wine and dine, entertain royally, regale
>     2 flatter

**ágil**
>     agile, lithe, quick, nimble, lively
>     *slow, lazy, clumsy*

**agitar(se)**
>     1 wave, flap, shake, brandish, stir, stir round, stir up
>     2 stir up, excite, rouse, disturb, worry, upset, make anxious
>     3 wave, wave to and fro, flutter, flap, shake, get rough
>     4 get excited, get worked up, get worried, get upset, upset oneself

**aglomerar**
>     agglomerate, crowd together, collect, pile up, accumulate
>     *separate, disperse*

**agobiar**
>     weigh down, bow down, oppress, burden, overwhelm, fatigue, tire
>     *relieve*

**agonía**
>     1 agony, death throes, death agony
>     2 *(fig)* anguish, agony, torment
>     3 *(fig)* desire, yearning

**agonizar**
>     bother, annoy, irritate, harass, molest, pester, plague, vex
>     *calm, comfort*

**agotar(se)**
>     1 consume, drain, finish, expend, spend, use up, deplete, empty
>     2 debilitate, weaken, exhaust, tire out
>     3 become exhausted, be finished, be used up, give out, run out, sell out
>     4 go out of print
>     5 exhaust oneself, wear oneself out

**agraciado**
>     1 beautiful, lovely, pretty, graceful, nice, attractive
>     *ugly*
>     2 lucky, fortunate
>     *unlucky, unfortunate*

**agraciar**
>     1 concede, favour, authorize, reward
>     2 grace, adorn, make more attractive
>     3 pardon

**agradar**
>     content, satisfy, please, delight, cheer (up), be pleasing to, be to the liking of
>     *displease, dissatisfy*

**agravar**
>     weigh down, make heavier, increase, make worse, aggravate, oppress, burden (with)
>     *lighten, diminish, lessen*

**agregar**
>     1 unite, join together, add, add up, augment, gather, collect
>     *subtract*
>     2 appoint, attach (to the staff of)

**agreste**
>     1 uncultivated, wild, country, rural, untamed, uncivilized
>     *cultivated, civilized*
>     2 *(fig)* rough, uncouth, rude, vulgar

**agriar(se)**
>     1 sour, turn sour
>     2 *(fig)* exasperate, exacerbate, vex, annoy
>     *assuage, calm, pacify, placate*

3 get worse, get exasperated, become embittered

**agrupar(se)**
1 group together, gather, assemble, crowd together
2 form a group, gather, come together, crowd together, cluster, bunch together

**aguantable**
tolerable, bearable, endurable, sufferable, supportable
*unbearable, intolerable, insufferable*

**aguantar**
1 bear, put up with, hold up, sustain, withstand, support, suffer, tolerate, endure
2 control oneself

**aguante**
1 strength, resistance, vigour, energy, stamina
2 suffering, patience, tolerance, fortitude

**aguar**
1 water down
2 *(fig)* spoil, mar, frustrate, perturb, disturb, upset, interrupt

**agudo**
1 sharp, pointed, acute
2 high, high-pitched, shrill, piercing
3 sharp, keen, acute, penetrating, smart, clever, trenchant, penetrating, ready, lively, acute, searching, sharp, pungent
4 *(grammar)* accentuated

**aguijón**
1 thorn, point, prickle, spine
2 *(zoology)* sting
3 point of a goad, goad
4 *(fig)* stimulus, goad, incentive, spur, incitement

**aguzar**
1 file, sharpen, whet
2 *(fig)* incite, stir up, stimulate, goad

**ahínco**
insistence, determination, perseverance, tenacity, firmness, emphasis, effort, earnestness, intentness

**ahogar(se)**
1 drown, asphyxiate, suffocate, smother
2 repress, extinguish, smother, put out
3 choke back, stifle, hold in
4 oppress, fatigue, weary, tire, burden
5 drown oneself

**ahorrar**
1 save, put by, keep, reserve
*spend*
2 economize, save
3 avoid, prevent
4 free (a slave)

**ahorro**
economy, saving, frugality, husbandry, parsimony, thrift

**ahuyentar**
1 drive away, frighten away, put to flight, keep off
2 banish, dispel

**airar**
annoy, irritate, anger, infuriate, make furious, provoke
*appease, pacify*

**airoso**
1 airy, draughty, windy, blowy
2 *(fig)* graceful, elegant, jaunty, successful

**aislado**
1 isolated, cut off, shut off (from), lonely, solitary, retired, remote, quiet
2 *(electricity)* insulated

**aislar**
isolate, separate, detach, cut off, shut off
*unite*

**ajar**
1 crumple, crush, mess up, ruffle, rumple, tamper with, spoil
2 *(fig)* abuse, disparage, humiliate

**ajeno**
1 outside, alien to, foreign to, inconsistent (with), inappropriate (for, to)
2 unaware of, unsuspecting

**ajustar(se)**
1 fit (to, into), fasten, engage

2 adjust/regulate (a machine), put right (an abuse)

3 *(fig)* adjust, adapt to

4 strike (a relationship), make (an agreement), arrange (a marriage), settle/reconcile (differences)

5 settle (an account)

6 fix (a price)

7 hire, engage

8 adjust oneself, get adjusted (to), conform (to), comply (with)

**alabar(se)**

1 celebrate, praise, eulogize, pay tribute to
*offend, injure*

2 think right, approve

3 boast, be pleased, be satisfied

**alarde**

1 *(military)* review

2 *(fig)* show, display, parade, ostentation, vainglory, bragging

3 supreme effort, *(sport)* sprint, dash

**alarmar**

1 alarm, frighten

2 *(military)* alert, rouse, call to arms

**alba**

dawn, dawning, daybreak, sunrise
*sunset*

**albedrío**

1 decision, election, judgement, desire, wish

2 whim, fancy, caprice

3 appetite, taste, pleasure

**albergar**

1 shelter, give shelter to, give refuge to, give hospitality to, give lodgings to, lodge, put up

2 cherish, have, experience

**albor**

1 whiteness

2 dawn, dawn light

**alborotar**

1 agitate, disturb, stir up, perturb, scandalize, shock, yell, shout, raise voices, proclaim
*pacify, soothe, mollify*

2 excite, incite, stir up, incite to rebel, rouse to revolt

3 excite, arouse the curiosity of

**alboroto**

1 tumult, sedition, revolt, uprising, mutiny

2 shouting, din, uproar, racket, brawl, riot

3 scare, shock, alarm

**alborozo**

merriment, rejoicing, pleasure, joy, content(ment)

**alcance**

1 reach

2 *(military)* range, scope, grasp, importance, significance

3 chase, pursuit

4 *(commerce)* adverse balance, deficit

5 stop-press (news)

6 intelligence, capacity, talent

**alcanzar**

1 catch, catch up (with), overtake, catch (train, post)
*lose, miss*

2 achieve, get, obtain, attain
*lose*

3 hit, *(ball, bullet)* strike

4 reach, amount to

5 reach to, perceive, take in

6 live into the period of, live on into the time of

7 grasp, catch hold of, get, obtain

8 grasp, understand, comprehend

**alegrar**

1 animate, excite, please, cause to rejoice, gladden

2 animate, brighten up, enliven, cheer up

3 excite, stir up

4 slacken (sail)

**alegre**

1 happy, merry, glad, carefree, cheerful, gay, sunny, good, *(news)* cheering, *(colour)* bright, *(day, period)* happy, *(weather)* pleasant

2 bold, reckless

3 risqué, blue

4 fast, immoral

**alegría**

1 happiness, joy, gladness, cheerfulness, gaiety, merriment, brightness

2 recklessness, irresponsibility

**alejar**
separate, remove, withdraw, retire, divert, sidetrack, turn aside
*approach, draw near*

**alentar**
1 encourage, cheer, inspire, *(LAm)* applaud, clap
2 stiffen, bolster up
3 *(spirits)* raise, buoy up

**aletargar**
make sleepy, make drowsy, make lethargic, put to sleep, numb
*enliven, animate, rouse*

**alevosía**
treachery, treason, betrayal, disloyalty, faithlessness, perfidy, perfidiousness
*loyalty, faithfulness*

**algarabía**
shouting, uproar, confusion, hullabaloo, gibberish

**álgido**
icy, chilly, crucial, decisive
*warm*

**alianza**
1 alliance, union, confederation, league, union
2 marriage, partnership
3 wedding ring

**aliar(se)**
1 unite, ally, combine, associate, merge, confederate
*disunite, separate*
2 form an alliance

**alicaído**
sad, downhearted, disheartened, dejected, downcast
*happy, optimistic*

**aliciente**
attraction, incentive, stimulus, spur, inducement, impulse

**aliento**
1 breath, breathing, exhalation, respiration
2 puff, gust, breath
3 *(fig)* spirit, effort, courage, mettle, resolution
*apathy, indifference, unconcern*

**aligerar**
1 quicken, hurry, accelerate
*delay*
2 lighten, alleviate, relieve, moderate, attenuate, lessen, minimize
*aggravate, intensify, make worse*

**alimentar**
1 feed, nourish, sustain, maintain
2 support, keep going, nourish, foment

**alimenticio**
nourishing, nutritious, strengthening, invigorating, wholesome
*unwholesome*

**aliñar**
1 garnish, season
2 beautify, deck, array, polish, dress up, embellish
*disfigure*

**alisar**
polish, burnish, touch up, smooth
*dull, tarnish, wrinkle, crease*

**alistar**
register, enrol, inscribe, matriculate, affiliate
*erase, obliterate, remove*

**aliviar**
1 lighten, unload, relieve, alleviate, ease
*burden*
2 moderate, mitigate, soothe, soften, improve, recover

**almacenar**
store, put in storage, stock up with, gather together, collect, assemble
*distribute, spend*

**alocado**
crazy, foolish, silly, idiotic, mad
*sane, sensible*

**alojar**
lodge, shelter, put up, accommodate, quarter
*eject, expel*

**altanería**
arrogance, haughtiness, disdain, pride, snobbishness, scorn, superciliousness
*humility*

**altanero**
arrogant, haughty, disdainful, overbearing, contemptuous, scornful, supercilious
*humble, servile*

**alteración**
1 alteration, disturbance, change, variation
2 start, scare, shock, perturbation, confusion, overturning

**alterar**
1 alter, change, move, disturb, vary
2 perturb, disturb, confuse, worry, trouble, overturn, upset

**alteza**
1 height, elevation, altitude
*bottom, depth*
2 sublimity, excellence

**altivez**
arrogance, haughtiness, pride, disdain, scorn, contempt
*humility, modesty*

**alucinación**
bewilderment, confusion, blindness, hallucination, illusion
*reality*

**alumbrar**
clarify, illumine, illuminate, brighten, light (up)
*darken*

**alza**
rise, increase, price increase, elevation, *(military)* sight, *(Am)* raise

**alzar**
1 raise, elevate, lift (up), turn up, *(agriculture)* gather, climb, *(LAm)* pick up
*lower, descend*
2 *(fig)* ascend, exalt
*descend*

**allanar**
1 smooth, level, roll flat, flatten, level off, even out
2 *(fig)* surmount, resolve, vanquish, subdue, overcome, master

**allegado**
1 relation, relative
2 partial, partisan
3 near, close, neighbouring, adjacent, adjoining

**allegar**
1 approach, come near, approximate, bring close
2 gather together, assemble, collect, aggregate, amass
*disperse, scatter*

**amabilidad**
amiability, kindness, benignity, friendliness, humanity, niceness, sympathy
*animosity*

**amable**
affable, courteous, attentive, affectionate, sociable, friendly, nice, congenial, sympathetic
*unkind, unsociable, unfriendly*

**amainar**
slacken, loosen, undo, relax, give in, yield, diminish, decline, grow weak

**amanecer**
dawn, dawning, daybreak, sunrise
*sunset*

**amaneramiento**
affectation, artificiality, mannerism, unnatural imitation
*artlessness, unaffectedness*

**amansar**
1 domesticate, train, tame, subdue
2 quieten, calm, reassure, pacify, mitigate, ease, tranquillize, *(Am)* tranquilize
*excite*

**amar**
love, adore, worship, like
*hate, abhor*

**amargura**
bitterness, affliction, pain, grief, sorrow, tribulation, distress, suffering
*sweetness, solace, comfort*

**amarrar**
fasten, tie up, secure, pinion, shackle, chain, moor, *(LAm)* tie
*loosen, untie, release*

**amedrentar**
intimidate, threaten, terrify, frighten, scare, alarm
*reassure*

**amenguar**
1 diminish, reduce, lessen, decrease, contract, curtail
*increase*
2 *(fig)* dishonour, discredit, humiliate
*honour, dignify*

**ameno**
agreeable, pleasant, delightful, entertaining, charming, friendly, amusing
*disagreeable*

**amigable**
amiable, friendly, cordial, fraternal, neighbourly
*ill-natured, unfriendly*

**amistad**
friendship, devotion, affection, fondness, intimacy, love
*enmity*

**amo**
master, proprietor, employer, boss, chief
*employee, underling*

**amoldar**
1 adjust, adapt, accommodate
2 conform, come to an agreement, reach a compromise, submit, accept
*disagree*

**amontonar**
assemble, amass, accumulate, pile up, put together, collect, gather together
*disperse, scatter*

**amor**
love, amity, affection, fondness, liking, passion
*hatred*

**amortiguar**
diminish, lessen, minimize, mitigate, moderate, alleviate, deaden, muffle

**amparo**
1 asylum, refuge, shelter, defence, help, aid
2 protection, favour, support
*abandonment*

**amplio**
ample, extensive, vast, spacious, wide, capacious, roomy, loose, baggy, full
*restricted*

**amputar**
amputate, cut off, curtail, lop, remove, sever, truncate

**amueblar**
furnish, equip, fit, provide, supply, stock

**analfabeto**
illiterate, uneducated, unlettered, untaught, untutored
*literate, educated*

**análisis**
1 analysis, breakdown, distinction, separation, segregation, dissection
*synthesis*
2 study, observation, examination

**anarquía**
1 anarchy
2 *(fig)* chaos, disorder, confusion, indiscipline, misrule, lawlessness, riot

**anatema**
anathema, excommunication, malediction, imprecation, curse, proscription, ban, prohibition
*blessing*

**ancho**
1 wide, ample, broad, capacious, spacious, vast, full
*narrow, constricted*
2 *(fig)* liberal, open-handed
3 *(fig)* arrogant, conceited, smug, self-satisfied

**andar**
1 go, walk, travel
2 function, *(machine)* work, go
*stop*

**andrajoso**
tattered, ragged, in rags, torn, broken
*neat*

**anegar**
flood, deluge, inundate, engulf, submerge, swamp, sink, drown, capsize

**anfitrión**
    host, landlord, proprietor, inn-keeper, entertainer
    *guest*

**angustia**
    anguish, distress, grief, pain, af-fliction, torture, agony
    *tranquillity*

**anhelar**
    crave, desire, be eager for, long for, yearn for, want
    *disdain, ignore*

**animación**
    activity, bustle, liveliness, ani-mation, spirit, vivacity
    *dullness, lifelessness*

**animado**
  1 animated, lively, spirited, stirring, vivacious
    *dull, torpid*
  2 encouraged, comforted
  3 agitated, heated, excited

**animadversión**
    animadversion, antipathy, ani-mosity, ill-will, antagonism
    *sympathy, friendliness*

**animar**
  1 animate, give life to, revive
  2 *(fig)* cheer up, liven up, brighten up, stimulate, provoke, move, en-courage, comfort
    *depress*

**ánimo**
  1 valour, intrepidity, bravery, cour-age, soul, heart
  2 intention, will-power, design, pur-pose, aim, idea, thought

**aniquilar**
    annihilate, destroy, exterminate, ruin, extirpate
    *construct, conserve*

**anónimo**
  1 anonymous, nameless, uniden-tified, unacknowledged, unattes-ted
  2 *(commerce)* limited

**ansia**
  1 aspiration, desire, eagerness, anxiety, yearning
  2 affliction, tribulation, anguish, distress, grief, anxiety

**antagonista**
    antagonist, adversary, rival, en-emy, opponent
    *ally, friend*

**antecedente** *(aj)*
    antecedent, anterior, preceding, previous
    *later*

**antiguo**
    old, archaic, remote, ancient, former
    *new, young, modern*

**antipatía**
    antipathy, dislike, aversion, ani-madversion, repugnance, abhor-rence, disaffection, ill-will, re-vulsion
    *sympathy*

**anudar**
  1 knot, tie, unite, join together, secure
    *untie*
  2 continue, renew

**anular**
  1 annul, revoke, repeal, cancel, abolish, suppress, remove
  2 deprive of authority, deny, inca-pacitate, render unfit, disqualify
    *authorize, confirm, consolidate*

**anunciar**
    announce, proclaim, predict, pre-sage, augur, prognosticate, *(com-merce)* advertise

**añadidura**
    addition, complement, extra, ex-tension, appendage
    *reduction*

**añejo**
    old, ancient, mature, *(wine)* mel-low
    *immature*

**aojar**
    bewitch, fascinate, charm, en-trance, captivate

**apacible**
    mild, gentle, pacific, tranquil, calm, quiet, restful, agreeable

**apaciguar**
    mollify, pacify, placate, appease, soothe, tranquillize, calm, quieten

**apagar**
    1 put out, extinguish, turn off, silence, muffle, suffocate, quench (thirst)
    2 repress, hold back, retain, stifle, contain
    3 reduce, lessen, soften, weaken

**apañar**
    1 pick up, collect, gather, save
    2 pick up, take hold of, grasp
    3 deck, array, compose, tidy up, dress
    4 mend, patch up, repair

**aparente**
    apparent, clear, evident, manifest, obvious, plain, unmistakable, suitable, adequate
    *dubious, uncertain, unsuitable*

**apartar**
    1 select, choose, pick
    2 separate, disunite, distance, divide, remove, extract
    3 estrange, turn aside, abandon, quit, withdraw
    4 dissuade, distract

**apasionado**
    impassioned, passionate, biased, prejudiced

**apasionante**
    thrilling, exciting, gripping, moving
    *tame, unexciting*

**apasionar**
    excite, arouse, incite, provoke, stimulate, stir up, whet

**apenar**
    afflict, sadden, grieve, distress, trouble, embarrass
    *console*

**apercibir**
    1 prepare, foresee, anticipate, get ready (for)
    2 warn, notify, advise, inform
    3 (*LAm*) notice, see, observe

**apertura**
    opening, inauguration, beginning, commencement

    *closure*

**apetito**
    1 appetite, necessity, hunger
    2 inclination, desire, craving, hankering

**apetitoso**
    appetizing, tasty, savoury, rich, delicate, tempting

**aplastar**
    1 crush, squeeze, squash flat
    2 confound, humiliate, shame, embarrass, depress

**aplaudir**
    applaud, cheer, clap, commend, praise, eulogize, celebrate

**aplazar**
    prorogue, postpone, delay, defer, put off
    *expedite*

**aplicación**
    1 adaptation
    2 assiduity, attention, study, perseverance, application

**aplicado**
    diligent, attentive, assiduous, studious, persevering, tireless, hardworking, industrious
    *lazy*

**aplomo**
    aplomb, gravity, serenity, circumspection, self-assurance
    *diffidence, self-effacement, timidity*

**apocado**
    pusillanimous, timid, cowardly, scared, bashful, recreant
    *brave*

**apocar**
    1 diminish, lessen, reduce, shorten, limit, narrow
    2 humiliate, beat down, humble, reduce
    3 scare, intimidate, frighten

**apócrifo**
    apocryphal, unauthentic, false, sham, fake, hypothetical
    *genuine, true, authentic*

**apogeo**
    apogee, splendour, plenitude, magnificence, climax
    *base, nadir, decadence*

**apoyar**
1 lean, rest (on), be supported by, load up, shoulder, bear
2 confirm, sustain, second, authorize
3 *(fig)* favour, help, support, back, defend, protect

**apoyo**
support, backing, favour, help, protection, patronage

**apreciar**
1 estimate, evaluate, value, rate, *(LAm)* be grateful for, appreciate
2 estimate, consider, deem, esteem, value
3 perceive, notice, see, observe, *(LAm)* become aware of
4 *(commerce)* appreciate

**aprehender**
apprehend, detain, capture, take hold of, catch, arrest, seize, imprison
*release, set free, liberate*

**apremiar**
1 squeeze, *(fig)* oppress
2 urge, urge on, hurry, compel, force

**aprensión**
apprehension, fear, distrust, scruple, suspicion

**aprestar**
prepare, arrange, get ready, dispose

**apresurar**
expedite, accelerate, speed up, quicken, hurry, precipitate

**apretar**
1 narrow, compress, squeeze, tighten, press together
2 oppress, afflict, importune, hound, pester, distress

**aprisionar**
1 capture, imprison, catch, arrest, seize
*set free*
2 bind, tie, seize, grasp, fasten, subject, subjugate
*untie, unbind, set free, liberate*

**aprobación**
approbation, approval, acquiescence, consent, assent, conformity
*disapproval*

**aprobar**
1 approve, assent, consent, admit, conform
2 pass (exams)

**apropiado**
appropriate, adequate, opportune, convenient, suitable
*inappropriate, inopportune, inadequate, inconvenient, unsuitable*

**apropiar**
1 apply, accommodate
2 appropriate, take possession of, usurp, arrogate, seize

**aprovechado**
diligent, studious, hardworking, industrious, thrifty, unscrupulous

**aprovechar**
1 serve, be useful, be worth, be of use
2 exploit, profit from, take advantage of

**aproximar**
bring close, bring near, approach, join, unite

**aptitud**
aptitude, capacity, disposition, sufficiency, competence, suitability
*inability, ineptitude, incompetence*

**apuesto** *(aj)*
1 decked, arrayed, adorned
2 elegant, graceful, neat

**apurado**
1 needy, poor, indigent
2 difficult, arduous, dangerous
3 exact, precise

**apurar**
1 purify, purge
2 finish, consume, exhaust, drain, use up
3 afflict, distress, grieve, annoy
4 compel, force, hurry, hasten, accelerate

**aquietar**
pacify, calm (down), quieten, appease, placate
*provoke, excite*

**arcaico**
   archaic, antiquated, old, old-fashioned, out-moded
   *modern, up-to-date*

**ardiente**
   1 burning
   2 *(fig)* fervid, fervent, vehement, spirited, passionate
   *cold*

**arduo**
   arduous, difficult, laborious, toilsome, exhausting
   *easy, simple*

**argumentar**
   argue, object, refute, contradict, discuss, impugn

**árido**
   1 arid, dry, sterile, unproductive
   *fecund*
   2 monotonous, boring, tedious, wearisome

**arisco**
   surly, unsociable, intractable, sullen, gloomy

**armonía**
   harmony, concord, consonance, conformity, agreement, concert, peace
   *discord*

**aromático**
   aromatic, fragrant, perfumed, odoriferous, scented
   *fetid, ill-smelling*

**arrasar**
   1 level, flatten out, smooth
   2 demolish, destroy, devastate, ruin, wreck
   *rebuild*

**arrear**
   urge, drive on, impel, instigate, press
   *deter*

**arrebatado**
   1 precipitate, impetuous
   2 violent, enraged

**arrebato**
   1 sudden start, sudden impulse, impetus
   2 fit of rage, fury, choler
   3 rapture, trance, ecstasy

**arreciar**
   augment, increase, enlarge, extend
   *abate, decrease*

**arriesgado**
   1 risky, dangerous, exposed
   2 daring, audacious, reckless, imprudent

**arriesgar**
   1 risk, expose, venture
   2 dare, take a risk

**arrogancia**
   1 haughtiness, arrogance, pride, scorn, disdain
   2 valour, courage, spirit, dash

**arrojar**
   1 throw, hurl, fling, fire, shoot
   2 emit, give out, send out, *(LAm)* bring/throw up
   3 *(commerce)* yield, produce
   4 attack, assault

**arrostrar**
   defy, confront, oppose, resist, challenge, face up to

**arruinar**
   ruin, wreck, destroy, demolish, devastate, *(LAm)* deflower
   *construct, erect, build*

**artero**
   astute, clever, smart, artful, crafty, cunning
   *artless, open, frank*

**asco**
   revulsion, repugnance, nausea, loathing, disgust

**aseado**
   clean, tidy, neat, smart, orderly, spruce
   *untidy, dirty*

**asediar**
   1 blockade, lay siege to, besiege, surround, fence in
   2 *(fig)* importune, molest, hound, pester, pursue relentlessly

**asegurar**
   1 consolidate, strengthen, secure, fix
   2 guarantee, warrant, pledge
   3 affirm, asseverate, certify, confirm, ratify, assure

**asenso**
assent, approval, approbation, acquiescence, consent
*dissent, disapproval*

**asentir**
assent, affirm, approve, agree, consent
*disagree, dissent*

**asequible**
available, accessible, attainable, approachable, reasonable

**aseverar**
asseverate, affirm, confirm, aver, declare, maintain, assert
*deny*

**asir**
seize, catch, take, grasp, grab, apprehend
*loose, release*

**asistir**
1 be present at, attend
2 help, support, favour
*desert, abandon*

**asociar**
associate, join, unite, reunite, affiliate
*dissociate*

**asolar**
1 destroy, devastate, demolish, raze, flatten
2 settle, *(liquids)* deposit

**asombro**
amazement, astonishment, fright, fear, scare
*indifference*

**áspero**
1 rough, uneven, *(fig)* difficult, tough
2 *(fig)* rigid, rigorous, rude, unpleasant
*civil, pleasant*
3 intractable, sullen, gloomy, surly

**asqueroso**
repugnant, nauseating, repellent, repulsive

**astucia**
1 astuteness, sagacity, subtlety, craftiness, slyness
2 ploy, trick, gimmick

**asustar**
startle, frighten, scare, intimidate, terrify

**atacar**
1 fill, stuff, pack, press together
2 attack, assault
3 oppose, refute, impugn

**atajar**
1 interrupt, detain, stop, hold back, contain
2 be ashamed, be embarrassed
3 *(LAm)* catch, catch in flight

**ataque**
1 aggression, attack, assault
2 accident, attack, fit

**atar**
bind, tie, tie up, secure, fasten
*loosen, untie*

**atascar**
1 obstruct, *(fig)* hinder, stop up, blind, bar, bolt
2 get stuck, get into a jam

**ataviar**
1 deck, array, compose, adorn, beautify, decorate, polish, dress (up)
2 *(LAm)* adjust, adapt, accommodate

**atender**
1 hear, listen, notice
2 care for, look after, watch over, be vigilant, keep watch, attend to
*neglect*

**atenerse**
abide by, adhere to, subject oneself, adapt oneself, adjust

**atropellar**
1 knock down, run down, run over, push
2 *(LAm)* make love to, seduce, dishonour

**aventar**
1 fan, blow, winnow
2 *(LAm)* throw (out), chuck out

**aviar**
1 equip, supply, provide, prepare, get ready
2 *(LAm)* advance money, lend equipment, provide with food

# B

**bajada**
slope, descent, drop, fall, declivity
*ascent*

**bajar**
1 diminish, decrease, lessen, decline
*increase*
2 lower, lower the price of, reduce
*raise, put up*
3 haul down (a flag)
4 get down, get out of, dismount, descend
*ascend, get into*
5 humiliate, humble, mortify, shame
*exalt*

**bajeza**
lowliness, abjectness, ruin, baseness, vileness, degradation
*dignity, pride*

**bajo**
1 cheap, moderate, reasonable
*expensive*
2 short, small, stunted
*tall*
3 faint, soft, low
4 abject, base, degrading, vile, menial, vulgar
*noble, lofty*

**bajón**
decline, decrease, diminish, fall, drop
*increase, rise*

**balancear**
1 balance, vibrate, sway, fluctuate
2 oscillate, swing, rock
3 vacillate, doubt, hesitate
*decide*

**balanceo**
1 balancing, fluctuation
2 oscillation, swinging, to-and-fro movement

**balbucear**
stammer, stutter

**baldío**
1 wild, deserted, uncultivated
*inhabited*
2 barren, infecund, infertile, unfruitful, unproductive
*fecund, fertile, productive*

**banda**
1 band, gang, faction, clique, set, group, party, coterie
2 band, strip, strap, belt, *(LAm)* fan belt

**bandera**
flag, standard, insignia, banner, streamer, ensign, pennon, pennant, colours

**bandido**
bandit, brigand, thief, marauder, outlaw, footpad, highwayman

**baratija**
trinket, trifle, junk

**barbaridad**
1 barbarity, barbarism, ferocity, cruelty, inhumanity, fierceness
2 atrocity, outrage, hugeness, immensity
3 foolish remark

**bárbaro** *(aj)*
1 barbarous, savage, fierce, ferocious, cruel, inhuman, brutal
*cultured, refined*
2 uncouth, coarse, rough, atrocious, awful
*refined*

**bárbaro** *(s)*
barbarian, ruffian, savage, boor, brute, philistine

**barco**
boat, ship, vessel, barque

**barranco**
1 ravine, gorge, gully, defile, pass, fissure, cleft, *(LAm)* cliff
2 difficulty, embarrassment, impediment, obstruction, obstacle

**barraca**
1 hut, cabin, cot, cottage, lodge, shack, shanty, hovel, den, booth
2 (LAm) large storage shed, market stall

**barrenar**
1 drill, bore, make holes in
2 infringe, contravene

**barrer**
1 sweep, sweep away, brush, clean, clear, remove
*dirty*
2 free, clear, make something disappear, remove

**barrera**
1 barrier, fence, hurdle
2 obstacle, impediment

**barullo**
1 confusion, disorder, muddle, mess
2 tumult, uproar, commotion, disturbance, row

**basura**
1 dirtiness, dirt, filth
2 litter, (Br) rubbish, (Am) garbage

**basto**
1 rude, bad-mannered, unpolished, crude, vulgar, coarse, common
*refined, cultured*
2 rough, coarse

**batir**
1 strike, knock, knock down, beat, punch, whip, spank
2 defeat, rout, vanquish, crush
3 fight, combat, battle, struggle, war
4 beat, mix, whisk
5 (medicine) explore, scan, probe, examine, search

**beato**
1 blessed, pious, devout
2 hypocritical, prudish

**belén**
1 crib, manger
2 crèche
3 confusion, disorder, muddle, mess, trouble, tangle, mix-up
*order*

**bellaco** (aj)
1 cunning, sly, crafty, tricky, wily, artful
*artless*

2 wicked, rascally, roguish
3 (LAm) brave

**bellaco** (s)
rogue, villain, scoundrel, scamp, knave
*gentleman*

**bello**
1 beautiful, lovely, handsome
*ugly*
2 elegant, exquisite, choice, admirable
*inelegant, unrefined*

**bendecir**
1 bless, adore, exalt, glorify, magnify, worship, extol
*abhor, execrate, curse, hate*
2 bless, sanctify, consecrate

**bendito**
1 blessed, sacred, holy, saintly
2 blessed, happy, lucky, fortunate
*cursed, unhappy, unlucky, unfortunate*
3 simple, natural, unaffected, candid, frank, naïve

**beneficiar**
1 benefit, be of benefit to, favour, help
*harm, damage*
2 exploit, use, utilize, profit by, profit from, take advantage of
3 (LAm) (animal) slaughter, (person) kill, shoot
4 (LAm) (land) cultivate, (mine) exploit, work, (mineral) process, refine, (agriculture) process

**beneficio**
1 benefit, advantage, boon, favour, service, good
*disadvantage, injury*
2 benefit, emolument, return, profit, gain, acquisition, winnings
*loss*
3 (LAm) killing, slaughter, slaughtering
4 (LAm) (agriculture) cultivation, (mine) exploitation, (mineral) processing, smelting, treating

**beneficioso**
    beneficial, profitable, useful, productive, lucrative, favourable, advantageous, fruitful
    *disadvantageous, unprofitable, useless, unproductive*

**beneplácito**
    1 approval, consent, permission
    *disapproval*
    2 acquiescence, agreement, assent
    *denial, refusal*

**benevolencia**
    benevolence, kindness, indulgence, hospitality, kindliness, generosity, beneficence

**benévolo**
    benevolent, kind, benign, indulgent, magnanimous, generous, bountiful, philanthropic, charitable, beneficent, obliging, helpful, propitious
    *egoistic, selfish*

**benigno**
    1 benevolent, kind, good, indulgent, human, humane, merciful
    *disobliging*
    2 temperate, mild, gentle, soft, sweet
    *harsh*

**berrinche**
    1 temper, tantrum, whim, fit, ill-humour
    2 *(LAm)* pong, stink

**bestia** *(aj)*
    ignorant, stupid, foolish, simple, brutish, barbarous, coarse, rough, uncouth, unpolished

**bestia** *(s)*
    1 beast, animal
    2 idiot, fool, simpleton, imbecile

**bestial**
    1 bestial, brutal, inhuman, barbarous, cruel, brutish, depraved, gross, vile, irrational
    *human, rational*
    2 marvellous, terrific, great

**bien** *(s)*
    favour, mercy, benefit, advantage, profit, gain
    *disadvantage, loss, evil*

**bienaventurado**
    1 blessed, saintly
    2 happy, fortunate, lucky
    *unhappy, unfortunate, unlucky*
    3 candid, frank, simple, naïve, innocent, unwary
    *artful, secretive*

**bienes**
    capital, riches, wealth, property

**bienestar**
    1 comfort, convenience
    *discomfort, inconvenience*
    2 abundance, riches, luxury, comfortable living, welfare, well-being, weal
    *poverty, penury, misfortune*

**bienhechor** *(aj)*
    beneficent, charitable, benevolent, munificent, bounteous

**bienhechor** *(s)*
    benefactor, protector

**bizarría**
    1 gallantry, valour, bravery, vigour, effort
    *cowardice, fear*
    2 generosity, show, magnificence, splendour, *(Am)* splendor
    *meanness, dullness*

**bizarro**
    1 valiant, brave, energetic, vigorous
    *cowardly*
    2 generous, splendid, magnificent
    *mean, dull*
    3 gallant, dashing

**blando**
    1 gentle, tender, mild, benignant, soft, sweet
    2 cowardly, weak

**blandura**
    1 gentleness, smoothness, softness, sweetness
    *harshness*
    2 tenderness, soft-heartedness, compassion, sympathy, humaneness, humanity
    *hardness, harshness*
    3 kindness, clemency, indulgence
    *cruelty*

**blasfemar**

blaspheme, swear, curse, vituperate

*praise, extol*

**blasfemia**

blasphemy, profanity, swearing, curse, malediction, oath

**bloquear**

1 block, obstruct, hinder, impede, stop, blockade, besiege, lay siege to, surround

*clear*

2 isolate

3 freeze, immobilize

**bobada**

nonsense, foolishness, foolish action, foolish statement, silliness, stupidity

**bobo** *(aj)*

simple, daft, naïve, silly, foolish, stupid, idiotic

*smart, clever*

**bobo** *(s)*

simpleton, fool, idiot

**bocado**

1 mouthful, bite

2 bit, bridle

**bochornoso**

1 sultry, muggy, thundery, stifling, oppressive

*cool, fresh*

2 embarrassing, disconcerting, distressing

**bofetada**

slap, smack, blow

**bombo** *(aj)*

stunned, surprised

**bombo** *(s)*

1 drum

2 praise, eulogy, encomium

3 poster, advertisement, advertising

**bondad**

1 benignity, benevolence, generosity, kindness, goodness, magnanimity, humaneness, humanity

*cruelty*

2 affability, indulgence, clemency, tolerance, gentleness, meekness, sweetness

**bonito**

beautiful, lovely, pretty, attractive, fair, elegant, bonny, comely, nice

*ugly*

**borde**

border, edge, margin, side, rim, hem, end, extreme

**borrar**

delete, expunge, efface, obliterate, cancel

**borrascoso**

1 tempestuous, stormy

2 disordered, uncontrolled, unbridled

**borrón**

1 stain, mark

2 stain, blemish, defect, imperfection, flaw

**borroso**

1 stained, soiled, blemished, tarnished

2 smudged, illegible, blurred, dimmed, obscure

3 confused, nebulous, vague, unclear

*clear*

**botar**

1 throw, hurl, bowl

2 dismiss, evict, throw out, fire, sack, *(LAm)* throw away, chuck out

3 jump, jump about, leap

**botón**

1 button, switch, knob

2 leaf bud, bud, shoot, tip

**bravío**

1 wild, untamed, fierce, indomitable, savage, ferocious

*tame*

2 wild, rough

**bravo**

1 brave, bold, daring, dauntless, intrepid, fearless, valiant, valorous, courageous, fine, splendid

*cowardly, craven*

2 fierce, ferocious, savage, untamed, wild, cruel

*tame*

3 wild, rough, stormy
*calm*

4 (*LAm*) hot, strong

**bravura**

1 bravery, valour, courage
*cowardice, timidity*

2 ferocity, fierceness
*gentleness*

**brega**

1 argument, brawl, quarrel, fight,
struggle, conflict, battle

2 hard work, bustle, labour, fatigue,
weariness

**breve** (*aj*)

brief, short, terse, concise, curt,
succinct, compendious
*lengthy, prolix, rambling, verbose,
wordy*

**breve** (*s*)

papal brief

**brevedad**

brevity, succinctness, conciseness,
terseness, shortness, condensation
*prolixity*

**bribón** (*aj*)

1 idle, lazy

2 dishonest, sly, cunning, mischievous, villainous

**bribón** (*s*)

rascal, rogue, scoundrel, villain,
swine, scamp
*gentleman*

**brillante** (*aj*)

1 brilliant, resplendent, shining,
refulgent
*dull, tarnished*

2 (*fig*) admirable, excellent, lucid

**brillante** (*s*)

diamond

**brillar**

1 shine, sparkle, dazzle

2 (*fig*) shine, excel

**brillo**

1 brilliance, shine, lustre, brightness
*opacity*

2 (*fig*) brilliance, splendour, renown, fame, glory
*obscurity*

**brío**

1 spirit, resolution, effort, strength,
courage
*indecision*

2 spirit, dash, grace, elegance, gal-
lantry

**brioso**

spirited, lively, bold, courageous,
energetic, vivacious
*calm*

**broma**

1 joke, trick, jest, quip, witticism

2 fun, merriment, sport, frolic,
diversion

**bronca**

1 row, dispute, quarrel, brawl, fight,
uproar, tumult
*peace, tranquility*

2 fuss, commotion, agitation, excitement, stir, bustle, flurry

3 reprimand, rebuke
*praise*

**bronco**

1 rude, surly, bad-mannered, uncouth, coarse, vulgar, crude
*polite*

2 harsh, hoarse, raucous
*gentle, tender*

3 harsh, rough, intractable, unsociable, sullen, gloomy

**brumoso**

1 nebulous, hazy, misty, cloudy
*clear*

2 obscure, incomprehensible, confused, hazy
*clear, comprehensible*

**brusco**

1 brusque, abrupt, curt, blunt,
harsh, unpleasant, rude, discourteous
*gentle, mild, pleasant, polite, cour-
teous*

2 sudden, unexpected, unforeseen
*foreseen, expected*

**brutalidad**

brutality, cruelty, bestiality, ferocity, rudeness
*humanity, culture*

**bruto** *(aj)*
  1 stupid, foolish, incapable
    *sensible*
  2 unbridled, uncontrolled, brutish,
    vicious, depraved
  3 coarse, unpolished, rude, bad-
    mannered, vulgar, crude
  4 *(LAm)* silly, foolish

**bruto** *(s)*
  1 brute, animal
  2 *(weight, income)* gross

**bueno**
  1 good, kind, indulgent, benevol-
    ent, charitable, virtuous, pleasant,
    compassionate
    *bad, unpleasant*
  2 right, exact, true, proper, suitable
  3 pretty, beautiful
    *ugly*

**bulto**
  1 volume, size, mass, bulk, body
  2 package, bundle, bale, load,
    burden, *(LAm)* briefcase, bag
  3 lump, swelling

**bulla**
  din, uproar, confusion, racket,
  row, commotion, rumpus, *(LAm)*
  quarrel, fight, brawl

**bullicio**
  bustle, noise, uproar, racket,
  rumpus, commotion, gibberish

**burla**
  1 jibe, taunt, jeer
  2 joke
  3 trick, hoax, fraud, practical joke

**burlas**
  1 mockery, ridicule
  2 joking, fun

# C

**cabal**
finished, completed, right, exact, whole, entire, honest, just , fair
*incomplete, dishonest*

**cábala**
1 cabal, intrigue, clique, coalition, conspiracy
2 conjecture, guess, supposition

**caballero**
gentleman, nobleman, aristocrat, peer

**cabaña**
cabin, hut, shack

**cabecera**
1 head, bedside
2 title, heading, headline

**cabeza**
1 head
*foot*
2 intelligence, talent, capacity, judgement, brains
3 person, individual
4 chief, director, superior
5 capital
6 beast, animal
7 origin, beginning, start, top, summit

**cabo**
1 point, extreme, extremity, end, limit
2 handle, haft, helve, stock
3 end, finish, close
*start, beginning*
4 promontory, cape
5 cable, rope, cord

**cacarear**
cackle, boast, brag, crow, exaggerate

**caco**
thief, pickpocket, *(fig)* coward

**cadena**
1 series, succession, continuation, link, connection, chain
2 *(fig)* subjection, dependence, slavery

**cadencia**
cadence, rhythm, movement, measure
*dissonance, discord*

**caducar**
1 become senile, become old
2 expire, go out of date, cease, terminate, stop, end

**caduco** *(aj)*
1 senile, very old, decrepit
*potent, strong, young*
2 *(botany)* deciduous
3 fleeting, passing, transitory, perishable
4 *(law, commerce)* out of date, expired, invalid

**caer**
1 decline, descend, go down, collapse, drop, fall down
*rise, lift, raise*
2 disappear, die, perish, succumb
3 suit, fall, *(clothes)* fit
4 collapse, fall

**caída**
1 descent, slope, decline, decadence, collapse, drop, fall
2 lapse

**calamidad**
calamity, disaster, misfortune, catastrophe, mischance, mishap, adversity
*fortune, good luck*

**calar**
1 soak, saturate, drench, permeate
2 penetrate, perforate, pierce, go through
3 size up, see through, penetrate
4 *(fig)* humiliate

**cálculo**
1 calculation, count, computation
2 conjecture, supposition, guess, hypothesis, assumption, theory, surmise
3 *(medicine)* gallstone, stone

**calibre**
1 calibre, bore, diameter, gauge, measure
2 *(fig)* scope, faculty, ability, talent

**calificar**
1 qualify, characterize
   *disqualify, discredit*
2 baptize, christen, call, brand (as)

**calma**
1 calm, fair weather
2 peace, tranquillity, repose, serenity, quiet(ness)
3 apathy, slowness, phlegm
4 *(commerce, finance)* calm, inactivity, lull

**calmante**
sedative, palliative, analgesic, narcotic, tranquillizer

**calmar(se)**
1 calm down, reassure, quieten, calm, put to sleep, pacify
   *excite, stimulate*
2 mitigate, moderate, palliate, soothe
3 *(wind)* fall

**calmoso**
1 calm, quiet, tranquil
2 apathetic, indolent, late, slow, phlegmatic
   *active, nervous*

**calor**
1 heat, warmth
   *cold*
2 *(fig)* ardour, fervour, vivacity, enthusiasm, energy, fever, passion, intensity, vehemence
   *cold, indifference*

**calumnia**
calumny, false accusation, false imputation, defamation, libel, slander, obloquy, vilification, vituperation
   *commendation*

**callado**
silent, uncommunicative, reticent, taciturn, reserved, discreet
   *communicative*

**cámara**
1 room, chamber, hall

2 *(nautical)* stateroom, cabin, saloon
3 *(agriculture)* granary, barn
4 *(politics)* Parliament, Spanish Cortes

**cambiar**
1 exchange, permute, swap, switch
2 vary, change, transmute, transform, alter, convert, modify, transfigure, transfer, move
   *stay, remain, place, locate, site, ratify*

**cambio**
1 alteration, change, move, switch, shift
2 change, exchange
3 *(commerce)* price, rate of exchange
4 exchange, barter
5 change, small change

**caminar**
1 go, travel, journey, cover, walk
2 cross, travel through, cover
3 *(LAm)(mechanics)* work

**camino**
1 track, route, course, path, way, road
2 *(fig)* manner, means, mode, procedure, way

**campeón**
1 victor, champion, winner
2 champion, protector, defender

**campestre**
country, rural, rustic

**campo**
1 country, countryside, cultivation, field
2 *(football)* pitch, course, camp
3 *(art)* ground, background, *(heraldry)* field
4 *(LAm)* space, room

**canal**
1 canal, channel, strait
2 tube, pipe, drainpipe, gutter, TV channel

**cancelar**
1 cancel, annul, abolish, wipe out the memory of
2 extinguish, pay off, sell off, settle, resolve

**candor**
candour, frankness, ingenuousness, simplicity, innocence, sincerity, artlessness, naïveté, honesty
*malice, villainy, shyness, craftiness*

**canijo**
weak, sickly, unhealthy, infirm, feeble, delicate, frail
*robust, healthy, strong*

**canjear**
change, exchange, swap, barter, trade, traffic

**canon**
1 rule, norm, precept
2 census
3 rent, *(commerce)* tax

**cansado**
1 tired, exhausted, fatigued, weary, jaded
2 tiresome, tedious, exhausting, wearisome, vexatious, boring

**cansancio**
1 fatigue, lassitude, *(Br)* puncture, *(Am)* flat (tyre)
2 weariness, exhaustion, tedium, boredom, annoyance

**cansar**
tire, tire out, weary, exhaust, bother, pester, anger

**cantidad**
quantity, amount, aggregate, part, portion, sum

**caos**
chaos, confusion, disorder, anarchy
*order, coherence, discipline, clarity*

**caótico**
chaotic, confused, disordered, untidy, disorderly

**capacidad**
1 capacity, space
2 aptitude, intelligence, talent, sufficiency, competence, suitability

**capar**
1 castrate (an animal), geld
2 *(fig)* reduce, cut down, curtail, diminish

**capaz**
1 capacious, spacious, roomy, extensive, vast, grand
2 intelligent, competent, expert, sufficient, apt, suitable
*incapable, inept*

**capital** *(aj)*
1 capital, chief, supreme, paramount, essential, principal, primordial, fundamental
2 *(LAm)* capital letter

**capital** *(s)*
1 *(finance)* capital, capital sum, wealth, riches, goods, money, property
2 *(politics)* capital, capital city

**capitulación**
1 pact, agreement, treaty, compromise, settlement
2 *(military)* capitulation, surrender, delivery

**capitular**
1 agree to, agree on
2 *(law)* charge (with), impeach
3 come to terms, make an agreement (with), cede, surrender, give in, submit
4 *(military)* capitulate, surrender

**capricho**
caprice, whim, fancy, humour, fantasy, vagary, notion
*steadfastness*

**caprichoso**
capricious, changeable, whimsical, fickle, inconstant, irresolute, mercurial, unsteady, volatile, variable
*steadfast*

**captar**
1 perceive, apprehend
2 *(water)* collect
3 attract, get, obtain

**captura**
capture, seizure, apprehension, imprisonment, arrest

**carácter**
1 nature, disposition, character, condition, idiosyncrasy
2 *(LAm)* *(theatre)* character, personage

**característica**
characteristic, peculiarity, singularity, particularity, distinctive trait, property

**característico** *(aj)*
peculiar, proper, particular, singular, distinctive

**carencia**
lack, shortage, want, privation, deprivation
*abundance, excess*

**carestía**
scarcity, shortage, want, need, penury
*abundance, plenty*

**carga**
1 weight, burden, load
2 tribute, imposition, tax, mortgage
3 obligation, care
4 *(military)* charge, assault, attack

**cargar(se)**
1 rest (on), be supported (by), lean (against), rest
2 face up to something
3 attack, assault, charge
4 attribute, impute
5 importune, upset, annoy, bother, irritate
6 tax

**cargo**
1 load, burden, charge
2 post, office, job, charge
3 obligation, care, custody, direction
4 accusation, recrimination, imputation
5 debit, debt

**caridad**
1 compassion, pity, mercy
*mercilessness, inhumanity*
2 charity, help, alms, aid
*miserliness*

**cariño**
1 affection, tenderness, fondness, love, endearment, friendship
*dislike, indifference, enmity*
2 adulation, flattery
3 *(LAm)* caress, stroke

**cariños**
endearments, show of affection

**caro**
1 costly, dear, expensive
2 dear, beloved, loved

**carrera**
1 run, race, *(bullfight)* running
2 course, route, stretch (of a journey), trajectory, way, *(LAm)* avenue
3 profession, career, *(study)* course
4 *(stocking)* ladder

**carta**
1 missive, epistle, letter, note
2 charter, instrument, deed, bond
3 map
4 menu
5 playing card

**casa**
1 dwelling, abode, mansion, home, residence, house, building
2 family, lineage
3 *(commerce)* company, firm, business

**casar**
1 marry off, give in marriage, pair, join, unite, fit (into)
2 abolish, abrogate, *(law)* annul, quash

**castigar**
1 penalize, punish, sanction
*pardon*
2 mortify, afflict, chastise
3 correct, amend
4 diminish, reduce

**castigo**
1 punishment, penalty, sanction, sentence
2 mortification, affliction, chastisement, castigation
3 correction, corrective

**castizo**
1 pure, correct
*impure*
2 traditional, authentic
*derived*
3 pure-bred, racially pure

**casto**
chaste, pure, undefiled, incorrupt, virtuous, honest
*impure, unchaste, corrupt*

**casual**

accidental, contingent, fortuitous, conditional, casual, chance, incidental
*foreseen, planned, essential, calculated*

**casualidad**

chance, accident, fluke, coincidence, luck
*forethought, certainty, confidence*

**casualidades**

*(LAm)* casualties

**catar**

1 try, taste, sample

2 examine, see, test, prove

**categoría**

category, class, sphere, hierarchy, rank, standing, condition

**categórico**

categorical, decisive, absolute, conclusive, downright, final, definitive
*indeterminate, relative*

**caución**

caution, security, guarantee, bail, surety, pledge

**causar**

1 cause, produce, originate

2 cause, motivate, occasion, provoke, determine, result in

**cautela**

1 caution, wariness, precaution, prevention, circumspection, distrust, reserve

2 astuteness, skill, dexterity, deceit, swindle, trick

**cautivar**

1 capture, seize, catch, arrest, imprison

2 *(fig)* captivate, attract, seduce

**ceder**

1 give in, yield, submit, compromise, make concessions
*insist*

2 fall back, retreat, drop, *(fig)* back down

3 diminish, reduce, lessen, decrease, mitigate

4 give, transfer, sell
*take, remove*

**cegar**

1 make blind, deceive

2 *(fig)* close, shut, cover, conceal, wrap, stop up, block up

**celebrar**

1 celebrate, solemnize, commemorate

2 praise, eulogize, pay tribute to, applaud, extol, exalt, glorify, laud, magnify

**célebre**

celebrated, famous, reputed, illustrious, glorious

**celebridad**

1 celebrity, fame, renown, reputation

2 celebration, festivity

**celeridad**

celerity, promptitude, diligence, speed, velocity, rapidity
*slowness*

**celo**

zeal, care, diligence, enthusiasm, devotion, ardour
*indifference, coldness*

**censura**

1 censure, disapproval, reproval, condemnation, criticism, blame

2 detraction, gossip

3 judgement, examination, censorship

**censo**

census, tax, tribute, leasehold, mortgage

**cerrado**

1 closed, shut, sealed

2 *(matter)* incomprehensible, obscure

3 *(sky)* cloudy, overcast, *(atmosphere)* heavy, *(night)* dark, black
*clear*

4 *(person)* quiet, silent, reserved, uncommunicative, secretive
*communicative, open*

5 obtuse, dim, dull, slow, thick, dense

## cerrar(se)
1 close, shut
2 block, obstruct, block up, stop up
3 stop, turn off
4 close, complete, bring to a close
5 close in, enclose

## certificar
1 affirm, confirm, asseverate, assure
2 guarantee, warrant, pledge, answer for

## cesar
cease, stop, finish, terminate, interrupt, suspend
*begin, initiate*

## cielo
1 atmosphere, firmament, sky, heaven
2 Eden, Paradise, empyrean, heavenly kingdom
*Hell*

## cierto
1 certain, sure, undoubted, unquestionable, positive, real
2 true, truthful, reliable, right, correct

## circumscribir
circumscribe, limit, restrict, encircle, surround, make more specific

## cisma
schism, discord, dissension, disagreement, quarrel, separation

## cita
1 appointment, date, meeting
2 mention, allusion, note
3 quotation, citation

## citar
1 make an appointment with
2 allude, mention, name
3 quote, cite
4 *(law)* summons

## claridad
1 clarity, brightness, radiance, luminosity, light
*obscurity, darkness*
2 transparency, limpidity, lucidity, translucence
3 *(fig)* frankness, sincerity, candour, openness, truth
*insincerity, falsehood*

## claro
1 luminous, brilliant, resplendent
*dull*
2 illuminated, lit up
3 transparent, limpid, crystalline, diaphanous, translucent
4 *(fig)* illustrious, famous, distinguished, enlightened, celebrated, eminent, renowned
5 perspicacious, shrewd, sharp, alert, astute, acute
6 evident, intelligible, manifest, unquestionable, obvious, plain
7 frank, open, sincere, truthful, candid, ingenuous
*artful, secretive, sly*

## coartar
limit, restrict, compel, coerce, restrain
*permit, allow, leave*

## cobrar
1 receive, earn, get, collect
*pay, disburse*
2 recover, recuperate, satisfy

## codicioso
1 interested, anxious, ambitious, avid
2 *(fig)* industrious, hard-working

## coercer
coerce, constrain, contain, limit, check, restrain, repress, subject, subjugate

## cohibir
check, restrain, repress, subjugate

## colocar
1 put, place, instal, situate, *(LAm)* put away, put back
2 employ, destine, occupy, accommodate
3 invest, employ, find a job for

## coloquio
conversation, dialogue, discussion, chat, lecture

## combinar
combine, unite, couple, join, coordinate, coalesce, merge
*separate*

## comenzar
begin, commence, start, initiate
*end, finish, terminate*

**cometido**
commission, task, assignment, mission, charge, obligation

**comodidad**
1 comfort, convenience, advantage, welfare, well-being
*inconvenience*
2 opportunity, facility, advantage
3 self-interest, usefulness
*disinterestedness, unselfishness*

**cómodo**
1 convenient, favourable, comfortable, well-to-do
2 adequate, appropriate, suitable, opportune

**compartir**
share (out), divide (up), distribute, apportion

**compensar**
1 compensate, balance, counterbalance, make equal, *(fig)* offset
2 indemnify, recompense, compensate

**competencia**
1 competition, rivalry, contention, dispute, emulation
2 authority, jurisdiction
3 competence, aptitude, sufficiency, capacity, ability, suitability
*incompetence, inability*

**complacer(se)**
please, satisfy, delight, cheer, liven (up)
*bother, grieve, disgust, displease*

**componer(se)**
1 arrange, prepare, accommodate, constitute, form
2 remedy, repair, restore, mend, *(LAm)* (bone) set
3 adorn, dress, decorate, season
4 outline, shape, dress up, give character to, compose, make up

**comprar**
1 acquire, procure, obtain, get, buy, purchase
2 suborn, bribe

**comprender**
1 embrace, contain, include, comprise, encircle, surround
2 understand, conceive, penetrate

**comprimir(se)**
1 squeeze, press (together), pack, crush
2 oppress
3 repress, subjugate

**comprobar**
verify, confirm, find out, make sure

**compromiso**
1 engagement, agreement, pact, accord, treaty
2 commitment, obligation, duty, pledge
3 embarrassment, difficulty, awkward situation, conflict, jam

**común** *(aj)*
1 general, universal, common
2 ordinary, vulgar

**común** *(s)*
1 community, commune
2 toilet, w(ater) c(loset)

**concebir**
1 comprehend, understand, perceive, penetrate
2 imagine, conceive, create, invent, think (up), plan
3 *(medicine)* conceive

**conceder**
1 concede, grant, confer
2 admit, agree, assent
*deny, disagree, dissent*

**concepto**
1 idea, notion
2 thought, sentence
3 opinion, judgement

**conciso**
concise, brief, terse, pithy, short, succinct, laconic, compressed
*prolix, verbose, wordy*

**concluir(se)**
1 conclude, finish, terminate, finalize, end
2 finish, finish off, *(commerce)* sell off cheap
3 consume, expend, exhaust, deplete, use up, drain
4 infer, deduce, conclude

**condición**
1 nature, condition
2 nature, character, disposition
3 state, situation, position, rank, class, category, quality
4 restriction, clause, stipulation, requirement, condition

**conducir(se)**
1 direct, guide, conduct
2 administer, govern, rule, manage, run
3 transport, carry, take, convey, lead
4 behave, conduct oneself, act

**conferencia**
1 conversation, colloquy, conference, dialogue
2 dissertation, disquisition, discourse

**confianza**
1 trust, confidence, faith
2 self-assurance, self-confidence
3 familiarity, intimacy

**confirmar**
confirm, corroborate, ratify, verify, substantiate, prove

**conflicto**
1 struggle, combat
*peace*
2 disparity, dissension, disagreement, difference, clash
3 difficulty, hardship, jam, squeeze

**confrontar**
1 bring face to face, confront
2 compare

**confundir(se)**
1 mix (up), confuse, confound
2 mistake, be wrong, make a mistake
3 deceive, bewilder
4 humiliate, disconcert

**confuso**
1 mixed up, in disorder
2 obscure, doubtful
3 disturbed, embarrassed, ashamed, flustered
4 confounded, mistaken, confused

**conjunto** *(aj)*
1 joined, united, contiguous

2 incorporated, mixed, mingled

**conjunto** *(s)*
total, totality, aggregate

**conocer(se)**
1 understand, know, comprehend
2 perceive, note, take account of, notice
*ignore, forget*

**consagrar**
consecrate, declare sacred, dedicate, destine, *(fig)* devote

**conseguir**
attain, secure, achieve, bring about, obtain, get

**considerable**
big, large, great, grand, substantial, considerable, important, numerous

**consideración**
1 attention, reflection, study, meditation
*thoughtlessness, inattention*
2 importance, total (sum)
3 urbanity, respect, deference, esteem, courtesy

**consolar**
console, comfort, calm, encourage

**constitución**
1 complexion, temperament, constitution, nature
2 statute, ordinance, constitution

**constituir**
1 constitute, make up, form, compose
2 found, establish, institute, erect, build, (put in) order

**consuelo**
1 consolation, alleviation, relief, solace
2 joy, pleasure, happiness

**consumir**
consume, eat up, destroy, wear away, waste away, use up, drain

**contar**
1 count, compute, calculate
2 narrate, relate, tell, recount

**contender**
1 contend, fight, struggle, battle
2 compete, rival, vie with

3 dispute, debate, argue

**contienda**
1 contest, fight, struggle, battle
2 dispute, quarrel, brawl

**contiguo**
contiguous, adjacent, next, adjoining

**contingencia**
contingency, possibility, chance, accident
*certainty, sureness*

**contrariar**
1 oppose, contradict, impede, obstruct, hinder
*facilitate, make easy, satisfy, be satisfied*
2 annoy, upset, vex, mortify

**contrario** *(aj)*
1 opposite, opposed, contradictory, contrary
2 harmful, damaging, detrimental

**contrario** *(s)*
enemy, adversary, antagonist, rival

**convenio**
agreement, contract, pact, compromise

**convenir(se)**
1 arrange, agree, agree with, agree on, agree to
2 suit, be suitable for, be good for, be appropriate, be convenient for
3 agree, come to an agreement
4 be advisable, be fitting

**copia**
1 abundance, plenty, copiousness, profusion
2 transcription, transcript, copy
3 plagiarism
4 reproduction, tracing
5 imitation, parody

**coraje**
1 courage, daring, valour, effort, impetus, impulse
*cowardice*
2 anger, ire, irritation, choler, fury, rage, annoyance
*tranquillity, peace*

**corriente** *(aj)*
1 running, flowing
2 present, current, everyday, standard
3 accepted, admitted, usual, ordinary, common
*extraordinary*

**corriente** *(s)*
1 *(water)* current, stream, flow
2 *(electricity)* current
3 course, tendency, drift

**corrupción**
1 corruption, rot, decay, decomposition, putrefaction
2 stink, stench, bad smell
3 *(fig)* corruption, depravity, perversion
4 corruption, graft, bribery
5 *(law)* seduction

**cortés**
gracious, courteous, polite, affable, friendly, urbane, refined, attentive
*impolite, unrefined*

**crear**
1 give birth to, create
2 institute, found, establish
3 produce, invent, make

**crédito**
1 credit, reputation, fame, prestige, renown, authority
2 responsibility, solvency, confidence
3 belief

**criar**
1 create, give birth to
2 *(animals, birds)* rear, raise, keep, breed, fatten
3 *(plants)* grow, tend, cultivate
4 *(land)* bear, grow, produce
5 suckle, feed, nurse
6 bring up, raise, educate, instruct
7 *(wine)* age, mature
8 *(fig)* foster, nourish, nurture

**cultivar**
1 cultivate, work, till, grow
2 *(fig)* cultivate, develop, improve

**cultura**
1 civilization, education
2 instruction, erudition, knowledge, learning, culture

**cumplir**

1 realize, carry out, effect, execute, obey, observe, fulfil
2 serve, discharge, carry out, attain, reach
3 occur, happen, come about, come to be

**cúmulo**

accumulation, agglomeration, multitude, mountain, crowd, total, heap

**custodiar**

guard, protect, defend, keep, watch over, take care of, look after

# CH

**chafar**
1 squash flat, flatten, crush
2 crumple, wrinkle, crease, spoil, make a mess of, ruin
3 confuse, shame, embarrass
4 *(LAm)* hoax, deceive

**chalado**
1 silly, crazy, dotty, touched
2 enamoured

**charlar**
talk, chat, chatter, gossip

**chasco**
1 prank, trick, joke, gibe, deception, deceit, swindle
2 disappointment, disenchantment, disillusionment

**chasquear**
1 tease, make fun of, trick, make a fool of, deceive, cheat, swindle
2 frustrate, disappoint, disillusion

**chillería**
1 noisy row, shouting, screaming
2 scolding, telling-off

**chirriar**
creak, squeak, chirp, sing, growl

**chispa**
1 spark, sparkle, ray, beam, lightning

2 penetration, sharpness, ingenuity, wit, humour, liveliness
3 drunkenness

**chocar**
1 shock, startle, be surprised
2 bump into, crash, collide
3 fight, quarrel, dispute

**choque**
1 bump, jolt, impact, crash, collision
2 fight, quarrel, row, conflict, dispute, contention

**chulo** *(aj)*
1 amusing, charming, attractive, winning
2 smart, showy, attractive, flashy, gaudy, vulgar
3 jaunty, swaggering
4 bold, outspoken, fresh, pert, saucy, obstreperous, truculent
   *delicate, correct*
5 slick, rascally, villainous
6 *(LAm)* pretty, attractive, elegant, graceful
   *unattractive, ugly*
7 *(fig)* brilliant, super

**chulo** *(s)*
rascal, scoundrel, pimp
*gentleman*

# D

**dar(se)**
  1 donate, present, surrender
  2 facilitate, offer, concede, grant, supply, provide, give
  3 produce, yield

**dato**
  fact, datum, piece of information

**debatir**
  debate, dispute, contend, quarrel, argue

**decencia**
  1 decency, decorum, dignity
    *indecency*
  2 composure, modesty, demureness, respectability, cleanness, cleanliness
    *filth, immorality*

**decisión**
  1 decision, decisiveness, resolution, determination, support
    *indecision, vacillation, doubt*
  2 *(law)*, judgement, sentence, verdict, ruling
  3 firmness, audacity, bravery

**declarar(se)**
  1 declare, state, explain, expound
  2 decide, resolve, pronounce sentence on
  3 *(law)* testify, depose, bear witness to, make a statement, give evidence

**declinar**
  1 decline, diminish, decay, lessen, grow weak
  2 decline, refuse, renounce, resign
    *accept*

**decorar**
  1 adorn, beautify, ornament, decorate
    *deface, disfigure*

**decoro**
  decency, respect, honour, estimation, dignity, propriety, decorum, respectability
  *indignity, shamelessness*

**dedicar**
  1 offer, consecrate, dedicate, devote
    *deny*
  2 employ, destine, apply, assign, occupy

**defender(se)**
  1 defend, shield, protect, preserve, sustain
    *attack*
  2 defend, advocate, justify, excuse, forgive, exculpate
    *attack, blame*

**deferencia**
  deference, consideration, respect, attention, condescension
  *rudeness, disrespect*

**degenerar**
  degenerate, decline, get worse
  *improve*

**degradar**
  degrade, humiliate, debase, depress, reduce, lessen, lower
  *ennoble, honour, exalt*

**delatar**
  denounce, accuse, inform against, uncover, betray

**delicado**
  1 attentive, courteous, watchful, refined, polite, gentle
    *discourteous, unrefined, impolite*
  2 sensitive, tender, ticklish, susceptible
  3 delicate, weak, ill
    *strong*
  4 hypersensitive, touchy, fastidious, squeamish
  5 slender, slight, fragile, frail
  6 dainty, exquisite, savoury, tasty
    *coarse*
  7 difficult, risky, exposed

**demasía**
  1 excess, surplus
    *scarcity*
  2 insolence, daring
    *courtesy, propriety, decency, decorum*

3 abuse, disorder, outrage

4 evil, wickedness, crime, offence

**demostrar**
prove, show, reveal, make evident, manifest, demonstrate
*hide, conceal*

**denigrar**
1 denigrate, vilify, revile, run down, discredit, debase
*honour, praise*
2 injure, offend

**denotar**
denote, indicate, signify, signal, announce

**depresión**
1 depression, sunken place, hollow, descent, drop, fall
2 sinking, collapse
3 humiliation, degradation
4 depression, melancholy, dejection, discouragement
*liveliness, sprightliness*

**depravación**
depravity, perversion, corruption, wickedness
*virtue*

**deprimir**
1 depress, press down
2 humiliate, degrade, humble, humiliate
3 depress, sadden, discourage
*animate, encourage*

**derecho** *(aj)*
1 right, right hand
2 straight, direct
*crooked, indirect*
3 just, legitimate
*unjust, illegal*
4 vertical, upright
*horizontal*

**derecho** *(s)*
1 right, claim, title, privilege
2 law, justice, fairness
*injustice*
3 *(coins, medals)* obverse, face

**derechos**
*(finance)* dues, fees, taxes, royalties

**derramar(se)**
1 disseminate, spread, scatter, spill, pour out
2 *(fig)* publish, divulge
3 flow into, result in

**derroche**
1 waste, squandering, extravagance, prodigality
2 *(fig)* abundance, profusion, plenty, copiousness

**derrotado**
1 defeated, ruined, broken
2 shabby, ragged, poor

**desacuerdo**
disagreement, discord, difference, quarrel
*pact, agreement, harmony, concord*

**desafecto** *(aj)*
disaffected, hostile, contrary, opposite

**desafecto** *(s)*
disaffection, disagreement, antipathy, aversion, animosity

**desagrado**
displeasure, dissatisfaction, discontent, disgust, bother, annoyance, trouble

**desaire**
disfavour, disdain, scorn, contempt, rudeness, discourtesy, slight, snub
*respect*

**desaliño**
negligence, carelessness, neglect, slovenliness, untidiness
*care*

**desánimo**
discouragement, depression, prostration
*encouragement, joy*

**desapacible**
unpleasant, disagreeable, hard, harsh
*pleasant, agreeable*

**desaparecer**
1 hide, conceal, get lost, vanish, disappear
*reveal, disclose*

**desaparecer**

2 flee, escape

**desaprobar**

1 disapprove (of), reprove, censure, condemn, vituperate

2 (examination) fail

**desarreglar**

disorder, discompose, alter, disorganize, disarrange, upset, confuse
*arrange, compose, fix (up)*

**desarrollar**

1 unroll, unfold, open out

2 (fig) develop, evolve, explain, expound, carry out

3 advance, progress, grow

4 extend, amplify, augment

**desarrollo**

advance, development, progress, growth, increase, unfolding

**desasosiego**

1 anxiety, worry, annoyance, uneasiness, disquiet

2 (politics) unrest

**desastre**

disaster, catastrophe, calamity, cataclysm, devastation, ruin, destruction

**desatender**

1 disregard, pay no attention to, ignore
*regard, pay attention to*

2 abandon, forget, neglect, overlook
*look after, care for*

3 slight, offend

**desatino**

1 foolishness, folly, silliness, tactlessness

2 blunder, mistake, error, foolish act

**desavenencia**

disagreement, difference, discord, friction, rift, quarrel

**desazón**

1 insipidity, tastelessness

2 (fig) discontent, annoyance, displeasure, frustration

3 restlessness, disquiet, uneasiness

4 (land) poorness

5 (medicine) discomfort, indisposition

**descansar**

1 rest, support, lean (on)

2 help, assist, aid

3 rest, sleep, lie down, repose

4 (agriculture) lie fallow

**descanso**

1 rest time, break, respite, relief, rest, repose

2 small table, side table, occasional table

3 (technical) rest, support, bench, bracket

4 (architecture) landing

**descarado**

shameless, brazen, barefaced, cheeky, saucy, insolent, foulmouthed

**descender**

1 lower, let down, get down, lift down, take down

2 descend, go down, come down, be demoted
*ascend, rise*

3 (fig) fall, reduce, demean oneself

4 drop, fall, diminish, decrease
*rise, increase*

5 descend from, be derived from, be descended from

6 proceed from, originate in

**desconfianza**

apprehension, distrust, suspicion, resentment, malice

**descontento** (aj)

displeased, upset, annoyed, dissatisfied, discontented
*pleased, satisfied*

**descontento** (s)

dissatisfaction, displeasure, anger, irritation, annoyance, discontent
*contentment, satisfaction, pleasure*

**descubrir**

1 discover, find, detect, spot, unearth, uncover, denounce

2 discover, ascertain, learn

3 discover, invent

4 disclose, reveal, manifest, show
*hide*

**descuidado**
1 slack, careless, negligent, forgetful
2 slovenly, untidy, unkempt, neglected, abandoned
3 unprepared, unready, off guard

**descuidar**
omit, forget, neglect, abandon, forsake
*remember, watch*

**descuido**
1 neglect, omission
2 negligence, inadvertence, carelessness, untidiness
3 lapse, slip, blunder

**desdén**
disdain, contempt, scorn, indifference, detachment
*admiration*

**desdeñar**
disdain, despise, scorn, slight, spurn, snub
*admire, appreciate, esteem, regard*

**desechar**
1 exclude, separate, set aside
2 scrap, cast aside, throw out, throw away, reject, expel
3 censure, reprove, scorn

**deseo**
desire, want, wish, appetite, ambition, aspiration, greed, lust, anxiety

**desgracia**
1 misfortune, mishap, setback, adversity, unhappiness
*happiness, good fortune*
2 disgrace, disfavour
3 entrails, offal

**desigual**
1 unequal, different, unfair, unequitable
2 uneven, irregular, unequal, broken
3 (fig) arduous, difficult
4 inconstant, variable, changeable, capricious, unpredictable

**desmembrar**
1 cut up, dismember
2 divide, separate, disintegrate, split, break up

**desmesurado**
1 excessive, enormous, inordinate, disproportionate
2 insolent, impudent, discourteous
*polite*

**desorientar**
1 mislead, misdirect, misguide
2 (fig) confound, confuse, bewilder

**despachar**
1 conclude, hurry, make haste
2 resolve, decide
3 send, send away, remit, despatch
4 sell, expend, deal in
5 (fig) kill, dispatch

**despedir(se)**
1 see off, show out
2 throw, hurl, launch, spread, scatter
3 despatch, send
4 fire, sack, discharge, dismiss, throw out, expel

**despierto**
1 awake
2 (fig) alert, sharp, ready, watchful, bright, quick, alive

**despótico**
despotic, tyrannical, arbitrary, lawless, absolute

**desprender**
1 separate, detach, unfasten, loosen
*unite*
2 renounce, give up, surrender
*accept*
3 deduce, infer, follow

**destierro**
exile, ostracism, deportation, proscription, banishment

**destinar**
destine, designate, dedicate, apply, employ, occupy

**destino**
1 fate, destiny, fortune, star, luck
2 end, purpose, aim, intention, objective
3 occupation, post, place, employment
4 destination

**detener(se)**
1 stop, suspend, intercept
2 arrest, apprehend, catch, capture, imprison
3 retain, conserve
4 linger, delay, slow down, be delayed, be late

**detestar**
1 detest, hate, loathe, abominate
2 condemn, execrate, curse

**detrimento**
1 detriment, deterioration, breakdown, fault, failure
2 loss, hurt, damage, harm, injury

**dicha**
luck, fortune, prosperity, happiness

**dicho** *(aj)*
above-mentioned, aforementioned, named, cited

**dicho** *(s)*
proverb, saying, adage, apothegm, maxim, dictum

**dictamen**
opinion, dictum, judgement, legal opinion, report

**dictar**
1 dictate, inspire, suggest
2 decree, pass judgement, pronounce, promulgate
3 *(LAm)* give, deliver

**diferente**
different, distinct, diverse, divergent, dissimilar, uneven, unequal
*even, equal, similar*

**difícil**
1 difficult, hard, arduous, involved, complicated
*easy*
2 rude, surly, unpleasant, rough, bitter, harsh

**dificultad**
1 obstacle, impediment, hindrance, obstruction, nuisance, bother, embarrassment, difficulty, inconvenience
2 conflict, opposition
3 doubt, objection

**digno**
1 worthy, fitting, proper, appropriate, adequate
2 worthy, upright, honourable
3 dignified, grave, serious, decorous, decent, honest

**dimitir**
renounce, decline, refuse, resign, relinquish

**dirección**
1 direction, way, *(fig)* course, trend
2 direction, guidance, control, administration, management, running, rule, leadership, government
3 address

**discreto**
1 discreet, prudent, cautious, circumspect, sensible, sane
2 sharp, clever, ingenious
3 quiet, sober, reserved

**disculpa**
1 excuse, defence, exculpation, plea, apology
2 excuse, pretext, dodge, subterfuge

**disculpar(se)**
1 defend, justify, excuse
2 pardon, forgive, exonerate, exculpate
3 excuse oneself (from), apologize (for)
*blame oneself (for)*

**disensión**
1 dissent, dissension, difference, disagreement
2 discord, contention, dispute, argument, brawl

**disgusto**
1 anger, annoyance, displeasure, vexation
2 grief, chagrin, sorrow, affliction, sadness, pain
3 disgust, repugnance, revulsion

**disimular**
1 hide, conceal, dissemble
2 disfigure, mask, feign, sham, fake, disguise
3 excuse, overlook, tolerate, permit, pardon

**dispensar**
1 dispense, give, concede, grant
2 excuse, pardon, absolve, forgive
3 exempt

**dispersar(se)**
1 disperse, disperse, disseminate, scatter
2 rout, drive off, frighten off, confuse

**dispuesto**
1 arranged, disposed, prepared, ready, forewarned
2 able, apt, suitable, wide-awake, bright, intelligent
3 neat, elegant, spruce

**disputa**
dispute, debate, altercation, contention

**distinción**
1 distinction, difference
2 distinction, honour, prerogative
3 elegance, refinement

**distinto**
1 distinct, different, diverse, dissimilar
*similar*
2 distinct, clear, precise, intelligible
*confused*

**distinguir**
1 distinguish, discern, make out, recognize
2 distinguish, differentiate (between)
3 distinguish, separate, single out
4 distinguish, mark, stamp, characterize
5 *(fig)* distinguish, honour, celebrate

**distracción**
1 distraction, amusement, entertainment, diversion, pastime, recreation, hobby
2 distraction, absent-mindedness, forgetfulness, omission, lapse, inadvertence

**disturbio**
disturbance, riot, tumult, row, uproar, mutiny, revolt

**diversión**
diversion, distraction, amusement, recreation, relaxation, pastime, hobby, entertainment

**diverso**
diverse, different, distinct, scattered

**diversos** *(aj)*
several, various, many, varied

**diversos** *(s)*
*(commerce)* sundries, miscellaneous (items)

**divulgar**
spread, circulate, publish, disseminate, popularize, *(pejorative)* divulge, disclose, let out

**dócil**
1 docile, submissive, obedient
2 gentle, peaceful, sweet, mild

**donaire**
1 cleverness, wit, sharpness
2 elegance, grace, charm, gentility

**dulce** *(aj)*
1 agreeable, delightful, gentle, sweet, pleasant, affable
2 indulgent, helpful, kind

**dulce** *(av)*
sweetly, softly

**dulce** *(s)*
sweet, sweetmeat, *(Am)* candy

**dulzura**
sweetness, gentleness, mildness, goodness, kindness

**duro**
1 resistant, strong, tough, consistent, compact
2 *(fig)* severe, rude, violent, cruel, inhuman, harsh, rough, pitiless
3 tiresome, tedious, boring, intolerable, unbearable, hard

# E

**echar(se)**
1 throw, cast, fling, pitch, toss, hurl, launch
2 emit, send forth, discharge, give off, give out
3 eject, throw out, chuck out, turn out, dismiss, fire, sack, discharge, expel
4 post, mail, dispatch, send
5 throw oneself (at), hurl oneself (at), rush
6 lie down, stretch out

**edificar**
1 construct, raise, build, erect
   *destroy*
2 (*fig*) edify, improve, uplift, ennoble

**educar**
1 educate, teach, guide, direct, show
2 develop, perfect, refine
3 raise, bring up
4 domesticate, train, tame

**efectivo** (*aj*)
1 effective
2 actual, real, true, certain, positive
3 regular, permanent, established

**efectivo** (*s*)
   cash, money

**efecto**
1 effect, result, consequence, product
2 purpose, end, objective
3 effect, impression, impact

**efectos**
1 bills, securities
2 effects, goods, things, (*finance*) assets, (*commerce*) goods, articles, merchandise

**eficaz**
1 efficacious, effective, telling, active, strong, energetic, powerful
2 efficient
   *inefficient*

**egregio**
   eminent, illustrious, celebrated, famous, distinguished
   *commonplace, ordinary*

**ejecutar**
1 execute, carry out, perform, obey, observe, fulfil, finish
2 execute
3 (*music*) perform, render, play
4 (*law*) attach, distrain on
5 (*computers*) run

**elegancia**
1 elegance, grace, smartness, stylishness, distinction, taste
2 (*portraiture, painting*) shape, form

**elemental**
1 elemental, fundamental, primordial
2 elementary, rudimentary, primary, natural, unaffected, simple
   *secondary, difficult*
3 obvious, evident

**elevar(se)**
1 raise, elevate, put up, lift (up), (*electricity*) boost
   *lower*
2 construct, erect, build
   *destroy*
3 (*fig*) exalt, magnify, ennoble, enlarge
   *humiliate*
4 rise, go up, soar, tower
5 be transported, go into a rapture
6 (*pejorative*) get conceited, become overbearing

**eliminar**
1 eliminate, suppress, remove, take away, exclude
2 (*medicine*) expel

**elogiar**
   praise, celebrate, pay tribute to, eulogize, extol, speak in praise of
   *denigrate*

**eludir**
   elude, avoid, escape, shun, dodge
   *oppose, confront, challenge*

**embarazar(se)**
1 make pregnant
2 hinder, obstruct, impede, hamper, get in the way
*facilitate, make easy*

**embarazo**
1 pregnancy
2 obstruction, impediment, difficulty, obstacle, snag
3 timidity, shrinking, shyness, embarrassment

**embeber(se)**
1 absorb, soak up, saturate, impregnate
2 insert, introduce (into), incorporate, contain, comprise, *(fig)* imbibe
3 be absorbed in, become engrossed in, be enraptured with, be enchanted with

**embestida**
1 attack, assault, onslaught, charge (of a wild animal)
2 importunate demand

**embrollo**
1 entanglement, tangle, mix-up, confusion, muddle, mess, fix, jam, row, uproar
2 fraud, trick, lie, fib

**embrollar(se)**
complicate, confuse, confound, disturb, mess up, embroil, get into a muddle, get into a mess
*clear up, resolve, put in order*

**eminencia**
1 height, elevation, eminence
2 projection, prominence, salient
3 *(fig)* excellence, sublimity, superiority

**eminente**
1 high, elevated, eminent
2 superior, distinguished, notable, illustrious, excellent, eminent

**empacho**
1 obstacle, impediment, hindrance
2 *(medicine)* indigestion, surfeited feeling
3 *(fig)* embarrassment, awkwardness, bashfulness, timidity, shame

**emplear**
use, employ, engage, hire, occupy, spend, put in, invest

**empleo**
1 use, employment, application, *(commerce)* investment
2 employment, work
3 occupation, post, charge, job, position

**emprender**
commence, begin, initiate, start, undertake, embark on, tackle
*finish, stop*

**empresa**
1 enterprise, project, design, undertaking
2 *(commerce, finance)* enterprise, company, firm, society, management
3 symbol, slogan *(chivalry)* motto, device

**empujar**
1 shove, push, *(mechanics)*, drive, move, propel
2 *(fig)* excite, incite, stimulate
*debilitate*

**encadenar(se)**
1 chain (together), put chains on, fetter, shackle
2 immobilize, paralyze, tie (up), tie down
3 *(fig)* enslave, subdue, subjugate
*liberate, set free, release*
4 join, unite, link, connect

**encantar**
1 bewitch, enchant, cast a spell on, charm
*disenchant*
2 *(fig)* charm, delight, enchant, captivate, fascinate, seduce, attract
*repel*

**encanto**
1 spell, enchantment, witchcraft, magic, bewitchment
2 delight, fascination, seduction
3 *(fig)* charm, delight, enchantment

**encarecimiento**
1 *(commerce)* price rise, price increase, high cost

2 stressing, emphasizing, insistence

3 exaggeration, overrating, extolling highly

**encargo**

1 assignment, job, post, charge, commission, responsibility

2 order, request, *(commerce)* order (for)

**encubrir(se)**

hide, conceal, cover (up), cloak, harbour, shelter, abet
*discover, reveal oneself, betray*

**enfadar(se)**

1 anger, irritate, annoy, upset, bother, trouble, become angry, be annoyed

2 *(LAm)* be bored, get bored

**engaño**

1 deceit, deception, fraud, trick, swindle, lie, falsehood

2 error, mistake, misunderstanding, delusion
*truth, reality*

**engaños**

wiles, tricks

**engendrar**

1 procreate, beget, breed

2 *(fig)* breed, cause, engender, generate, produce, occasion, start, originate

**engrandecer**

1 augment, amplify, increase, enlarge, magnify

2 elevate, highlight, accentuate

3 *(fig)* exaggerate, eulogize, extol, praise (highly), exalt

**enlace**

1 link, bond, connection, liaison, union, chaining together, relationship, *(chemistry, electricity)* linkage
*separation, disconnection*

2 marriage, nuptials, wedding

**enmendar(se)**

1 correct, rectify, repair, emend, reform
*pervert, corrupt*

2 make amends for, indemnify, satisfy, compensate, make good

**enorme**

enormous, colossal, huge, excessive, disproportionate, immeasurable, *(fig)* monstrous

**ensalzar(se)**

1 exalt, glorify, praise

2 eulogize, extol, praise (highly), pay tribute to

**ensayar**

1 test, experiment with, try out, *(medicine)* examine

2 train, teach

3 try, attempt, endeavour, try to, *(theatre)* rehearse

**ensayo**

1 test, trial, experiment, examination, search, attempt, practice, exercise

2 *(literature)* essay , exercise

3 *(theatre)* rehearsal

4 *(metals)* assay

**entender**

1 understand, comprehend, realize, grasp
*misunderstand*

2 intend, mean

3 think, believe, infer, deduce

4 hear

**entendido** *(aj)*

1 understood, agreed

2 expert, skilled, trained, wise, knowing, well-informed, clever, smart

**entendido** *(s)*

connoisseur, expert

**enterar**

1 inform, instruct, make known, advise, tell
*ignore*

2 *(LAm)* pay, hand over, make up, round off

**entero** *(aj)*

1 entire, whole, complete, exact
*incomplete, imperfect*

2 *(mathematics)* whole, integral

3 *(biology)* not castrated

4 *(fig)* honest, upright, straight, firm, resolute

5 *(fig)* healthy, strong, robust

**entero** *(s)*
1 *(mathematics)* whole number, integer
2 *(commerce)* point

**entorpecer**
1 stupefy, stun, disturb
2 impede, obstruct, hinder, retard, delay, slow down, embarrass

**entorpecimiento**
1 lethargy, torpor, dullness, numbness, confusion, disturbance
2 obstacle, difficulty, impediment, delay, embarrassment
*facility*

**entrar**
1 introduce, insert, fit into, penetrate, enter
*remove*
2 flow into, run into, empty into, drain into
3 be admitted to
4 begin, commence, start
5 *(military)* attack, invade, capture, enter
6 *(computers)* access

**entremeter(se)**
insert, introduce, implicate, involve, interfere in, meddle in

**entrever**
1 distinguish, make out, glimpse, catch a glimpse of
2 *(fig)* conjecture, guess, suspect (something of)

**envolver**
1 wrap (up), pack (up), tie up, do up, swathe, cover, enfold, envelop, muffle (up)
*unwrap, unfold*
2 *(military)* encircle, surround
3 *(fig)* imply, involve, implicate

**época**
era, time, season, period, age, epoch

**equilibrio**
1 balance, equilibrium, harmony, proportion, equality
2 equanimity, good sense

**equivocar(se)**
be wrong, make a mistake, be mistaken

**erróneo**
erroneous, mistaken, false, untrue, inexact
*correct, right*

**error**
error, mistake, lapse, fault, blunder, inadvertence
*correction*

**escabroso**
1 rough, rugged, uneven, unequal, abrupt
2 *(fig)* harsh
2 hard, difficult, tough, thorny
3 blue, dirty, risqué, impolite, unsuitable

**escarmiento**
lesson, example, warning, punishment

**escasez**
1 shortage, scarcity, insufficiency, exigency, lack
*abundance, plenty, sufficiency*
2 meanness, miserliness
*generosity, open-handedness*
3 penury, poverty
*riches, wealth*

**esclarecer**
1 light up, illuminate
2 *(fig)* explain, elucidate, shed light on, clarify, make clear, clear up
3 *(fig)* enlighten
4 make famous, make illustrious, ennoble

**escocer**
1 annoy, bother, hurt
2 sting, smart, redden
3 *(fig)* suffer, feel bitter about, feel sorry about, grieve

**escollo**
1 reef, rock
2 hidden danger, risk
3 trap, pitfall, obstacle, snag, difficulty, stumbling block

**esconder(se)**
1 hide, cover, conceal, conceal oneself
*open, uncover*
2 *(fig)* include, contain, enclose, shut up

**escrúpulo**
1 scruple, hesitation, doubt, suspicion, distrust, fear, apprehension
2 scrupulousness, exactitude, precision, (great) care

**escuálido**
1 skinny, scraggy, thin, weak, emaciated, feeble, gaunt, lean
2 squalid, filthy

**espantar(se)**
1 frighten, scare, frighten off, scare away, terrify, intimidate, appal, horrify
2 get frightened, get scared, be appalled, be amazed, be astonished (at)

**especial** (aj)
1 special, especial, singular, particular, peculiar
2 adequate, proper

**especial** (s)
1 (LAm) special offer
2 (LAm) show

**eslabonar**
link, connect, relate, join, tie, bind (together)

**espaciar(se)**
1 space out, spread, extend, stretch out, dilate
2 distance, separate
3 relax, enjoy oneself

**esparcir(se)**
1 scatter, spread, spread out, extend
2 propagate, publish, divulge, make public
3 relax, enjoy oneself, amuse oneself, distract oneself

**especie**
1 species, class, group, category, kind, sort
2 pretext, appearance, colour, shade
3 case, matter, subject, business, event
4 fame, rumour, piece of news, reputation

**espectáculo**
1 spectacle, show, function, representation, performance

2 contemplation, vision

**espíritu**
1 spirit
2 mind, intelligence, turn of mind
3 spirit, energy, dash, go
4 (religion) spirit, soul
5 spirit, ghost, phantom
6 spirits, liquor

**espléndido**
1 splendid, lavish, generous, liberal
2 splendid, ostentatious, magnificent, sumptuous, superb, rich

**esquela**
1 short letter, missive, note
2 obituary

**esquivar**
1 elude, avoid, shun, dodge
2 retreat, withdraw, retire, keep away, move away

**estación**
1 time, epoch, period, season
2 stop, station

**estancar(se)**
1 hold up, hold back, block, delay, suspend, detain, paralyze
2 stagnate, become stagnant, be held back
3 (commerce) monopolize, establish a monopoly in, corner

**estéril**
sterile, barren, arid, unfruitful, fruitless, ineffective

**estimación**
1 estimation, valuation, assessment
2 estimate, estimation, valuation
3 esteem, regard, respect, admiration, consideration

**estimar**
1 estimate, appraise, gauge, reckon, compute, evaluate, value, assess
2 esteem, respect, appreciate, consider
3 believe, think, judge, opine

**estirado**
1 stretched tight, taut
2 (fig) stiff, pompous, haughty, arrogant, proud

**estirar(se)**
1 stretch, pull out, lengthen, extend

2 delay, prolong, dilate, stretch out

**estorbar**
impede, obstruct, hinder, hamper, complicate, embarrass
*facilitate, permit*

**estorbo**
hindrance, impediment, obstruction, difficulty, obstacle, embarrassment, bother, snag
*help*

**estragar**
ruin, corrupt, spoil, pervert, deprave

**estrechar(se)**
1 narrow, make smaller, reduce, take in, draw tighter
2 squeeze, hug, embrace
3 compel, constrain, oblige, force, require, need
4 persecute, pester, hound, pursue relentlessly
5 narrow, get narrow, tighten, get tighter

**estrecho** *(aj)*
1 narrow, tight, close, cramped, small
*ample, wide*
2 reduced, limited, suffocated, smothered
3 rigorous, strict, austere, rigid
4 *(pejorative)* miserly, mean, mean-spirited

**estrecho** *(s)*
strait, channel, canal, passage

**estrépito**
noise, din, racket, commotion, rumpus, row, uproar

**estropear(se)**
1 wound, hurt, maim, cripple, injure
2 spoil, damage, ruin, mangle, mess up, make a mess of
*arrange, repair*
3 crumple, tear
4 pervert, distort
5 get damaged, be ruined, go bad, deteriorate

**estructura**
structure, framework, order, distribution, organization

**estruendo**
1 noise, racket, din, clamour, crash, clatter
2 *(fig)* confusion, turmoil, uproar
3 pomp, ostentation

**estrujar(se)**
1 squeeze, tighten, compress, press, crush
2 *(fig)* drain, bleed white

**estudio**
1 study
2 research, survey, investigation
3 book, work, monograph, text, manuscript
4 bedsitter, studio flat
5 *(art)* studio

**evacuar**
vacate, clear, free, abandon, desert

**evocar**
1 evoke, call forth, conjure up, invoke, call up
2 *(fig)* recall, remember

**eventual**
1 casual, accidental, chance, temporary
2 uncertain, possible, conditional (upon circumstances)

**evidente**
evident, obvious, clear, visible, manifest, ostensible, undoubted, unquestionable, axiomatic

**exagerar**
exaggerate, overdo, overstate, enlarge upon, carry to extremes, increase, put up the price of

**exaltar(se)**
1 exalt, glorify, praise, extol, elevate, raise
2 get excited, get carried away, get heated, get worked up

**examen**
1 examination, investigation, inspection, observation, analysis
2 test, trial

**examinar(se)**
1 examine, observe, study, analyse, inquire, investigate, inspect closely, consider pros and cons

2 test, question

3 take an examination, be examined

**exánime**
1 inanimate, lifeless, dead
2 unconscious, weakened, debilitated

**exasperar(se)**
1 exasperate, irritate, exacerbate, annoy, make worse
2 become angry, get exasperated, lose patience

**exceder(se)**
1 exceed, surpass
2 stand out, excel
3 go too far, overreach oneself

**exceso**
1 excess, surplus, redundancy, superfluity, pleonasm
   *scarcity, lack*
2 outrage, crime, infraction

**excitar(se)**
1 excite, stimulate, provoke, move, incite, induce
   *soothe, calm*
2 get excited
   *calm down*

**excluir**
exclude, rule out, reject, except, eliminate, separate, expel, shut out, suppress

**excusar(se)**
1 excuse, pardon, forgive, exculpate, exempt, justify
2 avoid, prevent
3 apologize

**exento**
1 exempt, free, clear
2 unobstructed, open
3 *(architecture)* free-standing

**exhalar(se)**
1 exhale, breathe out, breathe, heave, utter
2 emit, give off, give out
3 breathe hard, hurry, run

**exhortar**
exhort, plead, supplicate, ask for, counsel, advise, incite, excite, animate

**exigir**
1 order, command
   *obey*
2 require, demand, ask for, request, need, insist on

**exiguo**
scarce, insufficient, small, scanty, insignificant, reduced
*abundant, generous*

**eximir**
exempt, dispense, relieve of, pardon, release, set free
*oblige, condemn*

**exonerar(se)**
1 exonerate, free from blame
2 lighten, relieve, alleviate, unload, unburden oneself

**expansión**
1 expansion, extension, dilation, prolongation
2 development, growth
3 diffusion, circulation, divulgation
4 relief, relaxation, recreation, diversion

**expansivo**
expansive, communicative, effusive, affectionate

**expedición**
1 expedition
2 *(commerce)* shipment, shipping, consignment, sending
3 speed, promptitude, dispatch

**expedir**
1 send, ship, ship off, forward, dispatch, remit
2 draw up, make out, issue

**expirar**
1 expire, terminate, finish, conclude, finalize
   *begin*
2 die, breathe one's last, pass away
   *be born*

**explicar**
1 explain, interpret, expose, clarify, develop
2 declare, express, put forward a theory
3 teach, show, practise
4 satisfy, justify, exculpate

**explícito**
    explicit, clear, express, manifest, determined

**explorar**
    explore, investigate, *(medicine)* probe, *(radar)* scan, examine

**explotar**
    1 run, work, operate
    2 exploit, use, utilize, profit from, take advantage of
    3 explode, burst, go off

**exponer(se)**
    1 expose, lay bare, manifest, disclose, interpret
    2 display, exhibit, *(photography)* expose
    3 risk, run the risk of doing, lay oneself open to (danger), endanger, (ad)venture

**exposición**
    1 explanation, interpretation, exposé, narrative, account, statement
    2 presentation, display, *(art)* exhibition, *(commerce)* show, fair
    3 *(photography)* exposure
    4 petition, claim
    5 risk, danger

**expulsar**
    1 eject, throw out, fire, sack, expel, show someone the door
    2 expel, banish, *(sport)* send off

**extender(se)**
    1 unfold, open out, spread out, unwrap, extend
    2 amplify, enlarge, extend
    3 propagate, diffuse, divulge, spread, scatter
    4 issue, make out, draw up
    5 stretch oneself out, talk at length

**exquisito**
    exquisite, delicious, tasty, excellent, delicate

**extenso**
    1 vast, spacious, extensive
    2 *(fig)* long drawn out, prolonged

**exterior** *(aj)*
    1 external, extrinsic, outer
    2 foreign, alien

**exterior** *(s)*
    1 exterior, surface, periphery
    2 outward appearance, aspect, looks, bearing
    3 foreign countries, abroad

**extracción**
    1 extraction
    2 origin, birth, lineage, stock, class
    3 *(lottery)* draw

**extracto**
    1 extract, substance, essence
    2 abstract, summary, abridgement

**extraordinario** *(aj)*
    1 extraordinary, uncommon, singular, exceptional, rare, strange
    2 surprising, shocking, strange, odd

**extraordinario** *(s)*
    *(newspaper)* special number

**extravagante**
    extravagant, odd, eccentric, rare, shocking, outlandish

**extremo** *(aj)*
    1 last, ultimate, extreme, farthest, outermost
    2 extreme, exaggerated, excessive
    3 *(fig)* desperate, critical, extreme, utmost

**extremo** *(s)*
    1 extremity, end
    2 terminus, limit
    3 point, matter, issue

**exuberancia**
    1 exuberance, high spirits
    2 lushness, abundance, plenty, prodigality, copiousness, profusion, plenitude
    *scarcity, lack, shortage*

# F

**fábrica**
1 factory, edifice, structure, building, construction
2 manufacture, production

**fabricar**
1 manufacture, make, produce, prepare, elaborate
2 build, construct, devise
3 *(fig)* invent, imagine, forge, fabricate

**fábula**
1 fable, tale, myth
2 fiction, invention, falsehood, fib *truth, reality*
3 rumour, gossip

**fabuloso**
1 fabulous, mythical, mythological, legendary
2 imaginary, fictitious, false, invented, feigned
3 incredible, exaggerated, extraordinary, inadmissible

**fácil**
1 easy, simple, straightforward, comfortable, convenient
2 probable, likely
3 friendly, docile, manageable, compliant
4 easy, loose

**facilitar**
1 favour, prefer, facilitate, make easy *make difficult, complicate*
2 supply, provide

**facultad**
1 capacity, aptitude, ability, capability, faculty
2 power, authority, right
3 licence, permission, authorization, consent
4 *(University)* Faculty, School

**falaz** *(aj)*
1 deceitful, treacherous, lying *true, truthful, sincere*
2 deceptive, fallacious

**falsear**
1 falsify, forge, counterfeit, fake, adulterate, corrupt
2 buckle, sag, give way, *(fig)* flag, slacken

**falso**
1 false, deceitful, lying, imaginary, invented, feigned, erroneous, mistaken, deceptive
2 falsified, adulterated, apocryphal, spurious, bogus, sham
3 treacherous, disloyal, unfaithful *true, loyal, faithful, trustworthy*
4 feeble, flimsy, unstable

**falta**
1 fault, defect, flaw, imperfection, deficiency, shortcoming, failure
2 want, need, lack, privation, absence, scarcity, shortage
3 carelessness, negligence, fault, sin
4 fault, blunder, mistake, error, lapse

**falto**
1 defective, faulty, deficient, short, lacking, scarce
2 poor, wretched, mean

**falla**
fault, flaw, defect, imperfection, failure

**fallar**
1 ( *law*) judge, sentence, pronounce sentence on
2 fail, miss, go wrong, be lacking, be wanting

**fama**
1 name, renown, reputation, repute, glory, fame
2 report, rumour

**familia**
1 parentage, family, *(LAm)* relative
2 household, lineage, race, caste, stock
3 offspring, descendants, children

**fanático** *(aj)*
    fanatical, intolerant, intransigent, enthusiastic, worked-up, over-excited
    *tolerant*

**fanático** *(s)*
    fanatic, bigot, *(film, sport)* fan, admirer, supporter, enthusiast

**fantasía**
    1 imagination, fantasy
    *reality*
    2 whim, caprice, fancy
    3 conceit, vanity, airs

**fantástico**
    1 fantastic, phantasmagoric, imaginary, unreal, feigned, fictitious
    2 capricious, whimsical, fanciful
    3 fantastic!, great!, terrific!

**fastidiar**
    annoy, bother, vex, upset, sicken, disgust, weary, bore

**fastidioso**
    wearisome, tedious, boring, annoying, disgusting

**fatal**
    1 fatal, deadly
    2 inevitable, inexorable, predestined, inescapable
    3 adverse, ill-fated, fateful, disastrous, gloomy, unlucky, unfortunate, cursed
    4 awful, terrible, horrible

**fatalidad**
    1 destiny, fate, fatality
    2 adversity, misfortune
    *happiness*

**fatiga**
    1 fatigue, weariness, tiredness, breathlessness

**fatigas**
    1 nausea, disgust, repulsion
    2 hardships, troubles, toils, worries

**fatigar(se)**
    1 tire, exhaust, weary, weaken
    2 annoy, vex, bother, pester

**fatigoso**
    1 tiring, exhausting, fatiguing
    2 *(medicine)* laboured, difficult
    3 trying, tiresome, wearisome

**fatuidad**
    1 fatuity, foolishness, inanity, stupidity, silliness, frivolity
    *discretion*
    2 conceit, vanity, arrogance, presumption, petulance
    *modesty*

**favor**
    1 service, good turn, help, aid, succour, favour, *(Am)* favor
    2 protection, support, backing, sponsorship, favour, *(Am)* favor
    3 token, gift, favour, *(Am)* favor

**favorecer**
    1 help, aid, assist, succour
    2 protect, support, back, second, sponsor, prefer, favour, *(Am)* favor

**fe**
    1 religion, faith, dogma, belief
    2 assurance, confidence, credit, trust
    *distrust*
    3 security, asseveration, affirmation, witness, testimony
    4 fidelity, loyalty, rectitude, honesty
    *infidelity, disloyalty, dishonesty*

**felicidad**
    1 well-being, satisfaction, contentment, happiness, joy
    *unhappiness, sorrow, pain, disenchantment, disillusionment*
    2 luck, fortune

**feliz**
    1 happy, content, satisfied
    2 fortunate, lucky, successful
    3 opportune, timely, right, correct, effective

**fenómeno**
    1 phenomenon
    2 appearance, manifestation, portent
    3 prodigy, genius, monster
    4 *(fig)* oddity, freak, accident

**feo** *(aj)*
    1 ugly, plain, unsightly, nasty, foul, atrocious, horrible, monstrous
    *nice, handsome, beautiful*
    2 *(LAm)* disgusting, foul

**feo** (s)
  unattractiveness, rudeness

**ferocidad**
  ferocity, fierceness, savageness,
  cruelty, inhumanity
  *humanity, pity, kindness*

**feroz**
  fierce, cruel, inhuman, pitiless,
  wild, savage

**ferviente**
  ardent, fervent, enthusiastic,
  eager, fervid, hot, warm
  *cold, unenthusiastic*

**fervor**
  1 devotion, piety, fervour, (Am)
  fervor
  *incredulity*
  2 zeal, ardour, enthusiasm, passion
  *coldness, indifference, lukewarm-
  ness*

**festejar**
  1 feast, wine and dine, entertain,
  fête, treat well, shower with gifts,
  pamper, indulge
  2 celebrate
  3 court, woo, flirt with
  4 (LAm) thrash

**festividad**
  festivity, feast, solemnity, com-
  memoration, holiday

**festivo**
  1 festive, merry, gay, happy, joyful
  2 amusing, witty, clever, funny, humorous, facetious, (literary) comic,
  burlesque

**fiador**
  1 (law) surety, guarantor, (commerce) sponsor, backer
  2 fastener, catch
  3 (gun) trigger

**fianza**
  1 surety, security, bond, pledge,
  guarantee, caution, deposit
  2 guarantor, surety

**fiar**
  1 guarantee, warrant, stand surety,
  stand bail, vouch for, answer (for)
  2 confide (in), trust (in), rely on
  *distrust, suspect*

**fibra**
  1 fibre
  2 thread, grain, filament, (mining)
  vein
  3 (fig) energy, resistance, strength,
  toughness, vigour, (Am) vigor

**fibras**
  sinews, muscles

**ficticio**
  1 fictitious, false, invented,
  imagined, imaginary, fabulous,
  feigned, (pejorative) fabricated
  *real*
  2 conventional, hypothetical

**fiel** (aj)
  1 faithful, loyal, trustworthy, reliable, firm, constant
  *unfaithful, unreliable*
  2 exact, accurate, true, truthful,
  faithful
  *false, inaccurate*
  3 honest, upright, scrupulous
  *dishonest, unscrupulous*

**fiero**
  1 cruel, fierce, ferocious, sanguinary, brutal
  2 savage, wild, untamed
  3 horrendous, terrible

**fiesta**
  1 festivity, feast day, festival, com-
  memoration, holiday
  2 happiness, joy, celebration, entertainment, party

**figura**
  1 (art) figure, form, shape, configu-
  ration
  2 (mathematics) figure, drawing,
  diagram
  3 look, appearance
  4 effigy, image
  5 figure, personage, character, celebrity

**figurar**
  1 represent, delineate, form, shape,
  figure
  2 simulate, feign, pretend
  3 suppose, imagine, believe

**fijar**
  1 fix, fasten, secure, hammer in,
  drive in, thrust in

2 decide, settle, determine

3 fix one's attention on

**fin**

1 end, conclusion, finish, termination, boundary, limit
*beginning*

2 end, aim, purpose, objective, intention, design

**firme**

1 stable, solid, hard, firm, fixed, secure

2 *(fig)* firm, resolute, steady, constant, invariable

**flaquear**

1 become weak, grow weak, decay

2 *(fig)* cede, give in, give way, sag, loosen, slacken, faint, pass out, become discouraged, become downhearted

**flexible**

flexible, docile, manageable, adaptable
*hard*

**flojo**

1 weak, feeble, loose, slack, limp

2 lazy, negligent, indolent, careless

**fomentar**

1 foment

2 *(fig)* excite, promote, stimulate, enliven, increase
*discourage*

**fondo**

1 depths, bottom

2 *(fig)* at bottom, at heart, really

3 condition, character, nature, state of being, background

**fondos**

1 *(commerce)* funds, money, finance, resources, capital, wealth

2 *(fig)* reserves, fund, supply, reservoir

**florecer**

1 flower, bloom

2 *(fig)* flourish, prosper, progress, develop, thrive, grow

**forjar**

1 forge, beat into shape

2 invent, imagine, create, plan, design

**formar**

1 mould, manufacture, make, form, shape

2 constitute, compose, make up

3 institute, establish, organize

4 educate, instruct, teach, train, bring up

5 develop, grow, form, take form

**formal**

1 formal, courteous, correct, conventional, proper, well-behaved
*informal, ill-behaved*

2 express, explicit, precise, determined

3 *(fig)* exact, serious, wise, sensible, truthful

**formidable**

1 tremendous, imposing, smashing, marvellous, terrifying, fearful

2 enormous, colossal, gigantic

3 brutal

**fórmula**

1 norm, model, rule, guidelines, form

2 recipe, prescription

**fortalecer**

1 strengthen, tone up, invigorate
*weaken, get softer*

2 encourage, comfort, animate

3 fortify, consolidate

**fortuito**

unexpected, chance, accidental, random
*foreseen, essential*

**fortuna**

1 fate, chance, luck, accident

2 fate, destiny, fortune

3 wealth, fortune, goods, capital, estate
*misery, misfortune*

4 squall, storm, tempest

**fracción**

1 fraction, division

2 part, fragment, portion, bit, piece
*whole*

**fragmento**

fragment, part, piece, bit, fraction
*sum, totality, whole*

**franco**

1 liberal, generous, free

**franco**
2 open, sincere, ingenuous, natural, simple, straightforward
3 free, clear
4 exempt, excused, free

**franqueza**
1 liberality, generosity
2 frankness, openness, forthrightness, candidness, familiarity, freedom, intimacy, sincerity, ingenuousness, simplicity, naturalness
3 exemption (from)

**fraude**
fraud, forgery, falsification, dishonesty, lie, trick, swindle
*honesty, truth*

**frecuente**
1 repeated, reiterated, regular, constant, frequent, usual
2 common, ordinary, current, every-day, usual
3 *(LAm)* familiar

**fresco**
1 cool, fresh
2 recent, fresh, new
3 *(fig)* plump, round, healthy, fresh, ruddy
4 cool, calm, unabashed, serene, impassive
5 cheeky, saucy, insolent, impudent, shameless, forward

**frialdad**
1 coldness, cold, chilliness
2 *(fig)* coldness, coolness, indifference, unconcern, detachment
3 *(LAm)* impotence, frigidity, sterility

**frío**
1 indifferent, unaffected, detached, cold, cool
2 imperturbable, tranquil, impassive, fearless, intrepid

**fuego**
1 fire, blaze, conflagration
2 fireside, fireplace, hearth
3 *(fig)* fire, passion, ardour, vehemence, vivacity

**fuente**
1 fountain, spring, source
2 *(fig)* origin, beginning, source

3 serving dish, platter

**fuero**
1 municipal charter, regional law-code, exemption, privilege
2 jurisdiction, authority, power
3 *(fig)* arrogance, presumption, conceit

**fuerza**
1 energy, vigour, *(Am)* vigor
2 strength, resistance, solidity
*debility*
3 *(fig)* authority, power, coercion, compulsion
*passivity*
4 *(fig)* violence, intensity, impulse, impetus, impetuosity
*softness, tenderness, mildness*

**fulgor**
brightness, brilliance, splendour, gleam, shine, sparkle, twinkle
*obscurity*

**función**
1 function, operation, performance
2 function, performance, show, diversion, spectacle
3 office, profession, duty, job

**funciones**
duties, responsibilities

**fundar**
1 institute, establish, erect, build, found
2 base, found, lay the foundations of, rest on, be supported by

**fundir**
1 fuse, join, join together, unite
2 liquidize, liquefy, melt, smelt
3 *(LAm)* spoil, ruin, sink

**funesto**
1 unfortunate, ill-fated, fateful, fatal, unlucky, disastrous
2 sad, dolorous, wretched, miserable, gloomy

**furia**
fury, rage, choler, ire, anger, violence, frenzy, madness, passion
*tranquillity, serenity, peace*

**furioso**
furious, irascible, rabid, choleric, raging, violent, mad, frenetic
*calm*

# G

**gabinete**
1 study, library, private sitting room, boudoir, office, laboratory, museum, studio
2 *(politics)* cabinet, government, council, ministry

**gala**
1 full dress, best dress, court dress
2 pomp, ostentation, display, show
3 *(LAm)* gift, tip

**galas**
finery, trappings, jewels, adornments, regalia

**galante**
1 attentive, polite, thoughtful, gallant, flattering, charming
2 amorous, erotic, amatory, wanton, free, licentious

**gallardo**
1 elegant, graceful, free and easy, charming, courteous
2 dashing, brave, valiant, courageous, spirited
3 *(fig)* excellent, handsome, grand

**gana**
1 appetite, hunger
2 desire, longing, hankering, craving, wish, will

**ganar**
1 acquire, get, obtain, secure, collect, earn, win
*lose*
2 outstrip, surpass, exceed, leave behind, triumph, defeat, overcome
3 *(military)* conquer, take, capture
4 attain, reach, arrive at
5 attract, gain
6 prosper, improve

**garantía**
guarantee, pledge, security, undertaking, surety, *(law)* warranty

**garbo**
1 elegance, grace, charm, gracefulness, refinement

2 largesse, generosity, magnanimity, lavishness
*meanness*

**gastar**
1 spend, consume, spoil, deteriorate, waste, wear out
2 expend, lay out, disburse
*save, put into one's pocket*
3 spend, use, employ
*save*

**gemir**
groan, moan, wail, howl, whine, *(fig)* lament, moan

**género**
1 class, group, kind, type, sort
2 *(botany)* genus, species
3 *(literature)* genre, type
4 *(commerce)* cloth, stuff, material

**generos**
*(commerce)* products, merchandise, commodities, goods

**genio**
1 condition, character, nature, disposition, inclination, temper
2 genius, aptitude, talent, capacity
3 *(mythology, religion)* spirit, genie, demon

**gentil**
1 graceful, charming, courteous, neat, elegant, dashing, jaunty, humorous
2 *(religion)* gentile, pagan

**gloria**
1 paradise, heaven
2 glory, fame, honour, renown, celebrity
3 splendour, magnificence, majesty
4 pleasure, delight, transport, rapture, ecstasy
5 puff-pastry cake

**gobierno**
1 guidance, control, management, direction, running, handling
2 government, ministry
3 *(boat)* steering, rudder, helm

**golpe**
1 blow, hit, punch, knock, smack, bump, stroke
2 *(fig)* shock, clash
3 percussion
4 heartbeat, throb
5 *(fig)* multitude, crowd, mass, abundance

**gozar**
1 enjoy, have
2 enjoy oneself, have a good time, amuse oneself, be pleased, rejoice *suffer, grow sad*
3 come, have an orgasm

**gracia**
1 grace, favour, benefit, gift
2 *(law)* pardon, mercy
3 affability, friendship, kindness
4 grace, elegance, charm, delight, attractiveness
5 sharpness, wit, humour

**grande** *(aj)*
1 high, vast, spacious, large, deep, profound, extensive, voluminous *small, little*
2 *(LAm)* old, elderly

**grande** *(s)*
grandee, magnate

**grandeza**
1 magnitude, size, greatness
2 magnificence, splendour, grandeur
3 generosity, nobility, magnanimity, loftiness
4 majesty, splendour, glory

**gratificar**
gratify, reward, recompense, tip, remunerate, pay

**gratificación**
1 gratification, reward, recompense, bonus, tip, remuneration
2 *(LAm)* gratification, pleasure, satisfaction

**gratuito**
1 gratis, free, free of charge, gratuitous
2 arbitrary, unfounded, groundless

**gravamen**
1 burden, obligation
2 *(finance)* tax, impost, duty, tribute, leasehold, mortgage
3 *(law)* lien, encumbrance

**grave**
1 heavy, weighty
2 important, considerable
3 difficult, arduous, dangerous
4 grave, serious, dignified, sedate
5 *(fig)* grave, serious, critical, important, momentous

**grosero**
1 rude, bad-mannered, discourteous *polite*
2 crude, vulgar, coarse, rough, uncouth, common

**grueso** *(aj)*
thick, heavy, bulky, voluminous, fat, corpulent, stout

**grueso** *(s)*
thickness, body

**guardar**
1 guard, keep, protect, defend, preserve, watch over, look after *neglect, be careless*
2 keep, observe, obey, respect
3 keep, conserve, retain, save, hold *waste, spend, use up*

**guía**
1 guide, conductor, leader
2 guide, counsellor, director, adviser, mentor, teacher, master
3 guidebook

**guiar(se)**
guide, conduct, show, direct, indicate, steer, be guided by *be wrong, make a mistake*

**gustar**
1 taste, savour, try, relish
2 please, be pleasing

# H

**haber**
1 have, possess
2 *(finance)* capital, estate, wealth, fortune
3 *(commerce)* credit side

**habilidad**
1 ability, mastery, skill, expertise, cleverness, talent, wit, intuition, tact
*inability*
2 *(law)* competence

**habitar**
inhabit, occupy, live, dwell, stay, reside
*wander*

**hábito**
1 habit, custom
2 practice, use, usage

**habitual**
habitual, customary, usual, accustomed, ordinary, current

**hablador** *(aj)*
1 talkative, chatty, voluble, indiscreet, gossipy
2 *(LAm)* lying, loudmouthed

**hablador** *(s)*
gossip, chatterbox

**habladuría**
piece of gossip, nasty remark, tale, story, rumour

**habldurías**
gossip, scandal

**hablar**
1 say, tell, speak, talk
2 discourse, perorate, make a speech
3 converse, chat, talk, lecture
4 communicate, treat a subject

**hacedero**
practicable, possible, feasible, realizable
*impossible*

**hacer(se)**
1 make, do
2 produce, create, form, build, construct, manufacture
*break up, destroy*
3 dispose, prepare, arrange, compose
4 cause, occasion, motivate
5 execute, perform, realize, practise
6 augment, grow, increase
7 become used to, get used to, adapt oneself to
8 simulate, feign, affect

**halagar**
caress, cherish, treat well, entertain, feast, woo, pamper, indulge, flatter
*discredit, disparage*

**halago**
1 pleasure, delight, gratification, allurement, attraction
2 petting, courtship, adulation, flattery

**hallar(se)**
1 find, encounter, meet, bump into, run into
2 invent
3 discover, find out, ascertain
4 note, observe
5 be

**hambre**
1 hunger, famine, appetite, necessity, need
2 *(fig)* desire, yearning, longing, eagerness

**hambriento**
1 hungry, starving
2 greedy, eager, anxious, covetous

**harapiento**
tattered, torn, ragged, in rags, rent

**hartar(se)**
1 stuff, fill up, gorge, glut, satiate, sate, surfeit

*dissatisfy, starve*

2 *(fig)* sicken, disgust, annoy, bother, exasperate, tire, weary, bore, get fed up with

3 *(LAm)* malign, slander

**harto** *(aj)*

1 satiated, glutted, gorged, over-filled, replete

2 *(fig)* annoyed, bothered, exasperated, tired, wearied, bored, fed up with

**harto** *(av)*

enough, more than enough, excessive, superfluous

**hastío**

1 repugnance, disgust

2 *(fig)* annoyance, disgust, tiredness, weariness, boredom

**hechicero** *(aj)*

*(fig)* charming, fascinating, enchanting, seductive

**hechicero** *(s)*

1 wizard, sorcerer, necromancer, magician, enchanter

2 *(fig)* charmer, seducer

**hechizar**

1 enchant, bewitch, cast a spell on

2 *(fig)* charm, enchant, fascinate, captivate, seduce, *(pejorative)* bedevil

**hechizo** *(aj)*

1 artificial, false, fake, sham, spurious, feigned, simulated

2 detachable, separable

3 *(LAm)* rough and ready, home-made

**hechizo** *(s)*

1 witchcraft, magic, spell, charm, curse, enchantment, potion, philtre

2 attraction, fascination, enchantment, glamour

**hecho** *(aj)*

mature, perfect, finished, complete, made-up, ready-made, ready-to-wear

**hecho** *(s)*

1 deed, act, action

2 fact, factor, matter, event

**hediondo**

1 stinking, foul-smelling, smelly, foetid, putrefying

2 *(fig)* filthy, dirty, repugnant, repulsive, obscene

3 annoying, troublesome, vexatious, bothersome, unbearable

**herir**

1 hit, strike, beat, knock down

2 wound, injure, hurt

3 *(fig)* touch, move, sway

4 *(fig)* hurt, wrong, offend

**hermoso**

1 pretty, beautiful, lovely, handsome, gracious, precious, splendid, magnificent

*ugly*

2 *(LAm)* robust, stout, impressive

**hidalgo** *(aj)*

noble, illustrious, distinguished, *(fig)* gentlemanly, generous, chivalrous

*vile, low*

**hidalgo** *(s)*

nobleman, hidalgo

**hijo**

1 son, child, offspring

2 *(fig)* descendant, native

3 *(fig)* result, consequence, fruit, product

**hincharse**

1 swell, distend, enlarge, inflate, blow up, pump up

2 *(fig)* exaggerate, carry to extremes

*diminish*

3 get conceited, become vain

**hipocresía**

hypocrisy, fiction, simulation, pretext

*sincerity*

**hipócrita** *(aj)*

hypocritical, canting, deceitful, false, insincere, pharisaical, sanctimonious

**hipócrita** *(s)*
   hypocrite, deceiver, dissembler, imposter, pharisee, pretender

**hipótesis**
   hypothesis, supposition, theory, conjecture, presumption, assumption

**holgar**
  1 rest, take a break, be at leisure, be idle, be out of work, lie unused
    *work, be employed*
  2 exceed, be superfluous, be unnecessary
  3 be happy, be contented, enjoy oneself
    *make oneself sad*
  4 amuse oneself, entertain oneself

**holgazán** *(aj)*
  1 lazy, idle, indolent, slack, good-for-nothing
    *industrious*
  2 negligent, remiss

**homenaje**
  1 allegiance, fealty, loyalty, fidelity, homage, tribute
  2 respect, reverence, veneration, duty, deference, worship
  3 *(LAm)* celebration, gathering
  4 *(LAm)* gift, favour

**hondo** *(aj)*
  1 deep, low
  2 *(fig)* deep, profound, heartfelt, intense, extreme
  3 *(fig)* recondite, arcane, abstruse, mysterious

**hondo** *(s)*
   depths, bottom
   *top*

**honestidad**
  1 decency, decorum, propriety
    *indecency, impropriety*
  2 purity, chastity, modesty
    *impurity, immodesty*
  3 fairness, justice, equity
    *unfairness, injustice, partiality*
  4 honourableness, honesty, integrity
    *dishonesty*

**honesto**
  1 honest, decent, honourable, *(Am)* honorable
    *dishonest*
  2 chaste, modest, pure, virtuous
    *unchaste, impure, immodest*
  3 upright, fair, just, reasonable
    *unjust, unfair*

**honor**
  1 renown, reputation, fame, glory, honour, *(Am)* honor
    *dishonour, (Am) dishonor*
  2 honesty, chastity, virtue
  3 distinction, dignity

**honores**
   honorary status, honours, *(Am)* honors

**honorarios**
   honorarium, stipend, payment, fee, emolument

**honra**
  1 honour, *(Am)* honor
  2 honesty, chastity, modesty
  3 reputation, renown, glory, fame, good name

**honrar**
  1 respect, revere
  2 distinguish, enhance, praise, exalt, favour, *(Am)* favor

**horrible**
   horrible, horrifying, horrific, horrendous, hair-raising, awesome, dreadful, frightening, terrifying

**horror**
  1 aversion, phobia, repulsion
  2 horror, consternation, terror, dread

**hosco**
   harsh, grim, dark, sullen, gloomy, shy, unsociable
   *smooth, gentle, mild, nice, pleasant*

**hostigar**
  1 whip, beat, punish
  2 harrass, pester, annoy, bother, hound
  3 *(LAm)* *(food)* surfeit, cloy

**hostil**
   hostile, unfriendly, inimical, antagonistic

**hueco** *(aj)*
1 hollow, empty, void
2 fluffed up, spongy
3 affected, swollen
4 booming, echoing, resounding, resonant
5 *(fig)* vain, presumptuous, fatuous, pompous, affected, conceited

**hueco** *(s)*
1 hollow, cavity, hole, space, lacuna, discontinuity
2 vacancy, void

**huir**
1 escape, flee, evade
*stay, stay behind, remain*
2 avoid, elude, shun, shrink from
*face*

**humanidad**
1 humanity, human species, man, mankind
2 benignity, benevolence, compassion, charity, pity, mercy

**humanidades**
Humanities, Humanism, Belles Artes, Literature

**humano** *(aj)*
1 human, humane

2 *(fig)* benignant, benevolent, compassionate, generous, charitable

**humano** *(s)*
human, human being

**humilde**
1 humble, docile, obedient, submissive
2 humble, modest, obscure, poor

**humillar(se)**
1 humiliate, humble, embarrass, shame, subdue, subjugate, conquer, overwhelm
2 humble oneself, grovel

**humor**
humour, mood, temper, condition, character

**hundir**
1 submerge, sink, hammer in
2 confound, vanquish, shame, embarrass
3 destroy, ruin, wreck, demolish, smash, break up
4 sink, collapse

**hurgar**
1 move, stir, rumple
2 *(fig)* incite, excite, stir up, rouse, move, disturb

# I

**idea**
1 concept, representation, image
2 opinion, notion, judgement
3 plan, project, design, intention, purpose
4 imagination, ingenuity, inventiveness
5 doctrine, belief
6 mania, obsession, caprice

**ideal** *(aj)*
perfect, sublime, elevated, excellent, exemplary, pure, abstract, imaginary

**ideal** *(s)*
1 model, prototype, archetype, criterion, example, standard
2 desire, ambition, dream, hope

**igual**
1 equivalent, synonymous, equal, like
*unequal, heterogenous, antonymous*
2 flat, plain, even, level, smooth
*uneven, rough*
3 constant, invariable, regular, uniform, unvarying
*variable, irregular*

**ilegal**
illegal, unlawful, illicit, illegitimate, prohibited
*legal, lawful, legitimate, just, fair, right*

**iluminar**
1 light up, illuminate
2 illustrate, make clear
3 *(fig)* enlighten, inspire

**ilusión**
1 illusion, dream, chimera, fiction, delusion, hopefulness
2 hallucination, delirium, confusion
3 hope, expectation, eagerness, excitement, thrill
*despair, disappointment*

**ilusionarse**
deceive, seduce, trick, dazzle, attract, delude oneself

**ilustración**
1 illustration, explanation, clarification, commentary, exegesis
2 enlightenment, learning, erudition, instruction, culture, civilization
3 figure, plate, engraving

**ilustre**
noble, illustrious, celebrated, renowned, prestigious, eminent, distinguished
*undistinguished*

**imaginar**
1 represent, create, invent, forge
2 presume, suspect, suppose, conjecture
*know*

**imitar**
imitate, copy, follow, mimic, ape, plagiarize
*create, invent*

**impaciencia**
anxiety, uneasiness, disquiet, restlessness, impatience
*calm, patience*

**imperfección**
imperfection, defect, flaw, fault, vice
*perfection*

**impertinencia**
1 irrelevance, inappropriateness
*relevance*
2 fussiness, peevishness, petulance
3 impertinence, impudence, insolence, intrusion
*politeness*

**impertinente**
1 inconvenient, inopportune, inappropriate
*convenient, opportune, appropriate*
2 impertinence, impudence, insolent

**imperturbable**
imperturbable, impassive, intrepid, fearless, undaunted, ser-

ene, tranquil, immutable, unchangeable

**ímpetu**
1 impetus, impulse, *(mechanics)* momentum
2 rush, onrush
3 haste, violence, impetuosity

**impetuoso**
impetuous, impulsive, precipitate, violent, rash, hasty, vehement
*calm, collected*

**impío**
irreligious, unbelieving, sceptical, incredulous, godless
*pious, religious, devout, godly*

**implacable**
inexorable, inflexible, cruel, hard, inhuman, vindictive, heartless, merciless, relentless

**implorar**
beg, supplicate, implore, pray, beseech

**imponente**
1 terrifying, frightening, awesome, dreadful
2 respectable, venerable, majestic, grandiose, impressive, imposing, grand

**importancia**
value, significance, consideration, interest, scope, size, importance, magnitude

**importante**
important, significant, weighty, substantial, considerable, momentous, interesting, well-known

**importar**
1 be of interest, worth the trouble, of concern
2 be worth, amount to , add up, rise, *(price)* go up

**importe**
amount, value, price, cost, sum, final total

**importunar**
importune, entreat, press, solicit, bother, pester, annoy, tire, inconvenience

**importuno**
1 importunate, troublesome, bothersome, uncomfortable, annoying
*hesitant*
2 inopportune, ill-timed

**imposibilitar**
1 make impossible, impede, prevent, hinder
*enable*
2 make incapable, cripple

**imposible**
1 impossible, impracticable, fantastic
2 unbearable, insufferable, intolerable, unmanageable

**imposición**
1 imposition, compulsion, demand, requirement
2 tribute, tax, obligation, burden, charge

**imprescindible**
necessary, obligatory, indispensable, essential, vital
*accidental*

**imprevisto**
sudden, unforeseen, unexpected, unprepared, surprising
*foreseen, expected*

**imprevistos**
incidentals, unforeseen expenses

**impropio**
1 inappropriate, improper, inadequate, inconvenient
2 foreign, alien

**imprudencia**
imprudence, indiscretion, impudence, effrontery, insolence, rudeness, nerve, daring

**imprudente**
imprudent, precipitate, thoughtless, indiscreet, trusting, rash

**impuesto**
tribute, tax, charge, contribution, duty

**impúdico**
1 impudent, cynical, dishonest
*honest*
2 shameless, immodest, lewd, lecherous, libidinous, libertine

**impudor**
1 cynicism, dishonesty
2 shamelessness, immodesty, libertinism, lechery, lewdness

**impulsar**
1 push, drive, propel, impel
   *stop*
2 incite, stimulate, excite, instigate

**impulso**
1 impulse, push, shove, *(mechanics)* thrust, drive
2 instigation, stimulus, incitement, urge

**inaccesible**
1 unattainable, inaccessible, unapproachable, impossible
   *accessible*
2 impracticable, impassable
   *practicable, penetrating*

**inactivo**
1 idle, quiet, motionless, stopped, inactive
2 inert, inactive, lifeless

**inagotable**
interminable, endless, inexhaustible

**inaguantable**
intolerable, unbearable, insufferable, unendurable

**inaudito**
unheard-of, extraordinary, outrageous, scandalous, incredible, monstrous

**incapacidad**
1 incapacity, incompetence, ineptitude, inability, clumsiness
   *capacity, competence, aptitude, experience, knowledge*
2 insufficiency, scarcity, penury

**incapaz**
1 incapable, unfit, inept, incompetent, ignorant, awkward, dim, slow, clumsy
   *competent, clever, able*
2 insufficient, little

**incauto**
incautious, careless, credulous, simple, naïve, innocent, candid

**incertidumbre**
uncertainty, doubt, perplexity, irresolution, indecision, vacillation

**incesante**
incessant, continuous, uninterrupted, unbroken, constant, persistent

**incierto**
1 uncertain, doubtful, dubious, unsure, ambiguous, vague
2 inconstant, insecure, unsafe, unreliable
3 unknown, unpredictable
   *known*

**incitar**
incite, instigate, rouse, provoke, stimulate, move, induce
   *calm, appease*

**inclinación**
1 declivity, slope, obliquity, inclination
   *verticality, horizontality*
2 propensity, inclination
3 fondness, affection, liking, inclination, leaning
   *indifference*

**inclinar(se)**
1 incline, bow, nod
2 bow, stoop
3 *(fig)* persuade, move, incite
4 be inclined to

**incluir**
include, comprehend, contain, consist of, embrace, include, incorporate, enclose
   *exclude*

**incoherente**
incoherent, unconnected, discontinuous, separated, dispersed, disintegrated
   *coherent, in agreement*

**incomodar**
1 inconvenience, bother, trouble, anger, irritate, displease, molest
   *please*
2 put oneself out, get annoyed

**incómodo**
uncomfortable, embarrassing, disagreeable, bothersome, annoying, inconvenient

**incompleto**
truncated, fragmentary, incomplete, unfinished, imperfect, defective

**incomprensible**
1 incomprehensible, unintelligible, inexplicable
*comprehensible*

2 *(fig)* obscure, enigmatic, arcane, mysterious, confused, complicated

**inconsecuente**
1 inconsequential, illogical

2 inconstant, fickle, capricious, whimsical, inconsistent

**inconstancia**
1 inconstancy, fickleness, capriciousness, whimsicality, versatility

2 instability, unsteadiness

**inconstante**
1 inconstant, fickle, capricious, versatile

2 unstable, variable, changeable, varied

**inconveniente** *(aj)*
inconvenient, unsuitable, impolite, discourteous, rude, bad-mannered, incorrect

**inconveniente** *(s)*
1 obstacle, impediment, bond, tie, shackle, hindrance, difficulty, disadvantage, inconvenience

2 injury, damage, harm

**incorrecto**
1 incorrect, wrong, erroneous, imperfect, defective

2 discourteous, uncivil, rude, bad-mannered

**incorporar(se)**
1 unite, join, meet, integrate, gather

2 sit up, stand up, raise

**incrédulo**
1 incredulous, disbelieving, impious, sceptical

2 distrustful, suspicious

**indecencia**
1 dishonesty, obscenity, impropriety
*honesty, decorum*

2 insolence, rudeness, bad manners

**indecisión**
indecision, doubt, perplexity, vacillation, irresolution, hesitation
*resolution, certitude*

**indecoroso**
1 indecent, rude, insolent, undignified

2 obscene, indecorous, dishonest

**indemnizar**
indemnify, compensate, make up for, make amends for

**indeterminado**
1 indeterminate, indefinite, inconclusive, vague

2 indecisive, irresolute, perplexed, confused

**indicar**
1 *(technical)* indicate, show, register, record, denote, signal, signify

2 indicate, point out, point to, show, suggest, hint, intimate

**indignar(se)**
1 anger, make indignant, annoy, irritate, infuriate
*pacify, calm, soothe*

2 get angry, get indignant

**indiscreto**
1 curious, intrusive, meddlesome, interfering

2 gossipy, long-tongued, indiscreet, tactless
*discreet*

**indiscutible**
indisputable, unquestionable, incontrovertible, certain, sure, irrefutable, unanswerable, undeniable

**indispensable**
necessary, essential, needed, needful, obligatory, requisite, indispensable
*unnecessary, inessential*

**indisponer(se)**
1 upset, spoil

2 *(medicine)* upset, make ill, make unfit

3 make enemies of, cause a rift between

**inducir**
induce, instigate, incite, persuade, move, press, attract

**índole**
1 nature, character, disposition, condition, temper, genius
2 class, kind, sort

**indolencia**
indolence, sloth, laziness, apathy, listlessness, idleness

**indudable**
indubitable, unquestionable, certain, sure, evident, undeniable, incontestable, incontrovertible, unarguable
*doubtful*

**indulgencia**
1 indulgence, tolerance, forbearance, leniency, clemency
2 *(ecclesiatical)* pardon, forgiveness, remission

**indulgente**
indulgent, tolerant, forbearing, lenient, compliant, kind
*harsh*

**inevitable**
1 inevitable, inescapable, unavoidable, necessary, certain, sure
*avoidable*
2 inexorable, fatal

**inexplicable**
inexplicable, incomprehensible, indecipherable, mysterious, arcane, strange
*evident*

**inextricable**
inextricable, entangled, confused, complicated, intricate

**infamar**
defame, discredit, vilify, slander, revile, dishonour, affront
*honour*

**infame**
1 infamous, odious, evil, vile, perverse, base, shameful
2 dishonourable, discreditable
*honourable*

**infamia**
1 infamy, ignominy, vileness, villainy, obloquy, odium

2 dishonour, discredit, disgrace, disrepute
*honour*

**infectar(se)**
1 infect, transmit, pass on
2 contaminate, corrupt, pervert

**infeliz** *(aj)*
1 unhappy, unfortunate, wretched, miserable, unsuccessful, unlucky
*happy, fortunate, successful*
2 simple, kind-hearted, good-natured, *(pejorative)* gullible
3 *(LAm)* trifling, insignificant

**infeliz** *(s)*
1 wretch, poor devil
2 simpleton, fool

**inferior** *(aj)*
1 lower than, inferior to
2 low, bad

**inferior** *(s)*
inferior, subordinate, *(pejorative)* underling

**infiel** *(aj)*
1 unfaithful, disloyal, traitorous, treacherous, perfidious
*faithful, loyal*
2 unbelieving, infidel
3 inaccurate, mistaken, wrong, erroneous, faulty, incorrect
*accurate, correct*

**infiel** *(s)*
infidel, unbeliever

**inflamar(se)**
1 ignite, kindle, set on fire
2 *(medicine)* inflame
3 *(fig)* inflame, arouse, enrage, madden, infuriate, incense
4 become inflamed, catch fire

**inflexible**
1 inflexible, rigid, firm, unbreakable
*flexible*
2 *(fig)* unbending, unyielding, adamant, obstinate, stubborn, intractable, resolute
*complaisant, pliable*

**informar(se)**
1 inform, tell, announce, notify, advise, communicate, make known
2 give an opinion, pass judgement
3 *(law)* plead

**informe** *(s)*
 1 report, statement, announcement
 2 piece of information
 3 *(law)* plea

**infracción**
 infraction, transgression, infringement, breach, violation, offence, *(Am)* offense
 *compliance*

**infringir**
 infringe, violate, transgress, contravene, disobey
 *obey, respect*

**ingenio**
 1 ingenuity, inventiveness, talent, creativeness, wit, skill, ability
 2 *(mechanics)* apparatus, engine, device
 3 *(technical)* mill, plant

**ingenuo**
 1 frank, sincere, candid, ingenuous, unaffected, artless, open, simple
 *artful, insincere, sly*
 2 simple, credulous, innocent, naïve

**ingrato**
 1 ungrateful
 *grateful*
 2 *(taste)* unpleasant, disagreeable
 3 *(task)* thankless, unrewarding

**inhospitalario**
 1 cruel, inhuman, barbarous
 2 inclement, inhospitable, unpleasant, savage

**inhumano**
 1 inhuman, cruel, barbarous, ferocious, hard, inhospitable, merciless, heartless
 2 *(LAm)* dirty, disgusting

**iniciar**
 1 initiate, commence, begin, start
 *finish, diminish, decline*
 2 instruct, inform, tell
 3 promote, cause, provoke, arouse, instigate, stir up

**inicuo**
 1 unjust
 *just, moral*
 2 perverse, evil, bad, ignominious, wicked, iniquitous

**injuria**
 1 insult, injury, affront, outrage, wrong, offence, *(Am)* offense
 2 hurt, harm, damage

**injuriar**
 1 insult, abuse, revile, offend, denigrate, wrong, affront, vilify, outrage
 2 injure, harm, damage
 *benefit*

**injusticia**
 injustice, unfairness, iniquity, wrong
 *fairness*

**inmenso**
 1 limitless, infinite, immeasurable, innumerable, uncountable
 2 enormous, immense, huge, colossal, excessive
 *small, diminutive*

**inmóvil**
 1 immobile, motionless, still
 *mobile*
 2 immovable, firm, constant

**inmundo**
 1 dirty, nasty, repugnant, nauseating, filthy, disgusting, sickening
 2 *(fig)* impure, foul, dirty, defiled, unclean

**inmutable**
 immutable, constant, fixed, invariable, stable, changeless, permanent, unchangeable
 *variable, mutable, unstable*

**innoble**
 ignoble, abject, vile, despicable, worthless, low
 *noble*

**inocencia**
 innocence, candour, simplicity, purity, uprightness
 *impurity*

**inocente** *(aj)*
 1 innocent, harmless, innocuous
 *harmful*
 2 simple, naïve, artless, frank, ingenuous
 *sly*

**inocente** *(s)*
 simpleton, fool

**inquietar(se)**
    disquiet, alarm, agitate, bother, disturb, make uneasy, upset, worry

**inquisición**
  1 inquiry, investigation
  2 tribunal, Holy Office

**inscribir(se)**
  1 inscribe, engrave
  2 enrol, register, record, list, annotate, note (down)

**inseguridad**
  1 insecurity, unsteadiness
  2 risk, danger, unsafeness
    *safety*
  3 uncertainty, incertitude, indecision, vacillation

**insensato**
  fatuous, stupid, silly, senseless, foolish, absurd

**insensible**
  1 insensitive, unfeeling, callous, impassive, cold, indifferent
  2 imperceptible, indiscernible
  3 *(medicine)* insensible, unconscious, numb, without feeling

**insípido**
  insipid, tasteless, *(fig)* dull, uninteresting

**insolente**
  1 insolent, rude, offensive, disrespectful
    *respectful*
  2 insulting, arrogant, haughty, contemptuous

**insólito**
  unusual, infrequent, rare, strange
    *habitual, ordinary*

**inspeccionar**
  inspect, examine, audit, check, control, register, recognize

**inspirar**
  1 *(medicine)* breathe in, inhale
  2 *(fig)* suggest, infuse, instil, inspire

**instalar(se)**
  1 install, set up, erect, fit up, lay on
  2 establish oneself, move into, settle down

**instantánea**
  snapshot, photograph

**instantáneo** *(aj)*
  instantaneous, momentary, brief, rapid, fleeting

**instituir**
  institute, establish, found, set up
    *abolish*

**instrucción**
  1 instruction, education, teaching, doctrine, illustration
  2 erudition, culture

**instrucciones**
  norms, precepts, orders

**insuficiencia**
  1 incapacity, ineptitude, ignorance, incompetence
    *capacity, aptitude, ability*
  2 insufficiency, scarcity, lack, penury
  3 *(school/college grade)* unsatisfactory

**insultar**
  insult, abuse, offend, affront, outrage, injure
    *praise*

**intacto**
  1 intact, whole, entire, complete
    *incomplete*
  2 undamaged, unhurt
    *damaged, hurt*

**integridad**
  1 integrity, probity, rectitude, honesty
  2 entirety, wholeness
    *corruption, division*
  3 *(fig)* virginity, chastity

**íntegro**
  1 entire, whole, complete
  2 *(fig)* honourable, honest, upright, incorruptible, just, straight

**inteligencia**
  1 intelligence, intellect, understanding, reason, mind
  2 comprehension, knowledge, consciousness, meaning
  3 agreement, harmony

**inteligente**
  1 learned, educated, knowledgeable, informed, intelligent
    *ignorant, uneducated, uninformed, unintelligent*

2 ingenious, clever, shrewd, smart, perspicacious, sharp, alert, intelligent
*stupid, silly, foolish*

**inteligible**
intelligible, comprehensible, clear, legible, decipherable
*difficult, confused, incomprehensible*

**intención**
intention, aim, design, purpose, objective, meaning

**intenso**
1 intense, strong, deep, profound
2 vehement, sharp, vivid

**intentar**
intend, try, attempt, essay, try out, test

**intento**
intent, purpose, design, intention, end, attempt

**interés**
1 benefit, advantage, profit, import
2 *(commerce)* interest, return, yield, income, earnings
3 inclination, attraction, attention, concern, interest

**intereses**
fortune, capital, wealth, goods

**intervenir**
1 supervise, control, *(LAm)* instal government apointees in, take over the control of
2 *(commerce)* inspect, audit
3 *(medicine)* operate on
4 *(law)* confiscate, seize

**intrepidez**
intrepidity, valour, courage, daring
*fear, cowardice, hesitancy*

**inventar**
1 discover
2 *(pejorative)* invent, think up, imagine, feign, fabricate, concoct

**invertir**
1 invert, overturn, upset, alter, change
2 *(commerce)* invest, employ, spend
3 dedicate, occupy, employ

**invitar**
1 invite, offer, present, *(drinks)* treat, buy, pay for
2 incite, induce, provoke

**involuntario**
involuntary, instinctive, automatic, unintended

**ira**
ire, anger, wrath, choler, fury, rage

**iracundo**
irascible, furious, choleric, irritable

**irracional**
1 brutish, animal, beastly
2 irrational, absurd, foolish, stupid

**irreflexivo**
1 precipitate, hurried, hasty, confused, bewildered
2 involuntary, instinctive, mechanical, automatic

**irregular**
1 anomalous, abnormal, irregular
2 unequal, intermittent, discontinuous
3 variable, capricious, inconstant

**irresoluto**
1 indecisive, hesitant, doubtful, vacillating
*decided*
2 irresolute, perplexed

**irrespetuoso**
disrespectful, irreverent, inattentive, discourteous
*respectful*

**irritable**
irritable, irascible, catankerous, choleric, petulant, testy, touchy
*good-tempered*

**irritación**
anger, choler, rage, fury, annoyance
*tranquillity, peace*

**irritar**
1 anger, infuriate, exasperate, provoke, annoy
*soothe*
2 excite, inflame

# J

**jactancioso**
boastful, vainglorious, presumptuous, vain, petulant, fatuous, conceited

**jaleo**
1 *(flamenco)* audience participation, fiesta, drinking bout, spree, amusement, noise
2 row, racket, uproar, confusion, disturbance, disorder
*peace, quiet*

**jefe**
leader, chief, head, director, principal, superior, manager, boss

**jocoso**
jocose, jocular, humorous, witty, comic, cheerful

**joroba**
1 hump, hunchback
2 *(fig)* nuisance, bother, annoyance, impertinence, mortification

**judiada**
1 cruelty, inhumanity, infamy
2 *(finance)* usury, extortion, exploitation

**juego**
1 diversion, recreation, pastime, entertainment, game, play, gaming, gambling
2 action, movement, performance, function
3 set, assembly, union, joint, juncture

**juerga**
party, spree, drinking bout, binge, carousal, diversion

**jugar(se)**
1 amuse oneself, have a good time
2 frolic, romp, play
3 function, move, perform, work, operate
4 risk, venture, gamble

**junta**
1 junta, board, council, committee, meeting, assembly, session
2 *(technical)* union, joint, juncture, coupling

**juntar(se)**
1 join, assemble, couple, link, unite, tie up, fasten, clasp
*separate*
2 amass, agglomerate, accumulate, pile up, collect
3 meet, assemble, gather together, congregate
4 *(zoology)* mate, copulate
5 approach, approximate, come close
6 *(documents)* enclose, attach, annex

**justicia**
1 justice, equity, fairness, rectitude
*injustice, impartiality*
2 tribunal

**justo**
1 just, fair, right, correct, impartial, equitable, legitimate, legal, reasonable
*unjust, unfair, incorrect, illegal, unreasonable*
2 exact, precise, punctual, right, correct

**juzgar**
1 *(law)* judge, sentence, decide
2 believe, opine, discern, estimate, consider, deem, assess, evaluate

# L

**laberinto**
1 labyrinth, maze
2 *(fig)* confusion, chaos, web, entanglement, fuss, trouble, *(LAm)* row, racket

**labor**
1 work, task, duty, chore, occupation
2 farming, cultivation
3 needlework, sewing, stitching, embroidery, lacework

**laborioso**
1 diligent, hardworking
2 difficult, laborious, tough, painful, distressing

**labrar**
1 work, fashion, labour
2 till, cultivate, plough
3 *(fig)* cause, bring about, produce, originate, do, make

**lacerar**
1 strike, wound, bruise, hurt, lacerate
2 *(fig)* damage, hurt, harm

**ladear**
tip, tilt, incline, slant, overturn

**lamentación**
lament, clamour, complaint, groan

**lamentar**
lament, complain, deplore, moan, weep, regret

**lance**
1 event, incident, occasion, opportunity, emergency, mishap, difficult situation
2 encounter, duel, fight, quarrel
3 luck, fortune, throw

**lánguido**
1 languid, listless, weak, feeble, tired, fatigued
2 depressed, discouraged, downhearted

**lanzar(se)**
1 throw, cast, fling, hurl, fire, shoot, discharge, throw out, evict
2 *(finance, commerce)* launch, promote

**largar(se)**
1 unfasten, loosen, undo, set free, launch, let fly
2 go away, leave, slip away, run away, run out, beat it
   *stay, remain*
3 *(LAm)* start, begin

**largo** *(aj)*
1 long, lengthy, extensive, diffuse
2 generous, lavish
3 abundant, copious
4 sharp, shrewd, quick, astute

**largo** *(s)*
length, longitude

**lascivia**
lasciviousness, incontinence, lewdness, lechery, obscenity, lust, sensuality

**lástima**
pity, compassion, commiseration, mercy, shame

**latente**
1 latent, occult, hidden, invisible, recondite, secret
2 *(LAm)* vigorous, intense, alive

**latitud**
1 latitude
2 breadth, area, amplitude, width, extent

**lazo**
1 loop, lasso, bond, tie, bow
2 trap, ambush, snare
3 *(fig)* union, alliance, affinity, connection, obligation, dependence, link, bond

**leal**
frank, noble, constant, sincere, faithful, loyal, honest, upright, trustworthy
*disloyal, treacherous*

**legal**
legal, legitimate, lawful, authorized, just, trustworthy
*unjust, immoral*

**legítimo**
1 legitimate, legal, lawful
   *illegal, unlawful*
2 just, reasonable, equitable, fair
3 genuine, authentic, real, true,
   simple, plain
   *false*

**lejano**
   distant, remote, far off, far-away,
   far-removed

**lentitud**
   slowness, delay, pause

**levantamiento**
1 raising, lifting, elevation
2 *(politics)* revolt, rising, uprising,
   rebellion, mutiny

**levantar(se)**
1 stand up, get up, pick up, raise,
   straighten out
   *lie down, fall, lower*
2 construct, build, erect
3 uplift, hearten, cheer up
4 *(politics)* rebel, rouse, stir up
   *conquer, overwhelm, subordinate*
5 magnify, extol, exalt, elevate,
   praise highly

**léxico** *(aj)*
   lexical

**léxico** *(s)*
   dictionary, vocabulary, lexicon,
   word list

**leyenda**
1 legend, tradition, tale
2 legend, inscription, motto, key

**liar**
1 unite, bind together, tie, tie up,
   lace, fasten, moor
   *untie*
2 tie up, entangle, complicate, get
   involved, mix, blend

**liberal** *(aj)*
   liberal, generous, disinterested,
   splendid, lavish

**liberalidad**
   liberality, generosity, disinterestedness, lavishness

**libertad**
1 liberty, licence, freedom, emanci-
   pation, independence

2 liberation, rescue
3 familiarity, looseness, slackness
4 daring, insolence

**libertar**
1 liberate, redeem, rescue, release,
   set free
2 *(commerce)* redeem, cancel,
   exempt

**libertino**
   libertine, dissolute, licentious, vicious, uninhibited, permissive,
   loose-living, rakish, profligate

**librar**
1 preserve, save
2 liberate, set free, save, rescue,
   deliver from
3 *(law)* exempt, dispense, free,
   release from
4 *(commerce)* expedite, draw (let-
   ters of exchange)

**libre**
1 independent, emancipated, free
2 clear, free, unoccupied, vacant
3 liberated, freed
4 exempt, excused
5 *(pejorative)* licentious, immoral,
   loose, dissolute, bold, daring, uninhibited

**lícito**
   just, legitimate, legal, permitted,
   authorized

**liga**
1 union, mixture
2 *(politics)* league, confederation,
   alliance, federation, union
3 garter, suspender
4 *(metals)* alloy, mixture

**ligar**
1 tie, bind, fasten, moor
   *untie, separate, detach*
2 unite, link, bind together, marry,
   reconcile
   *separate, cause a rift between*
3 oblige, compel, force,
4 ally, confederate, join together,
   unite
5 *(LAm)* look, stare

**ligereza**
1 lightness

2 celerity, agility, promptness, rapidity, speed, liveliness, swiftness
*slowness*
3 imprudence, thoughtlessness
4 inconstancy, instability, superficiality, shallowness, fickleness, flippancy, frivolity

**ligero**
1 slight, trivial, unimportant
2 agile, nimble, lively, prompt, fast, quick, swift
*slow*
3 inconstant, fickle, unstable, superficial, shallow, flighty, flippant
4 thoughtless, imprudent

**limitación**
limitation, demarcation, boundary, region, district

**limitar**
1 limit, determine, demarcate, fix
2 limit, restrict, reduce, cut down, shorten, abbreviate

**límite**
1 limit, boundary, frontier, confines
2 end, conclusion

**limpiar**
1 clean, wipe, wash, shine, polish, tidy up
*stain, mark, soil, dirty*
2 purify, purge, clean up
3 rob, steal
4 *(LAm)* hit, beat

**limpieza**
1 cleaning, cleansing, polishing, cleanliness, pulchritude
2 integrity, honesty, rectitude, sincerity
3 purity, chastity
4 *(fig)* precision, perfection, dexterity, skill

**limpio**
1 clean, tidy, smart
2 pure, immaculate, uncontaminated, purified, purged, honest
3 *(commerce, finance)* free of debts, net, clear

**lindo** *(LAm)*
1 beautiful, fine, pretty, lovely, nice, attractive

2 perfect, exquisite, delicate

**lío**
1 bundle, parcel, pack
2 muddle, tangle, mess
*order, clarity*
3 *(fig)* entanglement, confusion, disorder

**liso**
1 flat, plain, level, even, smooth, polished
*uneven*
2 shameless, insolent, forward, impudent

**lisonjear**
1 flatter, compliment, praise, blandish
2 *(fig)* please, satisfy, delight, pamper, indulge
*displease*

**listo**
1 diligent, active, lively, nimble, quick, swift, prompt
2 prepared, disposed, perceptive, observant
3 intelligent, astute, shrewd, wise, informed, smart, clever

**liviano**
1 slight, trivial, unimportant
2 inconstant, fickle, easy
3 lascivious, incontinent, dishonest, shameless, immodest

**loco** *(aj)*
1 demented, insane, mad, disturbed, perturbed
*sane*
2 imprudent, stupid, foolish, absurd

**loco** *(s)*
madman, lunatic

**lucir**
1 glitter, sparkle, shine
2 shine, be outstanding, be distinguished, be exceptional, excel
3 show, display, demonstrate

**lucro**
gain, profit, benefit, advantage, achievement, success
*loss, disadvantage, failure*

**lucha**
1 contest, struggle, battle, conflict, fight
2 argument, brawl, fight, row, hubbub
3 debate, discussion, polemic, dispute, altercation
4 controversy, contention

**luchar**
contend, struggle, fight, battle, combat

**lugar**
1 spot, place, site
2 passage (of a book)
3 occasion, opportunity, chance, motive

**lúgubre**
mournful, lugubrious, dismal, sad, melancholic, gloomy
*happy, clear, bright*

**lujo**
luxury, opulence, ostentation, magnificence, profusion, splendour, abundance, sumptuousness, wealth, richness
*poverty, simplicity*

**lujoso**
opulent, sumptuous, ostentatious, magnificent, splendid, rich, lavish, generous

**lujuria**
lust, lasciviousness, lewdness
*chastity*

**lumbre**
1 light, flame, blaze, fire
2 brilliance, splendour, *(Am)* splendor

**lustre**
1 brilliance, shine, sparkle, splendour, *(Am)* splendor, glitter, glint
2 *(fig)* lustre, glory

# LL

**llamar**
1 acclaim
2 call, name, denominate, designate
3 call, beckon, summon, call upon, invoke, implore
4 cite, convoke
5 draw, attract, invite
6 call, ring up, telephone, knock, ring
7 *(military)* call up

**llano** *(aj)*
1 flat, smooth, plain, level
2 plain, straightforward
3 accessible, frank, simple, unsophisticated, friendly
4 clear, evident

**llano** *(s)*
plain, flat land

**llegar**
1 come, arrive
2 reach, touch

go, leave, depart, set out, set off
3 achieve, attain, bring about, perfect
4 draw near, bring near, approach
5 be enough

**lleno**
full, filled, complete, replete, abundant, overflowing
*empty*

**llevar(se)**
1 take, transport, move, carry
*bring*
2 guide, conduct, direct, lead
3 wear, bear
4 *(money, wages)* collect, draw
5 *(time, life)* spend, pass
6 exceed, surpass

**llorar**
1 shed tears, cry, weep
*laugh*
2 lament, deplore, regret

# M

**macilento**
1 faded, discoloured
2 weak, skinny, emaciated, lean, gaunt

**macizo** (aj)
solid, full, firm, strong, massive, stout
*hollow, weak, fragile*

**machacar**
1 crush, smash, pound, grind
2 insist, persist, bother, pester, go on about something

**madurez**
1 ripeness, maturity
2 (fig) maturity, mellowness, sageness, wisdom, good sense
*immaturity*

**maduro**
1 ripe, seasoned, mature, mellow
*unripe, immature*
2 (fig) mature, prudent, sensible, thoughtful, reflective
3 adult
*adolescent*

**maestría**
mastery, skill, art, ability, expertise

**maestro** (aj)
masterly, skilful, expert, skilled, clever, smart, capable

**maestro** (s)
pedagogue, professor, instructor
*pupil, student, disciple*

**magia**
1 magic, witchcraft, enchantment
2 fascination, attraction, spell, seduction

**mágico** (aj)
magical, fascinating, marvellous, amazing, seductive, charming

**mago** (s)
magician, wizard, enchanter, necromancer

**majestad**
majesty, loftiness, solemnity, stateliness, grandeur
*lowliness*

**majestuoso**
majestic, august, solemn, sublime, impressive, imposing

**majo** (aj)
1 beautiful, handsome, good-looking, dashing, attractive, nice
2 elegant, smart, natty, (pejorative) flashy, gaudy
3 blustering, bold, outspoken, amusing, easy-going

**majo** (s)
bully, braggart, dandy, fop, pimp

**mal** (av)
unjustly, incorrectly, badly, improperly, wrongly, poorly, with difficulty

**mal** (s)
1 calamity, misfortune, illness, harm, damage
*good fortune, good health*
2 evil, wrong
*good, goodness*

**malbaratar**
1 (commerce) sell off cheaply
2 (fig) waste, dissipate, squander

**maldecir**
1 curse, imprecate, execrate
2 loathe, detest
3 denigrate, defame, disparage, slander, criticize
4 curse, complain bitterly of

**maleficio**
curse, spell, enchantment, sorcery, bewitchment, charm

**maleta** (aj) (LAm)
1 naughty, mischievous, wicked
2 stupid, useless

**maleta** (s)
1 suitcase, case, travelling bag
2 bungler, clumsy novice

**malgastar**
dissipate, squander, waste, throw away
*save, keep*

**malicia**
1 wickedness
2 malice, malignity, spite, wickedness, evil intention
3 viciousness, vicious nature, mischief, mischievous nature
4 rougishness, naughtiness
5 slyness, guile

**malicias**
suspicions

**malicioso**
1 wicked, evil
2 ill-intentioned, spiteful, malicious
3 vicious, mischievous
4 rougish, naughty, provocative

**maligno**
1 *(medicine)* pernicious, malignant
*benign*
2 evil, vicious, pernicious, harmful, malicious

**malo/mal** *(aj)*
1 bad, evil, malignant, malicious, vile, perverse
*good*
2 low, contemptible, mean, sly, cunning, depraved

**malo** *(s)*
villain, rascal, rogue, scoundrel
*hero, good person*

**manantial**
1 spring, fountain, source, origin
2 *(fig)* origin, source, fountain, beginning

**manar**
gush forth, surge, spout, spurt, run, flow, abound in

**mancha**
1 spot, mark, stain, blemish, bruise
2 *(fig)* flaw, blemish, stain, dishonour
3 sketch, outline

**mandar**
1 order, decree, command
*obey, carry out, fulfil*

2 direct, govern, rule, subdue, rule despotically
3 send, remit
4 *(LAm)* throw (away), hurl
5 *(LAm)* give, strike, fetch, hit

**mandato**
order, mandate, precept, prescription

**manejar**
1 manage, handle, operate, run, use, utilize, employ
2 direct, rule, govern, administer
3 drive (a vehicle)

**manejo**
1 handling, operation, management, use, employment
2 direction, government, administration
3 stratagem, manoeuvre, gimmick, trick, crafty plan

**manera**
1 form, procedure, mode, method, way
2 fashion, style, manufacture

**maneras**
manners, comportment

**manía**
1 fixed idea
2 antipathy, ill-will, dislike, spite
*sympathy*
3 *(fig)* whim, fad, craze, rage, mania

**manifiesto** *(aj)*
manifest, clear, obvious, visible, patent, ostensible
*obscure*

**manifiesto** *(s)*
*(politics)* manifesto

**manifestar**
1 declare, expose, tell
*hide, keep quiet*
2 manifest, show, exhibit, reveal, present

**mano**
1 hand, foot, paw
2 *(game)* hand, round, turn
3 *(LAm)* misfortune, mishap

**mansedumbre**
gentleness, sweetness, mildness, meekness, tameness
*anger*

**manso**
1 tranquil, quiet, peaceful, calm, meek, mild
2 docile, manageable, tame

**mantener**
1 maintain, conserve, keep
2 sustain, nourish, feed
3 defend, support, protect

**maña**
1 skill, ability, mastery, dexterity
   *inability*
2 shrewdness, astuteness, cleverness, ingenuity
3 artifice, trick, ruse, knack

**mañoso**
1 able, skilful, clever, smart, crafty
2 *(LAm)* vicious, obstinate, nervous, shy

**maravilla**
1 portent, prodigy, marvel, wonder
2 marigold

**maravilloso**
marvellous, wonderful, admirable, prodigious, portentous, surprising, extraordinary, stupendous, astonishing, amazing

**marcial**
1 martial, military, warlike, bellicose, aggressive
   *civil*
2 *(fig)* virile, manly, brave
   *cowardly, timid*

**marcha**
1 speed, celerity
2 *(fig)* march, progress, course, evolution, development
3 procedure, method
4 *(automobiles, mechanics)* gear

**marchar(se)**
1 walk, travel
2 work, function, move, go

**marchitar**
wither, fade, dry (up), shrivel, crease, crumple

**marchito**
withered, faded, dry, shrivelled, shrunken, creased, crumpled, spoilt

**mareo**
1 sickness, nausea, dizziness, vertigo
2 *(fig)* bore, nuisance, annoyance, inconvenience

**margen**
1 border, edge, margin, river-bank, shore
2 occasion, motive, pretext

**marina**
1 coast, seaboard
2 seamanship, navigation, sailing
3 navy, fleet, armada

**máscara**
1 mask, disguise, veil
2 *(fig)* pretext, excuse, dissimulation

**materia**
1 substance, matter, material
   *spirit, unreality*
2 matter, subject, theme

**matriz**
1 uterus, womb
2 mould, die, matrix, *(LAm)* stencil
3 *(fig)* principal, chief

**máxima**
rule, principle, sentence, precept, aphorism, apothegm, maxim

**mayor** *(aj)*
1 main, major, chief, principal, superior
2 older, elder, adult

**mayor** *(s)*
chief, boss, elder

**mayores**
elders, ancestors, grandparents, predecessors, progenitors

**mediar**
1 mediate, intervene, interpose
   *abstain*
2 be in the middle, lie between

**medida**
1 measure(ment)
2 dimension, size
3 step, move, precaution, foresight, prevention
4 prudence, moderation, restraint

**meditar**
consider, reflect, think over, ponder, meditate on

**mejora**
1 improvement, advance, progress, growth, prosperity
2 relief, ease

**mejorar**
1 improve, better, make better
*worsen*
2 struggle, strain
3 relieve, alleviate, re-establish
4 progress, prosper, advance, thrive

**meloso**
honeyed, sweet, mellifluous, sickly, cloying, smooth

**mencionar**
mention, name, allude, cite
*omit, forget*

**menester**
1 necessity, need
2 profession, ministry, occupation, exercise, duty

**mengua**
1 decrease, decline, dimunition
*increase*
2 poverty, scarcity
3 *(fig)* discredit, dishonour
*honour*

**menguado**
1 cowardly, pusillanimous, recreant, faint-hearted
2 miserable, mean, contemptible

**menguar**
1 diminish, decrease, lessen, be consumed, waste away
*increase, grow*
2 *(fig)* discredit
3 diminish, get less, dwindle, decrease
*increase*
4 *(fig)* wane, decay, decline

**menoscabar**
1 reduce, lessen, diminish
*increase*
2 deteriorate, harm, impair, dull, tarnish
3 *(fig)* discredit, dishonour

**menoscabo**
1 reduction, decrease, decline
2 deterioration, detriment, harm, damage

3 *(fig)* discredit, dishonour

**mente**
1 intelligence, understanding, mind, spirit
2 thought, proposition

**mentecato** *(aj)*
silly, simple, foolish, stupid, idiotic

**mentecato** *(s)*
fool, idiot, imbecile

**menudencia**
trifle, small thing, triviality

**menudencias**
1 odds and ends, minute details
2 offal, waste

**meollo**
1 brains
2 *(anatomy)* marrow
3 *(fig)* substance, essence, basis
4 *(fig)* understanding, brain(s), sense

**mercadería**
commodity

**mercaderías**
merchandise, goods, articles, produce, wares

**mesura**
1 gravity, dignity, seriousness, composure
2 reverence, consideration, courtesy, respect
*discourtesy*
3 moderation, prudence, circumspection
*imprudence*

**meta**
1 terminus, end, conclusion, final, goal
2 end, aim, objective, purpose, intention, goal

**meter(se)**
1 put in, insert, introduce, include, fit (into)
2 interfere in, meddle in
3 annoy, bother, disturb, disquiet, mortify

**método**
method, procedure, norm, rule, system

**mezcla**
1 mixture, blend, aggregate
2 alloy
3 plaster, mortar

**mezclar**
1 mix, blend, mingle, incorporate, add, join, unite
*separate, individualize, disunite*
2 interfere in, meddle in, introduce

**mezquindad**
1 poverty, misery, shortage (of money)
2 meanness, stinginess, pettiness, paltriness, wretchedness

**miaja**
piece, portion, crumb, bit

**miedoso**
fearful, timid, timorous, frightened, cowardly, recreant, pusillanimous

**milagro**
prodigy, portent, marvel, wonder, miracle

**milagroso**
1 miraculous, supernatural
2 marvellous, prodigious, stupendous, portentous, amazing, astonishing

**mimar**
1 pamper, spoil, indulge
2 consent (to), get accustomed to bad habits

**mimo**
1 affectionate caress, nice remark, pampering indulgence
2 mime, mime artist

**ministerio**
1 ministry, office, employment, function(s), occupation
2 (*politics*) ministry, government, cabinet

**minucioso**
meticulous, thorough, scrupulous, very detailed, minute

**mira**
1 (*fig*) aim, intention, design, end, purpose
2 (*military*) watchtower, look-out post

**mirado**
1 circumspect, prudent, cautious, reflective
2 attentive, considerate, respectful

**miramiento**
1 caution, care, precaution, circumspection
2 courtesy, respect, attention, consideration

**miramientos**
courtesies, attentions

**mirar**
1 look at, watch, observe, not lose sight of
2 consider, think over
3 recognize, respect, acknowledge
4 protect, look after, take care of, keep watch over, shelter

**miserable**
1 unfortunate, unlucky, unhappy, wretched, miserable
*fortunate, lucky*
2 indigent, poor, needy, squalid
3 miserable, paltry
4 mean, stingy, miserly, contemptible
*generous*
5 perverse, infamous, vile, despicable

**miseria**
1 unhappiness, misfortune, misery
*happiness, good fortune*
2 poverty, indigence, scarcity, shortage (of money), squalor
3 stinginess, meanness, miserliness
*generosity*
4 fleas, lice, vermin

**misericordia**
1 commiseration, compassion, pity, charity
2 clemency, mercy, forgiveness

**misterioso**
mysterious, occult, secret, recondite, obscure

**mitigar**
moderate, temper, calm, placate, soften, smooth (out)

**modelo**
1 model, pattern, guideline
2 exemplar, example, type

**moderar**
moderate, control, restrain, curb, temper, mitigate, adjust

**modestia**
1 humility
2 modesty, decency, decorum, shame, honesty

**módico**
moderate, reasonable, limited, frugal, sparing

**modificar**
1 change, vary, transform, alter
2 correct, emend, rectify, modify

**moler**
1 grind, crush, pound
2 weary, bore, bother, annoy, mortify

**molestar**
annoy, bother, pester, molest, hinder, be in the way, tire, weary, fatigue
*make happy, pacify, calm*

**molestia**
bother, trouble, nuisance, inconvenience, *(medicine)* discomfort

**molesto**
1 troublesome, annoying, bothersome, trying, tiresome
2 discontented, restless, ill-at-ease, uncomfortable, upset, offended, embarrassed

**momento**
1 instant, moment
2 opportunity, occasion, present time
3 *(mechanics)* momentum, moment
4 *(fig)* consequence, importance

**monstruoso**
1 unnatural
2 enormous, phenomenal, colossal
3 execrable, hateful, abhorrent

**morder**
1 bite, gnaw, nibble
2 corrode, eat away, eat into
3 defame, criticize, satirize, discredit

**mortal**
1 perishable
2 mortal, fatal, deadly, lethal

3 *(fig)* tiring, overwhelming, distressing
4 decisive, conclusive

**mortificar**
1 pain, harm, damage, mortify
2 afflict, molest, wound, offend, grieve, sadden

**mostrar**
1 indicate, designate
2 present, exhibit, show, display, explain, demonstrate

**mover(se)**
1 move, transfer, change
2 induce, persuade, incite
3 cause, occasion, originate, provoke
4 *(LAm)* push (drugs)

**móvil**
1 movable, mobile
*immobile*
2 unstable, unsure, insecure

**móvil** *(s)*
motive, cause, reason

**movimiento**
1 movement, motion, activity
2 revolt, rising
3 *(music)* time, tempo

**muchedumbre**
1 abundance, multitude, infinity
2 mass, crowd

**mudar(se)**
1 change, vary, alter
2 stir, move, transfer
3 go away, leave

**muelle** *(aj)*
1 suave, bland, delicate
2 voluptuous, sensual

**muelle** *(s)*
1 spring, watch spring
2 wharf, dock, pier, quay, mole

**muerte**
1 death, decease, demise, transit
*life*
2 homicide
3 end, destination, conclusion, annihilation, ruin

**muerto** *(aj)*
1 dead, deceased, lifeless
2 terminated, finished, inactive

**muerto** *(s)*
    dead man or woman, corpse
**muestra**
  1 sign, proof, demonstration
  2 example, sample, pattern
**multiplicar**
    multiply, increase, propagate, re-
    produce, augment
    *diminish, lessen, decrease*
**mundo**
  1 cosmos, creation, universe, orb

  2 world, earth, globe
  3 star
  4 humanity, mankind
**murmurar**
  1 murmur, whisper
  2 grumble
  3 criticize, gossip
**mustio**
  1 languid, lank, withered, faded
  2 melancholic, gloomy, depressed,
    sad

# N

**nacer**
1 be born, hatch, germinate, sprout, emerge, rise
*die*
2 begin, emanate, originate, proceed
*finish*
3 deduce, derive, infer, follow

**narrar**
narrate, tell, recount, relate

**natural** *(aj)*
1 native
2 natural, frank, sincere, ingenuous, unaffected, simple
3 common, normal, regular, habitual, ordinary, current, usual

**natural** *(s)*
1 inhabitant, native
2 nature, condition, character, disposition, temperament

**nave**
1 ship, boat, vessel, craft
2 *(architecture)* nave

**necesario**
1 necessary, inevitable, inexorable
*evitable*
2 necessary, vital, essential, indispensable
*accidental*

**necesidad**
1 necessity, need
2 necessity, fix, jam, tight spot, awkward situation
3 need, necessity, want, poverty, penury, scarcity, misery
*plenty*

**necio**
1 silly, foolish, simple, stupid, ignorant
2 *(LAm)* touchy, hypersensitive
3 *(LAm)* obstinate, stubborn, pigheaded

**negar(se)**
1 deny, refuse, ban, prohibit
*affirm, ratify*

2 hide, conceal, dissimulate, dissemble
3 refuse (to)

**negociar**
1 negotiate
2 trade, traffic, treat, do business, deal in

**negocio**
1 *(commerce, finance)* deal, transaction, piece of business
2 *(LAm)* firm, company, place of business

**negocios**
*(commerce, finance)* business, trade

**negro** *(aj)*
1 black
*white*
2 *(fig)* black, awful, sad, melancholy, ill-omened
*clear, happy, lucky, fortunate*

**negro** *(s)*
Negro, native of Africa

**nervio**
1 nerve, tendon, vein
2 energy, vitality, vigour, strength

**nervioso**
1 nervous, restless, excitable, edgy, irritable
*tranquil, impassive*
2 vigorous, lively, energetic, strong

**nítido**
1 bright, clean, spotless, *(photography)* clear, sharp
2 *(fig)* pure, unblemished

**noble**
1 noble, illustrious, generous
2 worthy, esteemed, honourable, respectable
*unworthy, low, contemptible, mean*
3 excellent, outstanding, principal, main
4 noble, aristocratic, blue-blooded
*plebeian*

**noción**
notion, idea, understanding

**nociones**
 rudiments, elements, principles

**nocivo**
 bad, harmful, pernicious, prejudicial
 *inoffensive, healthy, good*

**nombrar**
 1 name, designate, denote, nominate, select, choose
 2 mention, cite, allude, refer

**nombre**
 1 name, denomination, designation
 2 *(fig)* name, fame, renown, reputation, notoriety

**norma**
 norm, rule, precept, guide, guidelines, method

**normal**
 1 normal, usual, habitual, common, natural
 *abnormal*
 2 regular
 *irregular*
 3 perpendicular

**nota**
 1 note, memo(randum), *(LAm)* promissory note, bill
 2 characteristic, sign
 3 fame, credit, renown, reputation, notoriety
 4 explanation, commentary, observation, preface, foreword

 5 *(school/college)* grade, marks, class

**notar**
 1 note, notice, observe, mark, indicate, point out, take account of, pay attention to, perceive, warn
 2 annotate, note (down)
 3 censure, reprimand, criticize, denounce

**noticia**
 piece of news, notion, idea, knowledge

**noticias**
 news, information

**notificar**
 notify, inform, make known, communicate, advise

**notorio**
 notorious, well-known, clear, visible, evident, manifest, public
 *obscure, private*

**novato** *(aj)*
 inexperienced, inexpert
 *experienced, expert*

**novato** *(s)*
 novice, beginner
 *master, expert*

**nulo**
 1 null, nil, null and void, invalid, useless
 2 inept, useless, slow, torpid, incapable, unfit

# Ñ

**ñango** *(LAm)*
1 awkward, clumsy. short-legged
2 weak, feeble

**ñapa** *(LAm)*
bonus, extra, tip

**ñato** *(LAm)*
flat-nosed, snub-nosed, nasal, bent, deformed

**ñoño**
1 characterless, insipid, insubstantial, spineless
2 shy, bashful, timid
3 fussy, finicky
4 *(LAm)* senile, decrepit
5 *(LAm)* thick, stupid

# O

**obcecación**
blindness, bewilderment, blind obstinacy, stubbornness, disturbance

**obediencia**
obedience, submission, subjection, docility, respect
*disobedience, rebellion, disrespect*

**obediente**
obedient, submissive, manageable, docile, compliant, respectful
*disobedient, unmanageable, recalcitrant, refractory*

**objetar**
object (to), oppose, contradict, answer, answer back, argue, refute, impugn
*agree, assent, bring together, reconcile, come to an agreement*

**obligar(se)**
1 oblige, force, constrain, drive, impel, bind someone (to)
2 agree, promise to do something, compromise oneself

**obrar**
1 make, manufacture, build, construct
2 work, operate, act, behave, proceed, have an effect
*rest, abstain*

**obsequio**
1 gift, present, presentation, *(commerce)* free gift
2 courtesy, attention, kindness

**obsequioso**
attentive, courteous, polite, obliging, helpful

**observar(se)**
1 observe, watch, see, notice, spot
2 observe, respect, keep, abide by, adhere to
*neglect, disregard, ignore*

**obstáculo**
obstacle, impediment, hindrance, difficulty, inconvenience, drawback

**obstinado**
obstinate, stubborn, insistent, persistent, pertinacious, tenacious

**obstruir**
obstruct, impede, hamper, hinder, block, plug, stop up, clog
*facilitate, open, vacate, unblock, unplug*

**obtener**
1 attain, get, obtain, secure, achieve
*lose*
2 produce, extract

**obturar**
close, obstruct, block up, stop, plug, seal off, *(dentistry)*fill
*open, uncover*

**obtuso**
1 obtuse, blunt
*sharp*
2 *(fig)* dim, slow, dull, obtuse
*sharp, smart, clever*
3 *(mathematics)* obtuse

**obvio**
obvious, visible, manifest, evident, patent, clear
*difficult, obscure, hidden, occult*

**ocasión**
1 occasion, time, juncture
2 opportunity, chance, occasion
3 cause, motive
4 *(LAm)* bargain

**ocasionar**
1 cause, motivate, produce, provoke, promote
2 stir up, excite

**ocaso**
1 *(astronomy)* sunset, setting
*sunrise*
2 *(geography)* west, occident
*east, orient*
3 *(fig)* decadence, decline, end, fall

**ocio**
leisure, idleness, inaction, inactivity, rest
*activity, occupation*

**ocios**
    pastime, diversion

**ociosidad**
    idleness, laziness, inactivity
    *work, diligence, occupation, activity*

**oculto**
1 occult, hidden, concealed, covered, veiled
2 unknown, incognito
3 *(fig)* secret, mysterious, occult, clandestine

**ocupación**
1 occupation, possession, seizure, taking
2 occupation, employment, profession
3 work, job, task, labour

**ocupar**
1 occupy, take possession of, appropriate, take over
    *leave, abandon*
2 fill, take up, occupy
3 occupy, employ, engage, keep busy
4 occupy, inhabit, live in
5 *(LAm)* seize, confiscate

**ocurrencia**
1 occurrence, incident, event, happening
2 opportunity, occasion, contingency, possibility
3 witty remark, witticism
4 idea, bright idea

**ocurrir**
    occur, happen, pass

**ocurrente**
    witty, bright, sharp, clever, ingenious, entertaining, amusing

**odiar**
1 hate, abominate, detest, execrate, loathe
    *love*
2 *(LAm)* irk, annoy, bore

**ofender**
1 ill-treat, wound, harm, injure
2 injure, insult, affront, abuse, wound, offend
    *ingratiate oneself, placate, make up, praise*

3 take offence, get angry, get annoyed, feel resentful
4 *(LAm) (woman)* touch up, feel, grope

**ofensa**
    offence, insult, wrong, injury, affront, outrage

**oferta**
1 offer, proposal, proposition, promise
2 *(commerce)* offer, tender, bid, special offer, bargain
3 present, gift, donation

**oficio**
1 job, profession, occupation, *(technical)* craft, trade
2 job, role, post, office, *(mechanics)* function

**oficioso**
1 semiofficial, unofficial, informal
2 kind, helpful, obliging
3 *(pejorative)* officious, interfering, meddlesome, intrusive

**ofrecer(se)**
1 offer, propose, volunteer, offer one's services
2 offer, present, give
3 offer, dedicate, consecrate, contribute
4 show, teach
5 occur, happen unexpectedly, present itself

**ofuscar**
1 blind, dazzle, obscure
2 *(fig)* bewilder, confound, puzzle, confuse, blind
    *calm down, reflect, clarify*

**olfatear**
1 smell, sniff
2 *(fig)* sniff out, pry into, investigate

**olvido**
1 forgetfulness
    *memory, remembrance*
2 neglect, omission, oversight, carelessness, inadvertence
    *care, carefulness*
3 relegation, postponement, delay
4 oblivion

**ominoso**
 1 ominous, fateful, ill-fated, disastrous
 2 abominable, execrable, odious

**omisión**
 1 omission, lacuna
 2 omission, oversight, neglect
  *attention*

**ondular(se)**
 1 wave, undulate
 2 swing, rock, sway, wriggle
 3 curl, ripple

**oneroso**
  onerous, burdensome, tedious, costly, expensive

**opaco**
 1 obscure, dark
 2 sad, melancholic, gloomy
 3 *(fig)* dull, lustreless, lifeless

**oportuno**
 1 opportune, timely, appropriate, suitable, convenient, expedient
 2 witty, quick

**oposición**
  opposition, antagonism, resistance, contradiction, obstruction

**oposiciones**
  competition for a post, public entrance examination

**opresor** *(aj)*
  oppressive, tyrannical, despotic

**opresor** *(s)*
  oppressor, tyrant, despot

**oprimir**
 1 squeeze, depress, press down, compress
 2 *(fig)* oppress, tyrannize, enslave, subdue, subjugate, dominate, burden, weigh down
  *help, free, liberate*

**optar**
  opt, prefer, choose, elect, select

**opuesto**
 1 opposite, contrary, contradictory
 2 refractory, stubborn, recalcitrant, obstinate
  *obliging*

**oración**
 1 discourse, reasoning, speech, oration
 2 proposition, sentence
 3 prayer, deprecation
 4 *(LAm)* pagan invocation, magic charm

**orden**
 1 order, sequence, arrangement, disposition
  *disorder*
 2 rule, method
 3 order, command, decree, mandate, precept

**ordenar**
 1 order, arrange, organize, dispose, regularize, classify, coordinate
 2 direct, give directions to, put right, straighten
 3 order, command, establish, prescribe, decree

**ordinario**
 1 ordinary, common, usual, habitual, frequent, regular, normal
  *extraordinary, unusual, irregular*
 2 low, vulgar, common, plebeian, coarse, crude, obscene

**organización**
 1 organization, disposition, structure, constitution
 2 *(fig)* order, arrangement, array, control, rule, regulation, regularization

**organizar**
  organize, arrange, dispose, structure, reform, constitute, establish, regularize

**orgullo**
  pride, arrogance, vanity, presumption
  *humility, modesty*

**origen**
 1 origin, beginning, cause
 2 origin, birth, lineage, stock, ancestry, descent, family

**original**
 1 new, original, fresh
  *old*

2 authentic, personal, proper

3 singular, strange, odd, peculiar, rare, original

**ornamento**
ornament, adornment, dressing, seasoning

**ornato**
ornament, adornment, decoration, attire, dress

**osadía**
1 audacity, daring, boldness
2 insolence, shamelessness

**oscilar**
1 vibrate
2 balance, fluctuate
3 (fig) vacillate, hesitate

**oscuro**
1 dark, dull, sombre, gloomy, opaque, obscure
2 (fig) confused, incomprehensible, unintelligible
*clear, intelligible*
3 (fig) humble, unknown
4 (fig) uncertain, frightening, dangerous

**oscurecer(se)**
1 obscure, darken, dim, black out
2 (fig) confuse, cloud, fog, overshadow, put in the shade, dim, tarnish

3 grow dark, get dark, become cloudy
*become clear, clear up, dawn*

**oscuridad**
1 obscurity, darkness, gloom, gloominess
2 (fig) obscurity, confusion

**ostensible**
obvious, evident, patent, visible, clear, manifest, public

**ostentación**
1 exhibition, manifestation, display
2 ostentation, show, display, boasting, vainglory
*modesty*
3 magnificence, pomp, sumptuousness
*sobriety, simplicity*

**ostentar**
1 show, display, exhibit
2 flaunt, show off, boast, display

**otorgar**
1 consent, concede, condescend, grant, confer, authorize
*prohibit*
2 offer, stipulate, establish, dispose

**oyente**
1 listener, hearer
2 (university) occasional student, (Am) auditor

# P

**paciente** *(aj)*
1 tolerant, resigned, patient, long-suffering, gentle, mild
*impatient, intolerant*
2 calm, quiet

**paciente** *(s)*
patient, sufferer, sick person

**pacificar**
1 pacify, reconcile, establish peace
*irritate, fight*
2 tranquillize, quieten, calm (down)

**pacífico**
pacific, peaceful, peaceable, quiet, tranquil, calm, rested, reposed

**pactar**
agree, arrange, make a pact, fix (up), settle, establish, treat, stipulate

**pacto**
1 stipulation, agreement, covenant
2 contract, treaty, agreement

**pagar**
1 settle (a debt), satisfy, pay for, defray, recompense, repay, remunerate, reward
2 be content with
3 boast, brag, be conceited about

**pago**
1 *(finance)* payment, refund, pay, salary, wages
2 satisfaction, recompense, premium, *(fig)* return, reward

**paliar**
1 dissimulate, hide, conceal, excuse, pardon
*discover, accuse, charge*
2 mitigate, alleviate, calm, lessen, minimize, soften, smooth out, palliate
*augment, increase*

**palma**
1 *(anatomy)* palm
2 *(botany)* palm, palm-tree
3 *(fig)* glory, triumph, victory

**palmas**
applause, (hand)clapping, acclaim

**palurdo** *(aj)*
rustic, rude, coarse, peasant

**palurdo** *(s)*
rustic, peasant, yokel, oaf, *(Am)* hick

**pánico**
panic, terror, dread, fright, fear

**pantano**
1 marsh, bog, swamp
2 dam, reservoir, lake, lagoon
3 *(fig)* difficulty, embarrassment, hindrance, obstacle, obstruction, jam, fix

**parada**
1 stop, stopping place, halt
2 stoppage, shutdown, delay
3 station
4 place, post
5 *(military)* parade, *(LAm)* civic procession
6 *(fencing)* parry
7 *(LAm)* vanity, pride, presumption

**paralizar**
1 make impossible, make incapable, cripple, paralyze
2 *(fig)* impede, immobilize, obstruct, hinder, intercept, stop, come to a standstill
3 become paralyzed

**parar**
1 stop, halt, suspend, detain, paralyze, intercept, park
2 finish, terminate, conclude
3 inhabit, be, live, lodge, stay

**parcialidad**
1 faction, party, group
2 partiality, prejudice, bias, preference, inclination, injustice, inequality

**parco**
1 short, scarce, insufficient
2 frugal, sparing, moderate, temperate, restrained

**parecer(se)**
1 appear, seem, present, manifest
*disappear*

2 be (situated)

3 resemble each other, look like

**parecer** (s)

opinion, judgement, view, impression

**parecido** (aj)

similar, analogous, alike, equal

**parecido** (s)

similitude, analogy, similarity, resemblance, likeness

**parentesco**

1 kinship, relationship

2 (fig) union, link, bond, tie

**paridad**

1 parity, equality, resemblance, similarity

*dissimilarity, diversity*

2 comparison, parallelism

**parsimonia**

1 parsimony, frugality, economy, saving, sobriety

*imprudence, waste, extravagance*

2 circumspection, moderation, restraint

**participar**

1 take part in, collaborate, contribute, co-operate

2 notify, inform, advise, give notice, communicate, make known

**particular** (aj)

1 particular, personal, private, proper

*general, common, ordinary, impersonal*

2 especial, singular, extraordinary, rare, strange

**particular** (s)

1 particular, detail, point

2 private, individual

**particularidad**

1 peculiarity, singularity, characteristic, particularity

2 circumstance, detail, particular

**partida**

1 departure, march, running, working, jump start, push start, sudden start

2 party, group, band, gang, clique

3 guerrilla band

4 (commerce) entry, item

5 certificate

6 (sport) game

**partido**

1 prejudice, bias

2 resolution, determination, decision

3 advantage, convenience, benefit, profit

4 favour, protection, popularity, sympathy

5 district, territory

6 (sport) game, match

7 (sport) team, side, (politics) party

**partir**

1 divide, share (out), distribute

2 open, cut, split (open), break (open)

3 distribute, share

4 leave, go (away), set off, set out, absent oneself

**pasajero** (aj)

brief, transient, transitory, momentary, ephemeral, fleeting, passing, (commerce) perishable

**pasajero** (s)

1 passenger

2 (LAm) ferryman

**pasar**

1 go (from one place to another), move, pass, (time) spend

2 occur, happen

3 cross (over), traverse

4 exceed, surpass, outstrip, do better than, overtake

5 suffer, endure, tolerate, put up with, overlook

6 dispense, pardon

7 cease, finish

8 carry, conduct, transfer, give, infect

9 strain off, sift, sieve

10 spoil, get damaged, be ruined, wither, (fig) fade away

**pasión**

1 suffering

2 vehemence, ardour, enthusiasm, heat

**pasmar**

1 amaze, astound, astonish

2 cool, freeze, chill (to the marrow)

**pasmar**

3 cripple, immobilize

4 *(LAm)* become infected, fall ill, catch a fever

**pasmo**

1 spasm

2 tetanus

3 marvel, amazement, wonder, daze, confusion, astonishment

**patán** *(aj)*

rustic, stupid, slow, coarse, rude, uncouth, vulgar

**patán** *(s)*

rustic, yokel, oaf, villager

**patente** *(aj)*

visible, obvious, evident, clear, manifest, ostensible, palpable, well-known, notorious

**patente** *(s)*

*(commerce)* patent

**patético**

pathetic, moving, sentimental, emotional, tender, touching, poignant

**patraña**

tall story, tale, fib, lie

**patrimonio**

1 inheritance, succession

2 property, goods

3 heritage, patrimony

**patrón**

1 patron, protector, defender, *(religion)* patron saint

2 landlord, proprietor, owner

3 master, principal, boss, chief

4 *(technology, dressmaking)* guideline, model, pattern

**pausa**

1 pause, break, interruption, stop, halt, stoppage, shutdown

2 *(music)* rest, silence

3 slowness, delay

**pausado**

slow, deliberate, sluggish, phlegmatic

**pavor**

fear, terror, dread, panic, fright
*valour, courage*

**paz**

1 peace, peacefulness, tranquillity, calm, quietness, stillness

2 concord, harmony, agreement
*discord, disagreement*

**peculiar**

particular, private, proper, characteristic, distinctive

**pedir**

1 demand, require, claim

2 beg, implore, supplicate, ask for, seek

3 desire, fancy

**pega**

1 *(fig)* ploy, trick, joke

2 problem, difficulty, obstacle, hindrance, delay

**pegar**

1 adhere, stick, fasten, glue

2 unite, join, fix together

3 bring close

4 communicate, contaminate, *(medicine)* infect

5 hit, strike, chastise, ill-treat

**pegajoso**

1 sticky, adhesive, viscous, glutinous

2 *(medicine)* contagious, infectious

**pelar**

peel, skin, shave, crop, pluck, shear

**pelea**

1 combat, battle, fight, contention

2 quarrel, brawl, argument, row

**pelear**

1 battle, combat, fight, contend, take arms against

2 dispute, quarrel, brawl, row, fall out, become enemies

**peliagudo**

intricate, difficult, tricky, complicated, involved, arduous

**pena**

1 correction, punishment, penalty, *(law)* sentence

2 pain, affliction, sadness, suffering, anguish, distress, grief, regret

3 difficulty, fatigue, hard work, trouble, hardship

**penar**

1 sanction, condemn, punish, penalize
*pardon*

2 suffer, endure, put up with, grieve
*be happy, get merry*

**pendiente** *(aj)*
1 hanging
2 pending, unsettled

**pendiente** *(s)*
1 earring
2 slope, declivity, incline, hill

**penetrar**
1 enter, insert, put in, penetrate, pierce
2 comprehend, understand, find out, get to know, soak up

**penitencia**
1 penitence, penance
2 expiation, correction, punishment, chastisement

**penoso**
1 difficult, laborious, fatiguing, hard, arduous
2 sad, dolorous, painful, distressing

**pensar**
1 consider, reflect, meditate, reason, ponder, think, ruminate
2 imagine, believe, figure, suppose
3 plan, propose, invent, think up

**penuria**
scarcity, lack, necessity, shortage, want

**pequeño** *(aj)*
small, little, scarce, limited, reduced, short

**pequeño** *(s)*
small child, infant, boy

**percibir**
1 *(commerce)*, draw, receive, earn, get
2 see, note, take account of, distinguish, notice
*be blind, blind oneself to, ignore, be ignorant of*
3 know, comprehend, conceive

**perder**
1 lose, waste, squander, dissipate
2 lose, miss, lose one's way, get lost, get confused
*be (situated), orientate oneself*
3 disappear, be lost to view

4 sink, capsize
*save oneself*
5 corrupt, rot, pervert, become corrupted

**pérdida**
loss, waste, wastage, harm, damage

**pérdidas**
*(finance, military)* losses

**perdurar**
endure, subsist, last, remain, still exist, stand

**perdón**
pardon, forgiveness, absolution, remission, grace, mercy, indulgence
*condemnation*

**perecer**
perish, succumb, die, extinguish, shatter

**peregrino** *(aj)*
1 wandering, travelling, migratory
2 rare, singular, strange, unusual, absurd

**peregrino** *(s)*
pilgrim, palmer

**perenne**
perennial, lasting, perpetual, continual, everlasting, permanent, incessant

**perentorio**
peremptory, urgent, decisive, conclusive, definitive, set, fixed
*slow, passive*

**perezoso** *(aj)*
indolent, idle, lazy, good-for-nothing

**perezoso** *(s)*
layabout, vagabond, good-for-nothing

**perfecto**
complete, finished, perfect

**pérfido**
perfidious, treacherous, felonious, disloyal, unfaithful
*loyal, sincere*

**perfume**
1 aroma, fragrance, scent, good smell
2 essence, balsam

**pericia**
  skill, ability, practice, experience, knowledge, expertise

**perjudicar**
  prejudice, damage, harm, injure

**perjuicio**
  damage, harm, injury, detriment, deterioration
  *advantage, favour, good*

**permanecer**
  remain, stay, be, persist, subsist, continue, reside
  *absent oneself, go*

**permanente** *(aj)*
  permanent, stable, fixed, firm, unalterable, invariable, immutable, constant

**permanente** *(s)*
  *(hairdressing)* permanent wave, perm

**permitir**
  permit, allow, approve, accede to, consent to

**permutar**
  1 *(mathematics)* permutate
  2 change, exchange, switch

**pernicioso**
  1 injurious, bad, malignant, harmful, wicked, prejudicial
  2 *(medicine)* pernicious

**perpetuar**
  1 immortalize, make eternal
  2 perpetuate, continue, propagate

**perplejo**
  perplexed, bewildered, indecisive, irresolute, vacillating, uncertain

**perseverancia**
  perseverance, persistence, constancy, tenacity, endurance

**perseverar**
  1 persist, insist, maintain
  2 last, endure, stay, remain, continue to be

**persistir**
  1 persist, insist, persevere, maintain, be obstinate
  2 last, endure, stay, remain

**personal** *(aj)*
  personal, particular, private, proper, single, for one person

**personal** *(s)*
  personnel, staff

**perspicacia**
  perspicacity, shrewdness, sharpness, sagacity, penetration, discernment, subtlety

**perspicaz**
  perspicacious, shrewd, sharp, penetrating, subtle

**pertenecer**
  1 correspond
  2 pertain to, belong to, concern, touch

**pertinente**
  1 pertinent, relevant, concerning, belonging to, relative
  2 adequate, appropriate, convenient, opportune

**perturbar**
  perturb, disturb, disorder, disarrange, upset, confuse

**pervertir**
  pervert, corrupt, vitiate

**pesadez**
  1 weight, heaviness, gravity
  2 grief, sorrow
  3 tediousness, bother, importunity, impertinence

**pesado** *(aj)*
  1 grave, ponderous, heavy
  2 slow, quiet, calm
  3 tedious, troublesome, annoying, bothersome, boring
  4 hard, insufferable, rough, tough

**pesado** *(s)*
  bore, boring person

**pesadumbre**
  1 heaviness, gravity
  2 grief, sorrow, pain, anxiety
  3 quarrel, contention, argument, brawl

**pesar** *(s)*
  1 affliction, pain, sadness, sorrow, regret
  2 repentance

**pesar** *(v)*
  1 weigh, weigh a lot, be heavy
  2 examine, consider, reflect, think
  3 repent

# peso
1 weight, heaviness, gravity
2 entity, substance, importance
3 scales
4 *(coin)* peso

# peste
1 pestilence, plague, epidemic
2 stench, bad smell, stink

# petición
1 request, petition, supplication, demand
2 claim, demand, requirement
3 *(law)* petition, demand, plea, lawsuit

# petulancia
petulance, silliness, fatuity, frivolity, vanity, conceit, presumption

# piadoso
1 pious, devout, religious
2 kind, compassionate, merciful, benignant

# picante
1 hot, highly-seasoned, spicy, piquant
2 caustic, pungent, satirical, biting, bitter, racy, spicy

# picar(se)
1 prick, pierce, puncture, sting, stab, shoot, bite
2 peck, nibble, pick
3 goad, spur on
4 follow, pursue, chase after
5 burn, sting
6 cut, slice, mince, chop
7 incite, stimulate, urge on, hurry along, move
8 bore into, eat into, get moth-eaten
9 turn sour, go off
10 be piqued, be annoyed

# piedad
1 piety, devotion
2 pity, compassion, commiseration, mercy, charity
*inhumanity, cruelty, fury, rage*

# pieza
1 piece, part, bit, portion
2 room, lodging-room
3 piece, roll of material

# pillaje
1 rapine, robbery, theft, stealing
2 pillage, plundering, sacking, looting

# pillar
1 steal, rob, loot, plunder, sack, ransack
2 catch, grasp, grab
3 trap, surprise, catch, hunt

# pillo *(aj)*
astute, shrewd, clever, villanous, naughty, mischievous, sly

# pillo *(s)*
villain, rogue, scamp

# pío *(aj)*
1 pious, devout, religious
2 compassionate, merciful, benign

# pío *(s)*
chirp, chirping

# pisar
1 tread, trample, leave footprints on, *(fig)* walk all over
2 infringe, transgress, violate
3 *(LAm) (woman)* cover, screw

# piso
1 floor, pavement, paving
2 floor, storey
3 flat, apartment, room, residence, dwelling
4 *(shoe)* sole

# pisotear
1 trample, leave footprints on, stamp
2 *(fig)* humiliate, ill-treat, abuse, infringe, transgress, violate

# placentero
pleasant, agreeable, cheerful, happy, gentle, mild

# plácido
placid, calm, tranquil, gentle, mild, agreeable

# plaga
1 *(medicine)* plague, pest, epidemic
2 calamity, misfortune

# plan
plan, idea, design, project, intention, basis

# plantar(se)
1 *(fig)* place, put, position, arrange, seat, set down

2 *(fig)* found, establish, implant
3 plant, set up, erect
4 establish oneself

**plegar**
1 fold, bend, crease
2 yield, submit, give in
3 *(dress)* pleat

**población**
1 population, inhabitants, residents, neighbourhood
2 village, town, city, place

**pobre** *(aj)*
1 poor, indigent, needy, miserable
2 scarce, lacking, short
3 *(fig)* unhappy, sad, unlucky, humble

**pobre** *(s)*
1 poor person, pauper, beggar
2 *(fig)* poor wretch, poor devil

**pobreza**
poverty, necessity, scarcity, indigence, penury, misery, stinginess

**poco** *(av)*
little, not much, scarce, limited, short
*much, sufficient*

**poder** *(v)*
can, be able to, possible

**poder** *(s)*
1 power, dominion, authority, rule, jurisdiction, command
2 vigour, capacity, strength, ability, power

**poderoso**
1 potent, powerful, strong, energetic, active, efficient
*impotent, weak, powerless, inactive, inefficient*
2 rich, well-off, wealthy

**polémica**
polemic, argument, dissension, dispute, controversy
*pact, agreement*

**política**
1 tact, circumspection, ability, diplomacy, sagacity, tactics
2 courtesy, urbanity, politeness
3 political manifesto, politics
4 policy

**ponderar**
1 weigh up, consider, ponder, estimate
2 balance, counterbalance
3 exaggerate, put up the price of, enlarge, increase
4 praise highly, speak in praise of, esteem
*denigrate, humiliate*

**ponderación**
1 attention, reflection, circumspection, consideration
2 exaggeration, *(commerce)* price increase

**poner(se)**
1 place, situate
2 bet, stake
3 accommodate, insert, introduce, put in
4 dispose, prepare, arrange
5 transpose, hide, conceal
6 go, transfer, move

**porción**
1 piece, bit, part, portion, share, amount, quantity
2 lots of, a great many, a large number of, mountain

**porfía**
1 dispute, contention, debate, discussion
2 insistence, persistence, tenacity, firmness, obstinacy

**porfiar**
1 dispute, contend, argue stubbornly, quarrel
2 insist, be obstinate, go on, keep on

**posada**
1 inn, guest-house, state-owned hotel
2 shelter, lodging
3 dwelling, home

**postergar**
1 postpone, delay
2 put aside, put behind, put below, pass over

**posterior** *(aj)*
later, latter, subsequent, following

**posterior** *(s)*
*(Br)* posterior, rear, *(Am)* backside

**potencia**
1 capability, potential
2 power, authority
3 vigour, energy, strength, fortitude, potency
*weakness, impotence, ineffectiveness*

**positivo** *(aj)*
1 positive, certain, sure, undoubted, unquestioned, true
2 real, effective
3 practical, utilitarian, pragmatic

**positivo** *(s)*
*(technology, photography)* positive

**potente**
potent, powerful, strong, energetic, vigorous, effective, efficient

**práctica**
1 practice, skill, ability, experience, expertise
*inexperience, inability, theory*
2 custom, use, habit
3 mode, method, procedure

**practicar**
1 do, execute, realize, effect, carry out, perform
2 exercise, practise, *(sport) (Br)* go in for, *(Am)* go out for

**práctico**
1 practical
2 expert, skilful, experienced, versed in, knowledgeable, practised

**preámbulo**
1 prologue, proem, preface, preamble, introduction
*epilogue, outcome*
2 digression, detour, evasion

**preciarse**
1 appreciate, esteem, value
*despise, scorn, slight*
2 presume, boast, brag

**precioso**
1 excellent, exquisite, delicate, esteemed, considerable
2 expensive, costly
3 beautiful, enchanting, lovely

**precipitar(se)**
1 throw, launch, hurl, throw down

2 accelerate, knock down, run down, hurry, rush, speed up, act rashly
3 throw oneself headlong, lie down, throw oneself at

**precisar**
1 fix, determine exactly, clarify, define, specify
2 need, be necessary, require
3 force, oblige, constrain

**preciso**
1 necessary, indispensable, inexcusable, essential, vital, obligatory
2 precise, exact, accurate, determinate, defined, fixed, certain, concise
*irregular, indeterminate*

**predominar**
1 prevail, dominate, preponderate
*obey, submit*
2 exceed, surpass

**prefacio**
preface, preamble, proem, prologue
*epilogue, end, conclusion*

**preferir**
prefer, choose, pick, select, opt for, place in front of

**pregonar**
divulge, publish, proclaim, announce, acclaim

**prematuro**
premature, precocious, early, (in) advance
*slow, mature*

**premiar**
reward, award a prize to, recompense, remunerate
*chastise, punish*

**premura**
urgency, hurry, haste, pressure, peremptoriness, last resort

**prenda**
1 guarantee, bail, surety, pledge
2 garment, article of clothing

**prendas**
1 gifts, talents
2 *(game)* forfeits
3 *(LAm)* jewellery

## prender

1 seize, grasp, grab, *(LAm)* take, catch
2 catch, capture, apprehend, arrest, detain, imprison, jail
   *release*
3 *(dress)* pin, fasten, attach, hook
   *unfasten, loosen*
4 establish

## prendimiento

capture, arrest, detention, imprisonment

## presa

1 prey, victim, catch
2 capture, apprehension
3 dam, lake, pool

## prescribir

1 order, command, determine, dispose
2 prescribe

## presencia

presence, aspect, appearance, figure, looks, disposition

## presentar

1 show, exhibit, display, expose, offer, present, introduce
2 present, offer, contribute
3 appear (in court), appear in person, turn up

## preservar

preserve, protect, safeguard, shield against
*desert, abandon*

## presteza

1 promptness, promptitude, rapidity, swiftness, agility, speed
   *slowness, irresolution, heaviness*
2 diligence, activity

## prestigio

prestige, authority, reputation, credit, influence
*discredit*

## presumir

1 presume, suppose, conjecture, suspect
2 be presumptuous, boast, brag, praise oneself

## presunción

1 presumption, supposition, conjecture, suspicion
2 vanity, pride, fatuity, petulance, conceit, boasting

## presuntuoso

presumptuous, vain, conceited, petulant

## pretender

1 seek, request, ask for, aspire to, try for
2 try, try to, endeavour
3 claim, allege
   *renounce*

## pretensión

1 aspiration
2 vanity, presumption, pretension
3 claim

## preponderancia

preponderance, superiority, supremacy, predominance, hegemony

## prevalecer

1 prevail, predominate, preponderate
2 increase, grow

## prevención

1 preparation, preparedness, readiness, providential means, disposition
2 foresight, forethought, precaution, distrust
3 warning

## prevenir

1 prepare, dispose, get ready
2 prevent, foresee, guard against
3 advise, warn, inform, announce, counsel, notify

## prieto

1 obscure, black, *(colour)* dark
2 tight, packed
3 *(fig)* mean, stingy, miserly

## primero *(aj)*

first, prime, primary, primordial, primitive, foremost
*secondary, subsequent, later*

## primero *(av)*

first

## primor

beauty, (great) care, ability, skill, mastery, perfection
*imperfection, carelessness, dirtiness*

**principal** *(aj)*
1 important, first, main, principal
   *secondary, accessory, subordinate, unnecessary*
2 illustrious, distinguished, noble, enlightened
3 essential, fundamental, capital, primordial

**principal** *(s)*
   chief, director, principal

**principiar**
   begin, initiate, commence
   *end, finish, conclude*

**principio**
1 origin, beginning, start, cause
2 base, foundation, basic idea, rudiment
3 norm, precept, rule, maxim, principle
4 preface, foreword, introduction, prologue

**prisa**
1 hurry, haste, speed, quickness, agility, promptness, celerity, rapidity
   *slowness, passivity*
2 (sense of) urgency, anxiety, pressure

**prisión**
1 apprehension, capture, detention, arrest
2 prison, jail

**privilegiado**
   privileged, preferred, favourite, very good

**probar**
1 experiment, test, try out
2 try, attempt, endeavour
3 taste, sample
4 demonstrate, justify, evidence, accredit

**probidad**
   probity, integrity, rectitude, morality, honesty, goodness

**proceder** *(s)*
   behaviour, conduct

**proceder** *(v)*
1 come from, stem from, arise from, have a beginning

2 be born, originate, emanate, derive, be derived
3 be fitting, be appropriate
4 proceed, act, be right (and proper)

**procedimiento**
1 procedure, method, manner, form, progress, course, process, means
2 (law) proceedings

**proceso**
1 process, succession, sequence, series, lapse (of time), transformation, development
2 (law) trial, prosecution, lawsuit, case

**producir**
1 engender, procreate
2 create, elaborate
3 fructify
4 yield, produce
5 occasion, cause, motivate, produce
6 explain oneself, show

**producto**
1 production, output
2 product, benefit, profit, gain, yield, interest, income
3 effect, result, consequence
4 produce, fruit

**proemio**
   proem, prologue, preamble, preface, introduction
   *epilogue, end, conclusion*

**proeza**
   feat, exploit, heroic deed

**profanar**
1 violate, profane, desecrate
2 (fig) dishonour, prostitute, tarnish, dull

**profano** *(aj)*
1 secular, lay
2 ignorant, lay

**profano** *(s)*
   layman, ignoramus

**proferir**
   utter, pronounce, articulate, say
   *keep quiet*

**profesión**
1 profession, career
2 employment, office, ministry

**profusión**
profusion, abundance, copiousness, exuberance, prodigality, extravagance

**progresar**
progress, advance, perfect, develop, prosper, flourish, improve, grow

**prohibir**
prohibit, ban, forbid, deprive, impede, prevent

**prolijo**
prolix, long-winded, dilatory, tedious, diffuse
*concise, moderate*

**prólogo**
prologue, proem, preface, preamble, introduction
*epilogue, end, conclusion*

**prometer(se)**
1 offer, bind oneself
2 assure, affirm, certify
3 expect, get engaged

**prominencia**
hump, hillock, salient, prominence

**promover**
promote, provoke, cause, initiate, instigate, stir up

**pronosticar**
predict, forecast, presage, prophecy, forecast, foretell, guess

**pronóstico**
prediction, forecast, prophecy, foreboding, divination, guesswork

**prontitud**
1 promptitude, promptness, quickness, speed, rapidity, velocity, acceleration, diligence, activity
*slowness, laziness, idleness, deliberateness*
2 vivacity, precipitation

**pronto** *(aj)*
1 quick, rapid, fast, prompt, light, agile
2 prepared, ready

**pronto** *(av)*
at once, promptly, quickly

**pronto** *(s)*
1 fit of rage, outburst
2 occurrence, outcome

**pronunciamiento**
rebellion, insurrection, revolt, uprising

**propagar**
1 multiply, reproduce
2 *(radio, TV)* diffuse, broadcast, spread
3 circulate, make public

**propio**
1 characteristic, peculiar, own, particular, proper, typical
2 convenient, adequate, pertinent, opportune
3 natural, real

**proponer**
1 propose, pose, raise, establish
2 consult, present
3 try, endeavour

**proporción**
1 correspondence, harmony, conformity, relation
2 opportunity, occasion, juncture, suitability, time

**proporcionar**
provide, supply, give, make available

**proscripción**
proscription, ban, prohibition, banishment

**provocar**
provoke, tempt, invite, bring about, lead to, rouse, stimulate

**proyectar**
1 hurl, throw, cast, shed, *(cinema)* screen, show
2 plan, design, project

**prueba**
proof, test, trial, tasting, sampling, *(clothes)* fitting

**punto**
1 point, spot, dot
2 *(dressmaking)* stitch
3 spot, place, point, moment
4 *(grammar)* *(Br)* full stop, *(Am)* period

**puntual**
punctual, exact, accurate, reliable

**puntualidad**
punctuality, exactness, accuracy, reliability

# Q

**quebrado** *(aj)*
  1 broken, rough, difficult, tortuous, uneven
  2 *(medicine)* ruptured
  3 run out, expired

**quebrado** *(s)*
  1 *(finance)* bankrupt
  2 *(mathematics)* fraction
  3 ravine

**quebradura**
  1 crack, split, break, breaking, opening
  2 *(geography)* fissure, gorge
  3 *(medicine)* hernia, rupture

**quebranto**
  1 damage, harm, detriment, deterioration, loss
  2 exhaustion, decline, decay
  3 affliction, pain, grief

**quebrar(se)**
  1 break, smash
  2 bend, twist
  3 *(finance)* fail, go bankrupt
  4 *(medicine)* be rutpured, have a rupture

**quedar(se)**
  1 remain, subsist, stay, stop
    *go*
  2 remain, be left, be wanting, be lacking
  3 remain, stay behind

**quejarse**
  1 moan, groan, whine, whimper
    *laugh*
  2 complain of, grumble about
  3 quarrel, dispute

**querella**
  1 quarrel, dispute, contention, disagreement, brawl, fight

  *concord, peace*
  2 charge, accusation, complaint, dispute, lawsuit

**querer** *(s)*
  love, affection
  *hate*

**querer** *(v)*
  1 determine, resolve, have the wish or desire to
  2 desire, claim, want, long for, aspire to, endeavour to
  3 love, esteem, appreciate
    *hate*
  4 need, demand, require, ask for, request

**quiebra**
  1 crack, slit, fissure, rift, breach, break
  2 *(finance)* bankruptcy, failure, *(economics)* slump, crash, collapse

**quietud**
  1 immobility
  2 calm, stillness, tranquillity, peace, quietude, quiet(ness)

**quimera**
  1 *(mythology)* chimera
  2 hallucination, illusion, fancy, fantastic idea, pipe dream
  3 unfounded suspicion
  4 contention, dispute, quarrel

**quitar(se)**
  1 liberate, free
  2 redeem, cancel, withdraw
  3 separate, remove, deprive, subtract
  4 get rid of, take off, remove, undress
  5 whisk away, make vanish, steal

# R

**rabia**
1 (*medicine*) rabies, hydrophobia
2 (*fig*) anger, ire, choler, fury, rage, annoyance
*serenity, tranquillity*

**rabioso**
1 (*medicine*) rabid, mad
2 choleric, furious, angry, raging
3 (*fig*) vehement, excessive

**racional**
reasonable, logical, rational, just

**racionar**
reason, consider rationally, argue, think, meditate

**radiante**
radiant, brilliant, resplendent, refulgent

**radical** (*aj*)
radical, complete, total

**radical** (*s*)
extremist, radical

**radicar**
1 take root, establish
*uproot*
2 be, be situated

**rajar**
1 open, crack, split, separate, divide, (*fig*) slash
2 desist, stop, go back, retreat

**ramplón**
vulgar, uncouth, coarse
*elegant, cultured, cultivated*

**rapto**
1 rapture, sudden impulse, sudden start, outburst
2 robbery, theft, seizure, abduction, kidnapping
3 ecstasy, rapture, transport

**rareza**
1 strangeness, oddness, singularity
2 anomaly, irregularity, abnormality
3 extravagance, eccentricity, absurdity

**raro**
1 rare, remarkable
2 strange, extraordinary, singular, odd
3 extravagant, eccentric, maniac(al)

**rascar**
scrub, rub, scratch, scrape, scratch oneself

**raso**
plain, flat, smooth, level, (*sky*) clear

**rastro**
1 track, trace, trail, sign, vestige, clue, indication
2 rake

**raya**
1 line, stripe, scratch, ray
2 (*grammar*) hyphen
3 (*hair*) parting
4 trouser crease
5 boundary, limit, frontier, terminus

**razón**
1 discourse, speech
2 rationale, argument, proof
3 motive, cause, reason
4 justice, rectitude, truth, right
5 (*mathematics*) ratio

**real** (*aj*)
1 real, existing, positive, effective
2 (*fig*) royal, regal

**real** (*s*)
1 a coin
2 camp

**realizar**
1 achieve, carry out, make, undertake, effect, execute, realize
2 (*commerce*) (*Br*) sell up, (*Am*) convert into money
3 come about, come true

**realzar**
1 (*technical*) emboss, raise
2 (*fig*) enhance, heighten, add to
3 (*art*) illustrate, carve in relief, highlight
4 (*fig*) magnify, extol

## reanimar
1 comfort, strengthen, encourage, *(military)* fortify
2 *(fig)* animate, console, encourage, bring to life, revive
*discourage*

## rebatir
1 repel, reject, resist, oppose
2 impugn, confute, refute

## rebajar
1 diminish, reduce, lessen, lower; *(commerce)* discount
*augment, increase*
2 *(fig)* humiliate, humble
3 *(drink)* dilute

## rebelde *(aj)*
1 revolt, rebel
2 disobedient, indisciplined, rebellious, unruly

## rebelde *(s)*
rebel, insurgent

## recalcar
1 insist, repeat, keep on, go on, press
2 *(fig)* stress, emphasize

## recalcitrante
recalcitrant, obstinate, stubborn, persistent, contumacious

## recatar
hide, cover, conceal, wrap up, enclose

## recelar
suspect, distrust, fear (that), be afraid (that)

## recelo
suspicion, distrust, mistrust, fear, apprehension
*faith, confidence*

## recepción
1 receipt, reception, welcome
2 admission

## receta
*(cooking)* recipe, *(medicine)* prescription, formula

## recibir
1 take, accept
2 admit, receive, welcome, entertain
3 collect, get, obtain

## reciente
recent, fresh, brand-new

## recio *(aj)*
1 strong, tough, robust, vigorous
2 corpulent, fat, thick, stout, bulky

## recio *(av)*
hard, loudly

## reclamar
1 claim, demand, ask, insist on, protest
2 *(law)* appeal

## reclamo
1 decoy, *(birds)* lure
2 incentive, attraction
3 propaganda, publicity, announcement, advertisement

## recoger(se)
1 collect, gather, pick, *(agriculture)* harvest
2 guard, keep watch over
3 congregate, meet, collect, stock
4 welcome, give shelter to
5 retreat, withdraw, retire, confine, shut up
6 shelter, take refuge
7 be absorbed, be lost in thought

## recomendar
recommend, suggest, commend, urge, entrust
*distrust*

## recompensar
1 compensate
2 repay, remunerate
3 reward, recompense, award a prize to
*chastise, punish*

## recóndito
deep, hidden, occult, secret, recondite, obscure

## reconocer
1 distinguish
2 inspect, search, *(medicine)* examine
3 confess, accept, acknowledge, declare, agree
*not know, be ignorant of*

## reconocimiento
1 recognition

2 acknowledgement, gratitude, thanks

3 examination, inspection, registration, admission

**reconvenir**
reprimand, scold, reproach

**recopilar**
1 summarize, abridge, cut down, sum up
2 compile
3 *(law)* codify

**rectificar**
1 rectify, correct, modify, emend, amend
2 purify, re-distil
3 correct oneself

**rectitud**
justice, integrity, impartiality, *(fig)* rectitude

**recto** *(aj)*
1 straight, right, direct
2 *(fig)* upright, honest, just, impartial

**recto** *(s)*
1 rectum
2 straight line

**recuerdo**
1 memory, remembrance, reminiscence
2 souvenir, gift, present

**recuerdos**
memories, regards, best wishes

**recuperar**
recover, rescue, save, recuperate
*lose*

**recusar**
reject, turn down, refuse, decline, cross out

**rechazar**
1 repel, drive back
2 refuse, turn down, reject
*accept*

**redimir**
1 redeem, rescue, free, liberate, set at liberty
2 *(commerce)* redeem, cancel

**rédito**
interest, income, benefit, advantage, utility, output, *(commerce)* interest, yield

**redoblar**
1 fold, bend
2 duplicate, double
3 repeat, reiterate
4 play a roll on the drums

**reducir**
1 reduce, diminish, narrow, shorten, cut short, limit
2 summarize, abridge
3 reduce, subjugate, conquer, dominate
4 convert

**referir**
1 tell, narrate, relate, recount, retell
2 relate, connect, link, chain together
3 remit
4 refer to, allude to, cite, mention

**reflexionar**
reflect on, consider, think, meditate, pause to think

**reformar**
1 reform
2 repair, restore, correct, amend, modify, mend, fix, alter
3 reorganize, re-order, repeat

**reforzar**
1 augment, increase, enlarge
2 *(architecture)* reinforce, invigorate, strengthen
*weaken*
3 animate

**refractario**
refractory, rebellious, contrary
*submissive, easy*

**refulgir**
shine, dazzle, shine brilliantly, be dazzling

**refutar**
impugn, confute, contradict, refute

**regañar**
1 reprimand, warn, scold, nag
2 quarrel, fight, row

**registrar**
1 look, examine, inspect, scrutinize, search, recognize
2 copy, inscribe, note (down), register, record, *(computers)* log

**regocijar(se)**
1 content, cheer, delight, please, divert, feast, rejoice, have a good time
2 entertain oneself, enjoy oneself
*make oneself unhappy, be bored*

**regular** *(aj)*
1 regulated, regularized
2 methodical, adjusted, settled, regular
3 mediocre, moderate, middling, average, ordinary
*immoderate, abnormal*

**regular** *(v)*
adjust, regularize, put in order, regulate
*disorder, disarrange, upset*

**regularizar**
standardize, adjust, order, measure, normalize, regulate

**rehacer(se)**
1 redo, repeat, reconstruct, rebuild
2 mend, repair, replace, restore
3 reinforce, strengthen, invigorate
4 *(medicine)* recover

**rehuir**
avoid, elude, shun, shrink from, get around

**rehusar**
refuse, decline, reject, renounce, repudiate, avoid, dodge, elude, shun

**reinar**
1 rule, govern, reign, dominate
2 predominate, prevail

**reintegrar**
1 reinstate, reintegrate
2 reconstitute, replace, put back, return (to), give back
3 *(commerce)* refund, reimburse

**relación**
1 story, tale, narration
2 list, enumeration, catalogue
3 connection, correspondence, link
4 communication, correspondence, friendship, relationship

**relaciones**
relations, connections, (sexual) intercourse

**relacionar**
1 recount, relate, narrate, tell
2 chain together, join, unite, bind together, link, connect
3 correspond, visit, treat
4 be connected, be linked

**relajar(se)**
1 relax, slacken, loosen, undo, distend, weaken, soften
2 become corrupted, go bad, pervert

**relatar**
relate, recount, narrate, tell

**relevar**
1 relieve
2 exalt, magnify, enlarge
3 absolve, pardon
4 exonerate, exempt, dismiss
5 change, substitute, replace
6 *(art)* carve in relief

**relieve**
1 *(art, technology)* relief, embossing
2 prominence, eminence
3 *(fig)* importance, merit, renown

**relieves**
excess, surplus, remains

**relumbrar**
shine, glitter, shine brightly, sparkle, dazzle

**rematar**
1 put an end to, finish, conclude, terminate, finalize
2 give a finishing touch to
3 *(commerce)* sell off cheap
4 *(sport)* shoot
5 *(LAm)* buy at an auction

**remediar**
1 remedy, correct, emend, repair, make good
2 help, aid
*desert, abandon, deprive*
3 avoid, prevent

**remendar**
1 mend, repair, patch
2 correct, emend

**remilgado**
prudish, prim, squeamish, finicky, affected

**remisión**
1 *(LAm)(commerce)* consignment, shipment

2 reference

3 pardon, absolution, remission

**remiso**

1 irresolute, timid, weak

2 slack, slow, remiss, lazy, stubborn

**remitir**

1 send, despatch, forward, remit

2 refer, relate, make reference to

3 forgive, pardon, exculpate

4 suspend, defer, postpone

5 refer to, subject oneself to, adhere to, abide by

**remolino**

1 eddy, whirl, whirlpool, whirlwind, hurricane

2 *(fig)* disturbance, anxiety, worry

3 throng, crowd

**remoto**

remote, distant, far away

**remover**

1 move, transfer, change, remove *place, put*

2 stir, agitate, shake, revolve, turn over, move round

3 dismiss, depose, *(LAm)* sack, fire

**remunerar**

remunerate, pay, recompense, reward, tip

**rencor**

rancour, bitterness, resentment, hate, enmity, abhorrence *love*

**rendir(se)**

1 vanquish, defeat, conquer, subjugate, dominate, overwhelm *resist, rebel*

2 tire, fatigue

3 *(commerce)* produce, yield

4 surrender, capitulate, submit, wear oneself out

**renegar**

1 detest, abominate

2 abjure, deny, renounce, turn renegade

3 blaspheme, swear, grumble

**renta**

1 *(commerce)* yield, benefit, profit

2 income, rent

**renuncia**

renunciation, resignation, abdication, withdrawal, retirement

**renunciar**

1 renounce, resign, desist, stop, refuse

2 abandon, reject

**reñir**

1 contend, fight, quarrel

2 become enemies, disagree with, fall out

3 reprimand, scold

**reparar**

1 restore, remedy, emend, fix, repair, mend

2 correct, remedy, make good, emend

3 satisfy, make amends

4 indemnify, compensate

5 note, notice, take note of, watch

6 observe, consider, reflect, attend to, think

**reparación**

1 mending, repair

2 satisfaction, amends, righting of wrongs

3 indemnification, compensation

**reparo**

1 mending, repair, restoration

2 defence

3 observation, warning, note

4 difficulty, objection, inconvenience

**repartir**

1 divide, distribute, share out *add up*

2 *(commerce, post)* deliver

**reparto**

1 sharing out, division, distribution, partition

2 *(commerce)* delivery

3 *(theatre, films)* cast

4 *(LAm)* building site, *(Am)* building lot, *(LAm)* housing estate, *(Am)* real estate

**repeler**

1 repel, reject, throw out, emit

2 contradict, repudiate

**repentino**
    sudden, unforeseen, unexpected, surprising

**réplica**
1 retort, reply, answer (to a charge), contradiction
2 copy, *(art)* replica

**replicar**
1 object, contradict, answer, reply, *(pejorative)* argue, answer back
2 impugn, assail, attack, challenge

**reponer(se)**
1 replace, restore, revive, re-establish, re-instal
2 replace, put back
3 reply, answer

**reposar**
1 rest, repose, sleep
2 calm, quieten
3 lie, be buried

**reprender**
1 censure, condemn, reprimand, warn, scold, reprehend, correct
2 reproach, recriminate

**repugnar**
1 nauseate, disgust, hate
2 repel, drive back, refuse

**reputar**
    esteem, judge, consider, deem

**reputación**
1 reputation, fame, notoriety
2 glory, renown, fame

**requerir**
1 intimate, declare, notify
2 ask, request, ask for, claim, require, send for, summon
3 need, be necessary

**rescatar**
1 rescue, save, redeem, liberate, set free, free, ransom
    *imprison*
2 recover, get back, recuperate

**rescindir**
    rescind, repeal, abolish, cancel, annul, leave without effect

**reserva**
1 reserve, provision, preparedness, readiness

2 *(finance, commerce)* reserve, stock
3 *(geography)* reserve
4 circumspection, caution, discretion, prudence
5 reservation, doubt
6 reservation, booking

**reservar(se)**
1 conserve, retain, keep
2 dispense, except, exclude
3 hide, conceal, keep quiet about
4 save oneself, keep to oneself

**resguardar**
    safeguard, protect, defend, shield, preserve, guard against

**resguardo**
1 safeguard, defence, protection, security, shelter
2 *(commerce)* guarantee, security, voucher, receipt, slip

**residencia**
1 residence, habitation, dwelling, domicile, abode
2 *(education)* hostel

**resistencia**
1 resistance, opposition, obstruction
2 firmness, strength, solidity, endurance, patience
3 defence
4 *(electricity)* resistance

**resistir**
1 resist, oppose, repel
2 struggle against, defend
3 support, sustain, endure, put up with, bear
4 refuse to, resist

**resolución**
1 valour, audacity, courage, daring, boldness
2 resolution, determination, decision

**respiro**
1 breathing
2 *(fig)* respite, reprieve, relief, alleviation, rest, calm

**responder**
1 answer
    *ask*
2 reply, respond, answer back
3 guarantee, stand surety, stand bail

**resquemor**
1 burn, heartburn, stinging
2 resentment, rancour

**restar**
1 (*mathematics*) subtract
2 diminish, reduce, lessen
3 return, turn back
4 remain, be left

**restituir**
1 restore, re-establish
2 return, replace, put back, give back

**restricción**
restriction, limitation, reduction

**restringir**
1 reduce, limit, restrict, circumscribe, shorten, surround, encircle
*enlarge, amplify*
2 constrict, bind

**resuelto**
1 resolved, determined, decided, resolute
2 audacious, daring, insolent
3 prompt, diligent

**resumir**
sum up, abridge, summarize, abbreviate, cut down, recapitulate, extract
*amplify*

**retardar**
1 retard, delay, slow down, hold back
*advance, move forward*
2 postpone, defer, put off

**retener**
1 retain, withhold, conserve, keep, guard, reserve
2 remember, memorize

**retirado** (s)
retired person, pensioner, senior citizen

**retiro** (s)
1 retirement, seclusion, retreat
2 shyness, remoteness, isolation, solitude, loneliness

**retornar**
1 return, give back, restore
2 return, turn back, go back, come back

**retraerse**
1 take refuge, take shelter
2 retire, retreat, withdraw

**revelar**
1 reveal, discover, manifest
2 (*photography*) reveal, develop

**reverencia**
reverence, respect, veneration

**revés**
1 reverse, back, wrong side, (*manuscript*) verso
2 (*fig*) reverse, setback, disaster, misfortune
3 (*sport*) backhand

**revocar**
revoke, abolish, annul, repeal
*validate*

**revoltoso**
1 lively, mischievous, naughty, unruly, disorderly
2 seditious, rebellious, turbulent, mutinous, revolutionary

**revolver(se)**
1 agitate, mix up , move (about), shake
2 disorder, disturb, alter, disorganize
3 worry, trouble, make enemies of, cause a rift between
4 rummage through, (*LAm*) revolve, turn (round), spin

**revolución**
1 revolution, turn
2 revolution, sedition, mutiny, revolt, insurrection, rising, row, uproar

**revuelta**
1 turn, bend, revolution
2 row, uproar, tumult, mutiny, sedition, insurrection

**rezagar(se)**
1 suspend, detain, retard, be slow, slow down, delay
2 remain behind, lag behind

**rico** (*aj*)
1 well-to-do, wealthy, well-off, rich
2 abundant, copious, exuberant, opulent, luxurious

3 exquisite, excellent, appetizing, tasty, delicious, lovely, cute, pleasant

**rico** *(s)*

rich person

**ridículo** *(aj)*

1 ridiculous, ludicrous, laughable, derisory

2 strange, grotesque, eccentric, outlandish

3 silly, stupid, trivial

**ridículo** *(s)*

ridicule

**rigidez**

1 rigidity, inflexibility, stiffness, hardness
*flexibility*

2 rigour, severity, austerity, harshness, strictness

**rígido**

1 rigid, inflexible, tight, taut, hard, stiff

2 *(fig)* rigorous, severe, austere, strict, stern

**rigor**

1 strictness, severity

2 rigour, harshness, roughness, coarseness
*mildness*

3 exactitude, precision

**riguroso**

1 rough, sharp, bitter, coarse

2 rigorous, harsh, severe

3 austere, strict, stern

4 inclement, extreme, cruel

5 strict, precise, exact

**riña**

argument, quarrel, dispute, altercation, brawl, fight, contention

**riqueza**

1 riches, wealth, opulence, well-being, comfortable living, luxury
*poverty*

2 profusion, abundance, copiousness, fertility

**risueño**

1 jocund, jovial, happy, cheerful, festive
*serious*

2 pleasant, delightful

3 prosperous, propitious, favourable

**rodear**

fence in, surround, encircle, go round

**rodeo**

1 deviation, diversion, detour

2 *(fig)* circumlocution

3 *(grammar)* periphrasis

4 evasion, subterfuge

**romo** *(aj)*

1 obtuse

2 flat, snub-nosed

3 *(fig)* dim, slow, rude, rough, coarse, blunt
*sharp, smart, clever*

**romo** *(s)*

blockhead, dunce, fool, idiot

**romper**

1 smash, break, fracture, tear, rip

2 ruin, vanquish

**rompimiento**

1 breaking

2 fracture, rupture, break, crack

3 quarrel, fight, disagreement

**rubor**

blush, shame, bashfulness, embarrassment

**ruin**

1 bad, vile, low, unworthy

2 mean, miserly, miserable, avaricious

3 small, sickly, weak

4 insignificant, despicable, contemptible

**ruina**

1 ruin, devastation, desolation, destruction, perdition, decadence

2 collapse, bankruptcy, loss, *(economy)* slump

**ruinas**

ruins, remains, debris

**rumbo**

1 direction, route, course, way

2 rout, defeat

3 *(fig)* pomp, magnificence, ostentation, show

4 liberality, generosity, disinterestedness
5 (*fig*) course of events

**rumboso**
1 splendid, lavish, magnificent, ostentatious, pompous
2 generous, liberal, disinterested,
   detached

**rumor**
1 murmur, low sound, buzz, whisper

2 rumour

**rústico** (*aj*)
1 rustic, rural, country
2 (*fig*) rough, rude, coarse, uncouth,
   vulgar

**rústico** (*s*)
   rustic, peasant, yokel

**ruta**
1 way, course, direction
2 itinerary, route

# S

**saber** *(s)*
    erudition, science, knowledge, wisdom, learning

**saber** *(v)*
1. know, find out, learn, know how to
2. taste of, taste like, *(fig)* smack of

**sabiduría**
1. prudence, judgement, brains
2. science, sapience, knowledge, wisdom, learning

**sabio** *(aj)*
1. sane, wise, prudent, judicious, sensible
2. erudite, expert, learned, sapient

**sabio** *(s)*
    learned man, scholar, expert, savant

**saborear(se)**
1. savour, relish, taste, sample
2. anticipate, relish the thought of
3. *(fig)* entertain oneself, be delighted

**sabroso**
1. tasty, delicious, appetizing, exquisite, rich, seasoned
2. *(fig)* racy, salty, daring

**sacar**
1. take out, extract, remove, *(fig)* get out
2. bring out, publish
3. quit, leave, leave off, take off, remove
4. obtain, receive, get, attain, reach, achieve, bring about
5. except, exclude, subtract
6. deduce, infer, conclude
7. *(LAm)* flatter, fawn

**sacrificar(se)**
1. sacrifice, immolate
    *pardon, redeem, liberate*
2. restrain oneself, deprive oneself, resign oneself to

**sal**
1. salt
2. *(fig)* grace, wit, charm, elegance

**salado**
1. salt, salty
2. *(fig)* gracious, clever, witty, amusing, lively, cute, charming, attractive

**salida**
1. leaving, going out, exit, emergence, departure
2. *(military)* sally, sortie
3. *(technology)* output, production
4. *(mechanics)* outlet, vent, valve, *(geography)* outlet
5. *(theatre)* appearance, entry, coming-on
6. *(commerce)* sale, sales outlet, opening
7. *(sun, moon)* rising
8. pretext, excuse, recourse, subterfuge, escape
9. issue, result, outcome
10. salient, projection, protuberance

**saliente** *(aj)*
    protuberant, overhanging, jutting out, projecting

**saliente** *(s)*
1. projection, shoulder, *(military)* salient
2. Orient, East, Levant

**salir(se)**
1. be born, sprout, emerge, come out, appear, manifest, reveal oneself
2. liberate, free, get rid of
3. spill, escape, free oneself
4. result, flow out
5. move away, start off, start out

**saltar**
1. jump (over), leap (over), vault
2. project, jut out
3. *(fig)* omit, skip, leave (out), jump
4. *(fig)* blow up, explode

**salvaje** *(aj)*
1. *(botany, zoology)* wild, uncultivated, untamed
    *cultivated, tamed*

**salvaje**
2 *(fig)* brutal, savage, fierce, barbarous, atrocious
*civilised, educated*

**salvaje** *(s)*
savage

**salvar**
1 save, rescue, salvage
2 free, exempt, liberate
*enslave*
3 resolve, overcome, vanquish
4 cover, cross, clear (an obstacle)
5 except, exclude
6 *(LAm)* pass (examination)

**saludable**
1 salubrious, healthy, good
2 convenient, profitable, beneficial, advantageous

**salvo** *(aj)*
free, safe

**salvo** *(av)*
save, except for

**sano**
1 healthy, wholesome, sound
2 robust, well
3 intact, whole, unhurt
4 sincere, well-intentioned, straight, upright, honest

**sanguinario**
sanguinary, bloodthirsty, ferocious, cruel, inhuman, vindictive, revengeful

**sangriento**
1 sanguinary, bloodthirsty
2 bloody, blood-stained
3 sanguine, red

**santo** *(aj)*
1 sacred, holy, venerable, inviolable, saintly
2 *(fig)* wonderful, miraculous

**santo** *(s)*
saint, saint's day

**saña**
fury, rage, choler, anger, ire, passion, violence, frenzy

**sazón**
1 time, occasion, opportunity, juncture
2 perfection, maturity, ripeness
3 flavour, taste

**secuaz** *(aj)*
partisan, partial

**secuaz** *(s)*
partisan, follower, supporter, addict

**secundar**
second, support, back, favour, assist, help, cooperate

**sedición**
sedition, rebellion, insurrection, revolt, rising, mutiny, tumult

**seducir**
1 seduce
2 *(fig)* attract, captivate, enchant, fascinate, charm
*repel, dissuade, disillusion*

**segregar**
1 segregate, separate, divide, remove
*unite, join together*
2 *(anatomy)* secrete

**seguido** *(aj)*
1 continuous, unbroken, successive, consecutive, incessant
2 straight, upright

**seguido** *(av)*
straight (on), after

**seguir**
1 succeed, follow, follow on, come after
2 follow, pursue, chase, persecute, hunt down
3 accompany, escort
4 initiate, copy
5 continue, carry on, go on
6 profess, practise, study
7 infer, deduce, derive

**seguridad**
1 security, safety, safeness
2 certainty, conviction, confidence
3 firmness, stability, steadiness
4 *(law)* guarantee, security, surety, bail, pledge

**seguro** *(aj)*
1 secure, safe, trustworthy
2 certain, sure, positive, unquestionable, indubitable
3 firm, fixed, stable

4 *(LAm)* honest, straight

**seguro** *(av)*
  for sure, certainly

**seguro** *(s)*
1 safety device, tumbler, *(military)* safety catch, *(technical)* catch, pawl, lock, stop
2 *(fig)* safety, certainty, assurance
3 *(commerce)* insurance
4 *(LAm)* safety pin

**sembrar**
1 sow, plant, scatter about, sprinkle
2 *(fig)* disseminate, scatter
  *harvest, collect*
3 *(fig)* propagate, spread, diffuse, divulge

**semejanza**
  similarity, affinity, analogy
  *dissimilarity, difference, inequality*

**sencillez**
1 facility
2 simple-mindedness, naturalness
3 sincerity, frankness, ingenuousness, simplicity

**sencillo**
1 easy
2 natural, plain, unaffected
3 sincere, frank, candid, ingenuous
4 simple, unsophisticated

**senda**
1 path, track
2 way, mode, method

**seno**
1 hollow, sinuosity, concavity
2 bosom, bust, breast, teat
3 *(geography)* gulf, bay, inlet, cove
4 *(fig)* haven, refuge

**sensato**
  prudent, discreet, circumspect, sensible, wise

**sensible**
1 impressionable, sensitive, responsive
2 perceptible, noticeable, appreciable, considerable
3 manifest, patent, ostensible
4 lamentable, deplorable, regrettable

**sensitivo**
1 sensual, relating to the senses
2 sensitive, impressionable

**sensual**
1 sensual, sensuous
2 tasty, pleasant
3 *(LAm)* alluring, sexy

**sentar(se)**
1 place, locate
2 suit, be suitable, agree with
3 sit down, seat, settle, *(fig)* establish
4 smooth (out), level (off), even (out)

**sentencia**
1 saying, proverb, maxim, aphorism, apothegm
2 resolution, decision, verdict, opinion, ruling
3 *(law)* sentence, judgement

**sentimiento**
1 feeling, emotion, passion
2 affliction, pain, regret, grief, sorrow, suffering
3 sentiment, affection

**sentir(se)**
1 perceive, notice, experience, feel, sense
2 deplore, regret, be sorry for, lament, grieve, feel sorry
3 judge, opine
4 suspect, have a presentiment of

**sentir** *(s)*
  opinion, judgement

**señal**
1 mark, sign, symptom
2 *(radio, telecommunications)* signal
3 landmark, boundary stone
4 sign, representation, image, picture
5 vestige, trace, footprint, track, trail, indication, sign, clue
6 guarantee, pledge, *(commerce)* advance, deposit
7 communication, advice, sign, password

**señalar(se)**
1 mark, determine

2 indicate, point out, designate, fix, settle
3 mention, allude (to), note (down)
4 be distinguished, become famous, become notorious, excel, stand out, be outstanding, be exceptional

**señor**
1 man, gentleman
2 master, proprietor, owner
3 sir, Mr.

**señorear**
1 dominate, rule, reign, order, lead, command
2 stand out, excel

**separar(se)**
1 separate, disunite, divide
   *unite, join*
2 deprive of, depose
3 distinguish, differentiate
4 separate, come away, come apart, come free, cut oneself off

**sepulcro**
tomb, grave, tumulus, sarcophagus, *(bible)* sepulchre

**sequedad**
1 dryness
2 *(fig)* brusqueness, roughness, curtness, harshness

**serenidad**
serenity, calm, quiet, tranquillity, fearlessness, sangfroid

**serio**
1 grave, formal, circumspect, restrained, sensible
2 grave, important, serious, considerable, responsible
3 severe, stern, frowning
4 real, true, effective, positive

**servicio**
1 utility, advantage, benefit
2 aid, favour, benefit, gift, service

**servicios**
lavatory, toilet

**sermón**
admonition, reprimand, scolding, warning, telling-off, *(religion)* sermon

**servidor**
servant, domestic

**servidumbre**
1 servitude, slavery, subjection, vassalage, yoke
2 service
3 obligation, burden, load
4 staff, servants

**sesgo** *(aj)*
oblique, aslant, twisted, sloped, biased

**sesgo** *(s)*
1 slant, twist, obliquity
2 course, route, direction

**severidad**
severity, rigour, harshness, seriousness, rigidity
*flexibility, amiability*

**severo**
1 severe, rigorous, rigid, inflexible, inexorable
2 exact, accurate
3 grave, serious, strict, harsh

**significar(se)**
1 mean, signify, denote, designate, represent
2 manifest, express, tell, notify, declare, make known
3 represent, have importance
4 be distinguished

**siguiente**
next, following, subsequent, later, farther, further
*preceding, previous*

**silencioso**
silent, taciturn, reserved, quiet, discreet, mute

**similar**
similar, analogous
*different, distinct*

**simple** *(aj)*
1 simple, unsophisticated, single, unique
2 simple, simple-minded, silly, foolish, stupid
3 simple, easy

**simple** *(s)*
simpleton, fool, idiot

**simpleza**
silliness, foolishness, stupidity

**simplicidad**
  simplicity, candour, ingenuousness
  *complexity, difficulty*

**singular**
  1 singular, single, unique
    *plural, many*
  2 *(fig)* exceptional, particular, special, outstanding
  3 rare, strange, peculiar, odd, extraordinary, excellent
    *ordinary, vulgar*

**siniestro** *(aj)*
  1 left, *(heraldry)* sinister
  2 perverse, ill-intentioned, *(fig)* sinister
  3 unhappy, funeral, funereal, ill-omened

**siniestro** *(s)*
  natural disaster, accident, calamity, catastrophe

**sirviente**
  servant, domestic, servitor
  *master, boss, landlord, proprietor*

**sitiar**
  besiege, lay siege to, blockade, *(fig)* surround, hem in

**situar**
  situate, place, put, position, locate
  *remove*

**sobra**
  excess, surplus, remainder

**sobras**
  1 residue, remains
  2 scraps, leavings, left-overs

**sobrar**
  1 exceed, surpass
  2 be idle
  3 remain, be left over, be more than enough

**sobrecargar(se)**
  1 surprise, intimidate, frighten
  2 surprise, startle, amaze, astound
  3 be scared, be overcome

**sobreponer**
  1 superimpose, put on top, add, apply
  2 dominate, contain
  3 win, pull through

**sobresalir**
  1 jut out, project, stick out
  2 *(fig)* stand out, excel, be distinguished, be outstanding, surpass

**sobresaltar**
  startle, scare, frighten, disturb, worry
  *pacify, quieten, calm*

**socarrón**
  1 astute, cunning, sly
  2 mocking, joking, witty, sarcastic, ironic(al)

**sociedad**
  1 society, association, group
  2 society, collective, corporation, syndicate, firm, company

**socorro**
  help, aid, assistance, favour, remedy, *(military)* relief

**soez**
  low, vile, obscene, vulgar, coarse, rude

**sofocar**
  1 suffocate, stifle, asphyxiate, smother, repress
  2 extinguish, put out
  3 *(fig)* shame, embarrass, make someone blush

**sojuzgar**
  conquer, subdue, subjugate, dominate, rule despotically

**solapar**
  overlap, hide, conceal, feign, dissimulate

**solaz**
  solace, rest, relief, recreation, relaxation, diversion

**solicitar**
  1 request, pray, press, urge, beg, plead
  2 apply for, ask for, seek, canvass
  3 attract, tempt, invite
  4 chase after, pursue

**solícito**
  solicitous, careful, concerned about, diligent, industrious

**solicitud**
  1 solicitude, affection

2 diligence, application, attention, care

3 petition, request, claim

**solidez**

1 solidity

2 hardness, firmness, consistency, resistance, strength
*weakness, softness, inconsistency*

**sólido**

1 firm, strong, resistant, consistent

2 dense, compact, solid

**solitario**

1 deserted, abandoned, uninhabited, lonely, desolate

2 lonely, solitary, shy, retiring, quiet

3 sole, unique

**solitario** *(s)*

hermit, recluse, loner

**solo** *(aj)*

1 alone

2 single, sole, unique

3 solitary, isolated

4 deserted, uninhabited

**solo** *(s)*

*(music)* solo

**soltar(se)**

1 untie, undo, detach, separate

2 loosen, unfasten

3 set free, put at liberty, release

**sombrío**

1 shady, dark
*clear, luminous*

2 *(fig)* sombre, sad, gloomy, sullen, melancholy
*happy*

**somero**

1 superficial

2 succinct, summary, slight, unimportant

**someter**

1 dominate, subjugate, subdue, reduce, defeat, conquer, overwhelm, subject to one's will

2 entrust, commit

3 give in, yield, submit

**somnolencia**

somnolence, sleep, sleepiness, drowsiness

**sonado**

1 famous, celebrated, renowned

2 sensational, talked-about

**sonoro**

1 sonorous, vibrant

2 loud, resonant, noisy

**soplar(se)**

1 blow away, blow off

2 blow out, inflate

3 *(theatre)* whisper, prompt

4 suggest, inspire, prompt

5 accuse, betray, inform on

6 *(fig)* steal, pinch, remove, take away

**sopor**

drowsiness, somnolence, sleepiness, sleep
*alacrity, vivacity, alertness, insomnia*

**soportable**

bearable, tolerable, endurable
*insufferable, unbearable*

**soportar**

1 sustain, carry, bear, support, hold up

2 *(fig)* suffer, tolerate, endure, bear, withstand, put up with

**sórdido**

1 dirty, squalid

2 *(fig)* impure, indecent

3 miserable, avaricious, mean, stingy, petty, contemptible

**sortear**

1 draw lots for

2 *(fig)* avoid, elude, shrink from, get round

**sosegar**

quieten, calm, pacify, placate, reassure, rest

**sosiego**

quiet, calm, tranquillity, serenity, repose, rest

**sospechar**

1 suspect, presume, conjecture, imagine, suppose, guess

2 distrust, fear, be afraid

**sostén**

1 support, prop, stand, pillar, post

2 brassière, bra

**sostener(se)**
1 prop up, hold up, support
2 sustain, nourish
3 maintain, keep up
4 defend, help
5 support oneself, keep going, continue, remain

**suave**
1 smooth, even, plain, flat, polished, fine
2 bland, soft, gentle, tender
3 sweet, agreeable, pleasant
4 quiet, tranquil, gentle, meek, mild
5 slow, moderate
6 docile, peaceful, gentle

**suavizar**
1 smooth down, polish
2 mitigate, moderate, temper, calm down, soothe

**subida**
1 climb, ascent, elevation
2 slope, sloping ground, hill
3 price rise, increase, exaggeration

**subido**
1 high, elevated
2 fine, bright, strong (colour)

**subir(se)**
1 ascend, go up, climb
2 mount, ride, get on board
3 grow, increase, step up (production)
4 rise, go up
 *fall, descend*
5 sum up, add up
6 raise, elevate, lift, hoist
 *lower*
7 make more expensive, increase in price

**súbito** *(aj)*
1 sudden, unexpected
2 precipitate, violent, impetuous

**súbito** *(av)*
suddenly, unexpectedly

**sublevar(se)**
1 incite, stir up, rouse

2 rise, revolt, rebel
 *obey, submit, yield*
3 irritate, anger, annoy, upset

**sublime**
sublime, lofty, eminent, elevated

**subsanar**
1 remedy, make good, correct, amend, repair, compensate
2 excuse (fault)
3 overcome (problem)

**subsidio**
1 subsidy, grant, allowance, benefit, aid, help
2 tax, contribution

**subsistir**
1 subsist, survive, remain, endure, persist, continue
 *get lost, disappear*
2 live, exist
 *die*

**suceder(se)**
1 happen, occur, come to pass
2 succeed, follow
 *precede*
3 inherit
4 replace, substitute
5 follow one another, be consecutive

**sucesión**
1 succession, sequence, series, continuation
2 inheritance
3 origin, descent, offspring

**suciedad**
dirt, dirtiness, filth, *(Br)* rubbish, *(Am)* garbage
 *cleanliness*

**sucio**
1 impure, sordid, stained
2 slovenly, filthy, dirty, disgusting
3 obscene, vile, mean, dishonest

**sucumbir**
1 succumb, yield, submit, give up, surrender
 *resist*
2 fall, perish, die
 *live*

**suelto** *(aj)*
1 light, swift, quick, fast, agile

2 free, untied, loose
3 fluent, flowing
4 free, daring, licentious, lax, insolent

**suelto** (s)
loose change

**sueño**
1 sleep
2 somnolence, sleepiness, drowsiness
3 (fig) dream, daydream
4 chimera, illusion, fantasy, dream

**suerte**
1 fortune, destiny, fate, chance, luck, star
2 sort, kind, class, genus, species

**suficiencia**
1 sufficiency, adequacy
2 conceit, smugness
3 capacity, aptitude, competence, suitability

**suficiente**
1 sufficient, enough
2 smug, conceited
3 competent, suitable, apt, capable

**sufrido**
1 long-suffering, patient, resigned, tolerant
2 tough, durable, long-lasting

**sufrir**
1 endure, put up with, bear, suffer
2 resign oneself to, conform to
3 permit, support, tolerate, consent to
4 sustain, resist

**sujetar(se)**
1 grasp, clamp, fasten, hold down
2 conquer, subdue, subjugate
3 subject oneself
   *rebel, free oneself*

**suma**
1 addition
2 total, sum
3 summary, abridgement, compilation, resumé

**suministrar**
supply, provide, provision, facilitate

**sumiso**
1 submissive, obedient, docile
   *rebellious, disobedient, indisciplined*
2 subjugated, subdued, defeated

**suntuosidad**
sumptuousness, magnificence, splendour, luxury, glory
*modesty, simplicity, economy, saving*

**supeditar**
subdue, dominate, oppress, subjugate, conquer, subject to one's will, subordinate

**superar(se)**
1 surpass, exceed, stand out, go beyond, do better than, excel
2 overcome, vanquish, gain

**superchería**
swindle, fraud, trick, lie, imposture

**suplicar**
1 beg for, petition for, plead for, beg, implore, press, urge
2 (law) appeal, plead, petition

**suplir**
1 supplement, complete
2 replace, substitute, make up for

**suponer**
1 suppose, presume, conjecture, think, imagine, believe, suspect
2 involve, require, entail

**suprimir**
1 abolish, annul, cancel, lift
2 remove, delete
3 omit, keep silent

**surgir**
1 arise, emerge, come up, crop up, sprout, soar up
2 spout, gush, run, flow
3 (fig) appear, get up, rise, show

**suspender**
1 suspend, hang up
2 detain, interrupt, stop
3 disapprove, reprove
4 knock over, (examination) fail
5 admire, marvel, amaze, astound, astonish

**suspensión**
1 suspension

2 *(fig)* stoppage, suspension, interruption, cessation, pause, detention

3 admiration, amazement, astonishment

**suspicacia**
distrust, suspicion, resentment, mistrust, misgiving
*confidence, credulity, sincerity*

**suspirado**
desired, longed-for

**sustentar**
1 sustain, bear, put up with, endure
2 support, defend, back

3 feed, maintain, sustain, nourish

**sustento**
food, sustenance, support, maintenance

**sutil**
1 subtle
2 tenuous, fine, slender, thin, light
3 *(fig)* sharp, perspicacious, ingenious, clever

**sutileza**
1 fineness, subtlety, sophistry
2 perspicacity, discernment, penetration, ingeniuosness, sharpness, shrewdness

# T

**tacaño**
mean, stingy, miserly, wretched, miserable, contemptible

**tacto**
1 touch, sense of touch
2 tact, diplomacy, sagacity, dexterity, skill, ability, tactic

**tachar**
1 erase, suppress, cross out
2 criticize, censure, blame, accuse, denounce

**taimado** *(aj)*
1 astute, cunning, sly, crafty
2 sullen, surly
3 lazy, indolent, idle

**taimado** *(s)*
rogue, scoundrel, rascal, crook, fox

**tajar**
cut, slice, divide, split, share

**taladrar**
perforate, drill, bore, punch, pierce

**talar**
1 cut, cut down, fell
2 *(fig)* lay waste, destroy, devastate, demolish, ruin, wreck

**talento**
1 talent, ability, capacity, intelligence, understanding
2 *(Bible)* talent

**talentos**
gifts, accomplishments

**tallar**
1 tailor, shape, carve, engrave
2 evaluate, value, assess, measure

**tambalear**
1 stagger, sway, swing, oscillate, vacillate

**tantear**
1 guess, estimate roughly
2 weigh up, consider
3 test, try (out), examine

4 *(art)* sketch in, draw the outline of
5 *(LAm)* lie in wait for

**tapar**
1 cover, close
*uncover, open*
2 obstruct, hinder
3 protect, shelter, cover, wrap up
*unwrap*
4 *(fig)* hide, cover up, conceal
*disclose, reveal*

**tardanza**
slowness, delay, procrastination
*alacrity, lightness, agility*

**tasar**
1 estimate, appreciate, value, evaluate, assess
2 limit, control, regulate, measure, graduate

**tasa**
1 estimate, valuation, evaluation, assessment, appraisal
2 measure, standard, norm
3 fixed price, official price, standard rate

**tema**
1 matter, theme, subject, topic, question, motive
2 *(linguistics)* stem
3 fixed idea, main, obsession
4 ill will, unreasoning hostility

**temerario**
rash, reckless, hasty, imprudent, bold, risky, daring, ill-considered

**temeridad**
1 temerity, rashness, recklessness, hastiness, imprudence
2 rash act, folly

**tempestad**
squall, rough weather, storm, tempest, tornado

**templar**
1 moderate, mitigate, smooth, temper

2 placate, calm, quieten, soothe, lessen, diminish

**temprano** *(aj)*
precocious, premature, advanced
*mature, delayed, late*

**temprano** *(av)*
early, quickly, at once

**tenacidad**
1 resistance, firmness, strength, toughness
2 constancy, obstinacy, insistence, persistence, stubborness, tenacity

**tenaz**
1 firm, strong, resistant, tough
2 *(fig)* constant, obstinate, persistent, insistent, stubborn, tenacious

**tender(se)**
1 unfold, spread out, extend
2 scatter, sow, spread, disseminate
3 tend, have a tendency

**tener**
1 have, possess, contain, comprehend
2 keep, maintain, hold, sustain, take hold of
3 consider, judge, estimate, appreciate, esteem

**tentar**
1 touch, feel, feel one's way, grope
2 induce, attract, tempt, incite, provoke, instigate
3 try, test, try out, attempt

**tenue**
1 thin, slim, delicate, slight, slender
2 tenuous, insubstantial, slight, thin, light, faint, weak

**terciar**
1 divide into three
2 place diagonally
3 intervene, interpose, mediate

**terco**
1 obstinate, stubborn, persistent, insistent, tenacious, constant, contumacious
2 *(material)* hard, tough, hard to work

3 *(LAm)* harsh, unfeeling, indifferent

**terso**
1 clean, polished, shiny, smooth
2 *(literary style)* terse, pure, fluid

**ternura**
tenderness, affection, fondness, endearment
*hardness, harshness, vulgarity*

**terquedad**
1 obstinacy, pertinacy, contumacy, stubbornness
2 hardness, toughness
3 *(LAm)* harshness, lack of feeling, indifference

**terrible**
1 terrible, dreadful, horrible, awful
2 atrocious, insolent, discourteous

**terror**
fear, terror, panic, horror, fright

**tesón**
tenacity, firmness, insistence, persistence, perseverance, determination, will
*inconstancy, flexibility, resignation*

**testarudo**
obstinate, stubborn, pigheaded, persistent, pertinacious

**testificar**
1 testify, attest
2 affirm, certify, asseverate, assure

**tétrico**
gloomy, dismal, pessimistic, sullen, wan

**tiempo**
1 time, opportunity, occasion
2 period, age, epoch, duration
3 weather, season
4 *(music)* movement, tempo

**tiento**
1 touch, feel
2 tentacle
3 *(fig)* prudence, circumspection, caution, wariness, care

**tierno**
1 flexible
2 recent, fresh, new

3 delicate, affectionate, endearing, tender, sweet

4 sentimental, moving, pathetic

**tierra**

1 orb, world, earth

2 territory, region, district

3 fatherland

4 country, land, soil, terrain, ground

**timbre**

1 stamp, stamp duty

2 seal, mark, brand

3 *(fig)* coat of arms

4 *(door)*bell

5 *(music)* timbre

6 *(LAm)* personal description, description of goods

**timidez**

timidity, shyness, irresolution, fear, pusillanimity

*resolution, audacity, courage, bravery*

**tímido**

timid, shy, nervous, bashful, frightened, afraid, cowardly, pusillanimous

**timón**

1 *(boat)* helm, rudder, steering

2 *(fig)* control, direction

**tinglado**

1 shed, covering

2 *(fig)* machination, intrigue, trick, plot, artifice

**tino**

1 skill, insight, ability, knack

2 *(fig)* prudence, tact, judgement, wariness

**tipo**

1 archetype, prototype, model, exemplar, pattern, type, kind

2 figure, frame, *(anatomy)* build

3 *(printing)* letter, character

**tirante**

tense, taut, stretched tight, stiff, rigid

**tirantes**

braces, *(Am)* suspenders

**tirar(se)**

1 stretch, pull out, spread out

2 attract, draw, pull

3 incline, tend

4 fire, throw, hurl, shoot, cast

5 drop, knock over, upset, knock down, demolish

6 squander, waste

*save*

7 trace, draw, plot, sketch, mark, show

8 print, stamp

9 hurl oneself, rush forward

**titubear**

1 stagger, totter

2 stammer, stutter

3 *(fig)* doubt, hesitate, vacillate, be perplexed

**titular** *(aj)*

titular, official

**titular** *(s)*

1 holder of an office, occupant

2 newspaper headline

**titular** *(v)*

1 name, designate, baptize, title, entitle, be entitled

2 *(university)* graduate

**título**

1 designation, denomination, heading, title, label, epigraph, inscription

2 professional qualification, university degree

3 motive, foundation, base, reason

4 *(fig)* title, right

**tocado**

touched, crazy, silly, idiotic, maniacal

**tocar**

1 touch, feel, pulsate

2 allude to, touch upon, concern

3 *(music)* play

**toldo**

1 awning, marquee, pavilion, cover, cloth, tarpaulin

2 *(LAm)* Indian hut, tent

3 parasol, *(Br)* sunshade

4 *(LAm)* hood, *(Am)* top

5 vanity, conceit

**tonto** *(aj)*
    simple, silly, foolish, stupid, ignorant

**tonto**
    simpleton, fool, clown

**tono**
    1 pitch, tone, tune
    2 shade, tint, tinge
    3 energy, vigour, strength

**tope**
    1 top, end, limit, maximum, buffer, bumper
    2 obstacle, impediment, snag, hindrance

**torcer(se)**
    1 twist, bend, turn, curve, incline
    *straighten (out)*
    2 turn aside, go astray, go wrong
    3 make sour, turn sour, go off, curdle, turn

**tormenta**
    1 squall, storm, tempest
    2 *(fig)* turmoil

**tormento**
    1 torment, torture, martyrdom
    2 torment, pain, suffering
    3 *(fig)* affliction, anguish, distress, grief, sorrow

**torpe**
    1 dull, dim, torpid, stupid, foolish, obtuse
    *astute*
    2 clumsy, awkward, inept, incapable
    *capable*
    3 rude, rough, plain
    4 indecorous, lecherous, obscene, vile

**tortuoso**
    1 tortuous, sinuous, winding, broken, rough
    *straight*
    2 *(fig)* astute, crafty, sly, cunning
    *sincere*

**tortura**
    1 torture, torment, martyrdom
    2 pain, suffering, anguish, distress, sorrow

**tosco**
    ordinary, rough, plain, vulgar, uncouth, coarse, uneducated

**traba**
    1 bond, tie, fetter, shackle, *(mechanics)* clasp, clamp, *(LAm)* hair slide
    2 *(fig)* bond, link, tie, *(pejorative)* hindrance, obstacle

**trabar**
    1 join, unite, coordinate, link, tie up
    2 clasp, grasp, grab, seize, fasten, fetter, tie down
    *set free, liberate, release*

**trabajo**
    1 labour, occupation, task, work
    2 farmwork, production
    3 *(fig)* effort, trouble, bother, hardship, difficulty

**trabajoso**
    laborious, difficult, arduous, hard

**traducir**
    translate, *(fig)* render, interpret, express

**tragar(se)**
    1 bolt (down), gobble, devour, consume, ingest, swallow
    2 *(fig)* bear, put up with, tolerate, dissimulate

**traidor** *(aj)*
    1 disloyal, traitorous, treacherous, felonious, perfidious
    2 false, sly

**traidor** *(s)*
    traitor, betrayer, quisling, *(theatre)* villain

**transcurrir**
    slip (by), pass, run, occur

**tranquilidad**
    tranquillity, quietude, calm, peace, serenity
    *work, activity, fear, anxiety, worry*

**tranquilo**
    tranquil, peaceful, serene, quiet, calm, still, restful, pacific, untroubled
    *disturbed*

**transgredir**
> transgress, violate, infringe, damage, harm, shatter
> *obey, respect, comply (with)*

**transitar**
> pass by, pass along, go (from place to place), move along, travel
> *remain, stay, settle*

**transitorio**
> 1 transitory, transient, transitional, temporary, passing, fleeting, provisional, accidental
> *eternal, enduring*
> 2 perishable
> *durable*

**transmitir**
> 1 transmit, broadcast, communicate
> 2 *(medicine)* transmit, pass on, infect
> 3 transfer, cede, sell

**transponer(se)**
> 1 transpose, change the place of, exchange, cross, cross over
> 2 transplant

**transportar(se)**
> 1 transport, carry, conduct, move
> 2 *(fig)* be enraptured, get carried away

**transporte**
> 1 transfer
> 2 transport, haulage, transportation, conveyance
> 3 *(fig)* exaltation, ecstasy, rapture
> 4 *(nautical)* transport, troopship

**trasladar**
> 1 move, transfer to another place, carry
> 2 defer, postpone
> 3 copy, transcribe
> 4 *(linguistics)* translate

**traslucirse**
> 1 be translucent, be transparent
> 2 *(fig)* be revealed, become clear

**traspasar**
> 1 pierce, go through, pass, cross (over), transpose
> 2 transfer, transmit, cede, sell
> 3 infringe, violate, transgress, damage, harm, shatter

**trastornar(se)**
> 1 overturn, upset, disarrange, disorder, discompose
> 2 *(fig)* worry, trouble
> 3 drive insane, go mad, go crazy, perturb

**trasunto**
> 1 copy, transcription
> *original*
> 2 image, imitation, likeness, carbon copy
> *reality*

**tratar(se)**
> 1 manage, handle, operate, use
> 2 communicate, relate
> 3 traffic, trade, negotiate, do business
> 4 spin, revolve
> 5 try, attempt, endeavour, try to, try out, test

**travesura**
> 1 anxiety, worry
> *tranquillity*
> 2 prank, lark, practical joke, trick
> 3 *(fig)* sharpness, wit, ingenuity, subtlety

**travieso**
> 1 lively, mischievous, naughty, unruly
> 2 *(fig)* ingenious, clever, subtle, sharp, shrewd

**trazar**
> 1 *(art)* sketch, trace, plot, delineate, design
> 2 *(fig)* plan, project, invent, think up, dispose

**tregua**
> *(military)* truce, *(fig)* lull, intermission, rest time, relief, interruption, suspension

**tremendo**
> 1 terrible, horrible, horrendous, frightening, terrifying
> 2 enormous, formidable, colossal, imposing, tremendous

**trepidar**
> trepidate, shake, tremble, shiver, vibrate

**tributo**
> 1 *(history)* tribute

2 *(finance)* contribution, tax, tribute, duty

**trinar**
1 trill, warble, sing
2 *(fig)* fume, rage, be angry, be furious, become irritated, get annoyed

**triste**
1 sad, gloomy, troubled, depressed, melancholic, distressed
2 unfortunate, ill-fated, fateful, disastrous, ill-omened
3 deplorable, lamentable, dolorous
4 insignificant, ineffective

**tristeza**
affliction, melancholy, grief, sorrow, pain
*happiness, joy*

**triunfar**
triumph, win, vanquish, conquer
*lose, come to grief, submit*

**tropezar**
1 stumble, trip, collide against
2 find, encounter
3 slip up, blunder, make a mistake

**trozo**
bit, piece, part, portion, fragment

**tumbar(se)**
1 knock down, knock over, fall over
2 stretch out, lie down, go to bed

**turbación**
1 disturbance, worry, perturbation, uneasiness
2 confusion, disorder, untidiness

**turbar(se)**
1 perturb, disturb, upset, worry
2 overturn, disarrange, alter
3 confuse, embarrass, shame, bewilder, dumbfound
4 be disturbed, be embarrassed, become embarrassed, get into a mess, get worried, get confused

**turbulento**
1 turbulent, troubled, unsettled, stormy
2 *(fig)* turbulent, unruly, excited, noisy, restless

**tutela**
1 tutelage, guidance
2 guardianship, protection, custody, defence

**tutor**
1 tutor, instructor
2 protector, defender

# U

**ufanarse**
    boast, brag, be vain, be conceited
    *crawl, humble oneself*

**ufano**
1 vain, conceited, proud, pompous, arrogant
2 satisfied, contented, happy

**ultimar**
1 terminate, conclude, bring to an end, finish, finalize
    *begin*
2 *(LAm)* finish off, kill

**ultrajar**
1 affront, insult, offend, injure, wrong, outrage, abuse
    *respect, honour*
2 spoil, crumple, disarrange

**ultraje**
    affront, insult, offence, injury, wrong, outrage, abuse

**único**
1 only, sole, single, solitary
    *several, various*
2 *(fig)* singular, extraordinary, unique, unusual

**unidad**
    unity, oneness, togetherness, conformity, concordance
    *plurality*

**unificar**
1 unite, unify, join
    *separate, detach, cause a rift between*
2 make uniform, make standard, equalize

**unir(se)**
1 bind together, tie, fasten, join, unite, fuse together
    *separate*
2 mix, combine, merge
3 add
4 ally, confederate, harmonize, agree
5 pair, join together, marry

**urgencia**
1 urgency, pressure, haste, rush
    *calm, slowness*
2 emergency

**usar**
1 use, utilize, spend
2 practise, be accustomed (to), be in the habit of, wear

**usanza**
    use, usage, practice, custom

**útil** *(aj)*
1 useful, fruitful, productive, beneficial, advantageous, profitable
2 suitable, fitting, available, usable

**útil** *(s)*
1 utility
2 utensil, instrument, tool

**utilidad**
1 utility, usefulness, advantage, benefit
    *uselessness, inconvenience, loss*
2 aptitude
3 *(commerce, finance)* benefit, gain, profit

**utilizar**
    utilize, use, make use of, employ, take advantage of
2 *(technical)* reclaim

# V

**vacilar**
1 swing, fluctuate, vary, be unsteady
2 vacillate, doubt, hesitate, falter, waver, stammer, stutter
*decide, make up one's mind, act*

**vacilación**
1 oscillation, fluctuation
2 vacillation, hesitancy, doubt, perplexity, irresolution, indecision, incertitude
*firmness, decision*

**vacío** *(aj)*
1 vacant, empty, hollow
2 idle, vain, empty, hollow

**vacío** *(s)*
emptiness, void

**vago** *(aj)*
1 idle, lazy, unoccupied, unemployed, wandering
2 indecisive, imprecise, indefinite, indeterminate

**vago** *(s)*
vagabond, tramp, idler, lazybones

**valentía**
courage, bravery, valour, spirit

**valer** *(v)*
1 be worth, cost, be useful, serve, be valid
2 shelter, protect, defend, support, sponsor

**valer** *(s)*
worth, value

**valimiento**
1 favour, goodwill, influence, power
2 help, protection, support, refuge, assistance
*desertion, defencelessness*

**valioso**
1 meritorious, excellent, esteemed, valuable
2 efficacious, useful, powerful, valuable
3 rich

**valor**
1 valuation, estimation, appreciation, merit, worth, value
2 importance, significance
3 cost, worth, value, price
4 valour, intrepidity, courage, daring

**valores**
*(commerce, finance)* bonds, assets, securities, stock

**valla**
1 fence, enclosure, defence, stockade
2 fence, hurdle, obstacle, hindrance

**vanagloriarse**
boast, brag, be vain, be conceited, pride oneself on

**vanidad**
1 vanity, pride, presumption, vainglory, boasting, conceit
*humility, modesty*
2 glory, splendour, ostentation, pomp
3 illusion, fantasy, fiction, futility, uselessness

**vano**
1 unreal, insubstantial, imaginary, vain
2 empty, hollow
3 useless, fruitless, unsuccessful
*useful, fruitful, successful*
4 shallow, superficial, frivolous, empty, inane, pointless
5 presumptuous, vain, conceited, fatuous
6 unfounded, unjustified

**vaporoso**
thin, slender, light, delicate, tenuous, filmy

**variación**
1 variation, alteration, transformation, change
2 variety

**variar**
vary, change, alter, transform, differentiate, differ

**vario**
1 various, diverse, different, distinct
2 variable, inconstant, unstable, unsteady, changing
*constant*

**vasto**
vast, huge, extensive, spacious, spread out
*minute*

**vecino** *(aj)*
neighbouring, *(Am)* neighboring, close, near, immediate, contiguous

**vecino** *(s)*
neighbour, *(Am)* neighbor, resident, inhabitant

**vejar**
vex, annoy, bother, pester, oppress, ill-treat, humiliate

**velar**
1 watch over, keep watch, take care of, look after
*neglect*
2 veil, hide, cover, conceal
*unveil, reveal, show*

**veleidad**
1 whim, caprice, fancy
2 fickleness, capriciousness, inconstancy
*firmness, constancy*

**velocidad**
1 velocity, speed, celerity, rapidity
2 promptitude, promptness, hurry, haste
*slowness*

**veloz**
1 swift, rapid, fast, quick
2 prompt, swift, speedy, quick

**vencer**
1 triumph, win, defeat
*lose*
2 vanquish, conquer, defeat, dominate, subject, subjugate, subdue, overcome, master
*submit, be defeated*
3 surpass, exceed, outstrip

5 *(commerce)* expire, end, fall due, mature

**vender**
1 transfer, sell, alienate, transfer property
*buy*
2 expend, sell
3 *(fig)* sell, betray

**venia**
1 pardon, forgiveness
2 consent, permission, authorization, approval, licence, leave
3 *(LAm) (military)* salute

**venir**
1 arrive, come
*leave, go*
2 proceed, infer, deduce, come from, stem from

**venta**
1 *(commerce)* sale, transfer, alienation, transfer of property
2 guest-house, country inn, state-owned hotel
3 *(LAm)* small shop, stall, booth

**verdadero**
1 certain, positive, sure, actual, real, genuine
*uncertain, unsure*
2 truthful, true, trustworthy, reliable
*untrue, untrustworthy, unreliable*
3 sincere, ingenuous
*insincere*

**vergonzoso**
1 shameful, vile, abject, low, ignominious, dishonourable
2 shy, timid, bashful

**vergüenza**
1 dishonour, shame, ignominy, disgrace
2 modesty, bashfulness, timidity, embarrassment

**verificar(se)**
1 verify, check, inspect, prove (true)
2 fulfil, effect, execute
3 occur, happen

**verosímil**
likely, probable, possible, credible
*uncertain, implausible, incredible*

**versátil**
1 versatile, adaptable
2 *(fig)* unstable, inconstant, variable, fickle, whimsical, unsteady
*constant, firm, consistent*

**verter**
1 pour, pour out, spill, drain, empty, scatter, spread
2 *(linguistics)* translate

**vía**
1 road, route, street, way, path
2 track, railway line
3 method, manner, means, mode, way, procedure
4 passage, tube

**vicio**
1 vice, bad habit
*virtue, perfection*
2 blemish, defect, flaw, *(law)* error, *(grammar)* solecism

**viejo** *(aj)*
1 old, ancient
*young, modern*
2 used, well-worn

**viejo** *(s)*
old man
*youth*

**vientre**
1 abdomen, belly, tummy, paunch
2 bowels, intestines

**vigilia**
1 vigil, watchfulness, wakefulness
2 insomnia
3 eve
4 *(ecclesiatical)* vigil, abstinence

**vil**
1 vile, low, evil, worthless, mean, contemptible
2 disloyal, treacherous, villainous, unfaithful
*loyal, faithful*

**villanía**
1 infamy, baseness, lowliness, meanness, vileness
*dignity, honesty, decency, goodness, kindness*
2 disloyalty, treachery, treason
*loyalty, fealty*

**villano** *(aj)*
1 rustic
2 *(fig)* rough, rude, coarse, crude, vulgar, ill-mannered
3 *(fig)* disloyal, base, contemptible, mean, shameful, unworthy, infamous, treacherous, traitorous, villainous

**villano** *(s)*
1 villein, serf, rustic, villager
2 *(fig)* cad, rotter, rat, swine
3 *(LAm)* villain

**vínculo**
link, tie, loop, bond, union

**violar**
1 violate, infringe, damage, harm, shatter
2 violate, force, rape
3 violate, profane

**violentar**
1 force, violate, assault, oblige
2 twist, bend, turn, distort, misrepresent

**violento**
1 violent, furious, vehement, fiery, irascible
2 awkward, difficult, embarrassing, painful, distressing
3 twisted, forced, bent, distorted, misrepresented

**visión**
1 vision, fantasy, apparition, spectre, ghost
*reality*
2 vision, eyesight
*blindness*

**vislumbre**
1 glimpse, brief view
2 gleam, glimmer
3 glimmer, slight possibility, conjecture, suspicion, sign

**viso**
1 glint, gleam, twinkle, reflection, sheen
2 *(fig)* aspect, appearance

**vituperar**
censure, disapprove, reprove, reproach, criticize, condemn
*praise*

**vivaz**
1 vivacious, lively, sprightly, vigorous, energetic
2 perspicacious, sharp, sharp-witted

**vivo** *(aj)*
1 living, alive, intense, strong
2 expressive, loud, showy
3 ingenious, clever, smart, sharp, astute, rascally, sly
4 diligent, prompt, quick, agile

**vivo** *(s)*
trimming, border, edge

**vocear**
1 shout, cry, vociferate, shriek, howl, scream
*keep quiet*
2 manifest, publish, proclaim, acclaim

**volar(se)**
1 blow up, demolish, explode, blast
2 irritate, upset, exasperate
3 *(LAm)* put to flight
4 *(LAm)* pinch, rob
5 *(LAm)* swindle, cheat
6 *(LAm)* flirt with
7 *(fig)* hurry, rush, fly, hurtle along
8 disappear, vanish, escape, flee
9 fly away

10 *(LAm)* get angry, lose one's temper

**voluntad**
1 will, will-power, free will
2 intention, desire, wish
3 consent, acquiescence
4 affection, love, benevolence, fondness
5 order, disposition, precept, mandate

**volver(se)**
1 return, restore, give back
2 pay, reply to, respond
3 turn, turn round, return
4 turn inside out, change
5 repeat, reiterate
6 *(wine)* turn sour, become acid

**voz**
1 voice
2 shout, cry, yell
3 word, diction, term, expression
4 *(fig)* rumour, fame
5 *(grammar)* word
6 *(grammar)* voice

**vulgar**
1 vulgar, common, ordinary, current, general
*distinguished, fine, elegant*
2 popular, plebeian

# Y

**yermo** *(aj)*
1 uninhabited, deserted, barren, waste, uncultivated
*inhabited, fecund*
2 uneducated, ignorant

**yermo** *(s)*
waste land, waste, wilderness

**yerro**
1 error, flaw, fault, failure, shortcoming, want, need

2 error, mistake, inadvertence, carelessness, negligence
*correction*

**yugo**
1 yoke, *(oxen)* team, *(horses)* girth, saddle strap, *(plough)* beam
2 *(fig)* submission, submissiveness, docility, slavery, bondage
3 *(fig)* despotism, tyranny, subjection, bond

# Z

**zafio**
  coarse, rough, uncouth, vulgar, crude, boorish, vulgar

**zaherir**
1 reproach, attack, lash, reprehend, criticize, satirize
2 wound, mortify, humiliate, shame

**zalamería**
1 flattery, cajolery, wheedling
2 suaveness, oiliness, soapiness

**zampar**
1 put away hurriedly, whip smartly into, dip into, plunge into
2 hurl, dash against
3 devour, eat greedily, bolt, gobble, wolf
4 *(LAm) (blow)* fetch, deal

**zángano**
1 drone
2 *(fig)* drone, loafer, good-for-nothing, scrounger, idler, lazy-bones

**zoquete**
1 block, chunk of wood
2 crust of old bread
3 squat person
4 blockhead, fool, ignoramus
5 *(LAm)* body dirt, human dirt
6 *(LAm)* punch, smack in the face

**zozobra**
1 *(nautical)* capsizing, overturning, sinking
2 *(fig)* anxiety, anguish, distress, grief, worry, restlessness, uneasiness

**zozobrar**
1 *(nautical)* be in danger of foundering, capsize, overturn, founder, sink
2 *(fig)* collapse, fail, be ruined
3 be anxious, worry, fret

**zumbón** *(aj)*
  waggish, funny, teasing, bantering, *(pejorative)* sarcastic
  *grave, serious, formal*

**zumbón** *(s)*
  wag, joker, tease

**zurrar**
1 *(technical)* tan, dress
2 tan, wallop, lay into, give a beating
3 sit heavily on, flatten
4 criticize harshly, defeat in an argument

# HARRAP'S SPANISH STUDY AIDS

Also available in this series

## SPANISH VOCABULARY
★ Ideal revision aid
★ Particularly suitable for exam preparation
★ 6000 vocabulary items in 65 themes

*142mm × 96mm/256pp/plastic cover*
*ISBN 0 245-54689-8*
*in USA 0-13-383266-X*

## SPANISH VERBS
★ Over 200 verbs fully conjugated
★ Index of 2400 common verbs
★ Notes on verb construction

*142mm × 96mm/256pp/plastic cover*
*ISBN 0 245-54688-X*
*in USA 0-13-383282-1*

## SPANISH GRAMMAR
★ Comprehensive grammar of modern Spanish
★ Suitable reference for study to university
level
★ Lively examples

*142mm × 96mm/256pp/plastic cover*
*ISBN 0 245-54690-1*
*in USA 0-13-383274-0*

## MINI SPANISH DICTIONARY
★ For quick and easy reference
★ Clear layout
★ Handy format

*142mm × 96mm/667pp/plastic cover*
*ISBN 0 245-54586-7*

## SPANISH IDIOMS
★ Up to date coverage of both Spanish
and English Idioms
★ Colloquial translation of each Idiom

*142mm × 96mm/320pp/plastic cover*
*ISBN 0 245-60039-6*